D1201410

FLORIDA STATE
UNIVERSITY LIBRARIES

JUN 15 1994

TALLAHASSEE, FLORIDA

DEATH FORETOLD:

THE JESUIT MURDERS IN EL SALVADOR

DEATH FORETOLD:

THE JESUIT MURDERS IN EL SALVADOR

Martha Doggett

Lawyers Committee for Human Rights

Georgetown University Press / Washington, D.C.

HV
6535
S2
D64
1993

© 1993 by the Lawyers Committee for Human Rights

All Rights Reserved

Printed in the United States of America

Lawyers Committee for Human Rights

Since 1978 the Lawyers Committee for Human Rights has worked to promote international human rights and refugee law and legal procedures in the United States and abroad. The Chairman of the Lawyers Committee is Marvin E. Frankel; Michael H. Posner is its Executive Director; and Arthur C. Helton is the Director of its Refugee Project.

ISBN 0-87840-545-3 ISBN 0-87840-546-1 (ppk.)

1. Assassination – Investigation – El Salvador. 2. El Salvador – Politics and Government – 1979- 3. Jesuits – El Salvador. 4. Victims of Terrorism – El Salvador. I. Title
HV6535.S2D64 1993
364.1'524'09728409047 – dc20

TABLE OF CONTENTS

PREFACE

Death Foretold is the tenth report prepared by the Lawyers Committee for Human Rights on the Jesuit case.* In this report, the Lawyers Committee seeks to summarize the crime and to evaluate efforts to investigate and prosecute its perpetrators. Since December 1989, the Lawyers Committee has served as legal counsel to the Jesuits on the case. We have collaborated closely with the U.S. Jesuit Conference, the Central American Province of the Society of Jesus and the Human Rights Institute of the Central American University José Simeón Cañas (IDHUCA). Having closely studied El Salvador's justice system, we were determined to work with the Jesuits and Salvadoran human rights advocates to press for justice in this case. We also aimed to encourage the international community, particularly the U.S. government, to support constructively the efforts of Salvadorans to investigate vigorously and prosecute this crime. With over $4.5 billion in U.S. aid over the last decade, the United States has played a major role in El Salvador.

Chapter I of this report looks at the history of attacks on El Salvador's Jesuits. Eighteen priests, five religious women, and scores of Catholic lay workers have been killed since the 1970s. More priests have been killed in El Salvador than in any country in the world. In March 1977, Salvadoran Jesuit Father Rutilio Grande was murdered along with two laymen. In June 1977, a death squad threatened to kill each of the 47 Jesuits in El Salvador unless they left the country within a month. Over a decade of civil war followed, in which some 75,000 Salvadorans died. Twelve years later, six more Jesuits were targeted for death along with two Salvadoran women, murdered simply because they could have given witness to the crime. In examining this history, it is clear that what happened at the UCA had indeed been foretold. Just days after the murders, San Salvador Archbishop Arturo Rivera Damas decried the "irresponsible campaign of accusations and slanders" directed for years against the Society of Jesus in El Salvador. "These accusations and slanders poisoned minds and ultimately put weapons in the hands of the assassins."**

---

* The Lawyers Committee has published 22 reports on El Salvador since 1980, when we began representing the families of four U.S. churchwomen raped and murdered that year by National Guardsmen.

** El Juicio de Dios, Grande y Terrible," Homilia Pronunciada por Mons. Arturo Rivera Damas, Arzobispo Metropolitano de San Salvador (Basilica del Sagrado Corazón), Sunday Nov. 19, 1989, at 5.

Since the beginning of the conflict in El Salvador the Jesuits had argued that only a negotiated settlement could end the fighting. Attacked and demonized for their stance, the Jesuits worked doggedly for peace. In an ironic twist of history, it was their violent deaths which propelled the peace process forward more than any other factor. The priests' wisdom and foresight was proven on New Year's Day 1992, when a peace accord was signed in New York City. It was, perhaps, this very rational end to the bloodshed that the Jesuits' killers sought to avoid. "For all its bestiality, the murder of the six Jesuits was not the irrational act of madmen," wrote George Black and Anne Nelson, two journalists who know El Salvador well and knew Father Ignacio Ellacuría, S.J., the UCA rector who was likely the principal target. "We believe it was a declaration of intent by the men who really run the country. Father Ignacio Ellacuría was one of the last, best hopes for peaceful dialogue in El Salvador. That is why he was killed."*

Chapter II describes the days surrounding the murders, placing the crime in the context of the guerrilla offensive. We trace the killers' steps as they left their base in La Libertad department and, within hours of arriving in San Salvador, reconnoitered the murder site. The chapter ends with an account of the crime itself, based on the extrajudicial confessions of the triggermen and officers, most of whom were acquitted of all criminal responsibility in September 1991. Despite a nearly two-year attempt by the court to investigate the crime, these confessions remain the most thorough account of what occurred that night.

"The Institutionalized Lie"**

Chapters III and IV chronicle and analyze the government's attempt to establish an "official story." Just months before his death, Father Ignacio Martín-Baró, one of the six murdered Jesuits, published a scholarly article on the psychosocial impact of the war on Salvadorans. He presciently described how his own murder case would be handled by authorities in San Salvador and Washington. Having witnessed

---

* Black & Nelson, "Why the Right Would Slay Priests in El Salvador," *Los Angeles Times*, Nov. 26, 1989.

** Excerpted from, Martín-Baró, "Political Violence and War as Causes of Psychosocial Trauma in El Salvador," in *International Journal of Mental Health*, Vol. 18, No. 1, at 11 (Spring 1989).

the treatment of scores of human rights cases, Father Martín-Baró recognized a pattern:

> The systematic screening of reality continues to be one of the fundamental characteristics of the Salvadoran war. This screening assumes various forms:
>
> 1. Above all, the object is to create an official version of the facts, an "official story," which ignores crucial aspects of reality, distorts others, and even falsifies or invents still others. This official story is imposed by means of an intense and extremely aggressive display of propaganda, which is backed up by all the weight of the highest official positions.
>
> 2. When, for whatever reason, facts come to light that directly contradict the "official story," they are "cordoned off." A circle of silence is imposed that relegates the facts to quick oblivion or to a past that is presumably superseded by the evolution of events. The continued violations of human rights by members of the armed forces enter this realm of blanketing silence.
>
> 3. Public statements about the national reality, the reporting of violations of human rights, and, above all, the unmasking of the official story, of the institutionalized lie, are considered "subversive" activities -- in fact, they are, since they subvert the order of the established lie. Thus, we come to the paradox that whoever dares to state the reality or to report abuses becomes, by this very act, a culprit of justice. What seems to be important is not whether the facts in question are true or not, which is always denied a priori; what is important is that they are stated. It is not the deeds that count, but the images.*

Just as Father Martín-Baró had described, in the Jesuit case inconvenient facts were "cordoned off" as the Armed Forces threw up an impenetrable "circle of silence." While much is now known about what happened, the military's coverup has to this day prevented a full investigation of those who ordered the crime.

Chapter III details attempts by El Salvador's Special Investigative Unit (SIU) to investigate the crime. The SIU, a U.S.-created and financed criminal investigative unit, is directed and staffed by active-duty members of El Salvador's

---

* *Id.* at 10-11.

Armed Forces. The United States government set up the SIU in 1985 to investigate serious human rights abuses.* Lamentably, as we discuss in Chapter III, the SIU's performance in the Jesuit case was poor. The SIU chief at the time, Lt. Col. Manuel Antonio Rivas Mejía, is himself implicated in the coverup of the crime. Despite his performance at the SIU, Lieutenant Colonel Rivas was promoted to full colonel in December 1990 and named second-in-command of the National Police. He now represents the government on the committee setting up the new civilian police force currently being trained by the United States and Spain.

Chapter IV, entitled "The Black Hole," covers the period in January 1990, when nine suspects were named. Now, three years later, it is still unclear how they were identified. During this crucial period, a "Special Honor Commission" of the Armed Forces was convened to determine criminal responsibility. In examining the record, we conclude that the Honor Commission was established as part of an effort at damage control.

Chapters V, VI and VII examine the efforts of Judge Ricardo A. Zamora to investigate the crime. "Courting Failure," **Chapter V**, chronicles the judge's earliest attempts to uncover the truth. At nearly every turn, these efforts were met with military obstructionism. It was not until May 1990, following the publication of U.S. Congressman Joe Moakley's "Interim Report of the Speaker's Task Force on El Salvador," that the court's efforts yielded some fruit. For all his diligence, Judge Zamora turned up evidence of a coverup but little new information on the crime itself.

Chapter VI, entitled, "From a Standstill to a Crawl," examines the court's work after Congressman Moakley charged that "the case had come to a virtual standstill. . . ." This phase was characterized by greater attempts by the court to investigate some aspects of the case, though little real effort to pursue the issues of higher orders and coverup. On August 15, 1990, Congressman Moakley charged that the High Command was "engaged in a conspiracy to obstruct justice in the Jesuits' case." This charge prompted President Alfredo Cristiani to convene a meeting among the Armed Forces High Command, the Supreme Court president and Judge Zamora.

---

* Bypassing the peace accords' provisions on the new National Civilian Police (PNC), Salvadoran officials, under U.S. pressure, plan to transfer the SIU and its current military personnel to the Attorney General's office, thereby ensuring the existence of two criminal investigatory bodies in El Salvador.

Chapter VII, "To Court," looks at the period following this unprecedented meeting, when Judge Zamora, feeling emboldened, attempted to examine key issues in greater depth. After President Cristiani testified in person, five colonels waived their right to avoid a court appearance and submitted themselves to cross examination. Yet the judge's efforts turned up little new evidence. He ended the investigatory phase on December 6, 1990, elevating the case to the trial or *plenario* phase.

Chapter VIII covers "The Final Act" when the case spent months in an appeals court. While the case was on appeal, the attorneys prosecuting the case in behalf of the Attorney General's office resigned in protest, saying they had been prohibited from seriously pursuing justice. Their subsequent hiring by the Jesuits as private prosecutors in the case brought new dynamism to the prosecution.

Chapter IX, "The Denouement," describes the trial itself, held in September 1991. The trial is also examined in greater detail in Appendix C by Professor Robert Goldman of American University, who observed the trial on behalf of the Lawyers Committee. The trial resulted in the conviction of two officers, including Col. Guillermo Benavides. This is the first time that officers had ever been convicted by a Salvadoran court for human rights violations. Seven others, including the confessed triggermen, were acquitted.

Chapter X, "Washington's Mixed Messages," describes and evaluates the role of the United States government in handling the case. The Jesuit murders presented the U.S. government with an unparalleled opportunity to use its considerable influence to effect the kinds of changes within the Salvadoran military that it sought for more than a decade. Yet we conclude that U.S. officials failed to avail themselves of this opportunity. Instead, they often responded to damaging testimony by attempting to discredit the messengers or to downplay inconvenient facts. While this account is by no means exhaustive, it does outline key actions by U.S. officials. The Lawyers Committee concludes that U.S. officials treated the case much as they have many other human rights crimes in El Salvador -- with an emphasis on political expediency rather than consistently pushing for a full disclosure of facts. At center stage in how Washington mishandled the Jesuit case was Maj. Eric Warren Buckland, a U.S. military advisor who provided the first testimony implicating those who later stood trial for the murders.

Chapter XI, "El Salvador's Legal System," outlines the steps in Salvadoran criminal proceedings and provides other information relevant to understanding how the Jesuit case was handled. This chapter is meant as a road map to the legal case. Readers interested in the technical aspects of the case may want to begin here. Speaking on the second anniversary of the killings, Father José María Tojeira, the Jesuit Provincial for Central America, told an UCA audience: "The verdict that was issued and the legal proceedings that followed their deaths do not hide the reality of how poorly the legal system functions. On the contrary, they make it patently evident. [. . . .] The institutions of justice function badly, and in this case, they functioned badly too."*

As several commentators have emphasized, the court's performance in the Jesuit case showed the justice system at its best. But, despite goodwill and unprecedented efforts, the results were modest and in many respects disappointing. Carefully controlled throughout, the case was shepherded through the system by Supreme Court President Mauricio Gutiérrez Castro. In retrospect, it is clear that the case placed in bold relief all the obstacles to justice in El Salvador. On one hand are the structural problems of an antiquated and neglected system that has grown into an ungainly hybrid in need of total overhaul. On the other is the military's well entrenched impunity, which Salvadoran courts have never seriously challenged. In part because of the Jesuit case, in part because the legal system figured in the UN-brokered peace talks, and in part because of the efforts of a few nongovernmental organizations, reform of El Salvador's judicial system is today receiving more serious attention than ever before.**

Finally, the report contains a series of appendices, some of which may be useful to consult along the way. **Appendix A** is a chronology of the UCA assassination case, beginning before the murders and ending as we go to press. **Appendix B** is a chronology of attacks on El Salvador's Jesuits. **Appendix C** contains the report of the Committee's trial observer, Professor Robert Goldman. **Appendix D** provides a brief profile of the nine men charged with murder, plus one officer charged in the coverup of the crime. **Appendix E** is a list of names of persons who figure in the Jesuit murder case. **Appendix F** is a list of

---

* José María Tojeira, "El caso de los Jesuitas dos años después," *Estudios Centroamericanos*, [hereinafter *ECA*], #517-518, Nov.-Dec. 1991, at 1036.

** A forthcoming Lawyers Committee report will examine recent judicial reform efforts by Salvadoran authorities and the Agency for International Development (AID) as well as changes in the judicial system stemming from the peace process.

acronyms and names used throughout the story. **Appendix G** provides a list of previous publications on the case by the Lawyers Committee and the UCA, as well as reports of trial observers from several organizations.

This report was written by Martha Doggett, who has followed the Jesuit case since the priests and women were murdered in November 1989. Ms. Doggett worked in close partnership with Margaret Popkin, who was the assistant director of IDHUCA, the human rights institute at the UCA, from 1985 to 1992. The Committee is indebted to Ms. Popkin for generously sharing her fact finding, analysis and careful monitoring of developments in El Salvador over the last three years. The report was edited by Michael Posner and Patricia Armstrong. We are also grateful to Patrick J. Carome and Ronald I. Meltzer, of the Washington, D.C., law firm Wilmer, Cutler & Pickering, for their expertise and counsel regarding the many Freedom of Information Act requests submitted during the course of our work. We wish to express appreciation to R. Scott Greathead, a member of the Lawyers Committee's Board of Directors. He undertook a series of missions for the Committee, and provided input which has been invaluable throughout our work on the case. We also wish to thank Anne Nelson for editing an earlier version of some of this material; Patrick Hayden for research assistance; Charles O'Byrne, S.J.; and the staff of IDHUCA, who graciously opened their office and resources to the Lawyers Committee staff. Finally, we wish to thank the members of the Central American Province of the Society of Jesus.

The Lawyers Committee's work on El Salvador and the Jesuit case was supported by the J. Roderick MacArthur Foundation, the Albert Kunstadter Family Foundation, the Arca Foundation, the U.S. Jesuit Conference, the General Services Foundation, the John Merck Fund, the Ottinger Foundation and the Samuel Rubin Foundation. Our sincere thanks goes to these donors.

February 1993
New York, NY

Lawyers Committee for Human Rights

DEATH FORETOLD: THE JESUIT MURDERS IN EL SALVADOR

INTRODUCTION

> *Why, we ask again, were the Central American Jesuits so determined to prosecute this case? Because it was by implication a class-action suit, brought on behalf of some 70,000 people tortured and executed by the "peacekeepers" in the last dozen years. This lawsuit was one last attempt to crack the facade of impunity, which has intimidated even the United States Government.*[1]

Three years after six Jesuit priests and two women were gunned down at San Salvador's Central American University José Simeón Cañas (UCA), the question posed by *America* magazine has taken on renewed importance as the people of El Salvador struggle to confront their recent past. In July 1992, a United Nations-sponsored Truth Commission began a six-month effort to break the facade of impunity and to document a number of cases where basic human rights were violated. In a decade of war in El Salvador, tens of thousands of civilian non-combatants were murdered, most at the hands of uniformed members of the Salvadoran Armed Forces. Most of the killers remain anonymous, and in most cases, no attempt was made at establishing their legal accountability. Like many Salvadorans before them, the Jesuits, their cook and her daughter, were forced from their beds and summarily executed. In the days following the UCA murders, a feeling of heightened fear and vulnerability enveloped El Salvador. If the military could enter the cloistered campus – the "closest thing in Central America to an Ivy League school"[2] – and murder world renowned Jesuit academics, anything was possible.

While the manner in which the priests died was typical, for a variety of reasons, the Jesuit killings *were* different, and provided, as *America* put it, an opportunity to "crack the facade of impunity." As was clear from the beginning, the plotters had employed the official command structure of the Armed Forces, altered only slightly in response to the guerrilla offensive. For this reason, identifying and urging the prosecution of all of

---

1 Editorial, *America*, Oct. 12, 1991, at 235.

2 Black & Nelson, "Why the Right Would Slay Priests in El Salvador," *Los Angeles Times*, Nov. 26, 1989.

those responsible for the murder of the Jesuits and the two women provides the Truth Commission with an opportunity to expose the systematic nature of the abuse of human rights. Those violations were both a root cause of El Salvador's civil strife and a tragic byproduct of the war. Effective action on the Jesuit case and other instances of gross violations remains key to resolution of the country's broader societal conflicts.

Because of national and international attention focused on the Jesuit case, there was a serious attempt by some in El Salvador to seek justice through the Salvadoran legal system. The trial of nine soldiers, including four officers, in September 1991 was the culmination of that process. The trial resulted in the conviction of two officers, one of whom was Colonel Guillermo Alfredo Benavides Moreno, the director of El Salvador's Military Academy when the murders occurred. The five-member jury acquitted the remaining seven defendants. This highly visible case became, as *America* said, something of a "class-action suit," which, while perhaps not able to deliver justice in the thousands of other cases, offered, at a minimum, the potential to provide some assurance that such crimes were now much less likely to occur. Yet two key issues have not been resolved: Who ordered the crime and who orchestrated and implemented the coverup?

The Case for Higher Orders

There is a wealth of circumstantial evidence indicating that Colonel Benavides was acting in accordance with a broader military conspiracy. The Lawyers Committee believes that the murders were planned and carried out by some of El Salvador's top military leaders. A still larger group of officers and soldiers aided the coverup of the crime. This coverup was abetted by the Cristiani government. The U.S. embassy in San Salvador also impeded a full investigation of the crime following a strategy of damage control which prejudiced the outcome. The failure of the Salvadoran government to fully investigate all aspects of this case lead to the acquittal of most of the murderers and effectively shielded the intellectual authors of the crime. Because the Jesuit murders were an institutional crime and because of the prominence of those who masterminded the plot, we believe that establishing the truth in this case would go a long way toward purging and reforming a system that has made these kinds of crimes possible.

Our assessment that Colonel Benavides was acting on higher orders is widely shared in El Salvador. A public opinion poll conducted in El Salvador in December 1991 by the UCA found that 62.4% of those surveyed who were aware that the

Jesuit trial had taken place believed that others who were not prosecuted participated in the crime; 75.8% of these same people believed that more should be done to investigate and prosecute the others who were also responsible. The U.S. State Department's 1991 report on human rights in El Salvador acknowledges that "[s]peculation continues that other high-ranking officers may have been the intellectual authors of the crime or acted to cover it up."[3] The United Nations Special Representative for El Salvador, José Antonio Pastor Ridruejo, observed in his 1991 report:

> The Special Representative shares with many sectors of local and international public opinion, especially local and international non-governmental humanitarian organizations, the justified misgivings that others may have planned the murders. It has to be asked whether a decision so fraught with consequences of every kind as that to murder the Jesuit priests could have been taken solely by a colonel who, by all accounts, was well known for his deep sense of duty and strict obedience to orders. In short, although the outcome of the trial for the murder of the Jesuit priests is a landmark in the recent history of criminal justice in El Salvador, it does not go far enough. *The Special Representative considers that the judicial investigation should continue in order to determine once and for all whether others were behind the crime, and, if so, to bring them to justice*.[4] (Emphasis added.)

---

3 Department of State, *Country Reports on Human Rights Practices for 1991*, February 1992, at 594. The possibility of higher orders is also mentioned at pages 593 and 598 of the report.

4 "Situation of human rights in El Salvador," UN Doc. A/46/529, Oct. 11, 1991, at 22. Professor Pastor Ridruejo's mandate as Special Representative ended in March 1992, when the UN Commission on Human Rights requested the Secretary-General to appoint an "Independent Expert" to provide "assistance in human rights matters to the Government of El Salvador, consider the human rights situation in the country and the effects of the Peace Agreements on the effective enjoyment of human rights and to investigate the manner in which both parties apply the recommendations contained in the final report of the Special Representative and those made by the United Nations Observer Mission in El Salvador and the committees established during the negotiating process." Situation of human rights in El Salvador," UN Doc. E/CN.4/1992/L.66, Feb. 27, 1992. Professor Pedro Nikken, a Venezuelan who served as an advisor to the peace talks, was named the "Independent Expert."

The challenge now for the Salvadoran government is to explore evidence of higher involvement and the coverup. As they consider whether to do so, we offer the following assessment of areas where leads need to be pursued.

An examination of events during the year preceding the UCA murders suggests that the decision to move against the Jesuits may have been taken months earlier. While the guerrilla offensive provided a last-minute impetus and suitable cover, hard-liners within the Army had long before resolved finally to act on their 10-year wish to silence Father Ignacio Ellacuría. The decision to kill Father Ellacuría was consistent with a longstanding pattern of attacks against the Jesuits. In that context, Father Ellacuría, an outspoken commentator and peace advocate, had become an obsession. Attacks on the Jesuits intensified after the ARENA party won the presidency on March 19, 1989.[5] Just days earlier, the UCA campus suffered its first bombing since 1983. The campus was bombed again in April and July 1989. For some on El Salvador's extreme right, ARENA's assumption of the presidency served as a green light for further violence. There were increasing attempts to link the Jesuits to FMLN violence and to portray the priests as apologists for guerrilla actions.

To the extreme right in El Salvador, the Society of Jesus was a guerrilla front, *una fachada del FMLN*. These so-called guerrilla fronts – which in their view include much of the church, many popular organizations, as well as leaders of trade unions and student and women's groups – have long posed a challenge to the Army. Because they were engaged in peaceful political work promoting social change, these activists gave the military no legal means to stop their work. Col. Francisco Elena Fuentes, an aggressively outspoken officer from the Army's rightist faction, said shortly before the 1989 offensive that "[w]e have the capacity to fight. But we can't move because [the guerrillas] hide themselves among the civilians. We have to be very careful to just pluck out the guerrillas."[6]

Constrained from suppressing these groups, Colonel Elena Fuentes and other like minded officers and civilians felt increasingly frustrated. By the fall of 1989, this frustration had intensified, backed by what they considered solid intelligence that a serious guerrilla offensive was about to occur. That offensive would target urban San Salvador for the first time in

5 *See infra* Chapter I: "Death to Intelligence!" *and* Appendix B: Attacks on El Salvador's Jesuits.

6 Lawyers Committee interview with Col. Francisco Elena Fuentes, First Brigade headquarters, Nov. 7, 1989.

nearly a decade. There is evidence to suggest that neither U.S. nor Salvadoran officials believed that an offensive would take place until just before it actually began. Yet Colonel Elena Fuentes was among those who believed the intelligence reports. "There are plans by 'the subversion' for an insurrection," he told the Lawyers Committee on November 7, 1989.[7] "They are preparing the conditions among the people for an insurrection. There has been a wave of [FMLN] terrorism in the last few days."

"Just plucking out the guerrillas," to use Colonel Elena Fuentes' phrase, is difficult. In the early years of El Salvador's civil war, the Army committed large scale massacres of civilians and made extensive use of aerial bombardment. Under U.S. tutelage, some within the Salvadoran Armed Forces came to see that high civilian casualties cost them dearly in popular support and often served as a recruiting device for the guerrillas. By the mid-1980s, new strategies of forced relocation were implemented to limit the possibility of civilian casualties by "draining the sea to catch the fish."[8] In this image, the guerrillas – "fish" – were swimming in a sea of civilians. In densely populated urban San Salvador, "draining the sea" was not practicable and officers like Elena Fuentes understood that routing the guerrillas from the capital necessarily meant risking high civilian casualties. Yet in painting the popular movement with broad strokes as part and parcel of the FMLN, these officers arguably sought to legitimize steps they viewed as necessary. Their argument appeared at times illogical and contradictory. While asserting that the guerrillas had little popular support, this faction of the right nonetheless portrayed any opposition group as an FMLN front or operative. In their polarized world view, you were either with the Army or part of the enemy.

One of the recent acts of violence that Colonel Elena Fuentes attributed to the FMLN was the October 31, 1989 bombing of the FENASTRAS trade union federation in which nine people died. According to the colonel, the guerrilla movement had detonated a powerful explosive in the offices of its own "front-group" in order to create martyrs and galvanize popular support for the military offensive it was about to launch. FENASTRAS was meant as a "spark," Elena Fuentes said. At the time, the attack on FENASTRAS was viewed by the opposition as the Armed Forces' response to the FMLN assault on

---

7 *Id.* "*La subversión*" is one of several ways in which the Army referred to the guerrilla movement.

8 This metaphor, paraphrasing Mao Tse Tung, was coined by Maj. Gen. Edward G. Lansdale, an expert in psychological warfare and counterinsurgency, during his experience in the Philippines in the early 1950s.

Joint Command headquarters on October 30 in which one person died and several others were wounded.

The bombing of FENASTRAS was, in fact, a watershed event. An explosive device had been placed between an outer closed gate and the inner door leading to a corridor which was used as a canteen.[9] The explosion occurred at lunchtime when the unionists had gathered to eat, thereby maximizing deaths. Bodies were literally blown to pieces and the ground floor of the building gutted. The bodies were moved outside, where the coffins were displayed for two days before being carried on November 2 through the streets of San Salvador in a march ending at the graveyard.

Before the march reached the grave site, FMLN leaflets appeared among the crowd indicating that the bombing had provoked the guerrilla leadership to pull out of the peace talks, scheduled to resume on November 20 in Caracas. The bombing of the trade union federation was one of several acts of serious violence during this period.[10] That same day, the offices of COMADRES were also bombed. COMADRES is an organization of women whose family members have been killed or "disappeared." On October 19, the homes of opposition leader Rubén Zamora and his sister-in-law, Aronette Díaz of the leftist UDN party, were bombed.

The bombing of FENASTRAS evoked memories of an earlier period when such attacks were commonplace. "It is pure carnage, just carnage," a worker surveying FENASTRAS told a reporter.[11] "This is getting like the early 80s all over again. We are living the nightmare of the past." The spectacle of the dismembered bodies and gutted building provoked an outcry

9 Lawyers Committee interview with Héctor Bernabe Recinos, FENASTRAS headquarters, Nov. 8, 1989.

10 In the preceding months, a number of targeted assassinations contributed to further polarization. Between March and October 1989, five prominent civilians on the extreme right, a colonel and the daughter of a colonel were murdered. And the home of Vice-President Francisco Merino López was dynamited on April 14, slightly wounding a young girl. Those killed were Dr. Francisco Peccorini (March 15); Attorney General José Roberto García Alvarado (April 19); Dr. José Antonio Rodríquez Porth, Minister of the Presidency (June 9); Edgar Chacón (June 30); Gabriel Payés (July 19); Ana Isabel Casanova Porras (October 17); Col. Roberto Armando Rivera Escobar, fire chief, (June 26). The FMLN assumed responsibility for the killings of Peccorini, García Alvarado and Rivera Escobar.

11 *New York Times,* Nov. 1, 1989.

abroad, and President Cristiani decided to appoint a special investigatory commission.

Among those he sought to name to this commission was Father Ignacio Ellacuría. Father Ellacuría had met with the new president on a couple of occasions. He was known to consider Cristiani as a leader capable of achieving a peace settlement. In retrospect, some have exaggerated the extent of the relationship between the two men. They have used the priest's positive statements about the president to buttress an argument that the FMLN could have sought to silence Father Ellacuría or punish him for his support of President Cristiani's efforts. In fact, Father Ellacuría remained critical of the right, but considered President Cristiani a modernizing businessman who would likely view a peace settlement in the best interests of the country. He also thought that the right-wing ARENA party – which includes a faction of former officers – could coax the military into a negotiated settlement, something the Christian Democrats were never able to do.

Father Ellacuría had left El Salvador on an extended European trip on October 21, 1989. Via the UCA, Colonel Juan Antonio Martínez Varela, then Minister of the Presidency, faxed the president's request to the priest in Salamanca, Spain on November 6. Father Ellacuría responded in a hand-written fax on November 9:

> I am crushed by the terrorist act, I am ready to work for the promotion of human rights, I am convinced that President Cristiani rejects these kinds of acts and that he in good faith proposes this mechanism for this case, I want to support all reasonable effort to continue the dialogue/negotiation in the most effective manner possible. Precisely for this reason, I want first to thank the President for having invited me, and secondly, to ask him to grant me a reasonable period of time in which to make my decision in a responsible manner in order to promote the country's process of peace and democratization. On my return to the country I will bring myself up to date on recent events and contact representatives of various sectors in order to determine the best way for me to contribute.[12]

Father Ellacuría's hand-written message – which included the date he would return to El Salvador – was re-typed at the UCA and relayed to President Cristiani's office.

---

12 Facsimile dated Nov. 9, 1989 from Father Ignacio Ellacuría to Colonel Juan Antonio Martínez Varela (on file at the Lawyers Committee for Human Rights).

The Guerrilla Offensive Begins

The whereabouts of top military and civilian leaders at the time the offensive broke out on November 11 reinforces the belief that they were caught unaware, or at least, did not realize that the guerrilla attack would be so extensive. Chief military spokesman Maj. Mauricio Chávez Cáceres and his brother, Fifth Brigade Commander Col. José Emilio Chávez Cáceres, had left that day for a vacation at Guatemala's Rio Dulce.[13] Several other top officers were also in Guatemala for a meeting of military officers from all of Latin America, among them, the country's top intelligence officer, Col. Iván Reynaldo Díaz. Col. Carlos Armando Avilés, chief psychological operations officer at the Joint Command, was vacationing in New Orleans with his wife and children. President Cristiani was at his vacation home at Lake Coatepeque, and Vice President Merino left San Salvador by helicopter on the afternoon of November 11, stopping at the Atlacatl headquarters about 3:00 p.m. before continuing on to San Miguel for a pre-scheduled meeting of the ARENA party.[14]

Among those officers who were out of the country was General Juan Rafael Bustillo, who had commanded the Air Force for an unprecedented 10 years. The Air Force, which patrols the area around their Ilopango base, has long been associated with a pattern of serious violations. A 1990 article in *The New Republic* reported that the CIA "provided money and training to elite air force ground units. . . ."[15] General Bustillo was in the United States when the fighting erupted in San Salvador. He returned to San Salvador in the early morning hours of November 13 in a small private airplane co-piloted by Félix Rodríguez, the former CIA operative who orchestrated the *contra*-supply operation out of El Salvador.[16] Rodríguez told a Miami

---

13 Lawyers Committee interview with Maj. Mauricio Chávez Cáceres, Estado Mayor, Feb. 14, 1990.

14 Vice-president Merino's visit to the Atlacatl headquarters at Sitio del Niño on the afternoon of November 11, 1989 was recorded in the battalion's registry, which was entered into the court record in July 1991.

15 Lane, "The Pilot Shark of El Salvador: The Cruelty and Corruption of Juan Rafael Bustillo," *New Republic*, Sept. 24, 1990. *The New Republic* said Air Force members were engaged in smuggling contraband and trafficking in stolen cars and apparently also cocaine.

16 *El Nuevo Herald* (Miami), Nov. 29, 1989. Two additional sources have confirmed to the Lawyers Committee that Félix Rodríguez flew with General Bustillo to El Salvador in November 1989. Beginning in March 1985, General Bustillo worked closely with Rodríguez, a Bay of Pigs veteran and former CIA operative who came to El Salvador to help the

newspaper in November 1989 that he arranged to borrow a private plane from a Miami businessman after it had proved impossible to arrange for the general to return to El Salvador in a U.S. military plane.[17] According to this account, which has been confirmed to the Lawyers Committee by another source, Air Force air traffic controllers at Ilopango first denied the plane permission to land, fearing that it might have been a guerrilla airplane.

According to a November 1991 statement issued by Congressman Joe Moakley, General Bustillo was a central figure in ordering the murders of the priests. Congressman Moakley said that top officers met on the afternoon of November 15, 1989. "Reportedly, the initiative for the murders came from General Bustillo, while the reactions from the others ranged from support to reluctant acceptance to silence."[18] Congressman Moakley and other sources say the meeting was also attended by Col. René Emilio Ponce, then head of the Joint Command, and Col. Juan Orlando Zepeda, the Vice-Minister of Defense. Both men have since become generals and Ponce now serves as Defense Minister. In an unexpected move, General Bustillo relinquished command of the Air Force just six weeks after the crime. In so doing, he avoided joining his fellow top officers on the witness stand. He was never questioned by the court about his alleged role in the killings.

Information about a meeting held on the afternoon of November 15, 1989 was contained in a letter published in May 1990 by an anonymous group of junior officers. The officers pointed out that "according to the regulations of our institution, Colonel Benavides' superior is Colonel Zepeda and above him, the Minister of Defense; the question is, who besides Colonel Benavides was involved in the operation? What happened at the meetings that were held at 3:00 p.m. and 5:00 p.m. in the office of Colonel Zepeda? Not only Colonel

---

Air Force make more effective use of helicopters in its counterinsurgency efforts. In September 1985, Rodríguez was asked by Oliver North to "set up a maintenance operation for planes flying supplies" from Ilopango Air Base to the *contras*. *See New York Times*, Aug. 5, 1992 and F. Rodríguez and J. Weisman, *Shadow Warrior*, at 256-290 (Pocket Books, New York: 1989).

17 *El Nuevo Herald* (Miami), Nov. 29, 1989.

18 Statement of Rep. Joe Moakley, Chairman of the Speaker's Task Force on El Salvador, Nov. 18, 1991. A more complete account of the evidence provided by Congressman Moakley is found *infra* in Chapter X: "Washington's Mixed Messages."

Benavides attended, but also junior officers. All this is known to the High Command."[19]

The military itself has reported that some 24 ranking officers met from about 7:30 p.m. to 10:30 p.m. on November 15, 1989 at Joint Command headquarters. At that evening meeting, the decision was made to step up the Army's counteroffensive, including the use of aerial bombardment of guerrilla-controlled neighborhoods.[20] According to one source interviewed by the Lawyers Committee, General Bustillo was seated next to Colonel Benavides at this meeting. As reported by this source, Colonel Benavides turned to General Bustillo and said: "This is a chance to go after" FMLN sympathizers. "I have the UCA in my sector." General Bustillo reportedly answered: "Well then, you know what you have to do."[21] What may have preceded this exchange was not reported.

The decision to kill the Jesuits – or to implement a plan adopted earlier – was likely taken at a smaller gathering of top officers following this meeting. Col. Sigifredo Ochoa Pérez, a retired officer who is a prominent leader of the ruling ARENA party, said shortly after Colonel Benavides was arrested that the "action involved much higher officers."[22] Ochoa, who placed the key meeting as occurring immediately after the larger evening gathering, later told the U.S. television program, *60 Minutes*:

> A group of commanders stayed behind. It seems each was responsible for a zone in San Salvador. They gave an order to kill leftists, just as Colonel Benavides did. I'll say it again. Benavides obeyed, it wasn't his decision.[23]

Shortly after these evening meetings broke up, Lieutenant Espinoza, the young Atlacatl officer who likely led the

---

19 Open Letter from the Movement of Young Officers "Domingo Monterosa Vive," May 1, 1990, *as reported in Diario Latino*, May 4, 1990.

20 For a more complete discussion of the November 15, 1989 meeting at Joint Command headquarters, *see infra* Chapter II: "Chronology of the Crime."

21 Lawyers Committee interview, May 25, 1991, anonymity requested.

22 Paris AFP in Spanish 2112 GMT, Jan. 12, 1990, *as reported in* Foreign Broadcast Information Service, *Daily Report* (Latin America) [hereinafter FBIS], Jan. 16, 1990.

23 *60 Minutes* (CBS News television broadcast, April 22, 1990) (transcript on file at Lawyers Committee for Human Rights) [hereinafter *60 Minutes*].

operation on the ground, was ordered by radio to cease patrolling the UCA area and bring his men back to the Military Academy. It has never been determined who placed the radio call.

Having completed his business at headquarters, Colonel Benavides returned to the Military Academy and called together his Academy officers plus the visiting officers who formed the special command structure established on November 13 in response to the guerrilla offensive. According to the High Command, 10 officers attended the briefing.[24] Sources with knowledge of what transpired at the meeting said Colonel Benavides told those in attendance that a decision had been made to go after the "ringleaders of the FMLN" and that "it's either them or us." Colonel Benavides said a decision had been made to "eliminate" leaders in the unions, political parties, and mentioned specifically the Jesuits. In reporting this decision, the colonel read from his personal "*agenda*," listing the titles of those officers with whom he had met earlier that evening. Among those present, said Benavides, were Colonels Ponce, Zepeda, León Linares, Montano, Elena Fuentes, Rubio and General Bustillo. Benavides' statements at this meeting contradict the military's contention that he spontaneously called the three lieutenants into his office between 11:00 and 12:00 that night and ordered them to murder the Jesuits.

An internal U.S. embassy memorandum obtained by the Lawyers Committee under the Freedom of Information Act reinforces the conclusion that Colonel Benavides received higher orders. A criminal investigator temporarily assigned to the U.S. embassy in El Salvador concluded that there had been a wider conspiracy to kill the Jesuits. He concluded that a November 13, 1989 search of the Jesuit residence was in fact reconnaissance for the murders two days later. Arthur M. Sedillo, a former DEA agent assigned by the State Department's Bureau of International Narcotics Matters to the U.S. embassy in Mexico City reported, "I firmly believe that circumstantial evidence exists indicating that the Nov. 13-16 incidents are interrelated. To prove or disapprove [sic] this theory, several investigative leads including the following should be developed."[25]

---

24 Letter from the High Command to Justice Minister René Hernández Valiente, Feb. 22, 1991 (on file at the Lawyers Committee for Human Rights).

25 Unclassified Memorandum to Richard J. Chidester, Legal Section Chief, El Salvador U.S. Embassy from Arthur M. Sedillo, TDY Criminal Investigator, U.S. Embassy Mexico City, Subject: Jesuit Murder Investigation. (Feb. 28, 1990) (on file at Lawyers Committee for Human Rights).

Sedillo then proposed a series of sound, logical investigative steps. He observed, for example, that Lieutenant Espinoza of the Atlacatl Battalion was "given additional instructions to report" to Joint Command headquarters. Given that other troops were also assigned to the Academy during this special period, Sedillo proposed to determine if other units were similarly instructed to report to the Joint Command. "If they did not have to go through the same chain of command, it would appear that the Atlacatl Commando Company was preselected for the UCA special mission."[26]

Mr. Sedillo stated that he also suspected the SIU was withholding information from the U.S. embassy, particularly concerning the role of Lt. Héctor Ulises Cuenca Ocampo, an agent of the National Intelligence Directorate. Lieutenant Cuenca Ocampo had inexplicably accompanied members of the Atlacatl on their November 13 search of the Jesuit residence. When Sedillo asked the SIU's Lieutenant Preza Rivas about Cuenca Ocampo's participation in the search, the SIU agent contradicted information in the court record. He told Sedillo "that Lieutenant Cuenca Ocampo happened to be walking in the area of the UCA when he had seen members of the Atlacatl Unit and had decided to join them. This is hard to believe."[27] Mr. Sedillo wondered if Lieutenant Cuenca Ocampo might have been the officer on duty at the main UCA entrance who identified Father Ellacuría when he entered the campus just 45 minutes before the search. Mr. Sedillo said Lieutenant Preza Rivas told him "that Lieutenant Cuenca Ocampo had become an informant in the development of this investigation and that the informant had provided valuable information implicating the defendants in this case."[28]

Sedillo also emphasized that according to the testimony of Lieutenant Espinoza, his men were issued rations about 10:15 p.m. on November 15 "so that they could leave the military school early the following morning."[29] Sedillo concluded that if at that point the Atlacatl had "terminated their temporary assignment under the command of Colonel Benavides [. . . .] it would appear that the Atlacatl Company assignment to the military school was a premeditated action targeting the UCA incidents." The Atlacatl commando unit was assigned to Colonel Benavides for approximately 62 hours, during which –

---

26 Id., "Observations and Recommendations," at 1.

27 *Id.*, at 2.

28 *Id.*

29 *Id.*, at 3.

according to the commandos' own testimony – they only conducted two significant missions, the search and the murders at the UCA.[30]

To the knowledge of the Lawyers Committee, no serious attempt was made, either by Salvadoran or U.S. officials, to pursue evidence produced by Mr. Sedillo and others on the issue of higher orders. A full investigation of the crime should also have included a careful look at the role of the National Intelligence Directorate (DNI).[31] As Mr. Sedillo pointed out, the participation of DNI agent Cuenca Ocampo in the search two days before the murders has never been explained. The fact that Cuenca Ocampo was able to provide the SIU with the names of the soldiers later charged with the crime raises the question of whether Cuenca Ocampo himself was at the murder site. Treasury Police agents under the command of the DNI were posted all around the UCA in the hours surrounding the murders. Some of these men manned a roadblock at the main gate of the UCA.[32] It has never been determined who was on duty at the UCA entrance when Father Ellacuría returned to the campus and may have been told to watch for his arrival.[33]

The DNI shares office space with the CIA in San Salvador. The CIA has played a major role in DNI's establishment, training, and in its day-to-day operations. The *San Francisco Examiner* reported that CIA agents "regularly attend [DNI] meetings as observers." It went on to say that if they are not present, "what transpires at DNI meetings is nonetheless routinely passed on."[34] The role of the DNI in the crime raises the question of what CIA agents stationed in the building knew about the murders and when. "The CIA did not want to

30 According to the diary of operations of the Security Command at the Military Academy, 26 of these men conducted a search near San José de la Montaña on November 15, 1989. According to Colonel Benavides, that search was ordered by the Joint Command, as were all the orders given to the Atlacatl commandos during the brief period they were assigned to Benavides as "reinforcement." According to Col. Benjamín Eladio Canjura, a unit sent as "reinforcement" (*refuerzo*) means that it is earmarked for a specific mission while a unit placed under operational command indicates an indefinite placement. *See* Testimony of Col. Benjamín Eladio Canjura, Fourth Criminal Court, Oct. 1, 1990.

31 *See infra* Chapter VI: "From a Standstill To a Crawl."

32 SIU interviews with Treasury Police agents stationed at the Democracy Tower, Nov. 17, 1989, provided to Fourth Criminal Court.

33 On Father Ellacuría's return to the campus, *see infra* Chapter II, "Chronology of the Crime."

34 *San Francisco Examiner*, Feb. 5, 1990.

push the issue with the DNI," a ranking embassy officer told the Lawyers Committee.

An Institutional Coverup

The first attempts to conceal the military's role in the Jesuit murders occurred before the soldiers even left the campus. One of those later charged with the murders turned over a cardboard sign attached to UCA's back gate and scrawled: "The FMLN executed the enemy spies. Victory or Death, FMLN." The letters "FMLN" were also written on walls and doors on the lower floor of the priests' residence. All while professing their desire to cooperate, top officers launched an extensive coverup of the murder plot. By August 1990, the evidence was so extensive that Congressman Moakley issued a statement charging the High Command with complicity in the coverup:

> I believe that the High Command of the Salvadoran armed forces is engaged in a conspiracy to obstruct justice in the Jesuits' case. Salvadoran military officers have withheld evidence, destroyed evidence, falsified evidence and repeatedly perjured themselves in testimony before the judge. I do not believe this could be done without at least the tacit consent of the High Command.[35]

Congressman Moakley's repeated assertion that the murders were an institutional crime and that an institutional coverup was launched has rankled Salvadoran officials perhaps more than any other point. The following evidence supports the theory of an institutional coverup:

- Several testimonies in the court record indicate that Atlacatl troops were posted in the area around the UCA in the hours surrounding the murders. Yet the Atlacatl was not mentioned by Chief of Staff Ponce when he first told the court which troops were posted in the area and some soldiers who first mentioned Atlacatl presence later backpedaled and said they had not seen these troops in the area. This suggests an attempt to hide the presence of the Atlacatl.

- Troops stationed in the UCA area, as well as officers in the Joint Command headquarters during the murder hours, testified that they heard the tremendous firepower used at the UCA. Some even said they were concerned that the Joint Command complex might have come under attack. Yet according to the record, no

---

35 Statement by Congressman Joe Moakley on the Jesuits' Case and the Salvadoran Negotiations, Aug. 15, 1990, at 1.

one made any attempt to investigate or respond to the shooting. This suggests that they knew the source of the explosions and the reason.

- Despite a lengthy court investigation, key facts surrounding the crime have not been established. The military claims not to know, for example, who was posted at the main UCA gate in the days surrounding the murder, suggesting either inept record-keeping or an attempt to conceal something. Over three years later, it is not clear when or why the search of the Jesuit residence was ordered. The military has suggested the search was ordered in response to some great potential danger lurking within the campus, yet by everybody's account – the men who conducted the operation and observers such as Scotland Yard who evaluated it – the search was superficial.

A strong argument can be made that the search was reconnaissance for the murders two days later, as U.S. investigator Arthur Sedillo in fact concluded. As indicated in the court record, those who launched the search felt obligated to secure the authorization of the country's highest authorities, both Chief of Staff Ponce and President Cristiani. This indicates that they were aware of the sensitive nature of the operation. Intelligence officers interviewed by the court make no mention of reports of guerrillas inside the campus, nor of the origin of false intelligence reports attributing the murders to the FMLN.

- In late 1989, teams of emissaries associated with ARENA and the military were sent to Europe, South America and the United States on a diplomatic offensive designed to combat the negative publicity the government was getting internationally as a result of the murders. One congressional staff person who met with the delegation in Washington recalls that the group argued that the FMLN targeted Father Ellacuría for death because he had been asked by President Cristiani to investigate the October 1989 bombing of the FENASTRAS union federation headquarters.[36] A briefing paper prepared by the Ministry of Foreign Relations for the delegations provides sample questions

---

36 According to the argument, the FMLN itself had bombed FENASTRAS, a trade union federation considered a "guerrilla front" by the Salvadoran government and army, in an attempt to create martyrs and thereby trigger the guerrilla offensive, which in fact broke out less than two weeks later. Asked to join a commission to investigate the bombing, Father Ellacuría would have uncovered the FMLN's role in the crime, and therefore had to be killed before he discovered the truth, went the delegations's explanation. Lawyers Committee telephone interview, June 2, 1992.

and answers.[37] If asked about the threats broadcast against the Jesuits in the hours preceding their murder, team members were instructed to portray the open microphone as "one more manifestation of the freedom of the press that exists in El Salvador."[38] Concerning the extensive circumstantial evidence implicating the Armed Forces in the crime, the Foreign Ministry offered the following:

> It should not be forgotten in any case that blaming the government or the Army [for the Jesuit murders] is without any moral or legal foundation and should not be taken as any more than a strategy of the terrorist groups as a means to destabilize the democracy of the Nation. We should take into account as well, that the immediate beneficiary of this crime is the FMLN, which is using it internationally in its favor.[39]

On December 16, 1992, Father José María Tojeira, the Jesuit Provincial for Central America, wrote to Roberto Angulo, President of El Salvador's Legislative Assembly, to officially ask for a pardon for Colonel Benavides and Lieutenant Mendoza. In so doing, Father Tojeira emphasized that "asking for a pardon does not mean that we consider the Jesuit case closed. We believe that it is for the good of El Salvador that the intellectual authors of this crime, as well as for other unsolved crimes, also go through the process of truth, justice, and pardon." While the Jesuit murders provided El Salvador with an unprecedented opportunity to "crack the facade of impunity," three years after the crime that system of impunity remains largely intact. We share Father Tojeira's view that the case has not been closed. In publishing this comprehensive report we offer an account of what went wrong as well as elements that might aid in identifying those who ordered the murders at the UCA on November 16, 1989.

---

37 Ministry of Foreign Affairs, Objetivos de las Misiones (undated).

38 On the death threats against the Jesuits broadcast on a government/military radio station after the start of the guerrilla offensive, *see infra* Chapter II: "Chronology of the Crime."

39 *Supra* note 37, at 12.

CHAPTER I : "DEATH TO INTELLIGENCE!"

– General Millán Astray, in a debate with the writer Miguel de Unamuno, University of Salamanca, Spain, 1936

> *The UCA . . . is a logistical center of Communist subversion. The Jesuits who direct this center of studies are agents of the Marxist conspiracy at the service of the Kremlin.*[40]
>
> *It is proven, and there are documents showing, that Ellacuría is the agent who directs all Marxist-Leninist strategy in Central America.*[41]
>
> *These are the intellectual authors who have directed the guerrillas for a long time.*[42]

El Salvador's right-wing has long been obsessed with the Society of Jesus and with Ignacio Ellacuría in particular.[43] Since the early 1970s, El Salvador's Jesuits have been subjected to a vitriolic campaign of public attacks, which at times erupted into violence. Father Ellacuría and others were regularly referred to in the media as "nefarious," "satanic" and "the Basque agitators at the UCA, headed up by Commander Ignacio Ellacuría."[44] An April 18, 1989 headline in *La Prensa Gráfica* read: "Jesuit Montes is Immoral, ARENA Affirms." Referring to Father Ellacuría, a *Diario de Hoy* columnist wrote that shortly "after World War II, a sinister person arrived in the country, and

40 A. Jerez Magaña, *La Infiltración Marxista en la Iglesia*, at 27 (Editorial Dignidad, Instituto de Relaciones Internacionales, San Salvador: 1989) [hereinafter Jerez Magaña].

41 Ing. José Hernández, president of the Association of Salvadoran Professionals, in *Diario de Hoy*, Aug. 18, 1988.

42 Col. Guillermo Alfredo Benavides, convicted for the Jesuit slayings, is reported by defendant Gonzalo Guevara Cerritos to have said these words when ordering the killings. *See* "Sentencia interlocutoria para detención provisional," Fourth Criminal Court, Jan. 18, 1990, 3:45 p.m.

43 Ignacio Ellacuría was regularly subjected to primitive attacks such as those that appeared in an unsigned article in *Diario de Hoy* on Oct. 4, 1987 under the title "Ellacuría Comes Out in Support of Totalitarianism." Ostensibly a straight news article covering a speech by the Rector, the piece parenthetically adds, "Ellacuría, who is the ecclesiastical instigator of the 1979 coup. . . ." Further, the newspaper offers that "Ellacuría, who wore a gray suit of a foreign cut, far afield from the appearance of a priest and more like a rich businessman. . . ."

44 *See*, among others, *Diario de Hoy*, Jan. 25, 1989, Feb. 16, 1989 and March 3, 1989. Father Ellacuría and several other Jesuits in the UCA community were born in the Basque region of Spain.

it wouldn't be much of a surprise if he turned out to be a KGB agent . . . ."[45] The history of these attacks against El Salvador's Jesuit community offers some explanation of what happened at the UCA on the night of November 15-16, 1989. An examination of that history leads to the conclusion that the murders were deaths foretold.

Attacks against the Jesuits first surfaced in the early 1970s, when teachers at the Jesuit elementary and secondary school, the Externado San José, introduced new curriculum. In keeping with changes promoted by Vatican II, Jesuit and lay faculty sought to educate their students about their country's social problems and to discuss the need for fundamental social change. A group of younger priests took over the leadership of the school and by lowering tuition fees, attempted to expand the student body beyond the sons and daughters of El Salvador's elite. On field trips to poor neighborhoods, students were exposed to how the majority of Salvadorans lived. Some Externado pupils participated in literacy campaigns.

The attacks against the Externado Jesuits began in the pages of *Orientación*, the official periodical of the Catholic Church, which at the time was edited by the conservative wing of the church. *Orientación* accused the school of teaching Marxism. Some Externado parents joined the chorus, and attacks began to appear in the daily press. The Jesuits were accused of corrupting the nation's youth and of turning parent against child. Some Salvadorans called for the priests' expulsion. The Salvadoran president, Col. Arturo Armando Molina, asked Jesuit superiors to send abroad the priests who taught at the school. "Ruin and Anarchy in the Externado San José," read one headline in spring 1973; another charged: "Marxist Tendencies in the Declarations of Jesuits."[46] The Attorney General's office launched criminal proceedings, and Father Juan Ramón Moreno, a Jesuit who at the time was the interim rector, was called in to testify about the school's curriculum. He was asked if a comic book called "The Popular Way of the Cross" – which the Jesuits' critics considered "subversive" – was used in classes.[47]

---

45 *Diario de Hoy*, June 13, 1988.

46 *Diario de Hoy*, June 19 & 21, 1973.

47 *See La Prensa Gráfica*, June 22, 1973. Father Moreno was among the six Jesuits murdered on November 16, 1989. Another victim, Father Segundo Montes, chaired the Externado's department of social studies and sociology in 1973. He later served as rector. The nation's Attorney General took testimony from Jesuits and parents of Externado students to see if there was a basis to charge the Jesuits under the Criminal Code for "making propaganda for doctrines which are communist, anarchic, or contrary to democracy. . . ." *See El Diario de Hoy*, June 10, 1973.

In June 1973, the Society of Jesus published "This is how the Externado Thinks," which appeared on six consecutive days in the newspapers.[48] The lengthy document laid out in detail the Jesuits' views on Salvadoran society, Christianity and pedagogy. Some discontented parents sent their children to other schools. The campaign subsequently seemed to run out of steam, and for a time, was forgotten.

1976 Attempt at Agrarian Reform

Densely populated, El Salvador has long had one of the region's least equitable patterns of land tenure. Pressure for arable land by the nearly 60% of the population who remained landless in 1979 is often cited among the root causes of the current civil war.[49] One study showed that six families held more land than 133,000 peasants together.[50] On June 29, 1976, El Salvador's Legislative Assembly adopted Decree #31, a modest agrarian reform program which would have affected only four percent of the country's land. The plan, which had the support of the U.S. Agency for International Development, was to be implemented by the newly created Agrarian Transformation Institute (ISTA), the military and the centrist peasant organization, the Salvadoran Communal Union (UCS).

The Jesuits publicly and forcefully backed the plan, drawing criticism from the Right as well as from the Left. Some leftist political leaders argued that the extremely limited proposal was not worthy of support. The UCA journal, *Estudios Centroamericanos* (*ECA*), opined that the plan

> left no shadow or doubt that the intent is serious and appears to respond to a decided will to change the country's socioeconomic structures, beginning with something so strategic as the agrarian structure.
>
> All other citizens, of any ideology or class, who do not favor or desire a social explosion in El Salvador,

---

48 The document also appeared as a pamphlet, "El Externado Piensa Asi" (Publicaciones de la Revista `Estudios Centroamericanos,' June 1973).

49 *See, e.g.*, T. Barry & D. Preusch, *The Central America Fact Book*, at 216-217 (Grove Press, New York: 1986); M. Gettleman, *et al*, eds., "Peasants and Oligarchs in the Agrarian Reform," in *El Salvador: Central America in the New Cold War*, at 157-187 (Grove Press, New York: 1981).

50 *See* Barry & Preusch, at 217.

> must logically – emotionally is more difficult – accept a concrete agrarian reform. . . .[51]

A special September/October 1976 issue of *ECA* was devoted to the proposal, which by October was withdrawn by President Molina in the face of vociferous opposition by large landowners. An historical *ECA* editorial, "A Sus Ordenes, Mi Capital," attributed the president's about-face to a campaign of "lies, slander, threats, all available methods against the country's authorities."[52] The editorial said that the "most reactionary sector of capitalism, the agrarian sector, had won the battle."

> In the face of the pressure of national capitalism, and possibly, Central American capitalism, the government has ceded, the government has submitted, the government has obeyed. After such an exaggerated show of strength and determination, the government ended up saying, "At your service, my capital."[53]

The UCA campus was bombed six times during 1976. The first bomb detonated about 10:00 p.m. on January 6 at the *ECA* offices. The administration building and *ECA's* quarters were each attacked twice that year. A death squad known as the White Warriors Union took credit for the December 3 bombing of the administration building. In *ECA* and elsewhere, the UCA community responded, writing in November 1976 that:

> injustice cannot last long. The social caldron will no longer stand the pressure. The Right can win some battles, but historically they have lost the war. This conviction [that they can win the war] leads them down an erroneous path: bomb the intelligensia, as if by doing so they could kill adverse ideas.[54]

The Campesino Movement in Aguilares

In 1972 a Salvadoran Jesuit named Rutilio Grande returned to the community where he was born to take up work as the parish priest in Aguilares, a rich agricultural area with some

51 "Por fin, Reforma Agraria," *ECA*, #334, Aug. 1976, at 343.

52 "A sus ordenes, mi capital," *ECA*, #337, Nov. 1976, at 637.

53 *Id.*, at 641.

54 "Las Derechas Ponen Bombas," *ECA* #337, Nov. 1976, at 704. *See also* "Por que nos ponen bombas?" *ECA* #338, Dec. 1976.

33,000 inhabitants.[55] Much of the land was in the hands of El Salvador's most powerful families who produced sugar, relying on day laborers. Throughout the 1970s, social unrest grew as agricultural workers organized to obtain better wages and working and living conditions. It was in this environment that a team of three Jesuits, headed by Father Grande, and several Jesuit seminarians began their pastoral work. The team quickly developed close working relationships with *campesino* organizations such as the Christian Federation of Salvadoran Peasants (FECCAS) and the Union of Rural Workers (UTC), which were expanding rapidly. FECCAS had in fact been born in the church in 1964, but quickly claimed its autonomy.[56] "Christian Base Communities," a new form of church organizing that was growing throughout Latin America in the wake of a 1968 meeting of bishops in Medellín, Colombia,[57] grew up throughout the zone. Small groups devoted to Christian study and action often made use of materials produced by the Theological Reflection Center, founded by Jesuits at the UCA in 1974.

To some outside observers – especially those on the Right – the distinction between peasant organizing and pastoral work was lost, especially as some Jesuit seminarians and other priests from the Archdiocese assumed leading roles within the *campesino* movement. The early attacks on the Jesuit team in Aguilares expressed the themes that have remained constant over the last 20 years. According to their conservative critics, foreign Jesuit intellectuals – described as crafty, nefarious and power hungry – have perverted the minds of Salvadoran clergy, peasants or students, who have then organized movements promoting fundamental social change. "The Jesuits have organized and demagogically directed FECCAS and the UTC," reported the Salvadoran daily *Prensa Gráfica* in May 1977.[58]

Many Salvadoran rightists have charged that had there been no Jesuits in the country, the Farabundo Martí Front for National Liberation (FMLN) would never have existed. Jesuit-run schools

55 On this period and the life of Rutilio Grande, *see* "El Salvador: Los Riesgos del evangelio, Iglesia y violencia politica," *ECA*, #355, May 1978; R. Cardenal, *Historia de una esperanza: vida de Rutilio Grande* (UCA Editores, San Salvador: 1987) [hereinafter Cardenal].

56 Cardenal, *supra* note 55, at 457.

57 The Medellín meeting, which lasted two weeks, was an attempt by Latin American bishops to interpret the reforms growing out of Vatican II and to adapt them to the reality of Latin America.

58 *Prensa Gráfica*, May 19, 1977, *as cited in* Secretariado Social Interdiocesano, *Persecución de la Iglesia en El Salvador*, at 24 (San Salvador: June 1977).

were the "launching pad for the revolutionary praxis of the Catholic schools," wrote one critic about this period.[59] Since Father Grande was Salvadoran by birth, his deviation was attributed to his having fallen under the influence of foreign Jesuits at the UCA, from whom he in fact often sought counsel.

> Everything that happened in Aguilares, as well as the rest of the country, is the direct responsibility of a group of foreign conspirators ensconced in [the UCA]. These Jesuits – above all Ellacuría and Txobrino [sic] – have been the real brains who have remained hidden behind all the subversive movements that have been stirred up by the clergy in our country.[60]

The Reaction to a Landowner's Death

Throughout 1976 and 1977, the military government and its Armed Forces continued to move against the peasant organizations and the Catholic Church. During the tenure of President Molina (1972-1977), five priests were arrested, 18 expelled and two killed.[61] On December 5, 1976, a reportedly accidental death of a local landowner quickly assumed nationwide repercussions when the killing was blamed on the Church and in particular on the Jesuit pastoral team in Aguilares.[62] That fall, a series of economic demands by the *campesino* movement led to protests and demonstrations, and ultimately the arrest of several activists. Peasants to the north of Aguilares had lost their small plots when the land was flooded by the Cerrón Grande hydroelectric project. Supported by FECCAS, peasants unable to achieve redress went to the hacienda of the Orellana family to discuss the matter. The Orellanas had received compensation for the lands flooded by the reservoir, but had failed to share any of the money with the displaced peasants.[63] At first refusing to speak with them, the Orellana brothers suddenly appeared on the scene, shooting their pistols into the crowd. According to the account that

---

59 F. Delgado, *La Iglesia Popular Nació en El Salvador: Memorias de 1972 a 1982*, at 42 (no date or publisher appears on the booklet, which circulated in late 1988) [hereinafter Delgado].

60 Jerez Magaña, *supra* note 40, at 23. The author is referring to Jesuit theologian Jon Sobrino, an UCA faculty member.

61 P. Lernoux, *Cry of the People*, at 69 (Doubleday, New York: 1980) [hereinafter Lernoux].

62 *See* Cardenal, *supra* note 55, at 536-542.

63 Russell, "The Church," in *El Salvador in Crisis*, at 112 (Colorado River Press: 1984).

FECCAS later gave to Archbishop Luis Chávez y González, Francisco Orellana accidentally shot his brother Eduardo in the stomach. Four Treasury Policemen who appeared on the scene shot into the air, instead of attacking the people, which FECCAS took as proof that they knew the death was accidental.

Though no one was ever charged in the killing, the Right used it as an opportunity to step up attacks on the Church and those they called "Third Worldist priests." One observer has said that "[f]rom the date of the Orellana killing on, religious and political repression became so intertwined that it was difficult to separate them."[64] Landowners' organizations and other business groups launched a vitriolic media campaign, often singling out the Jesuits and naming Rutilio Grande and Father David Rodríquez by name. By chance, Monsignor Rivera y Damas, then the auxiliary bishop of San Salvador, was in Aguilares the day of the killing to preside over the ordination of three Jesuits. The landowners charged that a hit team to kill Orellana had been organized during the ordination celebration. Government troops moved into Aguilares in a show of force. A few days after the incident, Archbishop Chávez met with several Jesuits, offering his support and asked Father Ellacuría to draft a communiqué in response to the events.

In the early months of 1977, two ex-Jesuit seminarians working in Aguilares were deported. Another former Jesuit, Juan José Ramírez, was tortured with electric shock during a 10-day detention. Several foreign Jesuits working in El Salvador were refused entry to the country, among them Ignacio Ellacuría, then a professor of philosophy and theology at the UCA. Born in Spain, Father Ellacuría moved to El Salvador in 1948 and by 1977 had become a Salvadoran citizen. On February 19, the director of immigration, Colonel Santibánez, suggested to Jesuit Provincial Father César Jerez that all the Jesuits in Aguilares be removed. In discussion with the three priests in Aguilares, it was decided that the two foreigners would leave while Father Grande would remain.

Rumors of plans to kill Father Grande circulated in Aguilares in early 1977; apprised of the threats, he dismissed them and continued his work. A lay teacher received a letter announcing plans to finish off the priests, and then her, in the same way rats are killed. One week later, on March 12, 1977, Rutilio Grande was assassinated along with two laymen, while en route to say mass in El Paisnal. In the back of Grande's vehicle were three children who survived the attack.

---

64 *Id.*, at 112.

A Justice of the Peace and the First Instance Judge of Quetzaltepeque conducted for a time a judicial investigation of the crime.[65] While no real autopsy was performed, a medical examination indicated that shots were fired from both sides of the road and that 9 mm. bullets were fired from a Mautzer, the type of weapon then used by the police.[66] The three surviving children were interviewed, and identified one of the gunmen as Benito Estrada. An arrest warrant was issued for Estrada, a 35-year-old resident of El Paisnal. He was a customs agent (*policía de aduana*) at a border post who had returned to his home community after he was wounded in a fight with co-workers. He was never apprehended. Judicial authorities also ordered ballistics tests,[67] took photographs of the crime scene and elaborated a map of the area. The investigation led nowhere, and the murder remains unsolved.

In May, four more Jesuits were detained, mistreated and deported. Flyers appeared on San Salvador streets saying "*Haga patría, mate un Cura*" – Be a Patriot, Kill a Priest. On May 19, the military launched "Operation Rutilio," sealing off a 500-square mile area around Aguilares. Each house was searched, and many belongings stolen. Those in houses with photos of Rutilio Grande or the New Testament were especially brutalized.[68] While the government officially recognized seven deaths, witnesses said at least 50 were killed during the month-long siege of Aguilares. Father Grande's three Jesuit co-workers were all deported after being mistreated in detention. In June, a death squad known as the White Warriors Union (UGB) threatened to kill each of the country's 47 Jesuits unless they left El Salvador within one month. "Our struggle is not against the Church but against Jesuit guerrillaism," read the communiqué. As the deadline drew near, an ominous voice

---

65 Arzobispado de San Salvador, Secretaría de Información y Prensa, Boletín Informativo No. 14 and 15, May 1977.

66 *See* Cardenal, *supra* note 55, at 576; on the killing in general, *see* at 570-577.

67 The medical examination revealed 12 gun shot wounds, none of which showed exit wounds. Lacking the proper surgical instruments, the doctor was unable to extract any bullets for analysis. The physician concluded that shots had been fired from a distance of 15-18 meters and from both sides of the road.

68 On the occupation of Aguilares, *see* Cardenal, *supra* note 55, at 596-599 *and* Lernoux, *supra* note 61, at 76-79. Like Ignacio Ellacuría, Rutilio Grande remains an obsession for the Salvadoran Right. In February and March 1988, *La Prensa Gráfica* ran a four-part series on Grande under the headline, "Marxist Infiltration in the Church: Rutilio Grande in the Church of Judas."

on the radio announced repeatedly, "In 12 hours, all Jesuits will be killed."

The Jesuits' General, Father Pedro Arrupe, said: "They may end up as martyrs, but my priests are not going to leave [El Salvador], because they are with the people."[69] In San Salvador, the Central American Provincial, Father César Jerez, wrote that "[w]e have not remained because we are obstinate, but because we are thinking of our brothers, especially the dispossessed, who have suffered more than we . . . . We have remained to make a small testimony to the loyalty of the church."[70]

In June and July 1977, the Jesuits published a six-part newspaper series, "The Jesuits before the Salvadoran People," a lengthy exposition of the Society's history and work in El Salvador and a response to their critics.[71]

> We do not know the reasons for which they have waged their fiercest battles against the Jesuits. Judging from the attacks, we Jesuits have always been liars, sectarian and two-faced [*mentiroso, sectario, falso*]. We are very clever at manipulating people and institutions with an eye to achieving our hidden goals. We are hypocrites. We are Marxists (that is, monsters of the most dreadful sort).
>
> In summary, what can be gleaned from this collection of insults and calumnies is that we Jesuits are the most terrible plague to descend on this country. And the remedy, as with all plagues, is to exterminate it.
>
> It is clear that the Church is changing, and it is clear that the Jesuits, as part of the Church, have changed. These changes have been little by little, but effective. The fundamental aspect of the change consists of the decision to serve the country's majority. . . .[72]

The 1980s

Throughout 1980, violence against the Jesuits and Jesuit installations increased in tandem with that directed against

69 Lernoux, *supra* note 61, at 77.

70 *Noticias de la Provincia Centroamericana*, S.I., July 1977.

71 The series subsequently appeared in *ECA*, #344, June 1977. The first installment appeared on June 14, 1977 in *La Prensa Gráfica* and *El Diario de Hoy*.

72 *Id.*

other sectors of society. Between 1980 to 1982, El Salvador's death toll would reach 800 per month.[73] Buildings used by Jesuits were sprayed with machine-gun fire in January and February 1980. On February 18, bombs destroyed part of the UCA library and another heavily damaged the printing press on June 29. The priests' home in Jardines de Guadalupe was badly damaged in two bombings on October 24 and 27. In the first attack, some 12 bombs were lobbed over a wall that had been installed after the building was machine-gunned in February. Father Segundo Montes narrowly missed death when one explosive left a meter-wide hole in the wall next to the bed where he was sleeping. A Jesuit who lived in the house at the time recalls that had Montes not changed the position of his bed one week earlier he would have been killed.

At 1:15 p.m. on March 22, National Policemen entered the enclosed UCA campus and opened fire, killing Manuel Orantes Guillén, a mathematics student, and capturing two others. In his last homily one day before his own murder, Archbishop Romero called the invasion of the UCA a "grave offense against civilization and the rule of law in our country." The Jesuit high school, Externado San José, was occupied and searched in July; two Externado teachers were killed in the school's doorway in September. In late November, the entire leadership of the Democratic Revolutionary Front (FDR), an opposition political grouping which subsequently became aligned with the FMLN, was kidnapped from the Externado. The tortured cadavers of the five men showed up that night on the shores of Lake Ilopango.[74]

The next day, Father Ellacuría fled El Salvador when he was tipped off about a military plot against his life. A friend in the military telephoned an intermediary who transmitted the message to Ellacuría, who had become the UCA rector a year

---

73 *See* Americas Watch & American Civil Liberties Union, *Report on Human Rights in El Salvador,* at xxxii (Jan. 26, 1982). This report offers the following tallies for 1979-1981. According to the Archdiocese of San Salvador, an estimated 1,000 persons were killed during 1979. The U.S. Department of State placed murders during 1980 at 9,000, while Socorro Juridico del Arzobispado de San Salvador placed the number for 1980 at 10,000. Over 9,000 were killed during the first half of 1981, according to Socorro Juridico's director. *Id.* at 37. In January 1982, Socorro Juridico placed the number for 1981 at 12,501. *Id.* at 278.

74 Those murdered were Manuel Franco of the Nationalist Democratic Union (UDN); Enrique Barrera of the National Revolutionary Movement (MNR); Humberto Mendoza of the Popular Liberation Movement (MLP); Juan Chacón of the Popular Revolutionary Bloc (BPR); and FDR President Enrique Alvarez, a wealthy dairy farmer who once served as Minister of Agriculture.

earlier: "The patient is in grave danger." When asked if it could wait, the caller said, "[n]o, the patient won't survive the night. He must be moved immediately." Ellacuría sought refuge in the Spanish embassy and left the country the next day. For security, the flight manifest listed him as I. Beascoechea, his second surname which he seldom used. He spent some months in Spain and Mexico, later serving as UCA rector from Nicaragua. He returned to El Salvador in April 1982.

Archbishop Oscar Arnulfo Romero

Oscar Arnulfo Romero was consecrated as archbishop of San Salvador just three weeks before Father Grande's death. Known as a cautious and conservative man, he was considered a safe choice to lead the Church at a sensitive time in El Salvador's history. The death of his friend and colleague, Rutilio Grande, was said to have a profound impact on Romero.[75] He grew increasingly outspoken, calling repeatedly on the government to stop the violence against its own people.

Just three years after he was appointed archbishop, on March 24, 1980, Oscar Romero himself was shot dead while saying mass at the Divine Providence cancer hospital in San Salvador. Ten years afterward, the investigation of his murder remains open, but as far as ever from resolution.[76]

That Oscar Romero did not turn out to be the archbishop they expected has been used by the Salvadoran Right as yet another example of the Jesuit conspiracy. According to a booklet published in 1988, a group of priests met with Romero behind closed doors just days after he took over the Archdiocese.

> During these days they analyzed the national situation seen through a Marxist analysis. They discovered Archbishop Romero's personal psychological limitation: insecurity. The Jesuits and the "Group" offered themselves as a support group in the pastoral government of the Archdiocese. [....] The Jesuits started to work feverishly in the Archdiocese after Monsignor

---

75 *See* J. Sobrino, *Monseñor Romero*, at 9-39 (UCA Editores, San Salvador: 1989); J. Delgado, *Oscar A. Romero, Biografía*, at 71-99 (UCA Editores, San Salvador: 1986).

76 *See* Lawyers Committee for Human Rights, "A Decade of Failed Promises: The Investigation of Archbishop Romero's Murder" (March 1990). The paper was published in Spanish in *ECA* #497, March 1990, at 191-207.

> Romero took over, something unprecedented and never before seen in this country.[77]

Years after Archbishop Romero's death, this theme continues to surface. In November 1988, a San Salvador daily cited another Salvadoran bishop who said that "[f]our clergymen directed by the Rector of the Central American University (UCA), Ignacio Ellacuría, manipulated to extinction Archbishop Oscar Romero and they prepared for him his controversial Sunday homilies."[78]

Where there were Jesuits, there was treachery, according to their rightist critics. While run by the Jesuits, El Salvador's seminary, San José de la Montana, "was gradually converted into a 'nursery' of future Marxist priests."[79] After the FMLN was founded in 1980, Father Ellacuría and other Jesuits were regularly referred to as "the intellectual authors of the guerrilla movement," the "ringleaders" or "brains" of the FMLN. In ordering the murders of the six Jesuit priests in 1989, Colonel Benavides is said to have stated, "It's either them or us, since they have been the intellectuals who have led the guerrillas for a long time."[80] Another defendant in the case quoted Colonel Benavides saying: "We are going to begin with the ringleaders, inside our sector we have the university and there is Ellacuría."[81]

The UCA itself continues to be a wound that will not heal. The institution was founded in 1965 as an alternative to the National University, which El Salvador's influential families considered too leftist. The Jesuit-run school was to be the country's elite institution of higher learning, divorced from the political fray. That the UCA's early supporters and donors feel betrayed crops up again and again: "The UCA is the Bulwark of Communist Confabulation," read a 1986 headline.[82] One critic charged the Jesuits with "converting the UCA into an instrument of their political ambitions, the university that was founded with money from the rich, landowners, and industrial-

---

77 Delgado, *supra* note 59, at 29-30.

78 *Diario de Hoy*, Nov. 6, 1988.

79 Jerez Magaña, *supra* note 40, at 13.

80 Extrajudicial confession of Gonzalo Guevara Cerritos, Jan. 13, 1990, *as reprinted in ECA*, #493-494 Nov.-Dec. 1989 at 1161.

81 Extrajudicial confession of Lt. José Ricardo Espinoza Guerra, Jan. 13, 1990, *as reprinted in ECA, id*.

82 *Diario de Hoy*, May 22, 1986.

ists in San Salvador."[83] Ellacuría devoted himself to "the mental deformation of our youth" and the UCA "has been converted into the spokesman for the guerrillas."[84] UCA, according to another critic, was an "academic facade to indoctrinate and direct inhumane subversion."[85] The 1979 "young officers coup" was planned within the UCA, rightists charged, and "the leadership of the FMLN has been indoctrinated in these centers of Jesuit instruction."[86]

ARENA's Rise in the Late 1980s

In mid-1986 ARENA deputies in the Legislative Assembly launched a campaign to strip Father Ellacuría of his Salvadoran citizenship, arguing that as a foreigner and a clergyman he had violated constitutional provisions barring both from political involvement. On September 10, Dr. Armando Calderón Sol, now the ARENA mayor of San Salvador, introduced a proposal that would establish a "Special Commission to investigate the activities of the Jesuit priest José Ignacio Ellacurya [sic]" . . . "to clarify if the priest Ellacurya is a foreigner and is intervening in Salvadoran politics, in this case he would be an undesirable alien. . . ."[87] Roberto D'Aubuisson, then retired from the Army and an ARENA deputy, said that: "With [Ellacuría's] declarations it can be confirmed what has always been said: that the real ringleaders of subversive movements like the BPR and the FPL are not in the mountains, but near the UCA."[88]

Some members of the Christian Democratic Party joined in the campaign, including President Duarte, who warned that Father Ellacuría could lose his citizenship "for having

---

83 *Prensa Grafica,* Sept. 24, 1986.

84 *Diario de Hoy*, Sept. 26, 1986.

85 *Id.*, Aug. 29, 1986.

86 *Id.*, June 13, 1988.

87 *El Mundo*, Sept. 11, 1986.

88 *Diario de Hoy*, Sept. 17, 1986. The Popular Revolutionary Bloc (BPR) -- founded in the aftermath of a July 30, 1975 student massacre -- gathered peasant, union, student, Christian and neighborhood associations in a new kind of grassroots organization. The Popular Liberation Forces (FPL), founded in 1970, is the oldest and largest of the five armed groupings which together make up the FMLN.

insulted the executive, the government, the president, and the people."[89]

In late 1988 and 1989, two books were published on the popular church in El Salvador and its alleged responsibility for the "communist aggression of the FMLN." Both focused on the Society of Jesus. Freddy Delgado, a Catholic priest who collaborates closely with the Armed Forces, published *La Iglesia Popular Nació en El Salvador: Memorias de 1972 a 1982* (The Popular Church was Born in El Salvador). Later, the rightist Institute on International Relations (IRI) issued Alvaro Antonio Jerez Magaña's *La Infiltración Marxista en la Iglesia* (Marxist Infiltration in the Church). The books' publication gave rise to numerous newspaper articles, revisiting the subject of the Jesuits' "brainwashing" of Archbishop Romero and making charges such as "more than 80% of the ecclesiastical hierarchy is managed ideologically by the Jesuits Ignacio Ellacuría, Jon Sobrino and their followers."[90] Paid advertisements in San Salvador's morning papers again denounced the Jesuits, mentioning some by name, and blaming them for all the country's ills. In March 1989, one newspaper reported that Freddy Delgado had received death threats from "Marxist priests" because of his book.[91]

The rhetoric against the Jesuits increased steadily throughout the late 1980s, and would take on new intensity after ARENA won the March 1989 presidential elections. A 1987 campaign attempted to paint Father Ellacuría as a defender of the FMLN's use of land mines because he stated that

---

89 *El Mundo*, Sept. 6, 1986. President Duarte's remarks were included in a front-page article entitled "Duarte Accuses UCA Rector of Being FMLN Spokesman." The article opened by reporting Duarte's comments on the next scheduled round of talks with the guerrilla movement and ended with attacks on Father Ellacuría:

> Duarte manifested that the UCA rector defends the Marxist project of the FMLN, and further, that he is the creater of the theory and concept of the guerillas' rebellion in order to maintain their process of rebellion, of indiscipline, for their objectives. Duarte said that "there are two projects: they incorporate themselves into the democratic process and become a political, social and economic force so they can have influence and make inroads on this process, or they choose the route of weapons and violence and taking power by force. Now, that which Ellacuría is proposing is the second model," the president emphasized because "I am proposing the first."

90 *See e.g., Diario de Hoy*, Jan. 25, Feb. 2 and 16, 1989.

91 *Diario de Hoy*, Mar. 21, 1989.

mines are a weapon of war directed against the Army and their use did not constitute acts of terrorism designed to hurt civilians. A news article which described wounds suffered by two *campesinos* in a mine explosion was entitled "Mines Which the Priest Defends Mutilate More Peasants."[92] The only other reference to Ellacuría was a clause in the last line of the article which mentioned "these infernal artefacts, that a Jesuit justifies." In late 1988, the Armed Forces ran signed, paid advertisements suggesting that Ellacuría supported the FMLN's use of car bombs.

In April 1989, ARENA conducted a similar campaign against Father Segundo Montes, director of the UCA's human rights institute, for his alleged support for terrorist acts on the part of the FMLN.[93] An ARENA press release accused Montes of supporting FMLN terrorism in "an arrogant and cold manner" during a television interview. "ARENA energetically protests this indescribable conduct by the Jesuit Segundo Montes, even more because he is a university professor and the director of the Human Rights Commission [sic] of the UCA."

A paid advertisement by the Salvadoran Armed Forces in April ran a quotation from Father Montes superimposed over a dead body. The headline read: "In El Salvador there are groups and persons who insist on defending the terrorism of the FMLN-FDR and their front groups."[94] In April, after urban commandos of the FMLN had killed the ARENA-appointed Attorney General, Col. Juan Orlando Zepeda, then commander of the First Infantry Brigade and now a general and the Vice-Minister of Defense, said that the murder had been planned inside the UCA. The UCA "is a refuge for terrorist leaders, from where they plan the strategy of attack against Salvadorans." [95]

One week later, the UCA printing press was again bombed. A month earlier, a grenade had exploded in the university's electrical plant, the first acts of violence directed against the Jesuits since 1983. *Diario de Hoy* downplayed the attack and suggested the dynamite had been placed to "fabricate martyrs and justify later acts of terrorism."[96] On April 28, several explosives were thrown at the complex housing the university's

92 *Diario de Hoy*, July 6, 1987. *See also Diario de Hoy*, May 23 and 30, 1987.

93 *See* April 13, 1989 issues of *Prensa Grafica*, *Diario de Hoy*, *Diario Latino*, *El Mundo*.

94 *Prensa Grafica*, April 16, 1989.

95 *Diario de Hoy*, April 20, 1989.

96 *Id.*, May 4, 1989.

printing press, located in one corner of the campus along the Southern Highway.

On July 19, 1989, Gabriel Payés, an outspoken rightist and friend of Colonel Zepeda, was shot and died a month later. Though the FMLN never acknowledged the killing, some held guerrilla urban commandos responsible. The next day, the right-wing Committee to Save the University of El Salvador, denounced "communist infiltration" at the UCA.[97] Shortly before 2:00 a.m. on July 22, the university printing press again suffered an attack, the most serious in the last decade. Two bombs exploded outside the building, one in the transformer and another under a parked bus. Two others went off around the computer and photocopier; three more were defused. The damages exceeded $60,000.

In 1981, Father Ellacuría had called for a negotiated settlement to the civil war, saying it was clear that neither side could win a military victory.[98] At the time, his view was considered heretical. Along with Archbishop Rivera y Damas, Ellacuría remained the most consistent proponent of negotiations over the years. Just over two months before his death, he reiterated his desire for peace and his call for a negotiated settlement to the conflict in the form of a letter to the editor of *Diario de Hoy*.[99] Memorializing their founder, the staff of *Proceso*, the UCA weekly, wrote that Ellacuría's

> extraordinary intelligence has been felled by the bullets of the country's most irrational groups, egged

---

97 For a summary of attacks leading up to the Jesuit murders, *see* "El Asesinato de los Jesuitas (1)," *Proceso*, #409, Nov. 29, 1989. On June 30, 1989, another prominent rightist, Edgar Chacón of the Institute of International Relations, was killed.

98 *See ECA*, Aug. 1981, at 741-752. In this article Ellacuría first laid out his analysis which later became known as the "third force" -- neither FMLN nor Armed Forces. Father Ellacuría sought to promote reconciliation and peace by avoiding the polarization which characterizes Salvadoran political life. Misunderstood, his views only gave rise to more attacks. Asked what he thought of Father Ellacuría's "third force," Sigifredo Ochoa Pérez, formerly a top Army officer and now a prominent ARENA leader, responded: "Indisputably, Father Ellacuría is someone who has come here to subvert public order. Spanish by birth, he is a nationalized Salvadoran, but this does not give him any right to use an institution of higher education to subvert the minds of our youth. I don't think there is any doubt that he favors the FMLN. For him, the 'third way' does not exist, for him, there's only the way of the FMLN." *La Vanguardia* (Barcelona), Aug. 16, 1987.

99 *Diario de Hoy*, Aug. 29, 1989.

> on by terrorist journalism which has always nourished ideologically the dirty war of the death squads.
>
> He was killed for defending dialogue as the most rational and civilized way to end the inhuman war which has been bleeding the country for 10 years. The ultra-right, which could never combat his ideas with anything but insults, has ended up doing so with bullets.[100]

The U.S. View

Throughout the years of U.S. involvement in El Salvador, U.S. officials often repeated pejorative characterizations made by the Salvadoran right and military. Cable traffic between the U.S. embassy and the State Department in the early 1980s indicated a preoccupation with the critical analysis of Salvadoran events and the U.S. role being published in *ECA*. A June 1982 cable reporting on an article examining the flawed elections of March 28, 1982 says that the

> sources and data used in the Jesuit editorial to support this argument are subject to criticism. The main purpose of the editorial is to discredit the March 28 elections and the resulting government in order to advocate negotiations between the [Government of El Salvador] and the FMLN/FDR. . . . This quasi-analysis claiming election fraud was previously developed in two internal Jesuit documents. . . .[101]

The embassy refers to *ECA* itself as "the most important of the very few non-clandestine pro-FMLN/FDR publications available in El Salvador."[102]

An internal State Department memorandum identified the media's "source" of information on irregularities in the March 1982 vote count as the

> strongly leftist Central American University (UCA) in San Salvador. From the beginning of the Salvadoran conflict, the UCA has sympathized with the

---

100 "In Memoriam de Ignacio Ellacuría," *Proceso*, #409, Nov. 29, 1989.

101 U.S. embassy San Salvador cable to the Secretary of State, June 9, 1982. A series of government documents on the Jesuits in El Salvador was obtained by the National Security Archive, Washington, D.C., under the Freedom of Information Act.

102 *Id.*

> Salvadoran armed left, and this sympathy is reflected in university publications. The attempt to discredit the Salvadoran elections indicates the UCA is striving to limit the damage from what remains a severe blow to the leftist cause.[103]

Another State Department cable in August 1983 discusses an *ECA* issue on the U.S. role in El Salvador. "The articles [material deleted] show a bias for a negotiated solution to the Salvadoran conflict which will ultimately lead to an authoritarian leftist (but not Marxist-Leninist) regime."

Chris Norton, a free-lance reporter who covered El Salvador for *The Christian Science Monitor* and other publications from 1985 to 1990, recalls that *The Monitor's* foreign editor received a telephone call in early 1986 from a State Department official who complained about his reporting.[104] Greg Lagana, a former embassy press attaché who at the time of the call was the spokesman for the State Department's Latin America bureau, told the *Monitor* editor that the State Department was unhappy that one of Norton's frequent unnamed sources was Father Ignacio Ellacuría, the UCA rector, who Lagana said should be identified. According to Norton, Lagana further stated that *The Monitor* should be aware of who Father Ellacuría was, identifying him as the "intellectual godfather of the guerrilla movement." Norton says that at the time he had not interviewed the priest, though he later did so.

*****

In his Sunday homily on November 19, 1989, the day the priests were buried, Archbishop Arturo Rivera y Damas directly addressed the campaign that had been conducted over the years against the Jesuits:

> There is no doubt that such an abominable action had been decided beforehand and the groundwork was laid by an irresponsible campaign of accusations and slanders – above all in some print media – against several of the distinguished academics of the UCA who now are dead. These accusations and slanders poisoned minds and ultimately put weapons in the hands of the assassins.[105]

---

103 Department of State Information Memorandum, June 11, 1982.

104 Lawyers Committee interviews with Chris Norton, Aug. 1990 & Aug. 1992.

105 As cited in *Proceso*, #409, Nov. 29, 1989, at 4.

"Ignacio Ellacuría and his companions did not die for a tranquil El Salvador," *America* observed after the trial. "They died for a just state of affairs, for social change. They refused to accept that curse of Latin America, the stratification of classes."[106]

Father Tojeira told an UCA audience in November 1991 that he thought the murdered Jesuits had "destroyed the plans of those who killed them."

> Those who murdered our brothers wanted no one to identify the assassins. . . . And yet, from the very beginning everyone accused the Army. . . . They wanted to bury them among El Salvador's 75,000 dead. They said: "Such a scandal being stirred up for eight people when 75,000 have died in this country! Why such a fuss for them and about the others, no one says anything?"
>
> And what did they achieve with this attitude? They resuscitated the 75,000.[107]

106 *America*, Oct. 12, 1991, at 235.

107 Tojeira, "El Caso de los Jesuitas Dos Años Después," *ECA*, #517-518, Nov.-Dec. 1991, at 1034.

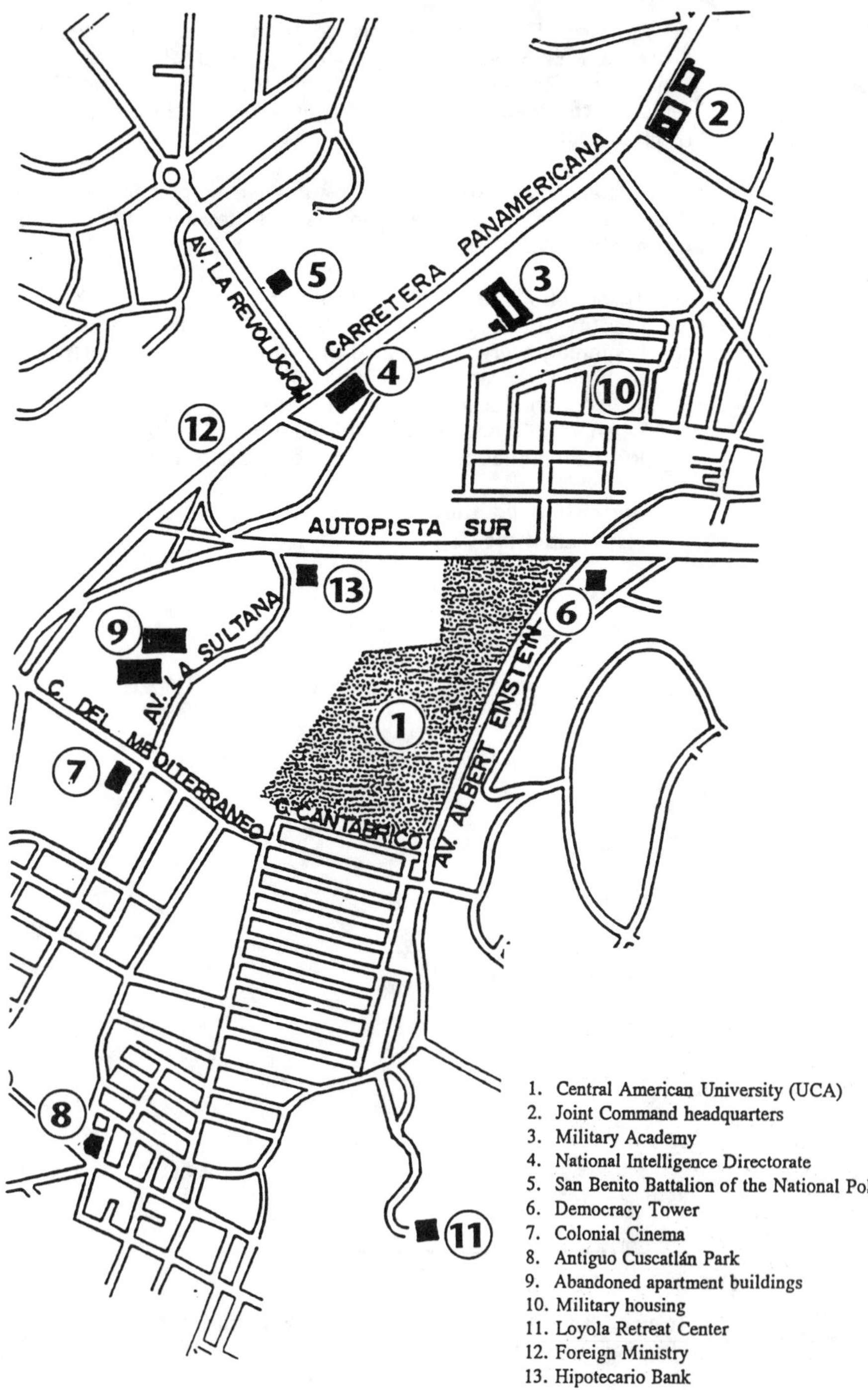
CARRETERA PANAMERICANA
AV. LA REVOLUCION
AUTOPISTA SUR
AV. LA SULTANA
C. DEL MEDITERRANEO
C. CANTABRICO
AV. ALBERT EINSTEIN
1. Central American University (UCA)
2. Joint Command headquarters
3. Military Academy
4. National Intelligence Directorate
5. San Benito Battalion of the National Police
6. Democracy Tower
7. Colonial Cinema
8. Antiguo Cuscatlán Park
9. Abandoned apartment buildings
10. Military housing
11. Loyola Retreat Center
12. Foreign Ministry
13. Hipotecario Bank

CHAPTER II: CHRONOLOGY OF THE CRIME[108]

Shortly after 8:00 p.m. on November 11, 1989, forces of the Farabundo Martí Front for National Liberation (FMLN) launched what proved to be their strongest urban offensive in the 10-year-old Salvadoran civil war. FMLN combatants struck simultaneously at scores of locations around the capital. Within minutes, fierce gun battles could be heard in many locations as the sky was illuminated with the military flares known as Bengal lights. Several places where fighting first broke out proved later to be largely diversionary. Heavy fighting took place that first night near the National University and the adjacent headquarters of the First Infantry Brigade. Army troops clashed with the FMLN briefly along the Autopista Sur (Southern Highway) at the Cuscatlán Stadium and at the entrance to a military housing development across from the Central American University José Simeón Cañas (UCA). The FMLN also attacked the residence of President Alfredo Cristiani,[109] and those of the president and vice-president of the Legislative Assembly, causing U.S. officials to report mistakenly that the goal of the offensive was to assassinate Salvadoran government officials and seize power.

It quickly became clear that the FMLN offensive was radically different from any combat previously seen in San Salvador. It is now estimated that some 1,500-3,000 combatants had entered the city in the preceding weeks. The troops seemed well prepared and able to resupply with both ammunition and food. Working class neighborhoods forming a ring around the capital soon became "rebel strongholds," occupied and controlled by the FMLN. Observers who visited these neighborhoods in the days immediately following November 11 described relaxed combatants chatting with residents, seemingly entrenched for the long haul. It was in poor *barrios* such as Santa Marta, Soyapango, Zacamil and Mejicanos, that the guerrillas took up positions, and consequently, the inhabitants suffered the most.

A number of military and diplomatic analysts contend that the Salvadoran Armed Forces performed poorly and were in

108 A chronology of the crime and its aftermath is also provided in Appendix A.

109 President Cristiani was in Coatepeque at the time, and according to *Proceso* had not been informed by the military of the impending guerrilla assault. *See Proceso*, #409, Nov. 29, 1989, at 11.

essence caught off guard. Though it is still not clear how much or when Salvadoran intelligence officers detected the guerrilla plans, by all accounts they had at least one or two full days' warning. According to Col. René Emilio Ponce, head of the Joint Command, the Armed Forces learned on November 9 of the scheduled offensive.[110] By the morning of Saturday November 11, U.S. embassy officials knew that something would happen that night. While Salvadoran military intelligence ultimately uncovered the scheme, the Armed Forces were clearly unprepared for the strength of the FMLN assault and the guerrillas' ability to hold large sections of the capital for days. Salvadoran military sources, as well as civilians with knowledge of the inner workings of the military, describe it as an institution in disarray during the first days of the FMLN action. Colonel Ponce and other ranking officers were reported to have said that the military seriously considered the possibility that they could lose power, or that San Salvador could become a divided capital, much like Beirut.

Broadcast Death Threats

In the first few hours, Salvadoran radio stations provided excellent coverage of the war raging around the city. Journalists as well as private citizens phoned in on-the-scene accounts of battles in many neighborhoods. Listeners monitoring the transmissions glimpsed the scope and severity of the guerrilla assault. But at approximately 11:00 p.m., all stations were instructed to tie into a nationwide network, which was actually Radio Cuscatlán, the station of the Salvadoran Armed Forces. Two stations which initially resisted hooking-in later did so under duress.[111]

---

110 Lawyers Committee interview with Col. René Emilio Ponce, Estado Mayor, Feb. 14, 1990. Colonel Ponce was appointed defense minister on September 1, 1990 and later named General.

111 One of those which resisted tying into the network was the Catholic Church's YSAX. The station's announcer reported receiving threatening phone calls from what he described as "fanatics." By Sunday morning, YSAX had joined the army network. Testifying in court on September 10, 1990, Maj. Mauricio Chávez Cáceres, chief of COPREFA, the military press office, said that the network was directed by Radio Cuscatlán and Radio Nacional. He said that Radio Cuscatlán is run by C-5, Psychological Operations of the High Command, which is in charge of "campaigns designed to raise the morale of the soldiers and lower the morale of the FMLN and to give tranquility to the civilian population." C-5 was headed by Col. Carlos Armando Avilés. *See Diario Latino,* Sept. 12, 1990.

Once under the control of the Armed Forces, programming changed radically and accurate coverage of the fighting was discontinued. Repeated messages from the governmental Center of National Information (CIN) provided assurances that the fighting was extremely localized and would soon be under control. The nature of the calls coming from private citizens also changed fundamentally. Salvadorans were no longer seeking information about relatives' well-being or sending word to family that they were safe. Instead, callers denounced opposition political figures, labor and church leaders, and members of nongovernmental organizations often labelled "FMLN fronts." The statements were vitriolic and vindictive, frequently urging violence against those named. One caller suggested that Dr. Guillermo Ungo, the head of the National Revolutionary Movement (MNR), be hanged. Rubén Zamora of the Popular Social Christian Movement (MPSC) and other opposition leaders were threatened and warned that they should "leave the country" or "go to Cuba."

In keeping with a long history of harassment and persecution of the Society of Jesus, Jesuits were also singled out. Father Ignacio Ellacuría, the UCA rector, was prominently mentioned by several callers. "Ellacuría is a guerrilla, cut off his head!" said one. "Ellacuría should be spit to death," said another.[112] Vice-president Francisco Merino of the ruling ARENA party accused Father Ellacuría of "poisoning the minds" of Salvadoran youth while teaching at the UCA and at the Jesuit high school, Externado San José.[113]

Reporting on these attacks, *La Prensa Gráfica*, a San Salvador morning paper, provided the following summary:

> All night on the radio network hundreds of condemnations could be heard against Humberto Centeno, Rubén Zamora, Guillermo Manuel Ungo, and other leaders of the Democratic Convergence and the FDR, who are responsible for what the FMLN is doing.
>
> Men and women who spoke on the radio asked the government to prosecute Centeno, Zamora, Ungo and others. Since [Zamora and Ungo] returned from exile to El Salvador, the subversives have taken greater direction from them to perpetrate acts of violence and all kinds of vandalism.

---

112 "*Ellacuría es un guerrillero. Que le corten la cabeza.*" "*Deberían sacar a Ellacuría para matarlo a escupidas!*"

113 *See Proceso,* Nov. 29, 1989, at 8.

> Also heard on the nationwide network were condemnations and severe criticisms of Archbishop Arturo Rivera Damas and against the Auxiliary Bishop, Gregorio Rosa Chávez, because every Sunday – instead of preaching the gospel – they give communist speeches in favor of the FMLN, the Convergence and FENASTRAS.
>
> These condemnations and criticisms categorically stated that it was of utmost urgency that the Jesuits be thrown out of the country because the UCA has been hiding weapons for about the last 10 years. The Spanish Jesuit priest, Ignacio Ellacuría, was named the principal person responsible.[114]

Asked about the threats broadcast over the network, Maj. Mauricio Chávez Cáceres – who as head of the military press office, COPREFA, played a major role in the provision and control of information during the offensive – denied responsibility since he had left for a vacation in Guatemala on the day the fighting broke out.[115] He said that the government's CIN was running the network and that responsibility lay with Mauricio Sandoval, who heads up the government press office, the Secretariat of National Information (SIN). "When I got to the radio station I realized they were giving an open microphone to anyone. I was told of the threats, that people were saying the Jesuits were responsible," Major Chávez Cáceres said. "I ordered that access be cut off to the public. From November 14, only military information was given." Explaining how the threats came to be broadcast, the major said that "no one had any experience with this. [Such a guerrilla offensive]

---

114 *La Prensa Gráfica*, Nov. 13, 1989. Humberto Centeno is a leader of the UNTS labor coalition. The MPSC of Rubén Zamora and the MNR of Guillermo Ungo formed the FDR, Democratic Revolutionary Front, in 1980 which entered into political alliance with the FMLN. With the Social Democratic Party (PSD), the two parties for a time comprised the Democratic Convergence, which participated in elections in 1989 and 1991. The MNR left the Democratic Convergence in mid-1992.

FENASTRAS is the National Federation of Salvadoran Workers Unions, a labor grouping often labelled an "FMLN front" by U.S. and Salvadoran authorities. Nine people died when a powerful explosion partially destroyed the FENASTRAS building at lunchtime on October 31, 1989.

115 Lawyers Committee interview with Maj. Mauricio Chávez Cáceres, Estado Mayor, Feb. 14, 1990. The major later died in a car accident.

had never happened in 10 years. Perhaps it was unwise" to open the microphone.[116]

Testifying before the Senate Foreign Relations Committee on November 17, 1989, Bernard W. Aronson, Assistant Secretary of State for Inter-American Affairs, said that when he was told of the threats on Tuesday November 14, he personally typed a cable to U.S. Ambassador William Walker asking him to "convey to President Cristiani the administration's wish that his government, within the limits of a free press, not permit such threats on government-controlled media."[117] But Assistant Secretary Aronson rejected suggestions that the Salvadoran government was responsible, saying, "I think it is a mistake to suggest that people who work for the government were issuing death threats over the airwaves."[118]

Jardines de Guadalupe from November 11

One of the first places fighting broke out on the evening of November 11 was Democracy Tower, a high-rise glass office building which has never been occupied. The tower is located at the corner of the Southern Highway and Avenida Albert Einstein just outside the UCA campus. Bombed by the FMLN, the building was regularly guarded by the Security Forces and its upper floors used for surveillance. Military sources report that their position along the Southern Highway at the entrance to the Arce community, a military housing project, was under guerrilla attack for 30 minutes. According to Jesuit residents of the neighborhood, there was also early combat at the Super Santa Clara, a small market at the corner of Río Lempa and Mediterráneo.

---

116 *Id.* In May 1991, the private prosecutors acting in behalf of the victims' families attempted to secure copies of the radio transmissions for the period November 11-16, 1989. On June 18, 1991, General Ponce provided the court with three brief, irrelevant transcriptions: a quote from Father Ellacuría in which he disagrees with the FMLN; a message from President Cristiani; and an announcement from the government stating its commitment to investigate the crime. The private prosecutors' attempt to summon for questioning those responsible for the radio programming was thwarted by the judge. In June 1992, Mauricio Sandoval was named to head the new State Intelligence Organization, the successor agency to the DNI.

117 Senate Foreign Relations Committee Hearing, Nov. 17, 1989; *see also New York Times*, Nov. 18, 1989.

118 *Id.*

Shortly after the offensive began, a group of FMLN combatants fled through the UCA campus, entering through a gate on Avenida Albert Einstein adjacent to the Jesuit residence. They opened the gate by setting off a low-powered explosive. Within 10 minutes, the Armed Forces were on the scene and "controlled the situation," according to a chronology prepared by the Jesuits.[119]

The next day, Sunday November 12, between 9:00 and 10:00 a.m., a military patrol of eight to ten men asked and were given permission to examine the scene. They were accompanied by Father Segundo Montes, one of the Jesuits who would be killed three days later. Montes told other Jesuits that the men belonged to the Belloso Battalion. The soldiers took away with them an unexploded device, apparently left behind by the FMLN which the Jesuits had found near the gate. Father Ignacio Martín-Baró, another of the victims, left in his computer a one-page description of some of these events. "From this moment," he wrote, "a group of soldiers was posted at the entrance to the university complex, checking [*registrando*] everyone who entered or exited, and from Monday November 13, prohibiting the entrance or departure of anyone." Martín-Baró also told a U.S. Jesuit with whom he spoke by telephone at 6:15 p.m. on Monday evening that "no one could enter or leave the university."

Given its proximity to several military installations, Jardines de Guadalupe, the comfortable middle class neighborhood in which the UCA is located, was heavily occupied by soldiers. UCA neighbors have testified that troops were posted throughout this first week on Calle del Cantábrico, which forms one parameter of the campus, and the adjacent Calle del Mediterráneo. One neighbor told the Lawyers Committee that men of the Belloso Battalion, an elite, U.S.-trained unit, were on Mediterráneo and other locations in Jardines de Guadalupe from Monday to the end of the week. Some members of the Jesuit order and other neighbors say Atlacatl troops were seen in the neighborhood on Wednesday.

119 *See* "Cronología de Acontecimientos Relacionados con el Asesinato de los Seis Jesuitas de El Salvador," Provincia Centroamericana de la Compañía de Jesús, San Salvador, Nov. 17, 1989 [hereinafter Cronología de Acontecimientos]; Ignacio Martín-Baró, "Cateo de la Universidad Centroamericana y la Comunidad Universitaria Jesuitica," San Salvador, Nov. 14, 1989.

Sunday November 12: Weapons Found at Loyola Center

At about 11:30 a.m. on Sunday November 12, 10 Treasury Police agents entered the grounds of the Loyola Center, a Jesuit retreat complex located on the edge of a coffee plantation one and a half kilometers from the UCA campus. The search of the center followed an anonymous telephone call which indicated that "delinquent terrorists of the FMLN had abandoned weapons in said place," according to the report Col. Héctor Heriberto Hernández, director of the Treasury Police, filed in response to the SIU's inquiry.[120] Father Fermín Saínz, the Jesuit who directs the center, stated that the soldiers brought along a young man, who was handcuffed, to locate the arms. The troops found equipment for four guerrilla combatants shallowly buried under a pile of ashes left from burning leaves.[121] Father Saínz, who was called to the scene by the center staff, says the lieutenant in charge told him, "Don't worry Father, we're finding things like this all over the city." FMLN combatants in flight were abandoning equipment rather than risk getting caught with it. The lieutenant suggested that the guerrillas probably intended to retrieve the weaponry the next day. President Cristiani told a group of visiting U.S. Jesuits accompanied by the Lawyers Committee in February 1990 that "nobody thought [the weapons] had anything to do with the Jesuits. We saw this in lots of places. The soldiers did find a few weapons, but they never gave it any thought because the guerrillas normally did this."[122]

Though the soldiers never suggested that the Jesuits were complicit in hiding the arms, U.S. and Salvadoran officials later cited the incident, offering it in justification of the November 13 search of the Jesuit residence, and, in some instances, using it to imply that the Jesuits were indeed involved in the armed uprising.

---

120 SIU records on file with Fourth Criminal Court.

121 The second lieutenant in charge of the patrol filed a report with the Treasury Police Director on the day of the search. Among those items found at Loyola were three AK-47s, one M-16, three 45 calibre pistols, three LAW rockets, two radios, four grenades, and ammunition for these weapons. Father Saínz, who also noted what was uncovered, says by contrast that the men found three AK-47s; one M-16; four 45 calibre pistols; four pistols of a smaller calibre; one LAW rocket; one radio; one grenade; and ammunition in four cloth bags.

122 Lawyers Committee interview with President Alfredo Cristiani, Casa Presidencial, Feb. 14, 1990.

Monday November 13: Atlacatl Commandos Arrive in San Salvador

On the afternoon of November 13, the Joint Command decided to create a *Comando de Seguridad*, a special security zone which included the area surrounding the UCA. Located within several blocks of the university are the Joint Command headquarters – which also houses the Ministry of Defense – the Military Academy, the National Intelligence Directorate (DNI, one of several intelligence bodies), the San Benito Battalion of the National Police, and two military residential neighborhoods, Colonía Arce and Colonía Palermo. Chosen as headquarters for this zone was the Military Academy and its director, Col. Guillermo Alfredo Benavides, was named commander. Colonel Ponce told the congressional task force headed by Congressman Joe Moakley (the Moakley task force) that "this military complex . . . was a permanent objective" for the FMLN, which "launched four attacks against these installations."[123]

In his third declaration to the court on October 23, 1990, Colonel Ponce said that commanders in the metropolitan region met at 2:00 p.m. on Monday November 13 and decided that part of the Atlacatl would be called into the capital to join this Security Command.[124] Atlacatl Commander Lt. Col. Oscar Alberto León Linares, who was present at the meeting, relayed these instructions to his men. Testifying before the judge on September 26, Lieutenant Colonel León Linares, said Colonel Ponce ordered him to send to the capital 90 men plus the commando unit, which was placed under the orders of the Joint Command.[125]

Despite optimistic predictions to the contrary, by Monday it was clear that the guerrillas would not be easily routed. Of paramount importance to the Armed Forces was protection of their key command centers. By chance, the UCA fell within those parameters. One unresolved question is why the Joint Command would have entrusted their most strategically important zone to Colonel Benavides, who was not known as a good commander and never held important combat posts.

---

123 Transcript of Moakley task force meeting with Col. René Emilio Ponce, Estado Mayor, Feb. 12, 1990, at 6. Following the 1992 peace accords, the Military Academy was moved to the facilities built for use as the National Police Academy in Santa Tecla.

124 Declaration of Col. René Emilio Ponce, Fourth Criminal Court, Oct. 23, 1990.

125 Testimony of Lt. Col. Oscar Alberto León Linares, Fourth Criminal Court, Sept. 26, 1990.

Named as "coordinator" of the zone's command was acting Academy deputy director, Maj. Carlos Camilo Hernández.[126] According to Hernández' testimony to Judge Zamora, the Military Academy took on battalion status in light of the guerrilla offensive. The normal command structure was duplicated at the Academy level, with officers assigned to head up S-1 (Personnel), S-2 (Intelligence), S-3 (Operations), and S-4 (Logistics).[127]

Since the Academy did not normally have combat-ready troops, portions of several other units were stationed at the school in the first few days of the offensive. Among those billeted at the Academy and nominally under Colonel Benavides' command were units from Military Detachments (DM) 6 and 7, Cavalry, Artillery, Atlacatl and Military Police of the Joint Command. Also pressed into service were students attending various Academy training courses.

Among those troops who were temporarily assigned to the Military Academy was a 47-man commando unit of the Atlacatl Battalion, an elite U.S.-trained force established in 1981.[128] On November 10, one day before the FMLN launched its offensive, 13 members of a U.S. Special Forces unit from Ft. Bragg, North Carolina, commenced a training course at Atlacatl Headquarters in Sitio del Niño, La Libertad. Among their students were these Atlacatl commandos, seven of whom were later charged with killing the Jesuits. According to information provided by the Pentagon to the Moakley task force, members of the Seventh Special Forces Group (Airborne) Deployment for Training were

---

126 Major Hernández was promoted to lieutenant colonel in early 1990 and named second-in-command at the elite Ramón Belloso Battalion based in Ilopango. In July 1990, Lieutenant Colonel Hernández was charged with destruction of evidence in the Jesuit case, detained and released on bail on July 31, 1990. He returned to active duty with the Belloso Battalion and on August 25, 1990, was wounded when his unit set up camp on a site near San José Las Flores, Chalatenango, that had been mined by the FMLN.

127 According to Hernández, those who held these command posts were: S-1: Lieutenant Nelson Alberto Barra Zamora; S-2: Major Vides Lucha; S-3: Major Castillo González; S-4: Lieutenant Gallardo Mata.

128 On the history of the Atlacatl Battalion, *see* Arms Control and Foreign Policy Caucus, "The Atlacatl Battalion and Alleged Human Rights Abuses" (April 25, 1990); "Trayectoria del batallón Atlacatl," *Proceso*, #415, Jan. 31, 1990. Forty-seven soldiers comprised the Atlacatl commando unit which was implicated in the crime. At least 88 other members of the Atlacatl who also came to the capital were billeted at the Military Academy as well and participated in the November 13 search of the Jesuit residence.

actually themselves being tested in "the annual evaluation of the Special Forces Detachment in its ability to conduct Foreign Internal Defense training missions."[129] The training was to be provided to some 150 Atlacatl members from November 10 to 20.[130]

During the afternoon of November 11, hours before the offensive began, Salvadoran Vice-president Francisco Merino arrived at Atlacatl Battalion headquarters in a helicopter.[131] Atlacatl Battalion records provided to the court indicate that Merino's visit lasted two hours.

All of the Atlacatl men charged in the killings participated in the special forces training course, as did Jorge Alberto Sierra Ascencio, a soldier who reportedly deserted in late December 1989 and was tried and acquitted of the crime *in absentia*. The course, which was in essence a teacher training exercise for the instructors, was interrupted on the afternoon of Monday November 13 when the commando unit was ordered to report for combat duty in San Salvador. Atlacatl commander Lieutenant Colonel León Linares testified that Joint Command

---

129 This untitled document, which was prepared by the U.S. Military Group at the U.S. embassy in San Salvador, was transmitted to Congressman Moakley on April 10, 1990 by Carl W. Ford, Jr., Acting Assistant Secretary of Defense for International Security Affairs [hereinafter Pentagon Report]. The quoted material is on pages two and three in the section responding to "Issue I: U.S. Training relationship with the Immediate Reaction Infantry Battalion (BIRI) Atlacatl and training received by members of the BIRI Atlacatl." There is no consistent pagination within the 25-page document, which appears as Appendix C to the Interim Report of the Speaker's Task Force on El Salvador (April 30, 1990) [hereinafter Interim Report].

130 Pentagon Report. The Atlacatl men were to receive training in the following areas:

Organization of Combat Patrols
Duties and Responsibilities of Patrol Members
Military Troop Landing Procedures
Combat Orders
Patrol Base Activities
Immediate Action Drills
Techniques of Fire and Maneuver
Rapid Fire Techniques (firing without looking through sights)
Preparation of Arms and Equipment for a Patrol
M16 Zero Fire (procedure to align sight of the M16 to the soldier's view of the target)
Practical Exercise in Combat Orders

131 Atlacatl Battalion registry (*Libro de Guardia de Prevención*), Nov. 11, 1989. The document appears in the court record.

Chief Ponce ordered him to bring his special forces unit to the Military Academy where they would provide "reinforcement" for the newly formed Security Command.[132] According to the testimonies of these commandos, they were called together about 4:00 p.m. that afternoon and told they would be leaving for the capital. Their commanding officer was Lt. José Ricardo Espinoza Guerra, one of three who later led the murder operation.

The November course was not the first U.S. training for the defendants in the UCA case.[133] According to the Pentagon, the defendants participated in the following courses:

> Lt. Yusshy René Mendoza Vallecillos: Course for Salvadoran officers at U.S. Army Infantry School, January-April 1982, Ft. Benning, GA; Commando Course, April 28-June 15, 1988, Ft. Benning, GA.
>
> Lt. José Ricardo Espinoza Guerra: Salvadoran officers course, January-April 1982, Ft. Benning, GA; Special Forces Officer's Course, November 11-January 21, 1989, Special Warfare Training Center, Fort Bragg, NC.
>
> Lt. Gonzalo Guevara Cerritos: El Salvador Cadet Course, June 13-September 30, 1988, Fort Benning, GA.
>
> Sgt. Antonio Ramiro Avalos Vargas: Small Unit Training Management, September 30-December 14, 1988.
>
> Cpl. Angel Pérez Vásquez: Small Unit Training Management, September 30-November 20, 1987, Ft. Benning, GA.

Lieutenant Espinoza's service record indicates additionally that he trained as a pilot at Oakland Air Force Base in San Antonio,

---

132 Col. Benjamín Eladio Canjura explained the difference between having a unit as reinforcement (*refuerzo*) and having it under one's operational command. According to Canjura, when a unit serves as a *refuerzo* it has been sent to fulfill a specific mission, while being placed under operational command indicates an indefinite placement. Testimony in Fourth Criminal Court, Oct. 1, 1990. *See* note 30 *supra.*

133 During 1989, the Atlacatl commando unit also received U.S. training in advanced marksmanship and sniping. Two Atlacatl men were "trained as actors," according to the Pentagon document. "The training's purpose was in how to put on "Skits" at civic actions. Students were trained in how to put on clown acts for children at Government and Army sponsored civic actions to aid the people of conflictive areas." *See* Pentagon Report, *supra* note 129, Response to Issues 4 and 5.

Texas in 1985-1986 and went on two other "official missions" to the United States in 1986 and 1988.[134]

According to the Pentagon, "[h]uman rights issues have been and continue to be a central issue in the US military effort in El Salvador. The very presence of US Military Advisors is a reminder to the Salvadoran Armed Forces of the US Government's commitment and insistence on human rights."[135] Generally describing the human rights training provided, the Pentagon observed that "in effect, almost all Salvadoran officers have received human rights training. This training is reinforced each time an officer goes to a US School."[136]

After the departure of the commando unit for San Salvador, the U.S. Special Forces remained at Atlacatl headquarters in Sitio del Niño, La Libertad, and continued teaching those Atlacatl members who "remained behind to secure the base. . . . " According to the Moakley task force report, these Green Berets later "spent a day barricaded in the San Salvador Sheraton" when the FMLN occupied the hotel on November 21, 1989.[137]

On arriving in the capital, the Atlacatl commandos went to the Military Academy to await orders. The lieutenants who

134 Lieutenant Espinoza's service record appears in the court file at page 4353, volume 22.

135 Pentagon Report, *supra* note 129, Response to Issue 3.

136 *Id.*

137 *Interim Report, supra* note 129, at 15. When combat in the up-scale Escalón section of San Salvador spilled into the Sheraton hotel, the FMLN found itself in an unplanned occupation of the hotel. Among those trapped in the hotel by the action were OAS Secretary General João Baena Soares and the 13 U.S. Green Berets. U.S. reporters were unable at the time to find out what these U.S. special forces were doing in El Salvador. *See Miami Herald,* Nov. 24, 1989, at 1A. In an April 20, 1990 letter to Secretary of Defense Richard B. Cheney, the Lawyers Committee urged that these U.S. trainers be made available for questioning. Given that they were said to be conducting a standard, pre-scheduled training exercise, why was information not released in late November about their activities while in El Salvador? Did U.S. personnel have any reason to suspect at this point that the Atlacatl trainees participated in the UCA killings? The Defense Department responded on May 17, 1990, providing the Committee with the Pentagon Report, *supra* note 129. The Defense Department also requested that the Committee not name Major Eric Buckland (discussed in more detail in Chapter X: "Washington's Mixed Messages") in future reports, referring instead to Buckland as a "U.S. Major." Additional letters to the Pentagon from the Lawyers Committee in June and September 1990 were never answered.

led the unit reported directly to the Joint Command, where they were given an order to search the Jesuit residence (see below). The fact that these lieutenants reported directly to the Joint Command and that the commandos searched the Jesuits' home within two hours of arriving in the capital suggests that the unit may have been brought to San Salvador specifically for this purpose. In his written statement to the court on September 5, 1990, Colonel Ponce said he "deduced that the officers of the Atlacatl immediate reaction battalion went to inform the Joint Command of their arrival on November 13, 1989 because the Joint Command ordered their transfer to the Military Academy and their assignment to the Security Command."

Col. Joaquín Arnoldo Cerna Flores, chief of C-3 (Operations) in November 1989, told the court on September 21, 1990, that he and Colonel Ponce decided it was "appropriate" to send the Atlacatl commandos to conduct the search because of their age, experience in combat and because they had no other mission assigned at the moment.[138]

Father Ellacuría Returns from Spain

On November 13 at about 5:45 p.m. the university rector, Father Ignacio Ellacuría, arrived at the UCA campus. He was accompanied by Father Amando López and Father Francisco Estrada,[139] who had met him at Comalapa Airport. When the fighting broke out, Father Ellacuría was in Spain, where he accepted an award for the UCA and attended a meeting of the Superior University Council of the Iberoamerican Postgraduate University. At that meeting he was elected president of the University Council. While in Europe he also addressed the West German parliament. In Barcelona, Father Ellacuría was interviewed by the Catalan newspaper, *Avui*. Asked if he was ever frightened by the death threats he had received, he replied, "Never. I'm not afraid. Fear is not a feeling which normally overcomes me. It would be too irrational to kill me. I've done nothing wrong."[140] During the three weeks that the rector had been gone, the country had changed greatly, and he told his

138 Testimony of Col. Joaquín Cerna Flores, Fourth Criminal Court, Sept. 21, 1990. *See also El Mundo*, Sept. 26, 1990.

139 Amando López, a Spanish-born Jesuit who once served as rector of El Salvador's seminary and of the Jesuit university in Managua, was at the time of his death teaching philosophy and theology at the UCA, where he chaired the philosophy department. Father Franciso Estrada, a Salvadoran Jesuit, would be named to succeed Father Ellacuría as rector of the UCA on November 28, 1989.

140 *Avui* (Barcelona), Nov. 15, 1989. Avui means "today" in Catalán.

colleagues, "We're returning to 1980," arguably the most violent year in modern Salvadoran history.[141]

The three men made their way from the airport, some 30 miles outside the city, to the campus without incident, arriving shortly before the 6:00 p.m. curfew, which had been imposed on Monday. Father Estrada recalls that Father López told Father Ellacuría about the death threats that had been broadcast over the radio. "Ellacuría was tense and very quiet on the return trip to the city," Estrada stated. "He hardly responded."[142] Entering by the main gate off the Southern Highway, the priests were stopped by soldiers who had been posted there since Sunday. No one had been allowed to enter the campus, and it was only after it was established that the car's driver was the university rector were the priests allowed to proceed up the hill. The Jesuit Provincial for Central America, José María Tojeira, told agents of the Special Investigative Unit (SIU), on November 28 that the man who appeared to be in charge of the patrol at the gate said, "*Dejenlo entrar que es el Padre*." (Let him pass. It's the Father.)[143] Though the soldier did not mention Ellacuría's name, the priests were left with no doubt that the officer recognized Ignacio Ellacuría, who often appeared on Salvadoran television and in newspaper photographs. An UCA watchman testified that he went out to unlock the gate when he heard the horn of Ellacuría's white Toyota.

Father Estrada recalls that the military man in charge came over to the car to see who was inside and said something like, "Oh, you've arrived, Father," leaving the impression that he recognized Ellacuría. When Ellacuría answered simply, "yes," the man gave the order to let the car pass through the gate.[144]

To date, it has not been established which unit was on duty at the UCA entrance that night. Interviews with these men could reveal whether they had been told to watch for Ellacuría's arrival and to whom they were told to report that the rector had returned. Answers to these questions could shed light on when plans for the murder were launched and by whom. Nonetheless, in May 1991, in response to a specific petition of the private

---

141 Lawyers Committee interviews with Jesuits in San Salvador, July-September 1990.

142 Lawyers Committee interview with Father Francisco Estrada, San Salvador, Sept. 4, 1990.

143 The declaration of Father José María Tojeira, recorded by the Special Investigative Unit on November 28, 1989, is included in the court record [hereinafter Tojeira Declaration].

144 Lawyers Committee interview with Father Estrada, Sept. 4, 1990.

prosecutors, Defense Minister Ponce replied that he could not identify the unit stationed at the UCA entrance at the time.[145]

The Monday Night Search of the Pastoral Center

At 6:30 p.m. that same evening, one half hour after the beginning of curfew, some 135 men surrounded the UCA campus. They did so with the intention of conducting a search of the Jesuit residence and the Theological Reflection Center housed in the same building.[146] Two patrols, about 20 men, entered the campus by breaking the lock on the back gate on Calle del Cantábrico.[147] Some soldiers jumped over the walls. Troops were already inside the Theological Reflection Center (CRT) by the time the priests detected their presence. The soldiers entered the lower part of the building – which is built into a hill – through a window and began kicking down the locked doors of offices which they aimed to search. Father Juan Ramón Moreno, whom these same soldiers would kill some 48 hours later, offered to unlock doors for them rather than have them destroyed. Soldiers later testified that one priest accompanied them, opening doors with keys.

Father Ellacuría asked the reason for the intrusion and requested the officer in charge to identify himself, which he declined to do. Ellacuría introduced himself, and the officer addressed Fathers Segundo Montes and Ignacio Martín-Baró by name. Lt. José Ricardo Espinoza Guerra, the Atlacatl officer in charge, had been a student at the Jesuit high school, Externado San José, while Father Montes was its rector, though Montes did not recognize his former student. Father Ellacuría challenged the Army's right to examine the building without a search warrant. The priest pointed out that the building belonged to the Society of Jesus and not the university. He asked that the Minister of Defense be called. The officer answered that according to the state of siege imposed the previous day, they could do anything they wanted, and added that they had orders to search the entire campus. Further, he promised not to force open locked doors or to harm the night watchmen. He also said the soldiers would stay all night on the campus, which according to statements later given to the SIU by the troops,

---

145 Written declaration of General René Emilio Ponce to the Fourth Criminal Court, May 31, 1991.

146 *See infra* Chapter VI: "From a Standstill to a Crawl" for a discussion of who ordered the search and why.

147 This account is based on Lawyers Committee interviews with Jesuits in San Salvador; on Father Martín-Baró's description of the search written on Nov. 14, 1989; and on *Proceso*, Nov. 29, 1989, at 8.

they did not do. Father Ellacuría suggested that the men come back in daylight to search the rest of the UCA, but they did not return the next day. Father Segundo Montes later told colleagues that the troops were members of the Atlacatl Battalion.

The Jesuits described the search as "correct" and said the soldiers behaved properly. Father Martín-Baró observed that the officer in charge "at all times conducted himself respectfully toward the professors . . . ."[148] In contrast to earlier searches, no questions were asked and they did not seem interested in papers or books. On previous visits soldiers had spent hours examining written materials to determine if they were "subversive." While in the residence, the priests accompanied the soldiers, who later searched classrooms and laboratories on their own. Nothing about the intrusion led the Jesuits to believe that this was anything more than a routine search. Father Tojeira told the SIU on November 28 that his colleagues believed that the search was conducted "because of the arrival of Father Ellacuría."[149]

The Jesuits quickly inspected the facilities the next day and discovered that the soldiers had forced open several locks to classrooms and laboratories, broken into the psychology clinic and damaged supplies, and smashed a window in the clinic.

During Father Ellacuría's absence, the rest of his community had moved into the newly built residence attached to the Theological Reflection Center. Ellacuría spent his first night back, Monday, November 13, in their old home on Calle del Cantábrico. In the course of Tuesday he began moving his belongings into his new room, and spent Tuesday night there. Thus, when he was killed early Thursday morning he had only spent one full night in the residence.

Shortly after the Atlacatl troops returned to the Military Academy, the adjacent National Intelligence Directorate (DNI) came under attack from rebel forces, a military source told the Lawyers Committee. DNI agents defending the complex sought reinforcement from the Atlacatl commandos, who entered the DNI grounds by walking through a gate which links the two institutions.

Salvadoran military officers have repeatedly said that neither weapons nor guerrillas were found during the search.

148 Martín-Baró, "Cateo a la Universidad Centroamericana y la Comunidad Universitaria Jesuitica," Nov. 14, 1989 (on file at Lawyers Committee for Human Rights). Father Ellacuría asked Martín-Baró to write a brief description of the search, which was found in his computer after his death.

149 Tojeira declaration, *supra* note 143.

Despite this fact, President Alfredo Cristiani told reporters on July 12, 1990 that the soldiers did discover some arms. Further, a November 13, 1989 cable by U.S. military intelligence agents to the Defense Intelligence Agency, which was released to the Lawyers Committee under the Freedom of Information Act, cited "initial reports that the following equipment was captured by the Salvadoran Armed Forces . . . in the Jesuit priests' dormitory at the Catholic University."

3 AK-47 (Soviet) rifles
3 RPG-18s (rocket propelled grenade)
2 M-16 rifles
4 .45 pistols
3 YAESU radios[150]

Though clearly untrue, this report inexplicably surfaced in Senate offices in the days preceding the October 19, 1990 vote on a U.S. foreign assistance bill, which included a 50% reduction in military aid to El Salvador.[151]

Atlacatl at the Loyola Center on November 15

On November 14, Atlacatl troops arrested someone near the Colonial Cinema, right behind the UCA, according to the Security Command's intelligence registries. Atlacatl members were also stationed in the Residencial Guadalupe, a neighborhood adjacent to the university.[152]

At mid-morning on Wednesday November 15, an Army officer posted in Jardines de Guadalupe commented to a Jesuit that there was going to be a lot of "movement" in the afternoon or evening.[153]

---

150 Cable, U.S. Defense Attaché's Office, San Salvador, to DIA, Washington, D.C., Nov. 13, 1989.

151 In late October 1990, Father Tojeira turned over copies of the Defense Intelligence Agency documentation obtained by the Lawyers Committee under the Freedom of Information Act to Judge Zamora, suggesting that the judge request the U.S. government to provide complete documents, since those released were heavily censored. *See El Mundo*, Oct. 31, 1990.

152 Members of the Treasury Police placed the Atlacatl soldiers behind the UCA in interviews with the SIU the day after the murders. Weeks later when their statements were officially recorded, they no longer mentioned the Atlacatl presence in the zone.

153 *See* Cronología de Acontecimientos, *supra* note 119, at 2.

About 3:00 p.m. some 120-130 members of the Atlacatl moved into the Loyola Center, the Jesuit retreat house which was searched by Treasury Police on November 12.[154] A housekeeper unlocked doors for the troops who rapidly examined the center's 45-odd rooms. One soldier asked, "This also belongs to the UCA, right? Here they are planning the offensive." Father Fermín Saínz, the director, immediately went to the center when he was informed of the soldiers' presence. A sergeant was waiting for the priest and ushered him to a lieutenant, who later commented that "it's possible to talk with this priest, but the ones down below just get furious." The officer was presumably referring to the behavior of Father Ellacuría and the others when they challenged the soldiers' right to search the Jesuit residence on the UCA campus on Monday night. For this reason, Father Saínz believes that these Atlacatl men may have been from the same unit later charged with the murders.

The soldiers occupied the center all afternoon; most just sat around resting and awaiting orders. Loyola's housekeeper served coffee and pastry to some 85 men. At about 5:15 p.m., a captain arrived and gathered the officers together. Looking at a large piece of paper which Father Saínz took to be a map, the captain pointed at the campus below. At about 7:00 p.m. – after the fall of curfew – the men moved out and headed down toward the UCA campus.

Before leaving Loyola, one officer said to someone present, "Yes, we're going to look for Ellacuría and all these Jesuits. We don't want foreigners. This has got to end!" Another soldier warned the staff that "tonight there is going to be a big uproar around here. Stay inside and keep your heads down!" Still another said that "we're going to look for Ellacuría, and if we find him we're going to be given a prize!"

Meeting at Army Headquarters on the Night of November 15

In an attempt to establish when the decision was made to kill the Jesuits – or perhaps when to implement longstanding contingency plans – attention has focused on a series of meetings held on November 15 at the Estado Mayor, the Joint Command headquarters. Top officers were known to be living at

---

154 The account of the occupation of the Loyola Center on the afternoon of November 15, 1989, is based on: F. Saínz, "El Martirio en la Iglesia Universal, Martirios Actuales: Padres Jesuitas" (Feb. 1990) (unpublished manuscript on file at Lawyers Committee for Human Rights); interviews with Father Fermín Saínz, February and September 1990.

the military complex during the offensive, and President Cristiani reportedly spent several nights there as well. Colonel Ponce told members of the Moakley task force during their February 1990 visit to San Salvador that beginning on November 9, when they became aware of the "possibility of broad FMLN action, we began meeting almost daily at night in order to evaluate the situation."[155] According to Colonel Ponce, some 24 top officers convened at about 7:30 p.m. on the evening of Wednesday November 15 "to analyze the positions we had lost since November 11. . . . We analyzed what we needed to do to regain them. We understood that we needed to take stronger measures."[156] Those who gathered that night included the Minister of Defense, the two vice ministers of defense, commanders of all the units in the metropolitan area, the commanders of special security zones set up during the offensive, Security Force chiefs, the head of the military press office, COPREFA, and members of the Joint Command and its chief, Colonel Ponce.

By their own account, top officers were in a state of near panic in the face of their inability to rout the FMLN decisively from the capital. Citing four attacks on the Joint Command headquarters and assaults on the military housing complexes where many officers live with their families, Colonel Ponce recalled that: "There were several skirmishes [on November 15] to the southwest of the UCA, in Antiguo Cuscatlán, there was one death and one injury. There was lots of confusion, lots of shooting. It's difficult to place yourselves in that moment, to relive that moment."

Some observers believe that these officers have in retrospect exaggerated the severity of the FMLN challenge as well as their despair at the time in an attempt to rationalize the Jesuit murders and extensive aerial bombardment. Self-serving or not, they describe an anguished mood that had gripped military ranks as the FMLN offensive entered its fifth day and showed no signs of abating. One participant told the *San Francisco Examiner* that the meeting on the evening of November 15 was "the most tense and desperate gathering of the country's top military commanders since the war against leftist insurgents

---

155 Transcript of Moakley task force meeting with Col. René Emilio Ponce, Estado Mayor, Feb. 12, 1990, at 4.

156 Lawyers Committee interview with Col. René Emilio Ponce, Estado Mayor, Feb. 14, 1990. Other participants in the meeting have said it started at 6:30 p.m.

began a decade ago."[157] There was early speculation that a decision to kill the Jesuits had been taken at this meeting, or that discussion of going after the "ringleaders" or "command posts" of the FMLN could have been misunderstood by Colonel Benavides. COPREFA chief Maj. Mauricio Chávez Cáceres, who attended the meeting, denied that the Jesuits had been mentioned, telling a group of visitors that

> UCA was not mentioned in any way. I would remember it perfectly because I am a former student at that university and also a friend of the priests whom they murdered. No, absolutely nothing was said, it would be a detail that I couldn't forget.[158]

He also said that the men joined hands in prayer at the end and asked for "divine enlightenment." Major Chávez Cáceres added, "If I believed that the decision to kill the Jesuits had been taken at that meeting, I wouldn't be here today. We are not so cynical that we would pray to God and then go out and kill priests."[159]

President Cristiani told a group of visiting U.S. Jesuits on February 14, 1990 that he "was spending a lot of time at the Joint Command then. I attended some of the meetings, but not that one." On August 27, 1990, Defense Minister Larios responded to Judge Zamora's request by providing a list of those Salvadoran officers present.

While denying that the Jesuits were mentioned on the night of November 15, Colonel Ponce and others admit that the officers decided to step up the use of air power, introducing 500 and 700 pound bombs. In early February 1990, well before participants in the meeting began to testify in court, accounts of what went on began to appear in the U.S. press. According to *The Boston Sunday Globe,* "the meeting ended at about 10:30 p.m." and President Cristiani was "awakened and asked to sign an order authorizing the use of the air force and artillery,

---

157 *San Francisco Examiner*, Feb. 5, 1990. For more on the November 15 meeting, *see Boston Sunday Globe*, Feb. 4, 1990; *Christian Science Monitor*, Feb. 7, 1990; *Baltimore Sun*, Feb. 4, 1990; *Miami Herald*, Feb. 5, 1990.

158 Transcript of Moakley task force meeting with Col. René Emilio Ponce, Estado Mayor, Feb. 12, 1990, at 6 (translated by Congressional Research Service).

159 Lawyers Committee interview with Major Chávez Cáceres, Estado Mayor, Nov. 14, 1990. The prayer was reportedly suggested and led by Col. Dionisio Ismael Machuca, an evangelical Christian who was then Director General of the National Police.

which he did."[160] Residents in Soyapango and other neighborhoods remember November 15-16 as the night of the worst aerial bombardment.

In August 1990, Judge Zamora submitted a list of questions concerning what transpired at the evening meeting on November 15 to Defense Minister Larios and Colonel Ponce.[161] The officers' written responses provided a few details, but no substantive information that could clarify how and when the murder scheme was launched. General Larios said that 24 commanders gathered at 6:00 p.m. and met non-stop until 10:00 p.m. He told the court that the meeting dealt with "nothing related to the priest Ignacio Ellacuría, other Jesuits or the installations of the José Simeón Cañas University nor about a meeting of union leaders inside said university."[162] The general added that "it was decided to expel the members of the FMLN from the areas in which aggression persisted, determining the methods of defense that would be employed to carry this out."[163]

After the meeting, Larios says he called President Cristiani, who arrived at Joint Command headquarters at 11:00 p.m. and remained until about 2:00 a.m. on November 16. If accurate, this means that President Cristiani was present at Joint Command headquarters while the Jesuit murder operation was in progress about one mile away. Thus, virtually the entire top military leadership of the country, Minister of Defense Larios, Vice-Ministers Zepeda and Montano, and Chief-of-

---

160 *Boston Sunday Globe*, Feb. 4, 1990. A source interviewed by the Lawyers Committee who saw Colonel Ponce's diary says it indicated that during the meeting Ponce had agreed with Air Force Chief Bustillo, who argued that it was unnecessary to consult President Cristiani about the increased use of air power. As an afterthought, Ponce decided anyway to secure the president's approval.

161 General Larios, a compromise candidate who had been considered a caretaker defense minister, was removed from the post on September 1, 1990 and named military attaché at El Salvador's embassy in Washington. At that time, Colonel Ponce took over as Defense Minister. Most recently, General Larios served as the military's observer to the Ad-Hoc Commission, mandated by the 1992 Peace Accords to review the records of the officer corps and recommend transfers or dismissal from the Armed Forces of those deemed unsuitable for continued service.

162 Written statement of Gen. Humberto Larios, Fourth Criminal Court, Aug. 29, 1990; INTERJUST, Sistema Informativo de la Corte Suprema de Justicia, Sept. 4, 1990. [hereinafter INTERJUST.]

163 *Id.*

Staff Ponce were meeting during these critical hours with President Cristiani.

Colonel Ponce presented written testimony asserting that the meeting "did not address or discuss the presence of the FMLN inside the UCA nor were decisions taken to carry out operations inside said university."[164] In response to a question, Ponce mentioned an alleged meeting of unionists inside the UCA, information that had not appeared in the public record. According to Colonel Ponce's statement, at 4:30 p.m. on November 15, the National Police passed intelligence to C-2 at the Joint Command indicating that at 6:00 p.m. trade unionists intended to gather at the UCA. In the months following the Jesuit murders a rumor circulated indicating that soldiers had gone to the UCA in response to a tip that guerrilla commanders were holding a planning meeting for the next phase of the offensive. According to this story, one of the priests was accidentally killed in the course of an argument and the rest had to be killed so they could not give witness.

On September 7, 1990, President Cristiani provided oral testimony concerning what occurred that night, appearing personally before Judge Zamora, an event termed "unprecedented in the contemporary history of the Salvadoran court system."[165] Waiving his right to submit a written statement, the President said he went to the Joint Command headquarters when called by General Larios. He was accompanied by his personal secretary, Arturo Tona, in whose home Cristiani was staying at the time. President Cristiani also said that the Jesuits were not mentioned at any point during the meeting, during which he was asked to approve the use of heavier weaponry,

> given that it was the first time that the use of armored vehicles and artillery was proposed, it was necessary to consult [with the President about altering] the decision made by the High Command in the first few days of the offensive not to use these types of weapons in order to protect the civilian population.[166]

President Cristiani told Judge Zamora that at 12:30 a.m. he and Arturo Tona went to the COCFA to receive a briefing on the military situation in the capital. In the center at the time

---

164 Written statement of Col. René Emilio Ponce, Fourth Criminal Court, Aug. 25, 1990.

165 *Diario de Hoy*, Sept. 10, 1990.

166 *Id.*

were "two or three North American military advisors," with whom the president said he did not converse.[167]

Other Meetings on November 15

Given the improbability that an order as explosive as the murder of six Jesuit priests would have been given in the presence of 24 officers, questions have been raised about other gatherings of top officers which may have occurred in the hours preceding the assassination. One lead was provided by retired Col. Sigifredo Ochoa Pérez, a former senior Army field commander and now a leading member of the ARENA party.[168] Colonel Ochoa, who headed the state-owned electrical company until September 1992, has made several public statements suggesting that Colonel Benavides was acting on higher orders when he ordered the Jesuit killings. In January 1990, *Agence France Presse* quoted Ochoa saying: "This action involved much higher officers, and even if a general or colonel is involved [the culprits] must be punished."[169]

Colonel Ochoa made a more explicit charge during an interview with the U.S. television program *60 Minutes* on April 22, 1990. According to Ochoa, a smaller group of officers gathered after the expanded High Command meeting on the evening of November 15. At this meeting, Ochoa said Colonel Benavides was given a direct order to kill the Jesuits. Ochoa said:

> A group of commanders stayed behind. It seems each was responsible for a zone in San Salvador. They gave an order to kill leftists, just as Colonel Benavides

---

167 Testimony of President Alfredo Cristiani, Fourth Criminal Court, Sept. 7, 1990.

168 In January 1983, Ochoa, then commander of Military Detachment 2 in Cabañas, led a rebellion against Defense Minister José Guillermo García when he attempted to send Ochoa into diplomatic exile in Uruguay. Known as a skillful commander trained in Israel and Taiwan, Ochoa has historically been resentful of U.S. advice and pressures on the Armed Forces. In the aftermath of the rebellion, Ochoa spent 18 months in Washington, before returning to head up the strategic El Paraíso base in Chalatenango. García was ultimately removed as Defense Minister. See *Washington Post*, Jan. 8, 1983; *New York Times*, Jan. 13, 1983; *Financial Times* (London), Feb. 13, 1985.

169 Paris AFP in Spanish 2112 GMT, Jan. 12, 1990, *as reported in* FBIS, Jan. 16, 1990.

did. I'll say it again. Benavides obeyed, it wasn't his decision.[170]

Colonel Ochoa's assertion was supported by a group of young military officers calling themselves "Domingo Monterrosa Vive."[171] They issued a five-page communiqué on May 3, 1990, which discussed the Jesuit case as well as other issues.[172] The anonymous group said that "[t]he Ochoa case should be considered more carefully; his position is supported by many young officers, and also by some of our superiors. He has said something which many of us cannot express because we would be punished."[173] The men also asked what "happened at meetings that were held at 3:00 p.m. and 5:00 p.m. in the office of Colonel Zepeda? Not only Colonel Benavides attended, but also junior officers. All this is known by the High

---

170 *60 Minutes, supra* note 23. Asked if Colonel Benavides would be capable of ordering such a murder, Colonel Ochoa responded, "No, I don't think so. Knowing him, he's a man who could never take or even conceive of making a move as big as assassinating the Jesuits. Benavides acted under orders. He didn't act alone."

171 Lieutenant Colonel Domingo Monterrosa and other senior eastern front officers died in October 1984 in a helicopter crash caused by sabotage. The helicopter went down over Cacaopera in northern Morazán province. Various versions circulated at the time suggesting that the FMLN, the military itself, or even the Duarte government could have been responsible, allegedly because Monterrosa was said to oppose peace talks with the guerrilla movement. He was known as an extremely effective field commander who was well liked by his men. *See N.Y. Times*, Oct. 25 and Nov. 28, 1984; *Christian Science Monitor*, Nov. 30, 1984. Speculation was finally laid to rest in 1992 with the publication of a firsthand account of the operation to assassinate Monterrosa by members of the ERP faction of the FMLN. *See* J. López Vigil, *Las Mil y Una Historias de Radio Venceremos*, at 310-338 (UCA Editores, San Salvador, El Salvador: 1992).

172 On the young officers' communiqué, *see* Lawyers Committee memorandum to U.S. Jesuit Conference of July 27, 1990, at 4-6.

173 Open Letter from the Movement of Young Officers "Domingo Monterrosa Vive" to the President of the Republic and Commander in Chief of the Armed Forces; to our Chiefs of the High Command; to Members of the Legislative Assembly and Cabinet Ministers; to the domestic and international press and to the Salvadoran people, May 3, 1990, *as printed in Diario Latino*, May 4, 1990.

Command."[174] To our knowledge, no serious attempt has been made to investigate these leads. The High Command rejected the group's letters as "gray propaganda" put out by the FMLN.[175] President Cristiani also suggested that the FMLN might be responsible and said he has never given "much credence to anonymous [letters] concerning political questions. . . ."[176]

U.S. Ambassador William Walker confirmed in April 1990 that the embassy had received reports of a second meeting held on the night of November 15. "But if they were not meeting in almost continuous session they should have been brought up for incompetence. It's hard to reconstruct what went on at meetings from this time distance."[177]

Joint Command Headquarters on the Murder Night

At the helm of the COCFA, the command center at Joint Command headquarters, from 8:00 a.m. on November 15 to 8:00 a.m. on November 16 was Col. Iván López y López, head of C-1 (Personnel). Also on duty in the COCFA were Lt. Raúl Antonio Mejía Chávez, representing C-2 (Intelligence), Maj. Oscar Joaquín Martínez Orellana representing C-3 (Operations),[178] an Air Force officer and a radio technician.[179] C-3 chief Col. Joaquín Arnoldo Cerna Flores was in the COCFA until between 1:00 and 2:00 a.m., he told the court on September 21, 1990. Two U.S. military advisors, whose office was adjacent to the COCFA, were in the command center during the night. Members

---

174 Colonel Juan Orlando Zepeda, a leading member of the clique which dominates the Armed Forces known as the *tandona,* is currently the vice-minister of defense. According to the State Department, Colonel Benavides would have reported either to Colonel Zepeda or to Colonel Cerna Flores, the head of Operations (C-3), on the night the Jesuits were murdered. In April 1989, Colonel Zepeda said that an attack carried out by FMLN urban commandos had been planned inside the UCA.

175 Canal Doce Television, May 4, 1990, *as reported in* FBIS, May 4, 1990; Canal Doce Television, May 22, 1990, *as reported in* FBIS, May 29, 1990.

176 *Diario Latino*, May 3, 1990.

177 Lawyers Committee interview with Ambassador William Walker, Washington, D.C., April 18, 1990.

178 These names were first supplied by General Ponce in June 1991 -- too late to be of any use during the investigation -- and were not confirmed by any other source.

179 Testimony of Maj. René Guillermo Contreras Barrera, Fourth Criminal Court, Nov. 1, 1990.

of the High Command remained in the COCFA until 2:00 a.m., when the killers were already on the campus.[180] The sounds of the Jesuit murder operation – the barrage of machine-gun fire and automatic assault rifles and the explosions of grenades and LAW rockets – were heard in Joint Command headquarters. "On hearing these explosions, there was extreme concern inside the Joint Command," remembers Col. Carlos Armando Avilés. "There was likewise concern that the vital centers of the Armed Forces, the Joint Command and the Ministry of Defense, were under attack."[181] Another officer present that night, counterintelligence chief Maj. René Guillermo Contreras Barrera, heard loud explosions near the Joint Command and said that he placed them by the UCA.[182]

Following the early evening meeting at Joint Command headquarters, Colonel Benavides returned to the Military Academy and gathered his staff. Benavides briefed 10 officers on the decisions made earlier at the larger meeting at the Joint Command.[183]

November 16 Meeting at DNI Headquarters

Another meeting that has been repeatedly mentioned as a clue to the case is the daily meeting of the National Intelligence Directorate (DNI), an intelligence agency located along the same corridor as the Joint Command headquarters and the Military Academy. The U.S. Central Intelligence Agency (CIA) shared office space with the DNI, and CIA agents generally attended DNI meetings.[184] One DNI agent told the Lawyers Committee that the unit's daily 8:00 a.m. meeting was moved back to 7:30 a.m. during the first week of the guerrilla offensive. On the morning of November 16, DNI agents gathered for their daily meeting, and among other items were to

180 Written testimony of Col. René Emilio Ponce, Fourth Criminal Court, Oct. 23, 1990.

181 Testimony of Col. Carlos Armando Avilés, Fourth Criminal Court, Oct. 31, 1990.

182 Testimony of Maj. René Guillermo Contreras Barrera, Fourth Criminal Court, Nov. 1, 1990.

183 Letter to Justice Minister René Hernández Valiente from the High Command, Feb. 22, 1991 (on file at Lawyers Committee for Human Rights).

184 *San Francisco Examiner*, Feb. 5 & April 15, 1990. Confirmation that agents of the CIA – which created the DNI – generally attend DNI meetings comes also from a DNI agent interviewed by the Lawyers Committee.

receive a report from their commander, Col. Carlos Mauricio Guzmán Aguilar, about decisions taken at the meeting the previous night at Joint Command headquarters.

The first version of the story that emerged after the murders placed the start of the meeting at 5:00 a.m. After the meeting was underway, an officer, later identified as Capt. Carlos Fernando Herrera Carranza, interrupted the proceedings to announce that Father Ellacuría had been killed resisting arrest.[185] Captain Herrera's source was the radio, he said. Later, the military asserted that the meeting actually took place at 8:00 a.m. The later hour does not seem credible, since the Jesuits were notified of the killings shortly after curfew was lifted at 6:00 a.m. and were on the scene well before 7:00 a.m. Journalists arrived around 7:00 a.m. as well.

One participant in the meeting told the Lawyers Committee that the session began at 7:30 a.m. and that only senior officers were present by the time Captain Herrera entered the room around 8:00 a.m. This explains, he said, why no CIA agents were present when the announcement was made. When asked if the CIA was represented at the November 16 meeting, Ambassador Walker told a group of U.S. Jesuits: "I have asked the question and they tell me no." *The San Francisco Examiner* reported in February 1990 that several contradictory accounts of the meeting had circulated. One source told the *Examiner* that the CIA was present, while "another source close to the CIA denied its agent had been there, although what transpires at DNI meetings is nonetheless routinely passed on."[186]

According to accounts in the U.S. press, the officers present "cheered and clapped" when Herrera announced that Father Ellacuría had died.[187] One officer, who defensively denied that the men had reacted in this fashion, told the Lawyers Committee he "couldn't see why the clapping would be relevant to who" murdered the priests. He added, however, that he "would not want to leave the impression that we were sorry [about Ellacuría's death] either." While nothing was made explicit, he said he was left with the distinct impression that the military could be responsible for the murders. By several accounts, DNI chief Colonel Guzmán Aguilar got into a heated

---

185 Captain Herrera is also the DNI agent who ordered Lieutenant Cuenca Ocampo to join the Atlacatl commando unit on the search of the Jesuit residence on Monday November 13. *See infra* Chapter VI: "From a Standstill to a Crawl."

186 *San Francisco Examiner*, Feb. 5, 1990.

187 *Boston Sunday Globe*, Feb. 4, 1990; *San Francisco Examiner*, Feb. 5, 1990.

discussion with Col. Roberto Pineda Guerra, who expressed the view that the killings would have serious negative repercussions for the Armed Forces. Capt. Luis Alberto Parada Fuentes, then a DNI officer who attended the morning meeting, said that "when he heard the word *arrest* from the mouth of Captain Herrera Carranza . . . I imagined that the authors of the murders of the Jesuit priests were members of the Armed Forces, because that is what the word [arrest] suggests."[188]

In a belated attempt to determine what went on at the meeting, Lieutenant Colonel Rivas of the SIU wrote to Colonel Ponce on February 13, 1990, "respectfully soliciting" permission to interview those men present at the early morning meeting. Not until June 4, 1990 did the SIU turn over their report to the judge.[189]

Narrative Account of the Crime[190]

On the afternoon of Monday November 13, a military cordon was established around the Joint Command headquarters, the Military Academy and the Arce neighborhood in San Salvador, which are directly in front of the main gate of the UCA. This military zone was under the command of Col. Guillermo Alfredo Benavides Moreno, director of the Military Academy. Troops assigned to various battalions, among them the Atlacatl as well as some troops belonging to other military detachments in Sonsonate and Ahuachapán were in this zone. This same Monday the order was given to conduct a search of the priests' residence at the UCA. The order to carry it out was given to Lt. José Ricardo Espinoza Guerra and his second-in-command, Second Lt. Gonzalo Guevara Cerritos, both on active duty with the Atlacatl Battalion.

---

188 Testimony of Capt. Luis Alberto Parada Fuentes, Fourth Criminal Court, May 28, 1991.

189 The SIU report appears in volume 10 of the court record at page 1933 *et seq*. The declarants provided no new information.

190 This account is an edited and abridged version of "Narración de los Hechos" which was prepared by the Jesuits in early 1990 and later appeared in *ECA* , #493-494, Nov.-Dec. 1989, at 1125-1132. The quotations and dialogue in this narrative are taken textually from the extrajudicial statements of those charged with the murders. Shortened versions of these statements appear in translation in an appendix to the Interim Report, *supra* note 129. *See also* "Documentación, 1.1 Sentencia interlocutoria para la detención provisional," *ECA*, #493-494, at 1155-1168.

According to the accounts in the extrajudicial confessions of the suspects arraigned before the judge, events unfolded in the following manner: At 11:00 p.m. on November 15, Lieutenant Espinoza was ordered to report to Colonel Benavides in the Military Academy. In the Academy he met Lt. Yusshy Mendoza Vallecillos, who repeated that the colonel wanted to see him and Second Lieutenant Guevara Cerritos. They found the colonel in the officers' quarters and walked with him to his office. According to their accounts, Colonel Benavides said: "This is a situation where it's them or us; we are going to begin with the ringleaders. Within our sector we have the university and Ellacuría is there." He immediately turned to Lieutenant Espinoza and said:

> You conducted the search and your people know the place. Use the same tactics as on the day of the search and eliminate him. And I want no witnesses. Lieutenant Mendoza will go with you as the man in charge of the operation so that there will be no problems.

Lieutenant Espinoza adds that he told the colonel that "this was a serious problem."

"Don't worry," Colonel Benavides reportedly responded. "You have my support." The accounts of the two other lieutenants differ from this version on a few points. Second Lieutenant Guevara agrees with Espinoza, but adds that Colonel Benavides also said: "These are the intellectual authors who have directed the guerrillas for a long time." In contrast, Lieutenant Mendoza asserts that when they called him into the colonel's office, Lieutenant Espinoza was already there and Colonel Benavides simply told him: "You are going to accompany Espinoza to carry out a mission. He already knows what it is."

Later, before they left the Military Academy, Lieutenant Espinoza says that he asked Lieutenant Mendoza for a bar of camouflage grease in order to paint his face. Lieutenant Espinoza graduated from the Externado San José, the Jesuit high school, at a time when Father Segundo Montes was the principal. While Montes did not recognize him during the November 13 search, it is not difficult to imagine that Lieutenant Espinoza would have recognized Father Montes. In his statement, Espinoza asserts that Lieutenant Mendoza offered him the bar of camouflage for his face.

As they prepared to leave, Lieutenant Mendoza offered an AK-47 to any man who could use it. Oscar Mariano Amaya Grimaldi, an enlisted man from the Atlacatl Battalion, who would be charged with using it, does not remember which of the two lieutenants – Espinoza or Mendoza – gave it to him because the two were together. But he says that he did receive the information from his commander, Espinoza, that they were going to kill "some delinquent terrorists who were inside the university UCA."

In their statements, the seven suspects state that a short while after the colonel gave the order, they left the Military Academy in two Ford 250 pick-ups. They got as far as the empty apartment buildings located on the west side of the UCA which have been left half-built. The group of soldiers congregated at this point before going into the UCA campus. Troops from DM 7, who were assigned to the Security Command, were stationed in these abandoned buildings.

The various testimonies indicate that the three lieutenants gave the instructions for the operation which was about to be carried out, including plans to provide cover and security for those who were going to kill the priests. It was at this point that they chose the individuals who would participate in the execution of the crime. Over 50 soldiers entered the campus, though not all of them played a direct role in the assassination; nearly 300 surrounded the university. Before leaving the unfinished apartment buildings, one soldier, Amaya Grimaldi, remembers Lieutenant Mendoza saying to him: "You are the key man."

Amaya Grimaldi, known among his friends as Pilijay,[191] understood "that he was the one in charge of killing the people who were inside this place." En route, walking beside Lieutenants Espinoza and Mendoza, Pilijay heard Lieutenant Espinoza say to him – in reference to the AK-47 – "Hide that shit."

Inside the UCA

The soldiers stated that they entered the UCA through the pedestrians' gate. For at least 30 minutes, they waited near the parking lot. At this moment, a plane passed low over the UCA, which awakened Father Fermín Saínz and several neighbors.

In front of the parking lot the soldiers feigned the first attack, damaging parked cars and launching at least one grenade. A night watchman who was sleeping in one of the buildings parallel to the parking lot later recounted that he

---

191 *Pilijay* is a Nahuatl word meaning "hangman." *See* "Qué te pasó, Pilijay?," *Carta a las Iglesias*, #243, Oct. 1-15, 1991, at 16.

heard two sentences: "Don't go over there, there are only offices over there" and "now is the time to go kill the Jesuits."

According to the soldiers' statements, the operation involved three concentric circles. One group of soldiers stayed in the area far removed from the Theological Reflection Center Archbishop Romero (CRT). Others encircled the building, some climbed on to the roofs of neighboring houses. Finally, a smaller "select" group was designated to actively participate in the assassinations. Only some of the members of this limited group were formally charged with the crime. After encircling the house where the Jesuit priests were sleeping, the soldiers began to bang on the doors. Simultaneously, they entered the lower floor of the building, the Theological Reflection Center, destroying and burning what they found. Those who encircled the Jesuit residence yelled at them to open the doors. Oscar Amaya (Pilijay) remembered having said at the back gate to the residence: "When are you going to come out? Do you think I have all the time in the world to wait?" In the testimony he stated that he saw a person stop in front of a hammock that was hanging on the balcony, who said to him: "Wait. I am coming to open the door, but don't keep making so much noise."

In his testimony, Pilijay remembers that "this man wore a brown nightshirt." Father Ellacuría was wearing a bathrobe of this color when he was killed. Antonio Ramiro Avalos Vargas, a sub-sergeant on active duty with the Atlacatl Battalion, testified that a soldier banged on the door with a piece of wood. After "ten minutes of banging on these doors and windows, a man with light colored hair wearing pajamas opened the gate which they were banging on with a stick . . . ." This man said to the soldiers that "they should not continue banging on the doors and windows because they knew what was going to happen to them." This second victim, probably Segundo Montes, was then taken to the lawn in front of the residence. When he arrived there, four of his colleagues – Amando López, Ellacuría, Martín-Baró and Moreno – were already outside.

At about the same moment, Martín-Baró went with another soldier to open the gate leading to the Chapel of Christ the Liberator. That is where the witness Lucía Barrera de Cerna saw five soldiers. There too, is probably where Martín-Baró said to a soldier: "This is an injustice. You are scum." Lucía Cerna heard this phrase perfectly, while another neighbor, a little further away, only managed to hear the words "injustice" and "scum."[192]

192 The word used by Father Martín-Baró was *carroña*, meaning carrion or rotting flesh. While common in Spain, the word is generally not used in Central American Spanish.

It could be that Martín-Baró said these words when he saw that a soldier had pointed his rifle at Elba, a cook for the Jesuits, and her daughter Celina. In fact, to get to this gate you have to pass by the room where the two women were murdered. Sub-sergeant Tomás Zarpate Castillo, another member of the Atlacatl Battalion, was guarding the door of this room on the orders of Lieutenant Yusshy Mendoza.

Antonio Avalos and Oscar Amaya say they ordered the priests to lie down at a moment when they feared losing control of the five priests because they were alone. The search of the house continued.

Meanwhile, Father Joaquin López y López had managed to hide in another room. It is unclear how long the priests were lying on the ground. Some neighbors heard whispers without understanding what was said. At one point, just before the gunfire that killed the priests began, one neighbor says she heard a kind of rhythmic whispering, like a psalmody of a group in prayer.

Killing of the Priests

In his statement, Antonio Avalos says that Lieutenant Espinoza, with Lieutenant Mendoza at his side, called him over and asked: "At what time are you going to proceed?" The sub-sergeant declares that he understood this sentence "as an order to eliminate the men who were lying face down." He approached Private Amaya and said to him: "Let's proceed."

They began shooting. Avalos vented his fury against Juan Ramón Moreno and Amando López. Pilijay shot Ellacuría, Martín-Baró and Montes. Espinoza and Mendoza remained 10 meters away, according to the testimony of one of the executioners. Pilijay would remember that "among these three men whom he shot first was the one who was wearing the brown nightshirt." Afterward he would give the *coup de grâce* to each one. According to Pilijay, Ignacio Martín-Baró only received the *coup de grâce*. The entrance and trajectory of the bullets suggests that some of the priests attempted to get up at the moment the execution started. Others, like Nacho,[193] appear not to have moved at all, even keeping his feet crossed until the end, like someone who lies down on the floor and finds a comfortable position.

While this was going on, Tomás Zarpate was "providing security" – according to his own testimony – for Elba and

---

193 Father Martín-Baró was known as Nacho, the nickname for Ignacio.

Celina. On hearing the voice ordering: "Now," and the following shots, he "also shot the two women" until he was sure they were dead, because "they no longer groaned."

At this moment, when the shooting was over, Father López y López appeared in the door of the residence. The soldiers called him and Pilijay says that he responded: "Don't kill me because I don't belong to any organization." And he then immediately went back inside the house. According to Corporal Angel Pérez Vásquez of the Atlacatl, Father López y López left his hiding place after he heard the shots. When he saw the corpses, he immediately went back into the house. The soldiers outside called to him: "*Compa*, come here."[194]

According to Corporal Pérez Vásquez' narrative, "the *Señor* paid no attention, and just when he had entered a room a soldier shot him." Pérez Vásquez says Father López y López fell down inside the room. When Pérez Vásquez went in to inspect the scene, he "felt Father López y López grab his feet. He moved back and shot him four times."

At the end of the shooting, the soldiers shot off a Bengal light, which was a signal to withdraw. When some did not move, they shot off another Bengal light. While leaving, Avalos Vargas – nicknamed "Toad" and "Satan" by his comrades – passed in front of the guest room where Elba and Celina were murdered and heard some people groaning. He surmised that some of the victims were merely wounded and would have to be shot again. According to Avalos Vargas' testimony, he "lit a match, seeing that inside the room . . . were two women lying on the floor, embracing each other and moaning, so he ordered the soldier Sierra Ascencio to shoot them again." Avalos Vargas testified that Jorge Alberto Sierra Ascencio, another member of the Atlacatl, "shot off a round of about ten cartridges toward the bodies of these women until they stopped moaning." Later, Sierra Ascencio realized that the investigation was focusing on his group and deserted.

According to Amaya Grimaldi, he heard Espinoza Guerra give an order to Corporal Cotta Hernández to "Get them inside even if you have to drag them." Corporal Cotta carried the body of Juan Ramón Moreno to Jon Sobrino's room and left him there. Lying next to him when his body was later found was the book *The Crucified God*, by the European theologian, Moltman. Going outside the house, Cotta noticed that the other soldiers had left and he too left the UCA, leaving the other priests lying on the grass.

---

194 *Compa* is short for *compañero*, meaning friend or comrade. *Compa* is used among FMLN members or affectionately by their supporters.

The entire operation took about one hour. As the soldiers left the scene of the crime, they feigned an attack on the Theological Reflection Center. It was part of the plan. The Joint Command's log contains the following entry: "At 12:30 a.m. on November 16, delinquent terrorists launch grenades from the San Felipe sand ravine, on the southeast edge of the University, damaging the Theology Building of this center of studies, no casualties reported." The Joint Command's report was only mistaken in the location from which the attack was launched and the hour. In fact, this record of the attack indicates it took place exactly two hours before it actually did.

On the doors and walls of the lower floor of the CRT, the soldiers wrote the initials "FMLN." Exiting through the pedestrians' gate to the UCA, one of them scrawled "The FMLN executed the enemy spies. Victory or Death, FMLN." Handwriting analysis indicated that the handwriting of Second Lieutenant Guevara Cerritos and that of Sub-sergeant Avalos Vargas "exhibits similar characteristics." Either of them could have been the authors of this grafitti. Several of the soldiers remembered having seen Guevara Cerritos write the message.

By the time the priests had been killed, the CRT had already been burned inside. Presumably Guevara Cerritos, who was not present at the scene of the assassination, directed the attack on the building. Later he set up an M-60 machine gun, brought from the Military Academy along with the AK-47, in front of the Center for Information and Documentation (CIDAI), the building opposite the Jesuit residence, and pointed it toward the CRT. Pilijay arrived in time to shoot off his anti-tank rocket, known as "LAW," which exploded against the iron gate on the balcony of the priests' residence. He added his own shots to those of the M-60. Other soldiers also took shots at the building and one threw two M-79 grenades against it. Neither Cotta Hernández[195] – who participated in the assassination by moving Juan Ramón Moreno's body – nor the sergeant nicknamed "Savage" and his patrol, who shot up the building, nor those soldiers who entered the Theological Reflection Center and burned and destroyed its equipment, were charged with any crime.[196] In his testimony, Lt. Yusshy Mendoza added one last memory of the crime scene. "An unidentified soldier took a light brown satchel," he said. The bag, containing $5,000 in prize money which had been given to Ellacuría a few days earlier, has never reappeared.

---

195 Cotta Hernández was reportedly later killed in combat in Zacamil.

196 Two engineers appointed by the court later assessed the damage to the building at 404,945 *colones*, over $50,000.

Lieutenant Espinoza Guerra states in his extrajudicial declaration that he left the crime scene with his eyes full of tears. He would cry again when he gave his declaration.

Back at the Military Academy

Back at the Military Academy, the operation was considered a success. Those participating in the operation had been led by "Satan, Accursed, Lightening and Corralled," nicknames of war given to the sergeants and sub-sergeants. The soldiers "Nahum," "Savage," "Samson," "Hercules" and "Lizard" were in the area and Savage participated in the operation. Espinoza, whose nickname is "Bull," related in his declaration that as soon as he arrived at the Military Academy he went to the office of Colonel Benavides "with the intention of confronting him, because he was angered by what had happened." He didn't find him. When at last he appeared, Colonel Benavides took the initiative: "What's wrong with you? You look worried."

My Colonel, I did not like what was done.

Calm down, don't worry. You have my support. Trust me.

I hope so, my Colonel.

There were over 300 officers and enlisted men around the UCA and surrounding neighborhood that night, without even counting those who participated in the assassination. Apparently not one of them informed his superiors, or tried to initiate an investigation of what had happened at the UCA. The soldiers of the Atlacatl who participated in the assassination were sent to fight in the neighborhoods of Mejicanos and Zacamil at 6:00 a.m. on November 16, rejoining their own battalion. There they told soldiers of the First Brigade what they had done. Between 2:00 p.m. and 3:00 p.m. this same day, Archbishop Rivera y Damas and Auxiliary Bishop Rosa Chávez heard a voice over a megaphone on a military sound truck saying, "Ellacuría and Martín-Baró have fallen. We're going to continue killing Communists." Minutes later, the same voice on the same microphone said, "Surrender. We belong to the First Brigade." Despite the public denunciation by Father Rosa Chávez and others, this lead was never investigated.

CHAPTER III: THE MYTH OF GOOD POLICE WORK
(November 16, 1989 to January 2, 1990)

On January 7, 1990, President Cristiani, flanked by the Army High Command, announced on Salvadoran television that "elements of the Armed Forces" were responsible for the Jesuit killings. At that time and in many subsequent accounts, this revelation was credited to the "good police work" carried out by the Special Investigative Unit (SIU).[197] Yet a careful examination of the SIU's performance reveals a pattern of missteps, failure to follow obvious leads and timidity. No doubt aware that it did not have a mandate to fully probe the crime, the SIU investigation lacked competence, zeal and good faith.

The court record – which includes the SIU's own account of its work – provides persuasive evidence that while the SIU carried out various investigative steps, it failed to do so in a thorough and timely fashion, allowing evidence to be disturbed, removed and even destroyed. The SIU's lapses gave military witnesses the opportunity to organize an extensive coverup. The consequences of these lapses were graphically illustrated by the destruction of the Military Academy's logbooks. Testifying before Judge Zamora on October 18, 1990, SIU Lieutenant José Luis Preza Rivas said that the SIU had planned to examine the Academy's logbooks in January 1990, but since by then the arrests had already been made, nothing was done. By late May when Judge Zamora requested the registries, it was revealed that they had been burned in December 1989. In addition to errors such as these, the SIU did not provide the court with a complete record of its investigation, omitting records of crucial visits and interrogations.

---

197 As late as November 1991, Representative Joe Moakley attributed the only partial success of the military's coverup to "good, preliminary police work carried out by El Salvador's Special Investigative Unit." *See* "Statement of Representative Joe Moakley, Chairman of the Speaker's Task Force on El Salvador," Nov. 18, 1991.

A lengthy attack on the work of the Moakley task force published by an unknown organization called the Central American Lawyers Group concluded that, ". . . suffice it to say that, without the important work done by the SIU, no progress would have been made on the case would [sic] and it would not be going to trial in 1991." Central American Lawyers Group, *The Rule of Law in Wartime El Salvador: The Jesuit Case in Context*, at 21 (Sept. 1991).

While the Jesuit investigation may represent the SIU at its best, its grave and obvious flaws demonstrate that an independent, professional criminal investigatory body is still sorely lacking in El Salvador. A top U.S. embassy official told the Lawyers Committee in July 1990 that the unit's work had been "too linear," only concerned with identifying the triggermen – or "material authors" of the crime – while not developing evidence or examining the chain of command above Colonel Benavides. "They found an answer, but they didn't build a case," he said.

"I thought that the SIU was technically going against the triggerpullers," a U.S. official who followed the case closely told the Lawyers Committee in May 1991. "They wanted a stand alone situation – the triggerpullers acting on their own with no conduit to the top. I felt that, and that's exactly what they are doing."

At no time did the SIU attempt to examine the key question of who ordered the murders. Lt. Col. Manuel Antonio Rivas Mejía, SIU chief at the time of the murders, stated this explicitly in court,

> that there was no investigation of the heads of the Joint Command of the Armed Forces, since this institution is in charge of the entire country, while the security command only [had] responsibility for the military complex. And having identified the suspects of the assassination under investigation, it was no longer necessary. . . .[198]

Other critics have suggested that the SIU's work was in fact aimed at damage control, more concerned with concealing the involvement of other ranking officers than with establishing the truth.

One telling statement on the quality of the SIU's work is that Lieutenant Colonel Rivas was repeatedly mentioned by judicial authorities and others as a potential defendant himself for his alleged role in the coverup. In a July 1990 interview with the Lawyers Committee, Supreme Court President Mauricio Gutiérrez Castro said he could not rule out the possibility that Lieutenant Colonel Rivas might face charges for improper conduct of the police investigation. Rivas was nonetheless

198 Testimony of Lt. Col. Manuel Antonio Rivas Mejía, Fourth Criminal Court, Oct. 19, 1990.

promoted to full colonel in December 1990 and named second-in-command of the National Police.[199]

Investigation Flawed from the Outset[200]

Shortly after the killings occurred, the SIU states that President Cristiani personally assigned it to investigate the crime. The SIU's investigation was flawed from the start, when its detectives neglected to seal off the crime scene before evidence could be disturbed. According to the unit's records, two SIU detectives arrived on the murder scene at 9:10 a.m. on November 16 – some seven hours after the killings took place. They proceeded to take photographs and to gather physical evidence: cartridges, shell fragments and fingerprints. They also began preparing maps and interviewing potential witnesses. They were joined at the site by technicians from the SIU's own Forensic Unit, members of the National Police's Explosives Unit,[201] the Third Justice of the Peace of San Salvador and her secretary, a forensic pathologist, the Second Criminal Judge of Santa Tecla and his secretary, and a prosecutor.

Although the U.S. State Department has reported that the SIU sealed the scene of the crime as soon as the agents arrived that morning, the scene was in fact not sealed until sometime on Saturday morning, November 18 during a memorial service. As a result, potential evidence was disturbed and removed by a variety of visitors. María Julía Hernández, head of the archdiocesan legal aid office, told Judge Zamora in mid-December that she took two projectile shells (*vainillas de*

---

199 Colonel Rivas is currently the government's representative on a commission charged with establishing the new National Civilian Police created by the 1992 Peace Accords.

200 Many of the details regarding the SIU's description of its investigation come from information it submitted to the court and from a paper it prepared in January 1990 entitled "Summary on the Murder of Six Priests of the Society of Jesus and Two Women in Their Service, on the Grounds of the "José Simeón Cañas" Central American University (UCA)" (on file at Lawyers Committee for Human Rights) [hereinafter SIU Summary].

201 On November 18, 1989, the National Police submitted its investigative report to the SIU regarding four explosions at the Pastoral Center which, according to a witness interviewed, took place at 12:30 a.m. on November 16. The report concluded that a LAW rocket and a grenade launcher had been used. National Police agents did not pursue their investigations further since according to the law regulating the SIU, all other Security Forces are foreclosed from conducting investigations parallel to that of the SIU. *See* El Salvador Ley de Creación de la Comisión de Investigación de Hechos Delictivos, Art. 10.

proyectil) from the area around the body of Father Ellacuría and two from the service area of the Jesuits' residence. Ms. Hernández' admission provoked attacks by the Attorney General's office (*Fiscalía*) and a rightist morning newspaper, which said she had "stolen and hidden" the evidence which she had obtained "fraudulently."[202]

Other potentially important physical evidence from the crime scene was ignored by SIU agents. Several days later, Father Tojeira picked up a Tecate beer can thrown against the wall of a neighbor's house. By the time SIU technicians examined the can, they found only Tojeira's fingerprints.

The SIU's next misstep was its failure to take statements from likely military witnesses and to act on important leads provided by its own investigators and the court. The SIU officers supervising the investigation knew from the start that the military had surrounded the UCA on the night of the killings. The SIU's files indicate that several military witnesses told the SIU on November 17 that Atlacatl troops had passed near the university that night. Days later, Jesuits informed them that the Atlacatl had carried out the November 13 search. Yet SIU agents delayed almost a month after the murders before officially interviewing any Atlacatl member.

In fact, as late as December 22, the SIU still entertained the possibility of FMLN involvement, or so they told the Jesuits in a private briefing. Perhaps awaiting a green light from the High Command before seriously following military leads, perhaps out of ineptitude, or perhaps a conscious attempt to conceal the truth, whatever the motivation, the SIU's failure to act gave the military time to ensure that soldiers around the UCA that night provided no useful testimony.

The first information implicating the Atlacatl Battalion was obtained by the SIU on November 17 when agents spoke to police guarding the Democracy Tower, located on the corner of the Autopista Sur and Avenida Albert Einstein. Sub-sergeant Germán Orellana Vásquez of the Monserrat Battalion of the National Police and agent Victor Manuel Orellana Hernández – who were on duty from midnight to 7:00 a.m. on November 16 – told the SIU they "saw tanks and troops from the Atlacatl Battalion pass by." They said that about 2:00 a.m. they had heard bomb explosions and firearms far and near.

Almost a month later, on December 11, the SIU finally recorded a formal statement from Orellana Hernández, who by that time only remembered hearing "sporadic shooting, but no

---

202 *Diario de Hoy*, Dec. 15, 1989; *El Mundo*, Dec. 15, 1989.

combat." Further, he saw no Bengal lights, and did "not recall that any military vehicles passed by, nor any movement of Army troops." On December 12, his colleague, Sub-sergeant Orellana Vásquez, gave his statement, saying that he did not see anything, but that he did hear the sound of engines coming from the direction of the Military Academy. The references to the Atlacatl Battalion had pointedly disappeared, strongly suggesting that between November 17 and December 11, the police were induced to "forget" the presence of Atlacatl troops.

Treasury Police agents on duty at Democracy Tower that night told the SIU on November 17 that members of the Atlacatl were patrolling Residencial Guadalupe, a neighborhood just south of the UCA. Not until December 5 were formal declarations recorded; by then, the Atlacatl troops were not mentioned. Further, in its public documents on the case, the SIU apparently sought to erase all early mention of the Atlacatl. The SIU's own report on their work summarizes testimonies recorded, but fails to report any mention of the Atlacatl. Yet the SIU went even further in distorting the information it had gathered. The entry for November 17, the day the unit interviewed members of the Monserrat Battalion stationed at Democracy Tower, incorrectly reports that these soldiers testified to "not having seen vehicles pass by, nor having heard the sound of engines, but they did hear shots in the UCA sector."[203]

In late November and early December, six Jesuits, most of whom were sleeping in another residence just off the campus on the night of the killings, testified in court that Atlacatl troops had searched the Jesuit residence within the UCA on the evening of November 13.[204] The Jesuits said that Father Ellacuría had returned to El Salvador late Monday afternoon, November 13, and that his car was checked by soldiers guarding the main UCA gate around 5:45 p.m. Only after Father Ellacuría spoke to the troops were he and his Jesuit colleagues allowed to enter the campus. At about 8:00 p.m. that evening, Father Martín-Baró called to advise Jesuits living on Calle del Mediterráneo behind the UCA that the search had occurred, suggesting that the soldiers might be en route to their house.

Two Jesuits told the court that the troops were from the Atlacatl Battalion. The priests also testified that Father Ellacuría had invited the soldiers to return in daylight to

203 SIU Summary, *supra* note 200, at 5.

204 Statements were taken from Jesuit Provincial José María Tojeira, S.J. (Nov. 20); Fermín Saínz, S.J. (Nov. 28); Rogelio Pedraz, S.J. (Nov. 21); Angel María Pedrosa, S.J. (Nov. 30); Francisco Javier Ibisate, S.J. (Dec. 8); Miguel Francisco Estrada, S.J. (Dec. 8).

conduct a thorough search of the UCA. In these judicial statements as well as Father Martín-Baró's written account, the beginning of the search is consistently placed between 6:30 p.m. and 7:00 p.m.

Father Fermín Saínz, an UCA psychology professor who directs the Loyola Retreat Center in the hills above the campus, told the court that on the afternoon of November 15, some 120 members of the Atlacatl Battalion occupied the Loyola Center just hours before they descended toward the campus.[205]

The testimony of the Jesuits supplemented by that of troops stationed in the area on the night of the murders means that well before the end of November 1989, the SIU had leads from a variety of sources suggesting that the Atlacatl Battalion should be investigated in connection with the crime. Yet it was not until mid-December that the SIU began to interview Atlacatl members. Given that the zone was totally under military control, an obvious first investigatory step should have been to interview troops stationed there and to question the zone commander, Military Academy Director Guillermo Alfredo Benavides. Testifying in court on October 19, 1990, SIU chief Manuel Antonio Rivas Mejía, was asked by a public prosecutor why Benavides had not been questioned immediately, and Rivas replied that there "was no indication that the men in the Military Complex were the authors of the crime."

Rivas' testimony in court, and that of his second-in-command, José Luis Preza Rivas, reads like a classroom exercise for beginning detectives learning to identify obvious leads and how to organize a criminal investigation.[206] Rivas Mejía offered that once the nine defendants were identified the SIU did not continue its work because they did not "feel" that there were "any other military officers superior to Colonel Benavides who could have given the order. . . ." Rivas said that the SIU work plan included asking for the Academy logbooks, but once the arrests were made he did not do so because he did not want

205 *See supra* Chapter II: "Chronology of the Crime," for an account of the Atlacatl's occupation of Loyola.

206 The SIU was created by the United States in 1985 and was originally trained by agents retired or on loan from the FBI. Since that time the unit has received extensive training under the International Criminal Investigative Training Assistance Program (ICITAP). According to AID, the SIU received $3.1 million in U.S. aid between 1985 and June 22, 1992. During that time the unit also received at least $2 million in Salvadoran counterpart funds generated by Economic Support Funds donated by the United States. The SIU's future is unclear, since the peace accords call for a new civilian criminal investigatory unit to be established within the Attorney General's office.

to "interfere with the judicial investigation."[207] By the time the logbooks were finally requested in spring 1990, they had been burned. As the record shows, the gaping omissions in the SIU's work allowed the military time to engage in an extensive and effective coverup.

Belated Investigation of Military Involvement

As noted by the Moakley task force, the "investigation of possible military involvement began slowly."[208] Investigators were even slower at examining the Atlacatl, and, at least according to the official record, did not consider the potential involvement of Military Academy personnel or of its director, Colonel Benavides, until confronted with the colonel's role by U.S. diplomats on January 2, 1990.

It is also noteworthy that Lieutenant Colonel Rivas chose to absent himself from San Salvador during the early critical days of the investigation. In late November, Rivas went to Miami to participate in FBI questioning of Lucía Barrera de Cerna, the Jesuit housekeeper who left the country after giving a full witness statement to the court. On returning to San Salvador in early December, Rivas instructed SIU agents to gather physical evidence in the Jesuit house where Mrs. Cerna and her family had been sleeping, in an apparent attempt to prove that they had never been in the house.[209]

Yet despite what the SIU has officially reported, Lieutenant Colonel Rivas, accompanied by three U.S. officials, visited the Academy in early December 1989, reportedly to obtain information about the location of troops around the campus. Richard Chidester, the embassy liaison to the SIU testified in August 1991 that he accompanied Rivas to the Academy.[210] Mr. Chidester told the Lawyers Committee a year earlier that

207 According to Article 143 of the Criminal Procedure Code, a police investigatory body must consign the suspect to the court within 72 hours of detention with its investigatory record, "without prejudice to continuing its investigation and advising the judge of its findings."

208 Interim Report, *supra* note 129, at 21.

209 For an account of what happened to Lucía Cerna, *see infra* Chapter X: "Washington's Mixed Messages."

210 Deposition of Richard J. Chidester, Aug. 6, 1991, *In Re Letters Rogatory From the Fourth Criminal Court Judge of San Salvador, El Salvador*, at 9 (D.D.C. 1991). The two other U.S. officials who accompanied Rivas and Chidester were Janice Elmore, a political-military officer at the embassy, and a DEA agent based in Mexico City who was brought in temporarily to work on the case.

Benavides, whom he found "forthcoming," used maps to illustrate the troops' location, and called in subordinates to supplement his own account.[211] On that occasion, Benavides provided the investigators with a map illustrating troop locations the night of the murders. In his August 1991 deposition, Mr. Chidester said the map was prepared by the SIU and that he did not know if it had been provided to the court.

Despite the SIU's legal obligation to report all investigatory steps, this visit was not reported to Judge Zamora, and Rivas Mejía actually denied in court on October 19, 1990 that he had any contact with Benavides before the colonel gave his defendant statement on January 11, 1990.

SIU personnel say that from the outset they considered three potential suspects: the military, the FMLN or a death squad. No substantial evidence ever supported the theory that the rebel movement was involved, despite the killers' feeble attempts to incriminate the FMLN: three of the priests were killed with a Soviet-made rifle of the type often used by the guerrillas; the soldiers scrawled "FMLN" inside the Theological Reflection Center; and a sign left on the UCA's back gate read, "The FMLN killed the enemy spies. Victory or death, FMLN." And, to date, it has never been established who made a mysterious entry in the registry of Army intelligence attributing attacks on the UCA at 12:30 a.m. to "delinquent terrorists using grenade launchers. . . ."

A $250,000 award offered by President Cristiani on December 11 prompted several would-be witnesses to come forward. These witnesses claimed to have overheard FMLN plans to kill the priests. No evidence was ever produced to suggest the involvement of a paramilitary group or death squad.

On November 28, 1989, public prosecutors from the Attorney General's office asked Judge Zamora to seek information from Joint Command chief Col. René Emilio Ponce about the location of all units on duty around the UCA on the night of the murders and the names of all officers and enlisted men. Writing to Colonel Ponce on December 5, the court expanded the request to include the troops who conducted the November 13 search of the Jesuit residence and the November 15 search of the Loyola Center. The court also asked the Joint Command to detail any combat in the UCA area on November 15-16 and provide any other information which might help establish what had happened.

---

211 Lawyers Committee interview with Richard Chidester, San Salvador, Aug. 16, 1990.

Colonel Ponce's December 8 response was filed in court on December 11, and described the formation of the Security Command of the military complex, of which Colonel Benavides was named director on the afternoon of November 13.[212] Curiously, the list provided by Ponce did not include the Atlacatl. According to Ponce, the following troops were assigned around the university between 6:00 p.m. on November 15 and 7:00 a.m. on November 16.

> **South and southwest**: Military Detachment 7 – Puma First Counterinsurgency Infantry Battalion led by Lieutenant José Ricardo Gallardo Mata.
>
> **South and southeast**: Miltary Detachment 6 – Jaguar Counterinsurgency Battalion.
>
> Both units were under the command of Captain Julio Armando García Oliva of the Military Academy.
>
> **North**: National Policemen were guarding the military neighborhoods, Arce and Palermo. Treasury Policemen were stationed at the Democracy Tower.

Colonel Ponce's statement also included information from the Joint Command log about incidents which allegedly occurred around the campus during the hours when the murder operation was unfolding:

> 1) at 12:30 a.m. on the sixteenth, delinquent terrorists using grenade launchers from the San Felipe Sand Ravine near the southeast side of the university in question damaged the theology building of this center of studies, without any casualties reported.
>
> 2) at 2 a.m. the same day, another fire fight was recorded with delinquent terrorists in the city of Antiguo Cuscatlán; two men from Military Detachment 7 were wounded.

The first entry concerns an incident that supposedly took place at the building where the Jesuits were killed, close to

---

212 Because of his rank and position, Colonel Ponce is not required by Salvadoran law to appear in court, but may instead submit a certified written statement. *See* Salvadoran Criminal Procedure Code, Art. 205.

The military complex (*complejo militar*) is the zone surrounding the Joint Command headquarters, which includes the Ministry of Defense, the Military Academy, the National Intelligence Directorate, the San Benito Battalion of the National Police and two military housing neighborhoods. The UCA falls within its parameters.

the time of the killers' arrival on campus. There is no record of any effort on the part of SIU investigators to discover the origin of the annotation once they received a copy of the statement and, to date, the court's efforts to establish its source have been unsuccessful. By all appearances, the entry is an early attempt to cover up the military's role. Adding to the mystery surrounding the first entry is that officers and soldiers involved in the second incident provided the SIU with extensive details.

SIU Requests to Joint Command

The SIU finally presented its own series of formal requests for information to the Joint Command, primarily between December 4 and December 15 – starting an entire week later than the court. It was not until December 16 that Lieutenant Colonel Rivas requested that Colonel Ponce provide the SIU with a copy of his statement submitted to the court on December 11. Furthermore, the SIU showed a consistent inability or unwillingness to follow up on leads in the information it received.

On December 4 the SIU asked Colonel Ponce to provide information about incidents that had occurred around the UCA starting on November 11; a reply came back on December 18. In the section entitled "Enemy Activity Registered" for the UCA area, marked confidential, the following entry appeared for 12:30 a.m., November 16:

> D/T[213] using machine guns (various kinds of rifles) assassinated the "JESUIT fathers," IGNACIO ELLACURIA (UCA rector), ARMANDO LOPEZ, [sic] IGNACIO MARTIN BARO, SEGUNDO MONTES, JUAN RAMON MORENO, JOAQUIN LOPEZ Y LOPEZ, Sra. ELBA JULIA RAMOS (maid) and her minor daughter CELINA RAMOS, inside the installations of the CENTRAL AMERICAN UNIVERSITY "JOSE SIMEON CANAS" (U.C.A.), SAN SALVADOR.

Again, there is no evidence of any SIU attempt to determine the origin of this entry, or even to identify who recorded it. Seeking to blame the FMLN with such notations was a routine practice of the military, but tracing it could have provided valuable information as to when and how the Joint Command first confirmed that the attack had taken place. The entry has never been explained; it should have prompted

213 The military frequently referred to FMLN combatants as "D/T" short for "delinquent terrorists."

SIU investigators to pose a series of questions about its source and timing.

On December 5, the SIU officially requested the Joint Command to provide a list of troops that carried out the search of the Jesuit residence and other parts of the UCA on November 13. The reply on December 10 consisted of a list of 35 names provided by Lieutenant Colonel León Linares, then commander of the Atlacatl Battalion – although all accounts indicate that these troops were not under his command at the time they carried out the search. The approximately 100 additional troops who also participated in the search were not mentioned. Lieutenant Colonel León Linares said the order for the search came at 8:50 p.m., in response to a report of an "undetermined number of D/T penetrating the UCA campus and . . . firing on an Armed Forces unit. . . ." Nothing was found in the search and the troops returned to the Military Academy.

León Linares' brief report did not explain who actually ordered the search, nor to whom the troops reported. Furthermore, it presents a significant inconsistency, stating that the search order was given at 8:50 p.m. while Father Martín-Baró had called Jesuits living nearby to tell them that a search had taken place between 6:30 p.m. and 8:00 p.m. Colonel Ponce's December 8 statement to the court stated that

> around 8:50 p.m. after receiving information that terrorist elements had penetrated the installations of the University "José Simeón Cañas" and that they were firing on military personnel, troops from the Atlacatl Immediate Reaction Infantry Battalion were ordered to enter the installations in pursuit of these delinquents.

The SIU again made no effort to clear up this inconsistency. In his written declaration dated June 5, 1991, Lieutenant Colonel Rivas said he "considered it unnecessary to investigate the origin of the search order, because he had been told the Joint Command authorized it."

Father Martín-Baró's written description of the search – discovered in his computer after his death – provided important evidence. He said troops had entered by breaking the lock on the gate that leads to Jardines de Guadalupe (the pedestrian entrance) and, it seemed, by jumping over one of the walls that surrounds the campus. Over the course of the investigation, military witnesses have offered several different explanations for why the search was ordered. While it was established that Colonel Ponce formally ordered the search, it is not clear who really instigated the operation, nor why.

On December 15, the SIU requested information from Colonel Ponce about an Army search at the Loyola Retreat Center on Wednesday November 15, apparently spurred by information provided by Father Saínz. On December 16, Colonel Ponce instead provided information about a November 12 search carried out by the Treasury Police during which weapons and equipment for four guerrillas were found at Loyola Center. In contrast to Father Saínz' testimony placing Atlacatl troops at Loyola on the afternoon and early evening hours of November 15, Colonel Ponce failed to make any reference to the Atlacatl in the area that night. Also on December 15, the SIU asked if the propulsion tube for the LAW rocket found at the murder scene had been assigned to the Armed Forces and if so, to which unit.

During December, the SIU recorded statements from National and Treasury Police agents guarding the military housing complexes across the highway from the UCA. They provided little useful information, confirming simply that guerrillas had fired on their position as the offensive began on November 11; they mentioned no shooting on November 12 or 13. Some said they heard gunfire from the direction of the UCA on the night of November 15-16, while many claimed to have heard nothing. No one had seen troops pass by and no one mentioned Atlacatl troops in the area.[214]

Another striking example of an obvious lead ignored by the SIU is the December 8 testimony of Pedro Anselmo Arévalo Coreas of the Monserrat Battalion of the National Police. Arévalo said that he and Sub-sergeant Hernández Reyes were assigned to patrol car #52, supplying and supervising the National Policemen guarding the Arce neighborhood. They spent the night of November 15-16 in the area. Around 6:00 a.m., just before the end of their shift, Arévalo Coreas testified that he heard interference on the patrol car's radio transmitter. "They said that they had killed Father ELLACURIA, they also said `NOW SWALLOW THAT ONE' and that he does not know

---

214 In his extrajudicial declaration of January 13, 1990, Lieutenant Espinoza states that he and Second Lieutenant Guevara Cerritos with two patrols were in or near the Arce neighborhood on the evening of November 15 until 10:15 p.m., when he received an order by radio to assemble his troops at the Military Academy. While Lieutenant Espinoza does not say who radioed to him, he does say he returned to the Academy with some of his units and the officers. These men would move out less than two hours later on the UCA murder mission.

who was giving that information. . . ."[215] This account indicates that the murders were being discussed over a military radio frequency near the end of curfew at 6:00 a.m., before the first civilians were on the scene.[216]

Inexplicably, the SIU appears to have made no attempt to identify the troops stationed at entrances to the UCA from November 13-16. Soldiers at the entrance on Southern Highway had identified Father Ellacuría before allowing him to proceed. Jesuit housekeeper Lucía Cerna and the UCA night watchmen leaving the campus from the back pedestrian gate passed troops at this position between 6:00 a.m. and 6:30 a.m. Timely interviews with these men might have yielded important leads. And after the killings, Treasury Police agents temporarily assigned to the DNI were ordered to stand guard at the main UCA gate.[217]

First Interviews with Atlacatl Soldiers

Once the Atlacatl commando unit was officially identified as the unit that carried out the November 13 search, the SIU called in for questioning the two lieutenants in charge of the unit – José Ricardo Espinoza Guerra and Gonzalo Guevara Cerritos. On December 13, a full month after the search, both men gave statements; other members of the commando unit were questioned later.

All the Atlacatl acknowledged leaving their base on the afternoon of November 13 with 40-odd members of the commando unit. Yet Lieutenants Espinoza and Guevara Cerritos said a total of 135 troops went to San Salvador. The officers left their men at the Military Academy and proceeded to the

215 According to the court record, Arévalo Coreas "...escuchó interferencia en el radio Trasmisor del Patrulla, en donde decían que habían matado al Padre ELLACURIA, asi mísmo dijeron "AHORA HARTENSELO" que ignora quién o quienes pasaban esa información, no dándole importancia a la noticia." (Emphasis in the original.)

Arévalo repeated this testimony in court on March 7, 1990, but added that his radio was experiencing interference from the guerrillas. He said he later learned that the FMLN had stolen two police vehicles "which is why they had interfered with the radios...."

216 Confirmation that the Jesuit murders were discussed on a closed military radio frequency before any civilians were apprised first surfaced in March 1991 when Capt. Luis Alberto Parada Fuentes gave a statement to the SIU.

217 Declaration of Mario Enrique Najarro Aguilar, Jan. 7, 1990.

Joint Command, where they were given the order to search the UCA. Espinoza said they went to the UCA "because there was information that an undetermined number of delinquent terrorists were there. . . ." Although the Jesuits had consistently fixed the November 13 search between 6:30 and 7:00 p.m., the Atlacatl commandos claimed to have begun the operation around 8:45 p.m. and finished around 10:30 p.m. DNI intelligence officers interviewed later also fixed the search at 6:30 to 7:00 p.m. All the commandos agreed that they rejoined the rest of the battalion early on the morning of November 16.

Yet on other important points, the statements of the Atlacatl members were riddled with contradictions. They could not agree on their manner of entry into the campus on the night of the search; whether they or their officers had conducted other missions between November 13 and 16; whether the electric power was functioning on November 13 when they conducted the search; whether other soldiers from the Atlacatl accompanied them; and whether they had gone by foot or by vehicle to the UCA. Some claimed to have entered the campus by crawling under the main entrance gate, a physically impossible feat.

Several statements refer to the participation of a Military Academy officer during the search, while others deny that officers from other units accompanied the commandos.[218] José Luis Martínez Carpio, a soldier who was wounded in subsequent fighting in Mejicanos, was the only soldier to admit that the search party had entered through the south pedestrian gate.[219] Martínez Carpio also reported that only eight rooms were searched and that he did not know why they did not enter the remaining buildings.

While inconsistencies in testimony are not uncommon, the sheer number of significant differences in the commandos' stories suggest that they had something to hide. Why could

218 It subsequently emerged that Lieutenant Héctor Ulises Cuenca Ocampo, an intelligence officer, accompanied the Atlacatl commandos on the orders of his superior at DNI, Capt. Carlos Fernando Herrera Carranza. *See San Francisco Examiner*, April 15, 1990, at A1 & A20. It was only 18 months later, during the eight-day evidentiary period in May-June 1991, that the court -- at the request of the private prosecution -- first solicited Cuenca's report. It emerged that Cuenca's written report to his superiors was dated December 13, 1989, a full month after the operation, and, perhaps not coincidentally, the first day members of the Atlacatl were questioned about the search.

219 Later testimony confirms that the search party entered through the south pedestrian entrance at the back of the campus and by scaling a wall on the west side of the UCA; the murderers used the same pedestrian entrance two days later.

they not agree, for instance, about their participation in other missions between November 13 and 16? Some recalled a second search in the Escalón section of San Salvador on November 14 or 15, while others claimed they did not set foot off the Academy grounds until the morning of November 16 when they rejoined the rest of the unit, which was fighting in Zacamil. Yet Sgt. Oscar Armando Solórzano Esquivel said the entire group set out at 7:00 p.m. on November 15 to reinforce other units stationed in the southern section of the complex – just beyond DNI headquarters – returning to the Academy around 5:00 or 6:00 a.m. on November 16.

The soldiers were almost unanimous, however, in claiming that they did not learn of the Jesuit killings until days afterward. Cpl. Angel Pérez Vásquez, who later confessed to killing Father López y López, told the SIU that "with respect to the assassination of six Jesuit priests he first learned about it 15 days after leaving the Military Academy by reading a newspaper." Pvt. Juan Antonio González Torres went so far as to claim that he had not heard of the death of the Jesuit priests until his statement was recorded on December 28.

By contrast, soldiers from other units generally said they learned of the killings through newspapers and radio reports within hours. The obvious deception observed in these early witness statements proved the norm, as hundreds of active duty members of the Salvadoran Armed Forces would later perjure themselves in court. Perjury charges were ultimately filed against four of them, among them, Sergeant Solórzano Esquivel, mentioned above.

On December 20, the SIU cited 10 additional members of the Atlacatl commando unit to give their testimony; statements from some 15 members of the unit had already been recorded.

On December 22, Lieutenant Colonel Rivas gave a briefing on the investigation's progress to Jesuit Fathers Tojeira and Estrada. The meeting was arranged by Col. Carlos Avilés, head of Army Psychological Operations (C-5) and a graduate of the Jesuit high school Externado San José.[220]

---

220 Colonel Avilés subsequently became a key figure in U.S. Major Eric Buckland's account implicating Colonel Benavides in the murders. According to the Buckland account, it was Colonel Avilés who had told him roughly two days before the meeting with the Jesuits that Colonel Benavides had confessed his involvement to Lieutenant Colonel Rivas and asked him for help. If Eric Buckland's original account is true, Benavides had already confessed to Rivas by the time the SIU chief met with the Jesuits.

By this time, former SIU chief Col. Ivan López y López had been seconded to the SIU to help Colonel Rivas with the investigation. At the time of the Jesuit killings, Colonel López y López was in charge of Personnel, C-1, of the Joint Command. While a former embassy official told the Lawyers Committee in May 1991 that López y López "had nothing better to do. . . ." a written statement provided to the court by General Ponce on June 3, 1991 suggests there may have been other reasons to place López y López in an oversight role. During the final eight-day evidence period of the plenary phase, Defense Minister Ponce answered a key unresolved question when he told the judge that López y López was in fact in charge of the command center at Joint Command headquarters at the murder hour.

By the time of the December 22 meeting with the Jesuits, the investigation was clearly focusing on the Atlacatl troops, but Lieutenant Colonel Rivas chose to tell the Jesuits that suspicion remained divided between the Army and the FMLN. Neither Colonel Benavides nor the Atlacatl troops were mentioned. Notwithstanding, a U.S. embassy chronology of the investigation called it a "full and detailed briefing."

That same day, Father Tojeira provided the SIU with additional evidence – a handwritten sign implicating the FMLN left on the pedestrian gate, some shells, an empty Tecate beer can he had retrieved from the crime scene, and two cigarette butts. The SIU immediately ordered lab analyses on these items, and directed that handwriting samples be taken from all Atlacatl commandos.[221]

In late December 1989, the SIU selected some of the Atlacatl commandos to participate in reconstructions of the November 13 search. The commandos not only contradicted each other, but several also contradicted their own prior statements.

Interviews with Other Units

Throughout December, the SIU conducted a series of interviews with soldiers attached to units other than the Atlacatl who were stationed in the UCA area. A careful reading of these testimonies suggests several leads which investigators

---

221 On January 14, 1990, handwriting analysts reported that the words "The FMLN executed the enemy spies. Victory or Death. FMLN," could have been written by either Second Lieutenant Guevara Cerritos or Sub-sergeant Avalos Vargas. Witness statements later indicated that Guevara Cerritos wrote the message.

failed to pursue, and also indicates that Lieutenant Colonel Rivas was basing his investigatory decisions on some *unofficial* information he apparently received prior to Colonel Ponce's *official* December 8, 1989 report on troop assignments.

On December 5, two lieutenants from Military Detachment (DM) 7 provided information which situated DM 7 troops at the abandoned apartment buildings used by the Atlacatl as a staging area before moving out for the campus. As noted earlier, the Lawyers Committee learned that Lieutenant Colonel Rivas and three U.S. embassy officials had gone to the Military Academy around this time to talk to Colonel Benavides about troops stationed in the area that night. The SIU record fails to mention the visit, although the recording of all investigative steps is obligatory. Without such a visit, it is difficult to explain how the investigators would have known that these DM 7 officers were in the vicinity that night before receiving Colonel Ponce's list of troop assignments.

In interviews with these DM 7 men and other troops, a series of discrepancies emerged and it appears that most soldiers went to great lengths to avoid placing themselves in the UCA area around the time of the killings.

Curiously, SIU investigators have never admitted that DM 7 troops were stationed exactly where the Atlacatl massed before and after the murders. Briefing a February 1990 delegation of presidents of U.S. Jesuit universities, Lieutenant Colonel Rivas Mejía mentioned military units stationed at Democracy Tower, the military housing neighborhoods and Antiguo Cuscatlán, but failed to list the DM 7 unit stationed at Cine Colonial and in the empty buildings. Yet an SIU map provided by the U.S. embassy, based on information provided by Colonel Benavides, did include the DM 7 men.

The testimony of those from DM 7 indicates that by November 15 three officers and 96 soldiers under the command of Lieutenant José Ricardo Gallardo Mata had been ordered into the capital and assigned to the Security Command based at the Military Academy. This unit and another from DM 6 were under the command of Captain Julio García Oliva of the Military Academy. For unexplained reasons, the location of the two units was switched hours before the killings.

According to these testimonies, around 6:00 p.m. on November 15, Lieutenant Gallardo Mata of DM 7 sent a six-man patrol under the command of Sub-sergeant Boris Ariel Rivas Contreras to the Cine Colonial behind the campus. At 9:00 p.m., they moved into the abandoned apartment buildings south of the Hotel Siesta, where they stayed until dawn.

In his extrajudicial confession on January 14, 1990, defendant Oscar Amaya Grimaldi recalled that

> . . . once ready, everybody at the Academy got into some Ford 250 pick-ups and together with the three officers already mentioned left for the university, having gotten out of these vehicles at the old buildings already mentioned, where the witness saw more men from their group who had already been posted in this place.

Yet no man in the DM 7 patrol admitted to having seen Atlacatl troops that night nor to hearing vehicles go by. In light of the subsequent declarations of Atlacatl members,[222] it is simply not credible that the DM 7 men could have spent the night in the same abandoned buildings where the Atlacatl met and planned their strategy prior to heading for the UCA without being aware of the Atlacatl presence.

Around 8:00 p.m., this same DM 7 patrol accidently killed a National Guardsman guarding the Economy Minister's house near the Cine Colonial. This episode underscores the impossibility of troops moving about in a militarized zone during curfew without prior coordination. Given the circumstances that night – which included a strict 6:00 p.m. to 6:00 a.m. curfew – it is simply not credible that the DM 7 troops were unaware of the presence and mission of the Atlacatl. Indeed, several Atlacatl patrols were nearby when this incident occurred, according to their January 1990 extrajudicial statements.

Testifying as an expert witness on May 27, 1991, Argentine Colonel José Luis García said that "each unit is given a geographic sector within the zone to defend, and in these sectors only those who know the password can circulate in order to avoid the enemy infiltrating the security zone itself without being detected. The conduct of military operations within a security zone is very rigid and controlled." Further, he said that "any movement not ordered or controlled by the higher command would immediately create a combat situation, as the troops stationed in the zone would consider those soldiers enemy troops." Colonel García's testimony was reinforced by an earlier statement recorded by the SIU. Treasury Police agent Juan Antonio Navarro Artiga told the SIU that any troops passing by would have to inform soldiers in the area by radio in order not

---

222 Extrajudicial confessions of the defendants, Jan. 13 and 14, 1990; *see also* testimony of Sub-sergeant Eduardo Cordova Monge, Fourth Criminal Court, Jan. 18, 1990.

to be shot. After the fall of the 6:00 p.m. curfew, Navarro said they were under orders to shoot any unidentified vehicle.[223]

DM 7 members also testified about the wounding of Pvt. Salvador Girón López at around 2:00 a.m. in Antiguo Cuscatlán, just five blocks south of the Cine Colonial. Some soldiers involved stated the incident occurred at the same time as the UCA operation, while others place the shooting and explosions on the campus a bit later. But according to all accounts, the wounded soldier was carried down to the cinema and evacuated in a Military Academy vehicle. Most versions place Lieutenant Gallardo Mata at that location; some also place Captain García Oliva there. Some refer to another Military Academy officer who participated in the evacuation of the wounded man. The inconsistencies about who was where and when suggest an effort to avoid mentioning any possible contact with the Atlacatl troops or knowledge of their mission. These inconsistencies warranted, but did not receive, serious examination by the SIU.

An obvious investigatory step should have been for the SIU to corroborate this testimony through Military Academy records. Second Lt. Juan de Jesús Guzmán Morales said he left the Academy in a pick-up about 2:30 or 3:00 a.m. on November 16. Mandated to pick up the wounded Girón López, Guzmán says he and three men providing security arrived at the cinema by the same route used by the Atlacatl. According to Guzmán, the area was quiet, while the wounded man testified that they had to take a detour to avoid the shooting. He said further that no Academy officer accompanied him.

Despite the important contradictions between the testimonies of these men – and that of Sub-sergeant Uto Rivas, a dental hygienist who accompanied the wounded soldier – the SIU apparently made no effort to secure the Academy's book of entries and departures. Nor did the unit interview the Academy officers responsible for troop movement. By July 1990 when they finally appeared in court, these officers uniformly denied having sent out any officers, troops or vehicles that night for any purpose. The logbooks, of course, had long since been incinerated.

These incidents illustrate the SIU's failure to follow the trail leading to the Military Academy. In fact, the most noteworthy aspect of the SIU investigation of the Academy is that, officially, it did not occur at all. The record does not reflect any effort by the SIU to determine early on which commander was responsible for the UCA neighborhood.

223 Declaration of Juan Antonio Navarro Artiga to the SIU, Dec. 6, 1989.

Although Lieutenant Colonel Rivas surely knew that Benavides was zone commander, this information was first provided officially by Colonel Ponce in his December 8, 1989 written sworn declaration to the court. The troops interviewed during December from DM 6 and DM 7 and the Atlacatl all said they had been billeted at the Academy, which served as zone headquarters.

Testifying in court on July 11, 1990, Colonel Benavides admitted that he had known Lieutenant Colonel Rivas for approximately 15 years, but did not remember seeing Rivas inside the Academy after the Jesuit killings. Beginning in December 1989, he said, he had answered several written requests from the SIU and recalled sending a list of military units assigned to the Security Command.

Lieutenant Colonel Camilo Hernández, acting Academy deputy director, told the court on June 15, 1990 that he remembered SIU agents conducting ballistics tests at the Academy in late December 1989 or early January 1990. Only when he saw these agents at the shooting range did he learn that the SIU was investigating the crime. He also acknowledged that the Military Academy had received letters from the SIU, but did not remember if they had received one or several. He did not recall having seen Lieutenant Colonel Rivas at the Academy.

The accounts of both Benavides and Hernández conflict with information provided by Richard Chidester, the U.S. embassy official who says that he accompanied Lieutenant Colonel Rivas to the Academy in early December 1989 to meet with Benavides. According to Mr. Chidester, Rivas apparently met with Benavides alone on at least one other occasion. Presumably, records of these visits were burned along with other logbooks.

These meetings are not on the public record, and testifying in court on October 19, 1990, Rivas denied going to the Academy or meeting with Benavides about the case. Rivas said he did not know if embassy legal officer Richard Chidester had made any such visits.

In many ways, Rivas' denial is curious, since the SIU investigation would look much better if the investigators had sought out Benavides early on. Yet concealing early contact between Rivas and Benavides is important if U.S. Major Eric Buckland's account is true that Benavides confessed his involvement to Rivas and asked for his help.[224] By admitting he had an early conversation with Benavides, Rivas would be admitting his role in the coverup.

The first recorded communication between the SIU and Colonel Benavides is dated January 3, 1990, when Lieutenant Colonel Rivas asked if any of Benavides' units launched the flares known as Bengal lights around the UCA between 6:00 p.m., November 15 and 7:00 a.m., November 16. Given the timing – the day after Major Buckland's revelations – the request may have served as an official warning that the SIU could no longer divert the investigation from Benavides. On January 4, 1990, Benavides replied that he had not authorized the firing of any Bengal lights. According to Benavides own account, the SIU questioned him on January 6 about Buckland's allegations.

Physical Evidence

A large part of the "myth of good police work" is based on the SIU's treatment of physical evidence gathered at the scene. According to the Moakley task force report, by late December,

> the SIU had taken 385 ballistics samples and 385 sets of fingerprints from soldiers assigned to the area of the UCA on the night of the murders, including 45 from members of the Atlacatl unit that actually perpetrated the crimes. In addition, 14 people had been polygraphed, 11 of whom were military officers, and 86 depositions from military personnel had been taken.[225]

These statistics were taken directly from the SIU's own summary of their work prepared for the Moakley task force.[226] Despite the volume of tests conducted, the evidence provided is really quite skimpy. No useful evidence was provided by the

224 *See infra* Chapter X: "Washington's Mixed Messages" for more on Major Buckland's account.

225 Interim Report, *supra* note 129, at 21.

226 SIU Summary, *supra* note 200.

scores of fingerprints lifted;[227] handwriting analyses were inconclusive; and by this time, ballistics tests had provided no useful results. Scotland Yard later criticized the SIU's treatment of evidence, which resulted in confusion in identifying where the evidence was found.[228] Moreover, to date the SIU has neither finished the ballistics testing nor linked any of the defendants to the crime through ballistics match-ups.

Not until December 7, 1989 did the SIU ask Colonel Ponce whether the ammunition used to kill the Jesuits belonged to the Armed Forces, and, if so, which units had been equipped with that type of ammunition.[229] Ponce answered on December 16, confirming that at least some of the shells and cartridges came from Army lots. On December 11, the SIU asked Colonel Ponce to order ballistics tests on the weapons of all soldiers assigned

---

227 An article in the November 19, 1989 issue of *The Baltimore Sun* cited church sources who said that "hundreds" of fingerprints were taken from inside the Jesuit residence. The SIU's own report of its fingerprint analyses mentions four tests: 1) positive match of priests' fingerprints taken after death with their drivers' licenses; 2) fingerprints lifted from desk drawers inside the residence did not match with priests' fingerprints; 3) digital prints taken from inside the house at Calle Cantábrico 16, where the witness Lucía Cerna and family spent the night of November 15-16, "display some characteristics with those of Jorge A. Cerna Ramírez, but . . . cannot be categorical in determining their identity." The final entry in the SIU's fingerprint report reads in its entirety: "4. Still pending study are the fingerprints gathered from the bedrooms of the Jesuit priests with possible suspects." *See* SIU Summary, *supra* note 200, at 3. The SIU report was apparently prepared in January 1990.

Of the fact that the SIU fingerprinted the victims, Scotland Yard commented: "This last task was carried out while the cadavers were *in situ*; Scotland Yard knows of no justification for conducting this procedure at this time as it only served to contribute to the contamination of the scene and the personnel involved. The cadavers, already identified before the investigating officials, should only have been carefully labelled and photographed." Scotland Yard Report, submitted to Fourth Criminal Court, Mar. 22, 1991, at para. 117, at 30 [hereinafter Scotland Yard].

228 Scotland Yard sent a three-man team to El Salvador in January 1990. Their extensive findings were delivered in part to the judge in February 1991 and the report first incorporated into the court record in May 1991, too late for their observations and concrete suggestions to have any impact.

229 While no bullets were retrieved from the cadavers, over 200 shell casings were gathered from the murder site and from the front of the CRT.

to the Military Complex between November 13 and December 6. For reasons unknown, it was not until December 29 that these units, with weapons, were ordered to report to the Academy. The first series using single shots yielded no positive results but a second series using automatic mode produced positive match-ups in early January. A U.S. ballistics expert brought in by the U.S. embassy observed the SIU technicians at work on January 7, verifying that match ups were correctly made on that day.

On January 3, the SIU noted that its ballistics experts had determined that some of the material found the day of the killings had been fired by the M-16 rifle assigned to Private Victor Antonio Delgado Pérez, one of the Atlacatl commandos. Fifty-three shells found on the west side of the CRT had been shot with this M-16. This left 73 shells to be matched with the samples taken from the Atlacatl commandos.[230]

On January 4, ballistics experts reported that a second M-16 provided by Atlacatl soldier Neftalí Ruíz Ramírez[231] matched with 41 shells found on the northwest side of the Pastoral Center, leaving 32 shells unidentified. Neither Lieutenant Preza Rivas nor Lieutenant Colonel Manuel Antonio Rivas could

230 In a statement taken by the SIU on January 15, 1990, Delgado Pérez admitted entering the UCA grounds the night of November 15, 1989, but claimed to have remained by the covered parking area and fired into the air when he heard others shooting. In subsequent court testimony on January 25, 1990, he denied that he even left the Academy on November 15. When the court tried to recall him as a witness to explore this contradiction and his possible role in the crime, the Joint Command chief, Colonel Rubio, replied by telegram on September 7, 1990 that Delgado Pérez had been dismissed from the Army on April 30, 1990. General Ponce later clarified in a June 18, 1991 response to an evidentiary request that Delgado Pérez was dismissed because he was "inappropriate for service" for having failed to return after a 72-hour leave. The military has apparently made no effort to investigate his whereabouts.

231 In a January 14, 1990 declaration, Ruíz Ramírez insisted that he was with the one Atlacatl commando patrol that did not go to the UCA the night of the killings and suggested that he must have accidentally switched rifles with someone else when they departed for Zacamil. The SIU promptly asked Atlacatl commander Colonel León Linares to inform them to whom the M-16 rifle serial number 5447811 had been issued. On January 15, Colonel León Linares replied that this rifle was assigned to Private Nelson Mauricio Morales Portillo of the Fourth Infantry Company, who had deserted on January 2, 1990. In court testimony of March 19, Ruíz Ramírez claimed to have picked up the rifle of Sierra Ascencio, the absent defendant; in a second court appearance on September 7, 1990, Ruíz Ramírez contradicted himself, asserting that he did not know whose rifle it was.

explain why only two M-16s were successfully identified through ballistics testing. Curiously, the soldiers who provided the two weapons that were matched have never been charged with any crime. The SIU failed to link any of the rifles provided by the defendants – five of whom allegedly fired at the priests or the two women – to the shell casings found at the crime scene.

Equally incomprehensible is the fact that the SIU had yet to finish the ballistics tests a year after the murders. Testifying in court on October 19, 1990, Colonel Rivas said he could not "explain the fact that only two M-16 rifles assigned to soldiers of the Atlacatl Battalion, have been implicated after having carried out the corresponding ballistics work and does not know who could explain this. . . ."

On November 7, 1990, Judge Zamora sent a letter to Colonel Rivas, asking that he send to the court, "as quickly as possible, the conclusions of the ballistics work carried out by the SIU's technical forensic unit and which according to the record of this criminal case . . . have still not been remitted." On November 12, Lieutenant Preza Rivas replied, explaining exactly what the SIU had reported 11 months earlier, that ballistics work carried out on 215 pieces of evidence collected at the crime scene yielded 73 matches on the M-60 machine gun; 19 matches on the AK-47; and numerous matches on two M-16 A1 rifles. Preza Rivas said 32 items had yet to be examined, and concluded that "for this reason it is not possible to provide you with conclusions about that work, but you will be informed as soon as it is finished."

Given Preza Rivas' reply, there is every indication that the SIU had done nothing to identify the remaining shells after it consigned the defendants to court in January 1990.

On November 29, 1990, Preza Rivas again wrote to the judge advising him that another rifle had been matched, but, in keeping with the earlier results, this rifle did not belong to any of the defendants. The M-16 rifle series no. 5370196 assigned to Private José Roberto Hernández Rochez was found to match one bullet taken from bedroom no. 13 (Father Ellacuría's) of the priests' residence. When Judge Zamora tried to cite Hernández Rochez to testify, the Ministry of Defense reported that this soldier had been dismissed from the Army in November 1990 and was imprisoned in Sensuntepeque Military Prison under the orders of the Military First Instance Court for violations of the Military Justice Code.

This information proved to be less than accurate. When Judge Zamora sought to locate Hernández Róchez through the military court, the military judge reported that he had no case pending against the former Atlacatl commando.[232] Apparently the Ministry of Defense was spurred by Judge Zamora's inquiries, since three days later Zamora received another letter from the military court saying that it had just received the case file from the Ministry of Defense. The Ministry sought charges against Hernández Rochez for abandonment of service on August 25, 1990.

It was not until January 6, 1990, after the Military Honor Commission began its work,[233] that the SIU asked Colonel Ponce for an up-to-date list of the M-60 machine guns assigned to the Atlacatl and the Military Academy, with their respective serial numbers. On January 11, ballistics experts reported their findings on five AK-47 rifles and one M-60 machine gun. The ballistics report indicates that all these weapons were obtained from the Military Academy. One of the AK-47 rifles matched shells found in different locations in the UCA; the tests of the M-60 machine gun also provided a match with 73 shells found on the north side of the Pastoral Center.

An important part of the evidence against Colonel Benavides consisted of the results of ballistics tests that identified the M-60 machine gun and one of the AK-47 rifles supposedly from the Military Academy as weapons used in the crime.

In a document dated January 11, 1990, an SIU detective affirmed that he had received the weapons in the Military Academy. Testifying in June 1990, Lt. Col. Carlos Camilo Hernández, assistant director of the Military Academy at the time of the assassination, confirmed that these weapons were turned over to the SIU.

The court nonetheless encountered difficulties in establishing the origin of these weapons. The SIU's carelessness in this regard is striking, given that a basic rule of any police investigation is to firmly establish and maintain the chain of custody of evidence. Lt. Francisco Mónico Gallardo Mata, head of S-4 (Logistics) at the Academy at the time, testified that the Academy had no AK-47s. To the court's surprise, when SIU officials testified in October 1990, they denied that the weapons were obtained at the Military Academy.

---

232 Letter to Fourth Penal Court from Military First Instance Court, dated Dec. 11, 1990.

233 On the role of the Military Honor Commission, *see infra* Chapter IV: "The Black Hole."

SIU Lieutenant Preza Rivas testified on October 18, 1990, that his unit had not received AK-47s or the M-60 machine gun from the Academy, though it had requested a list of weapons of this calibre assigned to the Academy and the Atlacatl Battalion.[234] He could not recall whether they ever received such a list. Preza Rivas further clarified that despite the SIU's January 11 statement that the weapons had been received by the SIU at the Military Academy, they actually had been turned over to SIU detective Catarino Lovato at the National Police headquarters by a member of the Honor Commission.

SIU detective Lovato Ayala said in his October 26, 1990 testimony that he received the weapons from Lieutenant Arias Ramos, at National Police headquarters. Lt. José Alberto Arias Ramos, subsequently testified that he had never witnessed the delivery of five AK-47 rifles nor of the M-60.[235] In a written declaration on November 13, 1990, National Police chief Col. Dionisio Ismael Machuca explained that the Military Academy had indeed sent several AK-47 rifles and an M-60 machine gun to the Honor Commission, which turned it over to the SIU the same day.[236] Yet, in his fourth sworn declaration provided in June 1991, Defense Minister Ponce, answering a question about one of the AK-47s, said it "did not belong to the inventory" of the Military Academy. In response to a request by the private prosecutors, the court obtained the Academy's records in June 1991. These records indicate that Lt. Nelson Alberto Barra Zamora delivered these weapons to the Honor Commission on January 11, 1990.[237]

On January 11, SIU agents went to National Guard headquarters to record Colonel Benavides' statement as a defendant. For reasons unknown, Benavides had been held at

234 Only a request for information about M-60 machine guns appears in the court record.

235 Testimony in Fourth Criminal Court, Oct. 30, 1990.

236 That the Honor Commission obtained these weapons suggests that its role was indeed more active than that described by its members. *See infra* Chapter IV: "The Black Hole."

237 One Salvadoran military officer suggested to the Lawyers Committee that captured guerrilla weapons often found their way into a garrison's arsenal, and were not always duly recorded.

the National Guard since January 8.[238] Officially, the SIU took this step based on the reports of its Forensic Unit indicating that weapons carried by Atlacatl members under Benavides' command were involved in the crime. Benavides denied any role, but said Colonel Cerna Flores, head of C-3 (Operations) at the Joint Command, had telephoned him on the afternoon of November 13 to inform him that he had been named to head the Security Command of the Military Complex. Given his new responsibilities, Benavides said he needed more troops, and in fact mentioned the involvement of some Atlacatl in an unrelated incident. Colonel Benavides said that at noon on November 14, he began to keep an Operations Diary of the Security Command of the Military Complex, in which he recorded all orders.

More significant than what the SIU did, is what it did not do. The failure to question Colonel Benavides prior to January is inexplicable, given that he was commander of the zone in which the university lies and that he had recorded shots and explosions at the UCA by the FMLN that night. Only one of Benavides' subordinates, Captain García Oliva – named by Ponce as the officer in charge of troops to the university's south and southwest – was questioned. There is no indication in the official record that the SIU interviewed then Academy Deputy Director, Lt. Col. Camilo Hernández. Well-placed to know what went on in the Academy that night, Hernández was ultimately convicted of destruction of evidence and sentenced to three years' imprisonment.

Nearly two months elapsed before attention publicly focused on Benavides and the Military Academy, allowing the Armed Forces plenty of time to close ranks, destroy incriminating evidence and "forget" events that might be incriminating.

"There were hundreds of units in the area," a U.S. embassy official close to the investigation told the Lawyers Committee. "Nobody was narrowing in on anybody. Somebody directed the SIU to turn back and zero in on the Atlacatl."

Despite all the evidence pointing to the military, the official line of military as well as civilian authorities throughout December 1989 was to blame the FMLN. Col. Heriberto Hernández, then director of the Treasury Police who

---

238 The SIU has maintained that Benavides' responsibility was determined by the extrajudicial statements of the Atlacatl troops, yet the recording of these statements supposedly began on January 13, two days after Benavides was interrogated as a defendant. This sequence of events suggests in fact that the Atlacatl troops had confessed their involvement earlier than the record reflects.

was implicated in the killings in a letter signed by "young officers," gave a sworn statement to the SIU on December 9 denying the accusation. He concluded his statement by saying that "the delinquent terrorists commit this kind of crime with the goal of discrediting the Armed Forces, making people believe that the Armed Forces have committed them. . . ."

In a December 12 press conference, Col. Inocente Orlando Montano, Vice-Minister of Public Security, made clear "that it was inconceivable that any member of the Armed Forces would opt to kill in cold blood innocent priests and their housekeepers."[239] Montano said the killings had most likely been carried out by a special FMLN command in order to blame the Armed Forces. On December 7, First Brigade Commander Francisco Elena Fuentes announced that the Army was "gathering evidence that involves the subversives in the crime."[240]

---

239 *La Prensa Gráfica*, Dec. 13, 1989.

240 *Diario de Hoy*, Dec. 8, 1989.

CHAPTER IV: THE BLACK HOLE
(January 1990)

With the wisdom of hindsight, it is now possible to identify the first two weeks of January 1990 as the most decisive period in the case. During that time, U.S. embassy officials confronted the High Command of the Salvadoran Armed Forces with information linking Colonel Benavides to the crime.[241] That revelation gave rise to the appointment of a "Special Honor Commission" on the case, which in retrospect played a major role in minimizing damage to the Army as an institution and in limiting the investigation. It was during these two weeks that the nine defendants were identified, though the process by which they were named remains obscure. It was also during this period that seven of these defendants confessed their roles in the murders to the SIU. Their extrajudicial confessions remain – over two years later – the most complete account of the crime.

Unfortunately, the institutional decision to provide information about the killings ended with the naming of the defendants. The testimonies of scores of officers and enlisted men who appeared before Judge Zamora over the course of the lengthy judicial investigation added nothing to the events described in the extrajudicial confessions. Only one member of the Salvadoran military provided any corroborating testimony,[242] while scores of officers and enlisted men, including the defendants, denied all knowledge of the events surrounding the killings described in the extrajudicial confessions. In many respects – including the key issue of who gave the order and when – not much more is known now about the murders than was established in January 1990. As such, it is fair to say that the military apparatus which defined the terms of the case in late 1989 and early 1990 and orchestrated an extensive coverup which continues to this day has been extraordinarily successful.

---

241 The information came from U.S. Major Eric Buckland. His role in the case is described in Chapter X: "Washington's Mixed Messages."

242 Testimony of Sub-sergeant Eduardo Antonio Cordova Monge, Jan. 18, 1990, Fourth Criminal Court. Cordova Monge admitted going into the UCA on the night of November 15-16, but claimed not to know about the murders.

Appointment of the Military Honor Commission

On January 5, Defense Minister Rafael Humberto Larios appointed a group of military officers to a "Special Honor Commission" on the case. The impetus for the commission was the January 2 visit to Colonel Ponce by Col. Milton Menjívar, chief U.S. military advisor, who notified the High Command of the embassy's knowledge of significant facts surrounding the case, including the role played by Colonel Benavides. In the ambassador's absence, Colonel Menjívar then briefed the deputy chief of mission about Major Buckland's story inculpating Colonel Benavides in the murders and the High Command's response. Unable to contain the leak further, the High Command now had to act. Also on January 5, Atlacatl commandos later identified as belonging to the unit implicated in the murder, were confined to different security force headquarters in San Salvador.[243]

At this stage, no one had been accused of any crime. There is no information on record indicating which Atlacatl troops were directly involved in the killings, nor had the name of one of the defendants, Military Academy Lieutenant Yusshy René Mendoza Vallecillos, surfaced.

On Sunday January 7, President Cristiani said on Salvadoran radio and television that the Honor Commission had been asked to "deduce responsibility in the case" and to "determine the exact circumstances [of the slayings] and clarify the truth in all its magnitude. . . ."[244] Cristiani also said that the group would work with the SIU.

The military Honor Commission concluded its work very quickly. On January 12 it presented a written report to President Cristiani. On January 13, Defense Minister Larios wrote SIU Lieutenant José Luis Preza Rivas informing him that the investigation had "determined the possible participation" in the killings of nine members of the Salvadoran Armed Forces. Providing the names, Larios concluded that "in view of the foregoing, I hereby place at your disposition the persons mentioned who are confined to the different" security force headquarters. That same day, President Cristiani appeared on nationwide television to announce the names, heaping praise

---

243 Other Atlacatl patrols which were also brought to San Salvador on November 13, 1989 and were apparently involved in both the search and the murders were never held for questioning.

244 *Diario de Hoy*, Jan. 8, 1990; *Miami Herald*, Jan. 9, 1990; Associated Press, Jan. 9, 1990, as printed in *The Independent* (London).

on the professionalism and impartiality of the SIU investigation.[245]

Commission Shrouded in Mystery

From the beginning, the purpose and actions of the Honor Commission were shrouded in mystery; the names of its members were not even revealed to the investigating judge until March 1990. On March 21, President Cristiani answered a request from Judge Zamora dated March 5, annexing a copy of a letter from General Larios in which the names appeared. Representing a spectrum of the officer corps, ranging from junior to senior officers, the commission consisted of:

- Gen. Rafael Antonio Villamariona, Commander of the Air Force
- Col. Dionisio Ismael Machuca, Director of the National Police
- Lt. Col. Juan Vicente Equizábal Figueroa, chief of Administration of Personnel, C-2 (Intelligence)
- Maj. José Roberto Zamora Hernández
- Capt. Juan Manuel Grijalva Torres
- Dr. Antonio Augusto Gómez Zarate, attorney
- Lic. Rodolfo Antonio Parker Soto, attorney[246]

As more information came to light about the Honor Commission, its role only became less clear. Lieutenant Colonel Rivas maintained that it was the Commission that narrowed the pool of suspects to the nine men ultimately charged. The Commission purportedly received the SIU file, which by that time had focused on the Atlacatl commando unit, and from those 47 names chose the murder suspects. Yet Commission members have denied this, first in interviews with members of the Moakley task force and subsequently in court.[247] According to the task force's *Interim Report*, both General Villamariona and Colonel Machuca denied that the Commission had done its own inquiry. Machuca told the congressional group that the Commission sought simply to "motivate the soldiers to tell the truth."[248]

---

245 *Diario de Hoy*, Jan. 15, 1990.

246 The two attorneys described their role as civilian legal advisors, in contrast to earlier reports that civilians also served on the Commission. The signatures of both civilian attorneys nonetheless appear on the report.

247 *See* Interim Report, *supra* note 129, at 35.

248 *Id.*

Commission members also stated explicitly that the names of the nine defendants were provided by Lieutenant Colonel Rivas Mejía, as chief of the SIU. Inexplicably, the SIU and the Commission each claimed that the other provided the names. And the record provides no help in solving the mystery since the first recorded relevant statements are dated January 13, after the Commission completed its work. Moreover, the names of the officers from the Military Academy had not surfaced in the SIU investigation, yet both were detained on January 8. This confusion leaves open the question of whether the defendants actually confessed their participation earlier than reported or whether the SIU received information from sources not reflected in the record. The absence of these statements from the official case record is inexplicable, and fuels doubt that the SIU sought to establish the full truth.

Somehow, between January 3 and 13, there was a "black hole" in the investigatory process that has still never been explained. Not only were the names of the defendants mysteriously produced, but seemingly there was also a tacit agreement between military and civilian officials that the investigation would be confined to these individuals. The SIU made no further serious effort to continue its investigation, despite its legal obligation to do so. Members of the Honor Commission deny having produced the names of the defendants through any investigatory process of their own, describing their role as merely "exhorting" the suspects to tell the truth. Nowhere is there any clear suggestion of how the names were produced, and by whom, or why this information should not be public knowledge.

Congressman Moakley's *Interim Report* states that the arrests might not have been made if it were not for the information provided by Major Buckland in early January 1990. While Major Buckland's information may have been crucial, it does not explain how the process worked in the case, and it is not adequate to explain the presentation of this group of suspects as a *fait accompli*, especially in a period of a little over a week. As Congressman Moakley pointed out in his August 15, 1990 statement on the case, even the Honor Commission lied with respect to its role in the case by "falsely" denying "it had written even the skimpy report it did prepare on the case, and has provided no other information about how confessions were obtained."

The Commissioners' Testimony

On May 4, 1990, just days after the *Interim Report* appeared, Judge Zamora asked Air Force chief Villamariona and

National Police chief Machuca to provide a sworn statement to the court explaining the Commission's findings, whether any of the defendants had confessed, other elements of proof considered, whether any report on their findings was prepared and to whom it was delivered.[249] Zamora also directed the remaining members to appear in court.

After initially failing to appear, Commission legal advisors Dr. Augusto Gómez Zárate and Lic. Rodolfo Parker Soto testified on May 14. Others cited later testified, also after failing to respond to an initial summons. According to their testimony, the Commission was sworn in on the afternoon of January 5 in the Defense Ministry. Later that day, they were briefed at the SIU by Lieutenant Colonel Rivas, who shared with them documentation on the case. According to Gómez Zarate, the SIU informed the Commission that Atlacatl weapons had matched with shells found at the murder scene.

Gómez Zárate said that during this briefing the SIU did not name individual suspects, but did show sketches of how the killers entered and exited the murder site. Lieutenant Colonel Equizábal noted that none of the documentation presented by the SIU included evidence against Colonel Benavides, while Parker said that Benavides' name appeared in the SIU documents. Gómez Zárate said further that the Commission did not have access to the extrajudicial statements recorded by the SIU, but did review drawings, maps and ballistics results that were posted on the walls. By contrast, Parker said they were given photocopies of SIU findings, including witness declarations.

On January 6, the group met at National Police headquarters, where they began "interviews" with some 30 soldiers, mostly Atlacatl commandos who had been placed under house arrest. Gómez Zárate said that Lt. Yusshy Mendoza was among those interviewed, yet inexplicably, he was not under arrest and remained on active duty at the Academy. While Gómez Zárate said the soldiers were chosen at random, Parker maintained that they were chosen on the basis of SIU documentation, but could not remember how Mendoza's name figured. Parker said that some of the troops who were "exhorted" to tell the truth had already given statements as shown in the documents given to the Commission by the SIU. Gómez Zárate could not explain why Colonel Benavides and Lieutenant Mendoza were among the suspects and noted that they had not been arrested at the time.

---

249 Neither officer could be required to appear in court because of article 205 of the Criminal Procedure Code, which permits officers with the rank of colonel or higher to provide sworn certified declarations.

There was agreement among Commission members that they had not played an investigative role. By contrast, "the object of these interviews was to try to exalt patriotic values, human rights, and military values, making those involved in the act see that they had to tell the truth, because the interests of the Fatherland were in danger. . . ."[250] Parker said the process of "exhortation" lasted about 10 to 20 minutes for each soldier, while Lieutenant Colonel Equizábal noted that the "exhortation was practically a monologue, since no questions were posed to the members [of the Armed Forces] being exhorted. . . ." Machuca's brief written statement reiterates that the Commission's role was

> exhorting each person to amplify his declaration, to tell the truth when interrogated by the SIU, paying attention to military honor and moral, civic, ethical and professional values, to get to the bottom of events and to preserve the prestige of the Armed Forces.

Attorney Parker described to the judge a three-stage process in the Commission's work: 1) his visit to the crime scene accompanied by Colonel Equizábal; 2) analysis of the SIU documentation and sessions with "selected military personnel whose names appear in this documentation, who individually received an exhortation to tell the truth . . ."; 3) delivery to President Cristiani of their recommendations, "which were based on the preliminary investigation carried out by the SIU in which they attributed responsibility [for the crime] to Colonel Guillermo Benavides, Lieutenants Espinoza and Mendoza, Sub-Lieutenant Guevara Cerritos, and five or six enlisted men." Their report was based exclusively on SIU documentation; the Commission collected no further evidence.

Several Commission members specifically stated that during their January 12 briefing, Lieutenant Colonel Rivas said that the SIU "had found elements of proof" against Benavides, the two lieutenants, and six enlisted men, "without the Special Honor Commission having participated in the investigation. . . ." Some claimed that no explanation was given concerning how the SIU had concluded that these nine men and no others were criminally involved.

Lieutenant Colonel Equizábal noted that Lieutenant Colonel Rivas mentioned no conclusive proof against Colonel Benavides, whom he said had called "two officers and given them `X' orders." They were not shown any kind of specific proof that directly implicated any Army member. According to

250 Testimony of Dr. Antonio Augusto Gómez Zárate, Fourth Criminal Court, May 14, 1990.

Equizábal, it was based on Rivas' briefing, during which he provided the nine names, that the Honor Commission elaborated its recommendations and named the suspects.

It was first in this round of court appearances by Commission members in mid-May 1990 that the existence of a written report was revealed. No written findings had been made public, provided to the court, or to the Moakley task force, which had specifically requested any such document. In late April – after interviewing President Cristiani, Defense Minister Larios, and several commissioners – Congressman Moakley concluded that there "is no known record of any kind concerning the proceedings."[251] President Cristiani never volunteered that he had such a document although on numerous occasions he had publicly urged anyone with relevant information to submit it to Judge Zamora. Once the report's existence became known, Cristiani stated his willingness to submit it to the court, and did so on May 25, in response to the judge's written request.[252]

The Honor Commission's seven-page report sheds no further light on the Commission's inner workings or on how it arrived at the findings that are on the public record. In broad strokes the document outlines the reasons for forming the Commission, explains that the SIU had "determined the possible participation of elements of the Armed Forces" and that the Commission was mandated to "support the investigation." In an understated fashion it lists the names of the soldiers and who they killed. In the report's conclusion, the Commission names the nine accused men as those "responsible" and "recommends" that they be turned over to the courts. Its description of events coincides with what is now on the public record. This is so despite the fact that the public record includes extrajudicial declarations recorded after the report was finalized; the document mysteriously offers no explanation of how it acquired this information.[253]

The January 12, 1990 report summarizes the group's work as follows: at the first meeting on January 5 at 4:30 p.m., commissioners were told by the High Command that they could count on all the support necessary to carry out their mission. At 5:30 p.m. they met at SIU headquarters for a briefing on the case

251 Interim Report, *supra* note 129 at 35.

252 *Diario de Hoy*, May 17, 1990.

253 The extrajudicial declarations of the seven defendants who admit having been on the UCA campus at the time of the killings were taken on January 13 and 14, 1990; the declarations of other Atlacatl soldiers and Lieutenant Mendoza's assistant were recorded on January 14 and 15.

and reviewed evidence assembled to date by the SIU. On January 6, an on site inspection was conducted at the UCA. Soldiers mentioned in the SIU documentation were summoned "selectively" and exhorted to tell the truth when they came before the SIU. The High Command was kept informed of the work of the Commission, which coordinated with Lieutenant Colonel Rivas so that the SIU could then take declarations from those soldiers who had received the board's "exhortations."[254]

The Commission further recommended that other military men held for questioning be immediately returned to active duty. The document leaves no doubt that commissioners placed no responsibility for the crime on the Armed Forces as an institution, commenting that "[b]oth morally and legally, these events can be attributed exclusively to those who carried them out."

Who Confessed and When?

Neither the Honor Commission document nor the testimony of its members has clarified the conundrum of when and how the names of the nine principal defendants were selected. The SIU is legally obligated to record all investigatory steps. Yet according to its record, the SIU did not obtain information linking individuals to specific roles in the killings until January 13. The Moakley task force reported that Lieutenant Colonel Rivas told them that "the honor board had questioned the soldiers from the Atlacatl and obtained confessions from them."[255] According to the Honor Commission, it was Rivas who on January 12 provided them with the nine names and, apparently, sufficient information to describe the role of each in its report to President Cristiani.

If the Honor Commission told the truth about its role, the SIU failed to reveal a crucial step in its investigation. And if Lieutenant Colonel Rivas told the truth and it was the Commission which named the nine men, then the Honor Commission failed to reveal a crucial piece of its investigation or, indeed, that it even had conducted an investigation.

By the time the case was turned over to the Commission on January 5, the SIU investigation was already focusing on the Atlacatl commando unit. Two M-16s assigned to members of that unit had produced shells matching those found at the UCA, although the soldiers who carried these rifles have never been

254 No record exists, however, of any Atlacatl declarations taken by the SIU during the period January 5 to 12, 1990.

255 Interim Report, *supra* note 129, at 35.

criminally charged. Commando testimonies concerning the November 13 search were full of contradictions, though they admitted participating in the operation.

As of January 5, the only evidence on the public record linking Colonel Benavides to the crime was that the Atlacatl troops had been billeted at the Academy and, presumably, under his command during the relevant period. The other evidence against Benavides, of a non-public nature, was provided by Major Buckland on January 2, indicating that Benavides had confessed to Rivas soon after the murders. No information on the public record as of January 5 even mentioned Lieutenant Yusshy Mendoza Vallecillos. Ballistics match-ups on weapons purportedly assigned to the Military Academy – the M-60 machine gun and the AK-47 – were not made until January 11.

The record suggests that between January 5 and 12, 1990 the SIU obtained detailed information from one or more sources who were at the crime scene, could identify Lieutenant Mendoza, and knew that Colonel Benavides had given the order to the lieutenants. To date, it is still unknown who provided this information. Could the source perhaps have provided admissible evidence against those tried in September 1991, or against others not yet charged?

Based on available evidence, the Lawyers Committee has concluded that the Honor Commission's role was to bestow an official Army imprimatur on the SIU investigation, perhaps in an attempt to make the controversial indictments more palatable within the military. Secondly, the group sought to limit the investigation, shielding others from scrutiny and, above all, avoiding harm to the Armed Forces as an institution. Events had overtaken the military's early attempts at coverup to a point where it was no longer possible to deny Army responsibility. The appointment of the Commission was an attempt at damage control.

Extrajudicial Confessions of the Defendants

Having now been provided with the suspects' names, SIU agents began recording their extrajudicial declarations on January 13, 1990; Colonel Benavides had already been interviewed on January 11. These statements provide the most extensive account of the killings to date and are generally consistent with one another, although each defendant clearly seeks to minimize his own participation. The accounts also differ on some factual details.[256] Despite the court's many attempts to deepen its knowledge of the crime, these testimonies remain the most authoritative source on what happened at the UCA on the night of November 15-16, 1989. Yet, given the lack of independent corroborating testimony, these declarations should be viewed with a skeptical eye.

In the following excerpts we have attempted to remain loyal to the language used by the deponent, but have made some adjustments in translation when necessary for comprehension. The details provided in these statements about how the operation was conducted warrant close examination for what they imply about repeated assertions by El Salvador's civilian and military leadership that the crime was planned and executed by individuals acting on their own. Soldier after soldier describes his place in the chain of command on the murder night as several hundred soldiers were deployed around the UCA.

The brazenly public nature of the crime is also clear, as are the lies told to cover it up. While several witnesses describe some 50 men grouping in the Academy courtyard in preparation to depart for the campus, sentries on duty at the gate as well as officers in charge of deploying troops have repeatedly testified that no men went out from the Military Academy that night. And while there are numerous accounts of several patrols of Atlacatl men converging on the abandoned apartment buildings just off campus where they were briefed on their murder mission by the lieutenants, soldiers attached to other units who spent the night in those same buildings claim there were no Atlacatl troops in the area.

The three lieutenants – Yusshy René Mendoza Vallecillos; José Ricardo Espinoza Guerra; and Gonzalo Guevara Cerritos – denied their guilt, but their own statements and those of the enlisted men left little doubt that they had directed the operation. All three implicated Colonel Benavides as the officer who had given them their orders; the two Atlacatl lieutenants said they were told to go to the UCA and "eliminate" Father Ellacuría.

---

256 An appendix to the Interim Report includes English translations of the portions of the testimonies used by the judge in decreeing provisional detention of the defendants. For the original Spanish, see "Sentencia interlocutoria para detención provisional," *ECA*, #493-494, Nov.-Dec., 1989, at 1155.

The Story of Lieutenant Yusshy René Mendoza Vallecillos

Military Academy Lt. Yusshy René Mendoza Vallecillos denied the charges against him. He explained, however, that between 11:00 p.m. and 12:00 p.m. on November 15, 1989, he complied with an order to report to Colonel Benavides' office and found two other officers there, one he recognized as Atlacatl Lieutenant Espinoza Guerra, an Academy classmate. Mendoza quotes Benavides as saying, "Look Mendoza, you are going to accompany Espinoza on a mission; he knows what it is." Mendoza proceeded to put camouflage paint on his face; then Espinoza borrowed the camouflage stick. Second Lt. Gonzalo Guevara Cerritos arrived with two other soldiers. He heard Espinoza tell them, "You remember where we went the day before yesterday." They left the Academy around 1:15 a.m. in two Ford pick-ups and were dropped off at the abandoned, partially constructed apartment buildings; the pick-ups returned to the Academy. Espinoza then rounded up some 20-25 men who were in this sector and met with seven or eight of them.

Mendoza places himself at the end of the column as they entered the campus through the south gate. He saw Lieutenant Espinoza's men surrounding the building and entered the residence garden through an open gate of metal bars. Mendoza saw soldiers conducting a search and two women sitting on a bed. Then he heard a series of continuous shots and thought they had been surprised by the enemy. Just as he got to some stairs he saw Lieutenant Espinoza and asked him what was going on; Espinoza said, "Let's go, let's go, they are giving it to some terrorist leaders." When Mendoza got to the street in front of the building he heard other shots like the first; he also saw soldiers retreating toward the south gate. Once outside the campus he heard rifle and M-60 machine gun volleys, LAW rockets and grenades exploding. He saw Bengal lights and smoke coming out of the building. He retreated by the same route, down Calle Mediterráneo to Cine Colonial and turned onto the street with the abandoned apartment buildings where he saw two parked pick-ups. Some of the soldiers climbed into the pick-ups.

The Story of Lieutenant José Ricardo Espinoza Guerra

The most complete story comes from Lieutenant José Ricardo Espinoza Guerra, head of the Atlacatl commandos and a student at the Externado San José when Father Segundo Montes taught there.

The Search: On Monday, November 13 Lieutenant Espinoza received an order that his unit and 88 other Atlacatl troops, all receiving a special training course, were to go to the Military Academy.[257] They left Atlacatl headquarters around 5:00 p.m. with 135 troops in four military trucks and arrived at the Academy around 6:00 p.m.[258] Colonel Benavides and Major Camilo Hernández, Academy deputy director, ordered him to report to the Joint Command, where he presented himself to the head of C-3 (Operations), Col. Joaquín Arnoldo Cerna Flores, who told him to wait. After 15 minutes, Cerna Flores told him, "You are to go to the university UCA. We have information that an undetermined number of delinquent terrorists are inside the installations." Their mission was to corroborate that information and, if no contact with terrorists was made, proceed to a general search of all the installations of the university. After having received the radio frequency and information about positions of other military units in the parameter of the Military Complex, around 7:30 p.m. he returned to the Military Academy and advised Major Camilo Hernández what he had been ordered to do.[259]

Lieutenant Espinoza then met with 12 patrol leaders to give them the necessary instructions.[260] Around 7:45 p.m. they left the Academy on foot through the south gate. Because the main university gate was locked, the unit went up the wide street that goes by the abandoned buildings and took Calle Mediterráneo to the pedestrian entrance on the south side of the UCA.

Atlacatl Sgt. Tomás Zarpate Castillo – who was about 75 meters east of the pedestrian gate – radioed that a soldier known as "Charley Coyote," Lieutenant Héctor Ulises Cuenca Ocampo, wanted to communicate with Espinoza and asked his

---

257 It later became known that the Atlacatl was being trained by U.S. Green Berets, who subsequently got caught in the guerrilla siege of the Sheraton Hotel. *See supra* Chapter II: "Chronology of the Crime" and Interim Report, *supra* note 129, app. B.

258 It was later determined that the Atlacatl commandos left their headquarters about 3:45 p.m. According to Atlacatl records, 110 men went to San Salvador on the afternoon on November 13, 1989.

259 It is noteworthy that Lieutenant Espinoza mentions that his instructions for the search included radio frequencies to be used and information about other units stationed in the area. While this is surely standard procedure, it casts additional doubt on the testimonies of units stationed around the UCA on the murder night who claimed they were not aware of the Atlacatl presence nearby. *See supra* Chapter III: "The Myth of Good Police Work."

260 A commando patrol is made up of six to seven men; other Atlacatl patrols are made up of 12-15 men.

location.[261] Five or six minutes after they arrived at the pedestrian gate, Lieutenant Cuenca Ocampo appeared and asked Espinoza what he was doing. When he explained, Cuenca Ocampo said he would accompany him. Espinoza claimed not to have known what Lieutenant Cuenca Ocampo was supposed to be doing. After they waited 15 minutes for a rain shower to pass, one of the soldiers began to force the gate. The two lieutenants entered, as did the troops who went to their assigned positions.

They walked to the right to a two-story building where they met a soldier from another unit who told Espinoza that he had seen a lighted room and some men who looked like gringos. He then approached cautiously and began talking to Father Ellacuría who asked, "What's going on? What is this uproar?" Father Ellacuría also argued that the soldiers were on private property belonging to the Society of Jesus, but finally allowed them to carry out the search. They searched the residence and offices downstairs, without finding anything.

Ellacuría asked if they were going to search other UCA buildings. Espinoza said yes, but they no longer needed his presence as they would only search places where doors were unlocked. The soldiers progressed to a classroom building marked with letters where they made a superficial search with flashlights, then to lecture halls. Espinoza began rounding up his troops to go to the main gate on the Southern Highway, which was locked. They went over it and returned to the Academy through the rear gate, arriving around 10 p.m. Lieutenant Cuenca went his own way.

Espinoza reported back to the Joint Command that they had found nothing except some priests, including Father Ignacio Ellacuría. He was ordered to await further orders at the Academy. After the UCA search, his troops were assigned other missions, including protecting the Military Complex and searches to corroborate information.

The Murders: On November 15 at 7:00 p.m. Lieutenant Espinoza's unit was occupying several positions in different sectors of the periphery of the military complex. The patrols of "Nahum" and "Rayo" were around the Colonia Guadalupe

---

261 The participation of this DNI intelligence agent in the search has never been adequately explained. *The San Francisco Examiner* reported that the DNI was "founded and funded by the U.S. Central Intelligence Agency. Its members rarely participate in such mundane military actions." *See San Francisco Examiner*, April 15, 1990, at A1 & A20.

shopping centers, just south of the UCA.[262] The patrol of "Satan" and "Hercules" were near the Panades hardware store across the Southern Highway from the UCA.[263] Espinoza, Guevara Cerritos, and the patrol of "Acorralado" were near the main entrance to the Arce neighborhood, also just across the highway from the UCA.[264]

Still holding these positions at 10:15 that night, Espinoza received a radio order to bring his troops back to the Military Academy. Unable to communicate with four patrols by radio, he returned to the Academy with the others. Between 10:30 and 10:40 p.m., the Atlacatl Battalion logistics officer told him they would be rejoining the rest of the Atlacatl in Zacamil the next morning. Around 11:00 p.m., he received an order to appear before Colonel Benavides.

Espinoza reported to the Academy's Center of Operations. Lieutenant Mendoza then arrived and asked for Lieutenant Guevara Cerritos, saying, "Colonel Benavides wants to talk to you." At 11:15 p.m. Benavides arrived and suggested they go to headquarters because there were too many people around. Benavides told them, "This is a situation where it's them or us; we are going to start with the leaders, and in our sector we have the university and Ellacuría is there." Benavides told Espinoza, "You did the search and your people know the place. Use the same set-up as on the day of the search and eliminate him, and I

---

262 Nahum is the nickname of Oscar Rafael Molina Aguilar. Of the soldier called "Rayo" it is only known that he led a patrol of the Fourth Company of the Atlacatl and was not a member of the commando unit.

Soldiers' testimonies are full of nicknames and some claim not to know the person's real name. Commenting on the practice, Scotland Yard said: "Based on the declarations one can observe that the use of nicknames is very common in the Salvadoran Army. During the investigation, the abundance of nicknames has made it difficult to identify individuals. Further, there is perhaps another reason for concern in some cases. Approximately half of the names suggest violence, for example, \`Destructor,' \`Satan,' \`Hercules,' and \`Savage.' Consequently, the Salvadoran Army can be seen as an unprofessional military force. The practice also encourages the Army's critics, who can point to these nicknames as an indication of the Army's lack of professionalism and even of the disregard for human rights that they accuse the Army of." Scotland Yard, *supra* note 227, para. 1261, at 353-354.

263 Satan is Sub-sergeant Antonio Ramiro Avalos Vargas; Sergeant Solórzano Esquivel is known as Hercules.

264 *Acorralado*, roughly translated as "corralled," is Cpl. Marcos González Rodríquez.

want no witnesses. Lieutenant Mendoza will go with you as the head of the operation to make sure there are no problems." Espinoza said this was a serious problem and the colonel replied, "Don't worry. You have my support." Mendoza offered them bars of camouflage grease. Mendoza asked if any man knew how to handle an AK-47 and Oscar Amaya Grimaldi said he could. "Come here, you're the key man," said Mendoza, giving him the rifle.

Espinoza recounts how they were ferried to the site of the abandoned buildings in two Ford pick-ups; each pick-up made two trips. Upon arrival he rounded up the patrols that were in these buildings, those of "Nahum," "Savage," and "Samson," some 30 men in all. Guevara Cerritos and Mendoza explained the situation to them. Approximately 66 troops advanced on foot to the Cine Colonial and proceeded along Calle Mediterráneo to the pedestrian entrance to the UCA.

Inside the campus, Espinoza attempted to distance himself from the action, claiming to have retreated from the Jesuit residence with tears in his eyes. He headed for the pedestrian gate, telling Guevara Cerritos he was indignant about what had happened and that they should leave this place without waiting for Lieutenant Mendoza. Mendoza had stayed behind directing the troops who carried out the execution. Espinoza claims to have been outside the campus near the cinema with 15-20 men when he heard strong detonations of LAW rockets, grenades, and M-60 machine gun fire; the area was lit up with Bengal lights. They were waiting for vehicles to arrive near the Cine Colonial when Mendoza arrived with his assistant, who was carrying a satchel.[265] Some of the troops went back in the pick-ups, while the rest returned to the Academy on foot with Guevara Cerritos.

Back at the Academy, Espinoza looked for Colonel Benavides to complain, but could not find him. When Benavides appeared he asked, "What's wrong, you're worried." Espinoza said, "My colonel, I did not like what was done." Benavides replied, "Calm down, don't worry, you have my support, trust me."

265 The Jesuits believe this satchel contained the $5,000 awarded to Father Ellacuría in Spain just days earlier. The money has never been found and it has never been determined who is responsible for the theft. Consequently, Judge Zamora dismissed robbery charges against the defendants in December 1990.

The Story of Second Lieutenant Gonzalo Guevara Cerritos

Second Lieutenant Guevara Cerritos confirmed that the search was done by the commandos and the additional Atlacatl patrols that accompanied them. He places the conversation with Benavides around midnight and that Mendoza was there too when Benavides said, "Well *señores*, we are playing for everything. It's them or us. These have been the intellectuals directing the guerrillas for a long time." He calculates that 80 Atlacatl troops were involved in the operation. At the abandoned buildings it was Mendoza who told the men about the order they had received from Benavides, and Mendoza began giving instructions.

Confessions of the Enlisted Men

The enlisted men admitted their participation in the killings, fleshing out the details and ascribing the lieutenants a more active role.

The Story of Sub-sergeant Ramiro Avalos Vargas

Sub-sergeant Ramiro Avalos Vargas, known as "Toad" or "Satan," who led the second patrol, was assigned to search inside the building with Lieutenant Espinoza and Sergeant Solórzano Esquivel. On November 15 around 10:00 p.m. they were grouped in front of the Academy's *Guardia de Prevención*[266] – patrols 2, 3, 4 and 6, plus two other 15-member Atlacatl patrols that had come to San Salvador with them – when the company commander told the patrol leaders that they had received higher orders to carry out a "delicate mission." The order was to locate some priests inside the UCA because they were the heads of the delinquent terrorists: they supported them with everything – logistics, transmissions, plans for attacks on military institutions and the civilian population. This mission was to be secret as they would also find subversive material there that would be useful, such as medicine, shoes and clothing. In this testimony, Avalos Vargas noted that if he did not follow the order he would be considered a traitor.

Avalos says Mendoza asked who could handle the AK-47. At the abandoned buildings Espinoza met with four of his patrols, plus two additional patrols and explained each patrol's mission. Avalos Vargas was ordered to enter the university with his patrol and told that he would eliminate the "D/T priests"

---

266 The *Guardia de Prevención* is the guard post at a garrison's entrance that records all comings and goings of people and vehicles.

but that he should await the lieutenant's order before opening fire. Lieutenant Mendoza said he would direct the entire mission.

Avalos Vargas and Oscar Mauricio Amaya Grimaldi, a member of his patrol who had been entrusted with the AK-47, stood guard over the five priests who had been ordered to lie face-down on the grass. Sergeant Solórzano Esquivel went inside with four soldiers to look for more people. Lieutenant Espinoza, who was by the stairs with Lieutenant Mendoza, called Avalos Vargas and asked, "When are you going to proceed?" Avalos then approached Amaya Grimaldi and said in a low voice, "Let's proceed." Amaya Grimaldi then shot three of the priests while Avalos killed the other two.[267]

At the same time, he heard shots inside the residence. Avalos began walking to the gate between the residence and the chapel when he was joined by Private Jorge Alberto Sierra Ascencio, who was standing guard. Before he got to the gate he heard groans coming from a room and told Sierra Ascencio to go check; upon lighting a match Avalos Vargas saw two women on the ground, embracing and moaning. Avalos told Sierra Ascencio to finish them off, which he did. When he and Sierra Ascencio headed for the gate, Lieutenants Espinoza and Mendoza were also leaving. Sergeant Solórzano Esquivel was still inspecting the rooms of the dead men.

He later learned that Corporal Cotta Hernández had been ordered to drag the dead men inside the residence. He heard one of the officers tell Cotta Hernández to shoot off a 40-mm illumination grenade as a signal to the rest of the troops. The operation took about one and a half hours. He saw Second Lieutenant Guevara Cerritos pick up a sign that had been on the gate and write something with the initials "FMLN" and then put the sign back on the gate.

The Story of Sub-sergeant Tomás Zarpate Castillo

Sub-sergeant Tomás Zarpate Castillo, the head of the third patrol known as "Samson," like the other enlisted men, also admitted his role in the crime. On November 15 at 5:45 p.m., he received an order from Lieutenant Espinoza to take up positions by the traffic light on the southeast side of the university, as they had information that wounded delinquent terrorists would

---

267 Avalos Vargas killed Fathers Juan Ramón Moreno and Amando López. With the AK-47, Amaya Grimaldi killed Fathers Ellacuría, Montes, and Martín-Baró.

be taken there.[268] With his men he walked past Democracy Tower, staying in the vicinity until 9:00 p.m., when he continued on to Cine Colonial.

At 1:30 a.m. on November 16, Lieutenant Espinoza contacted him by radio and told him to head east. Espinoza said they were going to the university because they knew that the people inside were terrorists and they had to be eliminated. Once inside the residence grounds, Lieutenant Mendoza ordered him to stay in front of a wooden door and not let anybody leave. He could see two women inside in the moonlight, one seated on a bed and the other lying down. Then he heard noise and a cry and several shots and then a voice saying "Now" and then a lot of shooting. He then shot the two women whom he was watching. He headed for the gate where he had entered, observing that the rest of his unit was simulating combat and that someone threw a Bengal light.

The Story of Corporal Angel Pérez Vásquez

Cpl. Angel Pérez Vásquez admitted having killed Father Joaquín López y López. According to his statement, on November 15 at 6:00 p.m. Lieutenant Espinoza ordered them to leave the Academy and assume a position on the west side of the UCA near the cinema, where they believed a group of subversives and wounded combatants would be. They were under orders to return to the Academy at 8:00 p.m. if there were no problems. Around this time, a National Guardsman was killed mistakenly by "friendly fire," prompting the patrol commander, Sub-sergeant Oscar Rafael Molina Aguilar, to alter their position to the south side of the cinema.

Around midnight, a soldier came and took them to the corner by the cinema, where Pérez Vásquez found the rest of the section, the two lieutenants and a third officer. Espinoza met with some of them and said he had received an order – without saying from whom – to eliminate the intellectual heads of the guerrillas who were inside the UCA and that the soldier Amaya Grimaldi, "Pilijay," had the mission to assassinate them with an AK-47. He also said that when it was time to retreat they would launch a Bengal light and simulate combat.

Pérez Vásquez entered the CRT with Sub-sergeant Molina Aguilar and they beat open a wooden door where they found only books. At that moment he heard several shots in the upper

---

268 Zarpate Castillo is likely referring to the corner of Calle Mediterráneo and Avenida Albert Einstein.

part of the building. Some eight minutes later he climbed up to the second floor, entering a hall off which were several rooms. When he went out the other side he could see several dead people and in this same instant saw a tall man with white clothing come outside. Soldiers called to him, saying, "Comrade, come here." The man paid no attention. When the tall man headed into a room a soldier shot at him and he fell to the floor. As Pérez Vásquez stepped over the man, he felt the man grab his feet, so he backed up and shot him four times. As they were leaving, he saw Guevara Cerritos writing on a paper with a felt pen. When all the soldiers had reunited at the Cine Colonial, they began walking in a column to the Academy.

The Story of Private Oscar Mariano Amaya Grimaldi

Private Oscar Mariano Amaya Grimaldi, "Pilijay," admitted to killing three Jesuit fathers. Around midnight on November 15 his patrol commander, Sub-sergeant Antonio Ramiro Avalos Vargas, awakened him and said he had been ordered to go kill D/Ts inside the UCA. A Military Academy officer told him he was the "key man." He walked with Lieutenants Mendoza and Espinoza to the UCA from the abandoned buildings. Espinoza said to him, "Hide that shit," referring to the AK-47.

When the priests came out, Sergeant Solórzano Esquivel, known as "Hercules," and Avalos Vargas were nearby; Avalos ordered the priests to lie on the ground. Amaya Grimaldi saw Espinoza and Mendoza about 10 meters away. He started shooting when he saw Avalos open fire. Amaya heard Espinoza say to Corporal Cotta Hernández: "Get them inside, even if you have to drag them."[269] He heard other shots inside and near the gate.

After killing the priests, he went to the kitchen where he found another soldier drinking a beer; the soldier gave him a beer too. Then Espinoza and Mendoza came and asked if he had not seen the signal to retreat, which he had not. He heard Espinoza tell Guevara Cerritos to shoot off the other Bengal light. Then the officers left the installations. Voluntarily, he joined the patrol of "Savage," Sub-sergeant Eduardo Antonio Córdova Monge, which stayed behind to shoot up the building and was the last to leave.

* * * * *

269 Pilijay and others testified that Corporal Cotta Hernández, who reportedly wounded Father López y López and dragged Father Moreno's body inside, was subsequently killed in an ambush in Zacamil.

The SIU proceeded to record more detailed declarations from other members of the Atlacatl, who basically supported this version of events. On January 16, 1990, the SIU notified the Fourth Criminal Court that it had terminated its work, and turned over the record of its investigations to date.

CHAPTER V: COURTING FAILURE
(January to April 1990)

In the first two weeks of January 1990, the Salvadoran Armed Forces selected those who would be held accountable for the Jesuit murders. Somehow, Security Force members assigned to the Special Investigative Unit working in concert with Army officers of the Honor Commission crafted the prosecution package. On January 16, the SIU consigned eight of the nine defendants to a civilian court, along with its original investigation records.

The SIU told the court that Colonel Benavides was detained at National Guard headquarters, while seven defendants were housed at the National Police headquarters. The ninth man, Jorge Alberto Sierra Ascencio, reportedly deserted in December 1989. The SIU also turned over to the court various pieces of physical evidence – including one M-60 machine gun, two M-16s and the AK-47 – which actually remained on deposit at the SIU. Maintaining that their work had been successfully completed, both the Honor Commission and the SIU bowed out of the case. The locus of activity now shifted to San Salvador's Fourth Criminal Court.

Judge Zamora immediately ordered that the eight suspects be held for 72 hours, the legal inquiry period. From the outset, the court's access to the defendants was tightly controlled by the military. For example, the SIU failed to follow standard procedure in presenting the men to the court, forcing the judge to petition the Security Forces to produce the defendants.

This problem persisted throughout the case. Salvadoran procedures dictate that the judge determines where defendants in a criminal case are held. While Article 700 of the Criminal Procedure Code provides that any defendant transfers must be cleared with the court, Articles 246 and 248 state that members of the Armed Forces who have not been discharged are to be held in detention sites selected by the military. In practice, this served to restrict access to the defendants by court officials and others.[270] Throughout their nearly two-year detention, the

270 On January 22, 1990, the director of the National Guard reported to the court that Colonel Benavides had been transferred to the National Police. The Security Forces were not always as helpful in notifying the judge. Court personnel encountered difficulties in serving required notices on the defendants, who had been transferred from the National Police to other Security Forces without notice to the court.

defendants remained active duty military men and presumably continued to receive a military paycheck. The military's failure to cashier the defendants – coupled with the collective defense provided – calls into question the Army's repeated assertion that there is no institutional responsibility for the crime.

On January 16, Judge Zamora began taking official statements from the suspects. Colonel Benavides ratified his extrajudicial statement, insisting that he first learned of the Jesuit murders from the media. He said that while he had been assigned the Atlacatl unit as a reserve, he gave them no orders on November 15-16. The Atlacatl did, however, seek to "verify the presence of terrorists in a ravine near San José de la Montaña," on the orders of the Joint Command. He said he did not order any unit to patrol the UCA area and no Military Academy officer accompanied the Atlacatl on their missions.

Six of Benavides' fellow defendants declined to give statements on January 16, saying they felt ill, confused, depressed, or that they had been "pressured" while at National Police headquarters. Cpl. Angel Pérez Vásquez said he was kept blindfolded in a dark room, and rarely fed. Sub-sergeant Tomás Zarpate Castillo claimed he was forced to sign a blank piece of paper and had been told that if he did not sign he would face charges for being a "delinquent terrorist," as the Army called FMLN members. Sub-sergeant Antonio Ramiro Avalos Vargas likewise said his captors threatened to label him a guerrilla if he did not sign. The following day, January 17, each of these three men gave his version of events surrounding the November 13 search and his role in it. None, however, admitted to participating in the assassination, as they had done earlier.

Second Lt. Gonzalo Guevara Cerritos also denied the charges against him, refusing to ratify his extrajudicial declaration. He too said he had been forced to sign a confession he was not allowed to read, and that he felt too ill to testify on January 16. The next day he told the judge that after arriving at the Military Academy on the afternoon of November 13, he and Lieutenant Espinoza had reported to the Joint Command. Espinoza was then ordered to search the UCA by "*el Señor C-3*," Colonel Cerna Flores, the head of operations. Guevara Cerritos also described other missions carried out by the commandos. He said he and the other defendants had been "held incommunicado in a dirty room" at the National Police. He signed his confession, he said, because he was under "strong psychological pressure."

Lt. José Ricardo Espinoza Guerra also denied the murder charges and refused to ratify his extrajudicial statement. He, too, pleaded illness. On January 17, he testified about the

November 13 search, claiming this time that he had been ordered by a major whose name he did not know to search the UCA, but that afterward he reported to Colonel Cerna Flores at the Joint Command.

In his initial court appearance, Lt. Yusshy René Mendoza Vallecillos also claimed to feel poorly, in bad spirits, tense, and consequently unable to testify. On January 17, he formally denied the charges against him. Mendoza said that on January 8, Military Academy Deputy Director, Lt. Col. Carlos Camilo Hernández, told him to take the Academy's Book of Orders and report to the National Police. There he was pressured into signing a confession, he said.

Unlike the others, on January 16, Pvt. Oscar Mariano Amaya Grimaldi denied the charges but ratified parts of his extrajudicial declaration. An Atlacatl member since 1982, Amaya Grimaldi is the soldier known as "Pilijay" who admitted to killing three of the priests. He confirmed that his unit came to the capital on Monday afternoon, November 13, and had searched the UCA in the early evening hours, returning to the Academy around 9:00 p.m. After that mission, he claimed not to have left the Academy until rejoining the rest of the battalion on the morning of November 16.

Amaya Grimaldi told the court that in early January his unit had been pulled out of combat and divided into three groups. He was sent to the Treasury Police with 13 other soldiers. Subsequently transferred to the National Police, he asserted that he was subjected to psychological pressure. If he refused to sign a blank piece of paper, he was told, he would be accused of guerrilla activity; he suffered "another kind of pressure that he does not remember." He noted that he had not been subjected to physical abuse. Amaya Grimaldi repeated several times throughout his January 16 testimony that if he had not cooperated with his superiors "they would have treated him like a guerrilla."

Since six of the defendants said they felt poorly on January 16, the court ordered that they be examined by a physician. Dr. Juan Mateu Llort, the court's doctor, found no physical problems but noted that all said they were depressed.

On January 17, the SIU detectives who had witnessed the defendants' extrajudicial declarations testified about what they had seen and heard. According to Article 496 of the Criminal Procedure Code, extrajudicial declarations are admissible as evidence if two witnesses attest that the statement was made voluntarily.

To date, only one member of the Armed Forces has given testimony in court placing the Atlacatl troops on the UCA campus on the night of November 15-16, 1989. On January 18, 1990 Atlacatl Sub-sergeant Eduardo Antonio Cordova Monge, not a commando, testified that all the Atlacatl patrols that came to San Salvador participated in the November 13 search. He remembered talking to Father Ellacuría, who asked that he identify their unit and commanding officer. Cordova Monge says he told Ellacuría that he was not obligated to provide any explanations, and that questions should be saved for the officer in charge who would soon arrive, a reference to Lieutenant Espinoza.

At around 5:00 p.m. on November 15, Cordova Monge says Lieutenant Espinoza ordered him to post his patrol near the Cine Colonial, a gasoline station, and some abandoned buildings. Around 1:00 a.m., he was awakened by a radio communication from "Bull," the code name used by Lieutenant Espinoza. Espinoza told Cordova Monge to round up his men because they were going to move out. Espinoza subsequently arrived, telling him they were going into the UCA, without saying why, and that he should stay by a staircase near the gate and return to the gas station when he saw a Bengal light.

Cordova Monge mentioned in his testimony that a Military Academy lieutenant accompanied the Atlacatl and that they returned to the Academy around 3:00 a.m. Espinoza told them at that point that they would be rejoining the battalion at 6:00 a.m. Around November 22, Cordova Monge said, he read in a newspaper that the Jesuits had been killed.

Provisional Detention Ordered

On January 18, Judge Zamora decreed the provisional detention of the nine defendants for the crime of murder. He based his decision on the establishment of the corpus delecti by the Justice of the Peace and the extrajudicial confessions of the seven defendants. Lacking a confession from Colonel Benavides, Zamora found nonetheless enough evidence to order his provisional detention as well. The judge based his decision on Colonel Ponce's December 8, 1989 declaration certifying that Benavides had been named commander of the zone that included the UCA. He also cited the extrajudicial declarations of the lieutenants, who asserted that Benavides ordered them to kill the Jesuits.

Attorneys for the Defense

Several attorneys promptly appeared to represent the defendants. The first lawyer to enter his appearance, Lic. José Oscar Caballero, promptly withdrew, leaving a defense team of Dr. Raul Méndez Castro, Dr. Carlos Alfredo Méndez Flores, and two law students, José Adalfredo Salgado and Joaquín Eulogio Rodríquez Barahona. Dr. Carlos Alfredo Méndez Flores was the lead counsel. Known to be close to the military, Dr. Méndez was reportedly the personal attorney for Col. Francisco Morán, who led the Treasury Police during its most repressive years in the early 1980s. Colonel Morán's deputy at the time was Col. René Emilio Ponce.[271] "When they named the defense attorneys, I knew that Benavides didn't act alone, that there were others behind him," a Salvadoran attorney told the Lawyers Committee in March 1990.

All of the defendants – the nine charged with murder as well as the four charged later in the cover-up – were represented by a single team of attorneys, despite their conflicting interests. For example, Yusshy Mendoza accused Camilo Hernández of responsibility for burning the logbooks, an offense for which both were charged. Hernández could serve three years for his role in the coverup, while Mendoza faced a potential 30-year incarceration for murder. Solórzano Esquivel only faced one to five years for perjury, while most of the defendants could have received the maximum 30-year sentence. From the beginning, the attorneys showed a clear tendency to favor those defendants who were officers, by expending far more effort on defending them in written pleadings, press statements and before the jury. Indeed, in June 1991, the defense asked that the service records of the officers, but not the enlisted men, be submitted to the court record.

In July 1990 when he was charged with having destroyed evidence, Camilo Hernández hired his uncle, Dr. Carlos Castellón, as his defense counsel. Castellón resigned within days, saying he had been threatened by "undetermined sectors." Sources close to the court told the Lawyers Committee that Castellón, who at times also represented the military, was pressured into resigning by the military's defense team.[272]

Since the defendants are far from wealthy, there has been consistent speculation about how the defense is financed. One source close to the Army told the Lawyers Committee that a

271 *See* Arms Control and Foreign Policy Caucus, "Barriers to Reform: A Profile of El Salvador's Military Leaders," at 13 (May 21, 1990).

272 Yet as late as March 9, 1991, Dr. Castellón accompanied Hernández when the officer was summoned to court.

system was established whereby each Armed Forces commander was assessed a portion of the legal fees. The commander would typically pay his assessment out of his unit's "slush fund," monies skimmed off the top of U.S. aid, according to the source.

On January 22, 1990, defense attorneys presented a motion to revoke the provisional detention order arguing that the extrajudicial declarations were not valid proof because they were taken after the 72-hour limit following detention.[273] In the case of Colonel Benavides, the defense argued that his position as head of the Security Command was not sufficient to indicate his criminal responsibility and that the declarations of his co-defendants are not valid proof against him in a murder case under Criminal Procedure Code, Article 499.[274]

The public prosecution, represented by the Attorney General's office, replied that while the defendants had indeed been detained between January 5 and 8, their arrest was ordered by the military for its own investigation conducted by the Honor Commission. It was not until January 13 that the suspects were transferred to the jurisdiction of an "auxiliary organ of the court" – the SIU – at which point the 72-hour period began.[275]

Agreeing with the Attorney General, on January 26 the court denied the petition to release the suspects. The judge buttressed his argument by citing Eduardo Cordova Monge's testimony placing the Atlacatl on the campus on the murder

---

273 *See* Criminal Procedure Code, Art. 496.

274 Article 499 of the Criminal Procedure Code prohibits the use of one defendant's statement against another; a 1986 amendment abolished this ban for crimes of kidnapping, extortion and certain kinds of drug offenses, but left the prohibition in place for murder cases. This ban on co-defendant testimony has proved a significant obstacle in prosecuting human rights crimes.

275 Article 11 of Salvadoran Criminal Procedure Code designates the country's three Security Forces as "auxiliary organs for the administration of justice." In practice, this means that only evidence gathered by detectives of the National Police, Treasury Police and National Guard has been admissible in court. The Special Investigative Unit does not have such status, but has assumed auxiliary organ status by virtue of the fact that its agents are drawn from the Security Forces. This has been a somewhat controversial point in contemporary Salvadoran jurisprudence and on at least one occasion an appeals court rejected the SIU's findings because it lacked this status.

night, and ballistics evidence which linked Atlacatl and Academy weapons to the crime.[276]

Challenge to Judge's Jurisdiction

Another tactic repeatedly used by the defense was an attempt to remove the case from the Fourth Criminal Court and Judge Zamora's jurisdiction, apparently motivated by the belief that they would get a more sympathetic hearing elsewhere. On March 22, 1990, they filed the first in what would prove to be a series of motions to change venue, arguing that the campus' location dictated that the case should be heard in the Second Criminal Court in Santa Tecla, Jurisdiction of Nueva San Salvador, La Libertad.[277] The defense offered supporting statements from the municipality of Antiguo Cuscatlán, where the UCA is located, and the National Geographic Institute.

On April 4, the Attorney General's office issued an advisory opinion on the venue challenge, stating that the Santa Tecla court clearly has jurisdiction over the UCA, but that an argument could also be made for leaving the case with the San Salvador court because of some of the subsidiary crimes. The Attorney General left the decision in Judge Zamora's hands. Dissatisfied with this equivocation, Zamora asked the prosecutors to "pronounce in a clear and precise fashion whether" the defense's request should be granted. On April 6, the Attorney General issued a second advisory opinion, this time siding with the defense's request to transfer the case to Santa Tecla.

On April 16, Judge Zamora issued his initial venue decision, ruling that since the crime had been planned in the Military Academy, which is in his jurisdiction, he could rightfully continue proceedings.

Although the defense had misguidedly chosen to challenge Zamora's jurisdiction under a procedure that does not allow for an appeal, they nonetheless renewed the petition on April 30,

---

276 Despite the judge's rejection of the defense attorneys' position, the defense recycled the same argument in its December 1990 challenge to Zamora's decision elevating the case to the plenary or trial phase. The theme was also mentioned repeatedly during oral arguments by the defense during the September 1991 trial.

277 The motion is known as a *declinatoria de competencia*. *See* Article 34 of the Criminal Procedure Code.

insisting that no crime was committed at the Academy.[278] On May 9, the prosecution once again expressed its support for the defense's motion, prompting the judge to confirm his earlier ruling by declaring the defense petition out of order.

Some four months after their first venue challenge – having gotten nowhere under the vehicle they had chosen – the defense launched another challenge on July 20, this time employing a section of the Criminal Procedure Code which affords an appeal.[279] In the meantime, far-right Attorney General Mauricio Eduardo Colorado had been replaced by Roberto Mendoza, a change which was reflected in the office's more active role in the case.[280] This time the public prosecutors urged Judge Zamora to enforce his decision, and warned the defense that it should stop making "malicious and dilatory petitions." They characterized the defense motion as a stalling tactic, noting that the defense itself was to blame for making a strategic error.

On August 17, 1990, Zamora ruled the defense attorneys' last petition out of order (*sin lugar*), ending their attempts to transfer the case to Santa Tecla.

The Investigation Period

Following provisional detention, a case remains in the "instruction" or investigative phase until the court determines that sufficient evidence has been gathered – largely in the form of oral testimony – either to dismiss the case or take it to

---

278 Perhaps seeking in part to strengthen his jurisdiction over the case, in December 1990 Judge Zamora added charges for acts of terrorism (against eight defendants); acts preparatory to terrorism (against six defendants); and conspiracy to commit terrorism (against four defendants), all crimes allegedly committed in the Academy.

279 This motion is known as "a dilatory exception for lack of competence." *See* Article 283 of Criminal Procedure Code.

280 On November 18, 1989, Attorney General Colorado wrote to Pope John Paul II, expressing his "fear for the lives of some of the bishops who . . . have persisted in keeping alive this questionable ideology of the `church of the poor'. . . ." Alluding to San Salvador's Archbishop Rivera y Damas and Auxiliary Bishop Rosa Chávez, Colorado suggested the two be sent out of the country in order to avoid more murders like those of the Jesuits. Embarrassed by the publicity at home and abroad, the government press office issued a statement to the press corps saying that Colorado's letter was "embargoed, please do no publicize it, as it is being analyzed by the National Information Center." *See New York Times*, Nov. 19, 1989.

trial.[281] For evidence to be admissible at the trial, the judge must elicit once again virtually the same testimony recorded during the police investigation. Attorneys for the defense and prosecution are entitled to be present when witnesses are giving their statements in court. During this phase the judge seeks to build a solid case against the defendants and investigate the possibility that others may have been involved. Based on his findings, he may add or subtract defendants and likewise drop or bring additional charges against existing defendants.

During the investigative phase, Judge Zamora encountered a series of obstacles that impeded an already cumbersome process. Witnesses, mostly soldiers, failed to appear when cited; some appeared without the necessary identification documents. In one case, the Armed Forces provided the court with the wrong witnesses. Several witnesses were outside the country on military assignment, while others had been transferred or left the Armed Forces.

The information-gathering process was further stymied because high ranking government officials and military officers are not required by Salvadoran law to testify in person, but can instead answer written questionnaires with written sworn statements. Should this written testimony raise additional questions, a new questionnaire must be sent out.

The greatest obstacle to progress, however, was the failure of military witnesses to tell what they knew. The record is replete with the testimony of soldiers and officers who saw nothing, heard nothing, remembered nothing and who patently engaged in perjury, contradicting themselves, each other, official military documents and common sense. In August 1990, Congressman Moakley lamented what he called a "Watergate-style approach to testifying in the case. . . ." Military witnesses "do not recall seeing, hearing or knowing anything that happened on the night of the crime," said his statement.[282]

Soldiers Testify in Court

One obstacle facing the court that emerged early on proved a perennial problem: repeated summonses had to be issued for

281 Article 123 of the Criminal Procedure Code establishes a period of 90-120 days for the investigative period, a deadline which is routinely ignored. In the Jesuit case this phase lasted from January 18, 1990 until December 6, 1990.

282 "Statement by Congressman Joe Moakley on the Jesuits' Case and the Salvadoran Negotiations," Addendum, at 1 (Aug. 15, 1990).

military witnesses, who typically failed to heed the initial requests. On January 16, Judge Zamora cited nine additional members of the Atlacatl commando unit who had given statements to the SIU and were still in detention at the National Police headquarters.[283] Yet it was not until February 16 – one month and four summonses later – that all of the soldiers actually made a statement in court.

The men first appeared on January 25, but four of them – Neftalí Ruíz Ramírez, José Napoleón Argumedo Gutiérrez, Orlando Martínez Dubón and Oscar Rafael Molina Aguilar – were unable to testify because they failed to bring their identification cards. The same day the court sent another letter to the National Police director, citing the men to appear again on January 26, this time with the proper identification. By February 1, the four had still not turned up, so the court sent out a third summons; a fourth letter was sent to the National Police on February 9.

Those who were carrying identification cards and therefore able to testify on January 25 were less than helpful. Victor Antonio Delgado Pérez, whose rifle had produced a match with shells found in the UCA, denied that he had left the Military Academy between November 13 and 16, even to conduct the search.[284] Manuel Osmar Garay Linares likewise maintained that he had spent that entire period inside the Military Academy. Lieutenant Mendoza's assistant assured the judge that he was near Mendoza in the Academy throughout the night of the murders.

It was not until February 16 that the remaining four Atlacatl soldiers finally appeared, offering nothing. Orlando Martínez Dubón maintained that after arriving at the Academy on November 13, he sat idle. Despite the myriad references to soldiers' nicknames and code names, he insisted that "in the military the comrades are known by their first names or last name but never by nickname or code name." Patrol leader Sub-sergeant José Napoleón Argumedo Gutiérrez also denied having left the Military Academy between November 13

283 These men were Oscar Armando Solórzano Esquivel, Oscar Rafael Molina Aguilar, José Napoleón Argumedo Gutiérrez, Neftalí Ruíz Ramírez, Rufino Barrientos Ramos, Orlando Martínez Dubón, Manuel Osmar Garay Linares, Héctor Antonio Guerrero Maravilla, Victor Antonio Delgado Pérez. José Heriberto Hernández Valle of the Military Academy was also cited.

284 Miguel Angel Soriano, who like Delgado Pérez was a member of the patrol under Zarpate Castillo, testified on March 19, 1990 that he indeed had participated in the November 13, 1989 UCA search.

and 16, while Sub-sergeant Molina Aguilar admitted to participating in the search.

Seeking to convert the SIU's investigation into admissible evidence, the judge cited 22 Atlacatl soldiers during March. Most admitted to participating in the November 13 search, but all denied returning to the UCA on November 15. Several claimed, however, that there had been no electricity the night of the search. In fact, there was electricity around the UCA on the evening of November 13, but service was suspended on the night of November 15-16.

The Judge and the SIU

During this period, both the U.S. embassy and the Moakley task force criticized Judge Zamora for not coordinating closely with the SIU. The *Interim Report* noted that "[s]ince the arrests were made in January, the judge and the head of the SIU, Lieutenant Colonel Rivas, have only met once (in late March); and that meeting was arranged by the U.S. embassy."[285]

In June 1990, Richard Chidester, legal officer at the U.S. embassy, proposed to set up a dinner meeting between Rivas and Zamora. That the dinner was proposed at all, and the strong rejection the idea received from Salvadoran judicial authorities, is indicative of a problem that plagued the process from the outset, particularly with respect to relations between Salvadoran and U.S. officials.

For Judge Zamora, schooled in the Salvadoran civil law tradition in which written procedures must be followed, such off-the-books approaches to doing business seemed highly improper. The propriety of such a meeting was also questionable given the fact that Lieutenant Colonel Rivas was at a minimum a witness in the case. In addition, El Salvador's judiciary customarily has not had contact with the Security Forces, and what contact does occur is carried out in writing. Yet to U.S. embassy officials, such a dinner meeting could help bridge the gap between military and civilian, paving the way for a good working relationship in the future. Such inability, or unwillingness, on the part of U.S. officials to understand how Salvadoran society functions has left its mark on the case, particularly with respect to the saga of Major Eric Buckland.[286]

---

285 Interim Report, *supra* note 129, at 37.

286 On Major Buckland, *see infra* Chapter X: "Washington's Mixed Messages."

Salvadoran judicial officials argue that according to Article 143 of the Salvadoran Criminal Procedure Code, the SIU was obligated to have continued its investigation, with or without directions from the judge and regardless of whether detentions had been made. Further, since its creation in 1985, many judges have expressed concerns about the independence of the SIU and the integrity of its investigations, given that it is staffed by active-duty career military men. The SIU's lackluster performance in the Jesuit case would seem to bear out these concerns. More seriously, according to the testimony of Major Buckland, SIU chief Lieutenant Colonel Rivas Mejía is himself implicated in the coverup of the crime.

Higher Orders

An examination of the SIU's work indicates that investigators did not probe the question of whether Colonel Benavides was acting on higher orders. While offering no evidence, the Honor Commission answered this question squarely in the negative. Only the court made any effort to examine this delicate yet pivotal question, unfortunately to no avail. While no solid proof has emerged concerning the involvement of other ranking officers, significant circumstantial evidence suggests that Colonel Benavides did not act alone.

One explanation that circulated early on was that Benavides could have misunderstood something that was said at a meeting of ranking officers on the evening of November 15 at the Joint Command, where a decision was made to take extraordinary measures to rout the guerrillas from the capital.[287] One source close to the Armed Forces told the Lawyers Committee that Colonel Benavides did indeed turn to the officer seated next to him, the hard-line chief of the Air Force at the time, General Juan Rafael Bustillo, and said, "I have the UCA in my sector, and Ellacuría is there." General Bustillo reportedly responded, "Well then, you know what you have to do."

Immediately after the *60 Minutes* program on the case was aired on April 22, 1990, the prosecution asked that

---

287 On the meeting on the evening of November 15, 1989, *see supra* Chapter II: "Chronology of the Crime." In late August and early September 1990, the court took testimony from some of the 24 officers in attendance; all denied there was any discussion of the UCA or the Jesuits at the November 15 meeting. On Benavides' alleged misinterpretation of the orders, *see San Francisco Examiner*, Feb. 5, 1990; *The Christian Science Monitor*, Feb. 7, 1990.

retired Col. Sigifredo Ochoa Pérez be required to provide written testimony.[288] As a member of the National Assembly, Colonel Ochoa could not be obliged to testify in person. Once a prominent and effective field commander and now an ARENA leader, Ochoa had asserted on the CBS television program that Benavides had been given a direct order to kill the Jesuits at a smaller meeting of officers later on the evening of November 15. A transcript of the program was published in *Diario Latino* on April 25 and subsequently entered into the court record. A May 3, 1990 *Prensa Gráfica* article cited Ochoa saying he knew which officers had participated in the second meeting. The Lawyers Committee has received confirmation of the second meeting from another source.

Apparently eager to hear his views, on May 7, 1990 defense attorneys supported the prosecution's request for Ochoa's testimony. Colonel Ochoa answered Judge Zamora's May 6 questionnaire on May 18, saying he based his view that Benavides did not act alone "on the procedures determining how decisions are taken in traditional military actions" and ran through the steps involved in carrying out an order. He said the murders had "their origin in the attitude of extremist sectors, and the number of people involved and the form of their execution indicates a pre-conceived plan. . . ." He denied, however, that he knew who specifically ordered Colonel Benavides to kill the Jesuits.

Reacting to strong suggestions in the *60 Minutes* program that Col. Juan Orlando Zepeda, Vice-Minister of Defense, was involved in the crime, Zepeda wrote to Judge Zamora on April 27, offering to "put himself at the judge's disposition to aid in the investigation of the crime." He was not cited to appear until September 18, 1990. On that occasion, he denied that the Jesuits had been discussed at the November 15 meeting, and suggested that Benavides was responsible for the murder by virtue of being commander of the zone where the killings occurred.

The first months of the judicial investigation did not provide much hope that the crime would ever be cleared up. All signs indicated that the Armed Forces' cooperation with the investigation had begun and ended with the identification of the nine defendants. The judge was apparently helpless to confront the military's stonewalling. He filed no perjury charges, instead allowing an endless stream of soldiers to simply lie in court. Yet the judge took tentative steps to

---

288 For a discussion of Ochoa's charges, *see* Lawyers Committee for Human Rights, "Status of Jesuit Murder Investigation in El Salvador," at 1-4 (July 26, 1990).

identify the members of the Honor Commission, bolstered by a request from the Jesuit Provincial.

Despite this initial effort to expand the investigation beyond the narrow parameters determined by the SIU and the utter lack of military cooperation, it remains unclear what would have happened had the Moakley task force not published its *Interim Report.* Just as the revelations of Major Buckland had forced the hand of the SIU in its investigation in January 1990, Congressman Moakley's findings and observations provided the necessary political cover for the court to persevere.

CHAPTER VI: FROM A STANDSTILL TO A CRAWL
(April 30, 1990 to August 20, 1990)

Publication of the *Interim Report of the Speaker's Task Force on El Salvador* – also known as the "Moakley report" – marked a turning point in the judicial investigation of the Jesuit case. Issued in Washington on April 30, the report is one of a series of factors and events outside the judicial process which have nonetheless had a profound impact on the course of the case.

The task force summarized its findings in five points: 1) The Jesuit killings reflect an institutional problem within the Salvadoran Armed Forces and major reforms of the institution are necessary.[289] 2) In some respects, the investigation shows "progress," in that at the outset "good police work was done." 3) Despite "good police work," arrests might not have been made if it were not for the testimony of a U.S. major who stepped forward in what proved to be a watershed event. 4) Little effort has been made to determine if Colonel Benavides was acting on higher orders. 5) The investigation and preparations for prosecuting the case had come to a virtual standstill at the time of publication.[290]

The *Interim Report* drew sharp criticism from political figures in El Salvador. For his part, President Cristiani emphasized that it was an interim report and that no one could predict the outcome of the case.[291] Reacting to the report's criticism that the case had stalled in the courts, the presidential spokesman said President Cristiani "expects that the case can be raised to the plenary or trial stage within 90 days."[292] The Associated Press quoted President Cristiani on May 10 saying that U.S. congressmen "can say [the case] is bogged down. But the truth is that it did not bog down." He lamented further that the Moakley report "gathered up speculations and sometimes

---

289 Perhaps not surprisingly, this remains one of the task force's most controversial points. On the reaction to Congressman Moakley's remarks at an UCA forum on July 1, 1991, *see infra* Chapter X: "Washington's Mixed Messages."

290 Interim Report, *supra* note 129, at 6-7.

291 *La Prensa Gráfica*, May 4, 1990; San Salvador Domestic Service, May 3, 1990, *as reported in* FBIS, May 4, 1990.

292 *La Prensa Gráfica*, May 3, 1990.

tries to present them as facts. And this makes things difficult because it obstructs the judicial process."[293]

The strongest critical reaction came from Supreme Court President Dr. Mauricio Gutiérrez Castro who said that the "flippant and irresponsible asseverations that the Jesuit case is stalled are a fallacy." Dr. Gutiérrez Castro offered his full support for Judge Zamora, who, he pointed out, as he had on numerous occasions, "also enjoys the confidence" of the Jesuits.[294] Throughout the process, Dr. Gutiérrez Castro expressed confidence in Judge Zamora and in the integrity of the proceedings. In response to Congressman Moakley's criticism that the case had come to a "virtual standstill," the Supreme Court began to issue frequent press releases, summarizing the court testimony and rulings along with other developments.

Based on the Moakley findings, Judge Zamora attempted to trace investigative leads concerning the participation of intelligence officer Lieutenant Cuenca Ocampo in the November 13 UCA search, as well as information provided by U.S. Major Eric Buckland. In the weeks following publication of the task force's report, more witnesses appeared more promptly in court, but the quality of information proffered remained poor. However, a series of steps initiated by Zamora led to significant disclosures concerning the coverup of the crime, and questions about the SIU investigation and the Honor Commission's role.

It was during this period that it became widely recognized that the Salvadoran Armed Forces were not cooperating with the investigation. Military witnesses failed to recall even basic facts surrounding the killings, blatantly contradicting one another as well as official Army records. One officer, not previously linked to the crime, was charged in the cover-up. Yet no progress was made in examining the question of whether Colonel Benavides was acting on higher orders. Nor did new evidence emerge against those already charged.

During this period, State Department and embassy officials repeatedly blamed Judge Zamora for the lack of progress in the case. On May 4, 1990 Ambassador William Walker told the Lawyers Committee that in "my opinion, the judge is doing nothing." Representative Bud Schuster, a Republican who accompanied the Moakley group to El Salvador, was

---

293 *Washington Post*, May 11, 1990.

294 *La Prensa Gráfica*, May 4, 1990.

quoted in *The New York Times* saying "The judge is sitting on his hands."[295]

The Jesuits assigned responsibility elsewhere for the lack of progress in the case. The Jesuit Provincial for Central America, Father José María Tojeira, said he was

> worried that the justice system of El Salvador is being blamed for everything. In my opinion, the judicial system of El Salvador is not the culprit. The system clearly has its drawbacks and weaknesses . . . but the major problem is created by groups which are stronger than the judicial system and which refuse to provide more information.[296]

Observing that Judge Zamora "is doing what he can with the options at hand," Father Francisco Javier Ibisate, dean of the UCA economics department, nonetheless said it is "as though [Judge Zamora is] wearing lead boots that do not permit him to move."[297]

On May 11, smarting from criticism that the military was not cooperating, Defense Minister Humberto Larios sent a letter to Judge Zamora asking that all future petitions to the military be channeled through the Defense Ministry "in order to impart the relevant orders and thus give you a quicker and better coordinated response. . . ." Judge Zamora subsequently credited Defense Minister Humberto Larios with a high degree of cooperation in securing timely responses to requests for witnesses and in facilitating their appearance.[298]

While the Lawyers Committee never shared the view that Judge Zamora was primarily responsible for the lack of progress in the case, the *Interim Report* unquestionably had a positive impact on the judicial investigation. Equally important, the public backing Zamora received in the face of the Moakley group's criticisms allowed him to investigate various aspects of the case that had previously been foreclosed. Given the dismal

295 *New York Times*, May 1, 1990. *See also* Interim Report, *supra* note 129, at 7.

296 San Salvador Channel 12 Television, May 16, 1990, *as reported in* FBIS May 16, 1990.

297 *El Mundo*, May 17, 1990.

298 Lawyers Committee interview, Aug. 24, 1990. An Addendum to Congressman Moakley's August 1990 statement observed that the "Minister of Defense has responded, often promptly, to direct requests by the Judge and other investigators for information, documents and other evidence in the case."

response to the court in the early weeks of the investigation, it is not clear how far the investigation would have gone without the pressure generated by the Moakley report. Zamora had been encountering enormous obstacles in taking testimony from soldiers and had taken steps to identify members of the Honor Commission as well as pursue leads about movements at the Military Academy the night of the murders. None of these efforts had yielded anything useful. It was only after publication of the Moakley report that Zamora was provided the names of the Honor Commission members.[299]

New Leads Pursued

Perhaps further encouraged by the military's renewed commitment to cooperate, Judge Zamora attempted to explore a series of leads concerning the National Intelligence Directorate (DNI), one of several Salvadoran intelligence agencies. DNI headquarters adjoin the Military Academy along the military corridor where the Joint Command-Defense Ministry complex is also located. DNI is known to work closely with the U.S. Central Intelligence Agency, which has offices in the same building.

The DNI figures in several different ways in the saga, and its role remains one of the case's major unknowns. The *Interim Report* mentions two incidents:[300]

1) A DNI officer, Lt. Héctor Ulises Cuenca Ocampo, accompanied the Atlacatl troops when they entered and searched the UCA on November 13, 1989. José Ricardo Espinoza Guerra, the Atlacatl lieutenant who led the search, said he did not know why Cuenca Ocampo came along, or even how he knew of the operation.

2) Task force members were told that "three members of military intelligence (DNI) witnessed the crimes from a nearby building, briefly surveyed the murder scene after curfew was lifted at 6:00 a.m. and

---

299 Father Tojeira had written to Judge Zamora on March 23, 1990, suggesting that the Honor Commission members be questioned. On April 5, the judge ruled Tojeira's request out of order, since the priest was not officially a party to the case. *See supra* Chapter IV: "The Black Hole" on the Honor Commission.

300 Interim Report, *supra* note 129 at 43, 47 & 48.

> informed their superior officers at DNI upon returning to headquarters."[301]

And a third incident was revealed in the U.S. press in February 1990:

> 3) DNI officers meeting early on the morning of November 16 reportedly applauded when an officer announced that Father Ellacuría had been killed.[302]

Lieutenant Cuenca Ocampo testified in court on June 1, 1990. His name had first appeared in the extrajudicial statement of Lieutenant Espinoza, who mentioned that Cuenca Ocampo had radioed to him and then appeared just as the commandos were about to enter the campus on November 13. While Espinoza did not mention Cuenca's unit, the Moakley report identified him as a DNI agent and urged that he be called to testify.

Cuenca Ocampo told the judge that Capt. Carlos Fernando Herrera Carranza, then head of operations at DNI, ordered him to observe the search of the Jesuit residence on November 13, 1989, and that he went to the UCA around 7:00 or 7:30 p.m., considerably earlier than the time given by the Atlacatl. Afterward he reported back to Captain Herrera.

Cuenca Ocampo testified the search was ordered because "it was supposed that shots were being fired from inside this place, or that there might be weapons inside." He could not explain why he had been ordered to accompany the Atlacatl troops, "as it is rather unusual for a member of the National Department of Intelligence [sic] to be present during any search."

According to the testimony of another DNI officer, Cuenca Ocampo could have been chosen for the mission because he was once a member of the Atlacatl, and "could know those who were conducting the search."[303]

In an earlier statement to the SIU, Cuenca Ocampo had stated that he learned of the search when he went to the Military Academy on November 13 around 7:00 p.m. to receive instructions concerning defense of the military complex. Returning to DNI, he told Captain Herrera that the Atlacatl

---

301 *Id.* at 47-48.

302 *San Francisco Examiner*, Feb. 5, 1990; *Boston Sunday Globe*, Feb. 4, 1990.

303 Testimony of Capt. Luis Alberto Parada Fuentes, Fourth Criminal Court, May 28, 1991.

planned to search the UCA, and Herrera ordered him to accompany the group. Afterward he reported to Herrera, and also provided a written report to DNI Director Colonel Guzmán Aguilar.[304]

It was only during the eight-day evidentiary period in May-June 1991 that the court – at the request of the private prosecution – asked the DNI to deliver a copy of Cuenca Ocampo's written report. It was thus 18 months after the search that investigators discovered that Cuenca's report to his superiors was actually dated December 13, 1989, one month after the search and the first day that Atlacatl officers were questioned about the operation.

Capt. Carlos Fernando Herrera Carranza, testifying on July 13, 1990, maintained that there was no relation of any kind between the Security Command and the DNI.[305] According to Herrera, Cuenca Ocampo went to the Academy to obtain the password when he happened to hear of the search plans.[306] Without consulting with his superiors, Herrera ordered Cuenca Ocampo to accompany the men, informing Guzmán Aguilar after the fact. Contradicting Cuenca Ocampo, Herrera said that it was quite normal for DNI agents to observe a search of this nature. He said he sent Cuenca Ocampo along to see if there were "explosives or something similar inside the UCA." Herrera specified that his motivation for sending Cuenca Ocampo to

---

304 Colonel Gùzmán Aguilar was assigned as military attaché to the Salvadoran embassy in Costa Rica in January 1990.

305 This information contradicts the testimony of Capt. Luis Alberto Parada Fuentes, who told the SIU on March 20, 1991 that the Atlacatl was called on to defend the DNI from a guerrilla attack just after the men returned from the UCA to the Academy on November 13. The DNI and the Academy are separated by a wall, through which there is a gate. DNI agent Cuenca Ocampo also testified that he continued to visit the Academy in the days following the search, suggesting that there had been some level of cooperation between the DNI and the Security Command based at the Academy. According to Parada Fuentes, he was told on November 14 by Herrera Carranza that the DNI loaned the Command five MX radios for use during the offensive.

306 It is noteworthy that Cuenca says he needed a password in order to be able to circulate freely within the special security zone. The existence of this security precaution makes it unlikely that the Jesuits' killers could have conducted their mission without other troops in the area being aware of their presence.

the UCA was not the fact that he had been fired on from inside the campus on November 11.[307]

Finally testifying on October 5, 1990, Guzmán Aguilar recalled that Herrera ordered Cuenca Ocampo to accompany the search party based on information that weapons, propaganda and guerrillas were inside the UCA. He, too, claimed it was not unusual for a DNI officer to observe a search.

The DNI officers' testimony instead of clarifying the situation served merely to confuse it further, adding several new justifications for the November 13 search, and failing to explain DNI's interest in participating.

DNI Meeting on the Morning of November 16, 1989

In April 1990, the SIU initiated the first of only two investigations the unit conducted after the defendants were consigned to court the preceding January. It questioned participants in a DNI meeting that reportedly took place at 7:30 a.m. on the morning of the murders. Yet it was not until June 8 that the SIU shared its findings with Judge Zamora, who had instructed the unit on May 29 to provide the court with all its information. It is telling that it was only after U.S. prodding that the SIU pursued a lead they should have looked into as soon as news of the meeting surfaced.

Lieutenant Colonel Rivas had sought Colonel Ponce's authorization to conduct this investigation on February 13, 1990, and on March 2 was provided with a list of 17 officers on duty at DNI on November 15 and 16, 1989. All but two gave statements to the SIU in April and May 1990; Colonel Guzmán Aguilar and Captain Luis Alberto Parada Fuentes, both assigned abroad, gave declarations to the SIU one year later, during the SIU's only other investigation after the detentions.

Curiously, one officer on duty at DNI that night was not included on Ponce's list and was never asked to testify in court. That Colonel Roberto Pineda Guerra attended the November 16 meeting had been known since early February 1990, when the news circulated that he had had a heated discussion with

---

307 Herrera stated that on November 11 around 8:00 p.m. he heard over the radio that President Cristiani's daughter was trapped near the Albert Einstein University, close to the UCA. While attempting to reach Einstein, he came under fire for 15-20 minutes while passing the UCA. Encountering Treasury Police units and some members of President Cristiani's security detail on the same mission, he decided to return to DNI headquarters.

Colonel Guzmán Aguilar at the meeting when he voiced the opinion that the Jesuit murders were apt to have seriously damaging consequences for the Armed Forces. Yet Pineda Guerra's presence was first officially confirmed only on May 28, 1991, when Captain Parada told the court that Pineda, who was serving as director of the National Intelligence School in November 1989 had attended the meeting.

Most, but not all, of those who attended the early morning meeting on November 16, 1989, recalled that Captain Herrera had delivered news of the Jesuit killings; most said the men had commented on the problems the murders would cause El Salvador.

Herrera himself claimed that on a day during the offensive around 7:30 a.m. he heard on a "civilian band radio a comment that it seemed that Father Ellacuría had been killed." He then interrupted the officers' meeting to report the news.[308]

It was not until late March 1991 when Captain Parada finally appeared before the SIU, that it was established that Captain Herrera's source for news about the murders was a limited access radio frequency used by the military, not a commercial radio station. The captain said he did not know if the source was the DNI's internal frequency or one used by the entire Armed Forces. According to Parada, Captain Herrera was the acting Director of Operations for DNI in November 1989.

Parada's testimony contradicted that of every other soldier questioned on the subject. Had it been known in November 1989 that the Jesuit killings were being discussed on a military frequency before any civilians had time to arrive on the scene, the investigation of the crime might have taken a different course.

Herrera himself was shot dead in the early morning hours of November 20, 1990, in San Francisco Gotera, Morazán, where he was serving as intelligence officer. According to Colonel León Linares, the former Atlacatl chief who was transferred to DM 4 in Gotera, Herrera died "from a bullet fired by a terrorist sniper" near a displaced persons camp on the edge of town.[309] Press accounts, which appear to be based on a military communiqué, said Herrera died in combat along with four other soldiers during the November 1990 guerrilla offensive. Rumors at the

308 For an account of the varying versions of what went on at the November 16 DNI meeting, *see supra* Chapter II: "Chronology of the Crime." No civilian radio stations were allowed to broadcast during this period.

309 Written declaration of Colonel León Linares, Fourth Criminal Court, June 6, 1991.

time suggested that he had been silenced by the military because of what he knew about the Jesuit case.[310]

Major Buckland's Account

The other major lead provided to Judge Zamora by Congressman Moakley's *Interim Report* was the story of Major Eric Buckland, the U.S. military advisor whose revelations unleashed a series of events which culminated in the arrests of eight soldiers in January 1990.[311] While the congressional task force honored the wishes of the U.S. Defense Department and did not name Buckland, the report referred to a written statement submitted to El Salvador's Defense Ministry on January 3, 1990. The content of Buckland's statement had circulated in Washington and San Salvador since January, but it was only after the story was told in part in the April 1990 report that Zamora felt free to request a copy from the Defense Ministry; Major Buckland's statement was subsequently incorporated into the judicial record.

Provided with the lead, Judge Zamora then went about trying to test out the major's story, citing first Colonel Carlos Armando Avilés Buitrago, the Salvadoran officer whom Buckland said was his source. When originally summoned in May, Colonel Avilés was reportedly in Taiwan; he finally appeared in court on June 27. According to the Moakley task force, Avilés and Buckland, both psychological operations officers, "worked side by side," and Avilés had "specifically requested" Buckland for his unit; yet Avilés did not describe a particularly close relationship with the North American.

In court, Colonel Avilés said he knew something "of the technical side" of the investigation because he accompanied Fathers Tojeira and Estrada to their SIU briefing on December 22, 1989. He explicitly denied providing Buckland with information about Benavides confessing to SIU chief Lieutenant Colonel Rivas Mejía. Avilés said he "would like to have a crystal ball to know why Major Buckland would make such a claim," and chose to believe that the major had "taken leave of his senses" as a result of the guerrilla offensive.

Avilés said he recalled attending a meeting at the Joint Command between 8:00 and 9:00 p.m. on November 15, but did

310 During the September 1991 jury trial, a defense attorney asked the jurors to remember that several soldiers connected to the case had since been killed under unclear circumstances.

311 For the story of Major Buckland, *see infra* Chapter X: "Washington's Mixed Messages."

not remember whether Colonel Benavides was present. The UCA was not discussed, but Avilés said he could not comment further as the meeting was "classified." He recalled additionally that at a meeting at the Joint Command at 7:00 a.m. on November 16, those present – who did not include Benavides – did not know of the Jesuit killings, which he said he heard about on a commercial radio station around 8:30 a.m.[312]

On July 12, 1990 the public prosecutors requested that the two remaining links in Buckland's chain of information – Col. Iván López y López[313] and Lt. Col. Manuel Antonio Rivas Mejía – be cited to testify. They also requested a court appearance by Buckland himself, and by Col. Milton Menjívar, chief of the United States Military Advisors Group in El Salvador; Menjívar was not summoned at that time, however.

Throughout the spring and summer of 1990, Judge Zamora continued attempting to bolster the case against the defendants and to uncover new information that might lead to the identification of others implicated. These efforts yielded little fruit, as the military consistently stalled, withheld and destroyed evidence, and repeatedly lied to the court.

As part of its effort, the court requested military records that should have been obtained by the SIU early on. These included the Diary of Operations which Colonel Benavides mentioned in his January 11, 1990 statement to the SIU; the Military Academy Book of Orders that Lieutenant Mendoza reported taking to the National Police on January 8, 1990; and Military Academy records showing entries and exits of military personnel, visitors, vehicles and weapons.

---

312 As noted, commercial radio stations were not broadcasting at that time. Avilés' account lost still more credibility when Major Buckland waived his diplomatic immunity and returned to El Salvador to testify on September 28, 1990. *See infra* Chapter VII: "To Court."

313 Colonel López y López testified on September 14, 1990, having been called as a witness because he attended the November 15, 1989, meeting at the Joint Command. He roundly denied that he told Colonel Avilés that Colonel Benavides had confessed to Lieutenant Colonel Rivas. Rivas himself did not appear in court until October 19, 1990, when he too denied that Benavides had confessed to him. Major Buckland has consistently maintained that he received this information about December 20, 1989, as he reiterated in his September 28, 1990 court testimony. That he received this information around December 20 and shared it with others prior to January 2 was corroborated by his sister, Carol Buckland, and by U.S. Captain Carlos Puentes, both of whom testified in response to letters rogatory in August 1991. *See infra* Chapter X: "Washington's Mixed Messages."

The court had little success in obtaining these documents. Those that were provided by the military raised further questions, most of which remain unanswered.

The Cadets

During this period, Judge Zamora sought to establish who had entered and exited the Military Academy on the murder night, both through the testimony of those on guard duty and through the Academy's normal records. While the judge's efforts disclosed virtually nothing about who was at the Academy in the critical hours, they revealed a good deal about the coverup and the extent of the military's unwillingness to cooperate.

Four cadets whom the military originally claimed were on guard duty at the main Academy gate testified that in fact they were not on duty that night. For reasons difficult to justify, months passed before Judge Zamora was able to record the testimony of the men who actually were on duty and when he did, they failed to provide any useful information.

On March 29, 1990, SIU chief Lieutenant Colonel Rivas Mejía responded to a request from the judge by providing the names of four Academy cadets who supposedly were posted at the main Academy gate on November 15-16, 1989. The SIU document gives no indication of Rivas' source for the information. In the first week of May, Colonel Ricardo Alfonso Casanova Sandoval, Academy director, sent the court a note indicating that the four cadets cited were abroad for training, three at Ft. Benning, Georgia and one in Panama.

The absence of the cadets generated speculation that they had been sent out of the country to avoid testifying and suggestions that the Army was throwing up roadblocks in the judge's path.[314] In early May, before the court had a chance to formally request their return, the four cadets were brought back to El Salvador. On May 8, Zamora for the second time summoned two of the cadets. Erick Othmaro Granados Moran and José Wilfredo Aguilar Alvarado testified on May 11. Both insisted they had not been on duty at the Academy gate on the night of the killings, and that they were not aware any Atlacatl troops were billeted there. Granados Moran assured the court that the Academy has no Ford pick-ups. Aguilar Alvarado noted that he had not heard any explosions from the direction of the UCA on the night of the November 15-16.

---

314 *See, e.g.* Associated Press, May 9, 1990, as printed in *Washington Times* and *El Mundo*; *New York Times*, May 9, 1990.

The remaining cadets, César Moises Rivera Pérez and Raúl Galán Hernández, arrived at the court on May 15 accompanied by the attorneys representing the nine military defendants, and gave their statements.[315] Both denied being on duty that night.

On May 14, the public prosecutors asked the court to seek an explanation from the SIU as to how the erroneous names had been obtained, requesting that the Academy chief provide the correct names. Judge Zamora made the request to Casanova Sandoval in writing on May 25, and also sought a list of Ford 250 pick-ups assigned to the Academy. The same request was made of Lieutenant Colonel Rivas. Additionally, Zamora asked the Defense Minister to identify the real *comandantes de guardia*.

On May 25, Lieutenant Colonel Rivas responded, explaining that on the basis of a news article published in *La Prensa Gráfica* on May 17, the Academy director had ordered a thorough investigation of service orders and determined that through an "involuntary error" the service assignments for December 15-16, 1989 had been copied instead of those for November 15-16. Rivas further provided the names of those who actually were listed as on duty, based again on information provided by Colonel Casanova. On May 29, Casanova provided the same information directly to the court, along with the current posts of the four cadets.

Apparently dissatisfied with what he was told, Zamora again instructed Lieutenant Colonel Rivas on July 11 to inform the court of the identity of those who had provided false information. All of the first group of cadets named were second year students. Since generally only third year Academy students are assigned to serve as *comandante de guardia*, the error should have been easily detected. (Those who relieve them during breaks are normally second year cadets.) Yet no one in a position to know about the error came forward to state that the wrong names had been provided, despite the considerable attention given by local and U.S. news media to the fact that the cadets had been sent abroad.[316] The mistake was not even acknowledged until after these cadets had been sent back to El Salvador and told the court that they were not on duty. As a result, over two months passed before the correct guards appeared before Judge Zamora.

Second Lieutenant Elio Ernesto Munguía Guillén, who had been posted onward to the First Infantry Brigade, finally

315 *La Prensa Gráfica*, May 16, 1990.

316 *See, e.g.*, *Washington Post*, May 8, 1990; *New York Times*, May 9, 1990; Associated Press in *El Mundo*, May 8, 1990.

testified on June 8, 1990, saying he had been assigned to guard duty at the main Academy gate for the 24-hour period beginning at 7:00 a.m. on November 15, 1989. He told the court that members of the Atlacatl Battalion, Cavalry Regiment, Artillery Brigade and Military Detachments 6 and 7 were all at the Academy that night, but he did not recall seeing any of these units leave the premises. He slept from 1:00 a.m. to 5:00 a.m., but his replacement advised him that nothing occurred during his absence. Munguia's substitute, Walter Alberto Merino Vaquerano, still a cadet, also testified on June 8 and confirmed that nothing had happened on his watch.

Thus according to the testimony of these men, they failed to note the presence of Atlacatl troops, who by their own account gathered in the Academy courtyard and exited the grounds by the main gate. Nor did the guards note the departure of the vehicle sent out to pick up the wounded DM 7 soldier at the Cine Colonial, though his injury is duly recorded in military registries as well as in court proceedings. The guards' failure to recall even this event suggests a complete lack of candor.

In a strongly worded editorial published in the May 30, 1990 issue of the UCA weekly *Proceso*, the University Center for Documentation and Information (CIDAI) observed:

> At the end of March, the SIU also gave Judge Zamora the names of the four cadets who were asleep on the night of the assassination. As a result, the questioning of those who really were on guard duty that night has been delayed yet another month, to the detriment of memories prone to forgetfulness. At best, the cadets in question will give their testimonies more than six months after the date that the SIU should have questioned them if it had acted in a professional manner.[317]

The Missing Logbooks

On March 15, 1990, Judge Zamora belatedly asked the SIU to provide him with the Academy's book of exits and entries of personnel for the period November 12-16, 1989. On March 29, Lieutenant Colonel Rivas informed the court that the book had been "misplaced," without offering any further explanation or details of his efforts to locate the document. On May 23, Rivas revealed that the book of occurrences, entrances and exits of officers and others kept at the Academy guard post had been

---

317 *Proceso*, #430, May 30, 1990, at 4.

burned. Rivas said that this information was based on an investigation ordered by the Academy's current director.

According to Rivas' letter to the court, the Academy archivist claimed to have been ordered between December 1 and 16 by the Academy's deputy director, then Major Carlos Camilo Hernández, to round up all the 1989 books because they were to be burned. One night around midnight Lt. Yusshy René Mendoza Vallecillos and four cadets came to take the books to the incinerator. Judge Zamora promptly summoned the archivist, Yusshy Mendoza (who was already charged with murder) and Lieutenant Colonel Hernández to testify. On May 29, Zamora further requested that Defense Minister Larios use his good offices to see that the registries of entries and exits of officers and others kept in the Academy guard post during November 1989 be delivered to the court.

On June 4, archivist Juan René Arana Aguilar testified in court. He confirmed the story as told by Lieutenant Colonel Rivas, and added some details. During the five years that he had been in charge of the general Academy file, he knew of no other incinerated documentation.

Defendant Yusshy Mendoza was brought to court to amplify his original declaration on June 6, 1990. Acknowledging his role in the logbook burning, Mendoza attempted to make it sound like a routine practice. He said Major Hernández had ordered him to burn the books in mid-December "in compliance with a standing order" of the Academy. Mendoza claimed that this order had existed since 1987, when the Academy acquired computers, which stored some of the information in the hand-written logbooks. He also mentioned that some data is stored on microfilm.

Archivist Arana and Lieutenant Mendoza both implicated Major Hernández, yet when Hernández appeared in court on June 15, 1990, he denied having ordered the burning. Hernández said that at Colonel Benavides' request he had asked the archivist if the logbooks from 1989 were at the Academy. He reported to Benavides that they were in fact stored at the Academy and claimed that he had no further knowledge of the order to burn them. He said he did not know why the archivist and Yusshy Mendoza had "involved him in the matter," and asserted that they were lying. He did not know whether there was a standing Academy order to burn registries.

Testifying on July 11, 1990, Colonel Benavides denied knowledge of any standing order to incinerate Academy records. He said some data had been microfilmed and books subsequently burned, but could not specify which books were destroyed. He denied knowledge of any burnings between December 1 and 16, 1989.

On June 14, Defense Minister Larios put to rest the dispute over the standing destruction order by sending Judge Zamora a copy of a letter from Academy director Colonel Casanova Sandoval. Casanova Sandoval said that according to longtime archive personnel, no such order existed.

Coverup Charges Filed

Judge Zamora now had enough evidence to file charges for destruction of evidence, or *encubrimiento real*.[318] On June 26, he ordered the provisional detention of Lt. Col. Carlos Camilo Hernández, then executive officer or second in command at the Belloso Battalion based outside San Salvador in Ilopango. Following standard procedure, Zamora notified immigration authorities that Hernández should not be allowed to leave the country.

Lieutenant Colonel Hernández was not actually detained for quite some time following the arrest warrant; the military was even slower in presenting him to the court.[319] Yet promptly on June 27, Dr. Carlos Castellón, an attorney acting in behalf of the officer, petitioned the court for the reinstatement of Hernández' right to travel freely, so that he could make a pre-planned family trip to the United States. Zamora ruled that this petition was out of order, arguing that Castellón was not a party to the proceedings. On June 29, Castellón petitioned to have Hernández released on bail.

---

318 According to Article 471 of the Penal Code, *encubrimiento real* is punishable by six months to three years in prison. These charges are considered by the judge, not the jury.

319 Lieutenant Colonel Hernández is said to be a well respected leader among the younger officers. Several informed sources have told the Lawyers Committee that implicating him in the case provoked a strong reaction among his peers. Around the time Hernández was implicated, there were even rumblings of a young officers' coup. Some speculate that involving Hernández was meant to cause the officer corps to close ranks. Many young officers blame the senior officers who make up the *tandona* -- who they view as corrupt and complacent -- for the Jesuit killings and ensuing political problems. Four communiqués allegedly issued by young officers, using different signatories, appeared during the six month period after the murders. None have appeared since charges were filed against Hernández. *See* Lawyers Committee for Human Rights, Memo to the U.S. Jesuit Conference, at 4-5 (July 27, 1990).

Remarkably, by mid-July Judge Zamora did not even know whether his prisoner was in custody. On July 12, he asked Defense Minister Larios to inform him whether Hernández had in fact been detained, and "if so, to see that he were consigned to the court as soon as possible to give his statement." According to a subsequent note from the National Guard, Hernández had been detained at its headquarters since July 5.

According to a source close to the Army consulted by the Lawyers Committee, Hernández originally sought to conduct an independent defense, telling one friend that "he would not take the fall" for the Jesuit killings, and would "go down fighting." For about 24 hours, he attempted to raise funds for his defense. His attorney, his uncle Carlos Castellón, withdrew from the case on July 17, citing "moral coercion." He told the press he had been threatened by "undetermined sectors."[320]

The defense team representing the defendants in the murder case immediately began representing Hernández, thereby guaranteeing that he would be a part of the common, institutional defense strategy. Any hope that Hernández might have testified against Benavides or others was thereby dashed.[321] The potential for conflicting interests is striking, given that Hernández was defended by the same attorney who is representing Lieutenant Mendoza, who had implicated Hernández in the crime to start with. Mendoza faced a 30-year sentence for murder, while Hernández only three years for destruction of evidence.

On July 18 – more than three weeks after Zamora had ordered his detention – Hernández was finally brought to court, where he pleaded innocent, but did not give a defendant's statement because he had no official legal representation at the time. He ultimately testified on July 27, and was released on 30,000 *colones* (about $3,750) bond on July 31.

At the suggestion of the public prosecutors, on July 19 Judge Zamora asked Defense Minister Larios to inform the court how many logbooks were burned, and what they had recorded. He also sought the number and name of the registries which remained in the Academy files.

General Larios responded on July 23, annexing Academy lists which indicated that some 22 logbooks for November and December 1989 had been destroyed. Larios' letter outlined the

---

320 *El Mundo*, July 17 & 18, 1990; *Prensa Gráfica*, July 18, 1990.

321 The rule excluding co-defendant testimony would not apply, since Hernández was not charged with murder, as were the original nine defendants.

various registries kept by the guards as well as records relating to the cadets. Larios itemized 14 categories of logbooks for that period which remained on file, including books of entries and exits of chiefs and officers.

According to information received by the Lawyers Committee, the logbooks may not in fact have been burned during the first two weeks of December. A source who spoke with Major Buckland in early January 1990 told the Committee that "Buckland mentioned the logbooks even then [January 2, 1990]. It was already an issue then. Buckland had indicated, `[t]hey are concerned about the logbooks.'"

One U.S. official close to the investigation told the Lawyers Committee:

> The logbooks proved that the Atlacatl departed for the UCA at a certain time. [The Army] doesn't throw anything away. They record religiously what goes on. But there must be something more than just the Atlacatl leaving, because they could lie about where they were going. It must be something strictly out of the ordinary, names of people who didn't belong there.

Academy Chain of Command

In his June 15, 1990 testimony, Lieutenant Colonel Hernández provided valuable information about how the Academy was organized at the time of the assassination. He explained that in response to the guerrilla offensive, a "Security Command" had been created, with battalion status. The normal command structure was duplicated with officers assigned to head up S-1 (Personnel); S-2 (Intelligence); S-3 (Operations); and S-4 (Logistics). He himself was the coordinator of the Security Command. Hernández claimed not to have been authorized to give orders to the troops assigned to the Academy, saying that only Colonel Benavides or the head of S-3, Operations, could do so.

He denied that Lieutenant Espinoza had briefed him on the November 13 search, or even knowing the mission was conducted. He noted that the head of Operations was responsible for recording any incident or activity related to any operation, as well as messages to or from superiors.

Hernández said further that units could only leave the Academy on Benavides' orders and only Benavides could issue Academy weapons; S-4, Logistics, would deliver the weapons.

The S-4 officer would also have been responsible for turning over the Academy's AK-47s and the M-60 to the SIU.

The Testimony of Colonel Benavides

On July 2, 1990, Colonel Benavides appeared in court, saying he was too ill to amplify his prior declaration. On July 11, he testified at length. Benavides described the formation of the Security Command, and said the Atlacatl commandos were among a number of units assigned to him. Further, he said that Lieutenant Colonel Hernández could give orders on his own initiative or transmit the orders given by Benavides. Benavides claimed that he never issued orders directly, always making use of the chain of command. He reiterated that the head of S-3 kept a Diary of Operations from the time the Security Command was created.

During this court appearance, Benavides also made a variety of statements seemingly designed to distance himself from the November 13 search, possibly because it could be interpreted as a reconnaissance mission for the murder. Benavides said he knew nothing about the operation, and that no unit could leave the Academy without his knowledge. He said that if a unit under his command had effected such a mission, they would be obliged to report back to him, which they did not do. He later clarified that the Joint Command could have ordered the search without him knowing about it, if the commandos were not yet officially under his command. The order, he asserted, would have had to come from Chief of Staff René Emilio Ponce. Operations chief Colonel Cerna Flores testified on September 21, 1990 that he did not inform Benavides of the search order because he assumed that the Atlacatl officers would and because the Security Command was still in formation.

Benavides' denial that he even knew the search had occurred contradicts the testimony of the lieutenants whom he allegedly ordered to murder the Jesuits. According to Lieutenant Espinoza, Colonel Benavides said, "You conducted the search and your people know the place. Use the same tactics as on the day of the search and eliminate" Father Ellacuría.

Benavides said he authorized loaning some Academy weapons to units temporarily housed there, but that his institution had no AK-47s.[322] Asked to clarify who was posted at the university entrances, the colonel said he ordered no one to these positions. He was not informed of any combat near or

322 It was subsequently established that while the Academy did have AK-47s, they were not officially registered to the institution.

in the UCA in the early morning hours of November 16. He did not recall exactly when he learned the Atlacatl was involved in the assassination, but thought it was in late December or early January 1990. Personally, he conducted no investigation of the crime, leaving the matter to the police.

That Benavides made no attempt to find out how eight civilians were murdered – in a military operation that involved dozens of troops, hundreds of rounds of machine gun fire, explosives, and Bengal lights – in an area under his command remains one of the most damaging pieces of evidence against him. Entrusted with the Army's most sensitive zone, the colonel had either allowed the enemy to penetrate his territory or his own men had committed the crime. Either possibility is a serious stain on an officer's record. Colonel Benavides apparently felt no need to establish what had happened, nor felt any special responsibility.

Who Ordered the Search?

For reasons unknown, President Cristiani decided some eight months after the November 13 search to publicly assume personal responsibility for the order directing it. At a July 12, 1990 press conference, Cristiani said that the High Command had ordered the search with his authorization and that the Atlacatl commandos were not yet under Benavides' command. Cristiani reportedly added that in the UCA "weapons were found and evidence that terrorists took refuge there, but that this did not signify that the entire Jesuit university was terrorist."[323]

In his second written statement on August 25, 1990, Colonel Ponce acknowledged that he authorized the search by Atlacatl troops at 8:50 p.m. on November 13, after consulting with Defense Minister Larios, who consulted with President

323 *Diario de Hoy*, July 13, 1990; *Prensa Gráfica*, July 13, 1990. The military has never asserted that arms were found in the UCA, and President Cristiani did not respond when the Jesuit Provincial sought an explanation for this assertion for which there has never been any proof. Much later, on June 2, 1991, Cristiani answered a written request from the private prosecutors clarifying that "at no point was he officially informed" that "weapons, uniforms and related items" had been found at the UCA during the search, adding, however, that "war material" had been found at the Loyola Retreat Center.

Cristiani.[324] Ponce said that inside the Armed Forces Joint Operations Center (COCFA) he had been advised of reports that "terrorist elements" had penetrated the campus and were firing on military personnel, although he did not know the origin of this information. He relayed the decision to order the search to Operations chief Colonel Cerna Flores.

In his third written declaration on October 23, 1990, Colonel Ponce clarified that the order to search the UCA was given in two stages. He said that about 6:00 or 7:00 p.m., he asked Cerna Flores to send some troops to check out a report of "terrorist" presence on the campus. The Atlacatl commandos, the unit dispatched, later radioed for permission to search the UCA, which was granted about 8:50 p.m. This belated attempt to explain the discrepancy in the hour of the search contradicted the testimonies of Lieutenant Espinoza, Colonel Cerna Flores and several DNI officers.

Testifying on September 21, 1990, Colonel Cerna Flores claimed that C-2 (Intelligence) had informed him of telephone calls from civilians and military personnel saying that "terrorists" were inside the UCA. On cross-examination he clarified that most of this information came from civilians who said that some 100-150 guerrillas were in the UCA and that police guarding the Arce military neighborhood reported coming under fire from inside the campus. Curiously, however, none of the police guarding the Arce housing complex who testified in the case recalled shooting from the UCA on November 13, 1989.

Intelligence records submitted in response to a request during the plenary evidence period reflect no such intelligence reports of "terrorist activity" for November 13. Defense Minister Ponce acknowledged in his fourth written declaration submitted in June 1991 that he could not identify the unit which came under fire on November 13.

Cerna Flores also recounted having discussed with Colonel Ponce which units should be sent to search the UCA. They chose the Atlacatl, he said, because they were "an experienced combat unit" which was not otherwise assigned. He claimed to have

---

324 According to the Moakley task force, it "appears that President Cristiani's permission to conduct the search of the University on November 13th was sought and obtained after, not before, the search took place." *See* Statement by Congressman Joe Moakley on the Jesuits' case and the Salvadoran Negotiations, at 2 (Aug. 15, 1990). It remains a mystery why Colonel Ponce chose to alter the hour that the search commenced.

received the order from Colonel Ponce to order the search around 8:00 p.m.

Testifying on May 29, 1991, Lieutenant Espinoza said he had been ordered to search the UCA by a major at the Military Academy whom he did not know. The order originated with the Joint Command, Espinoza testified. Espinoza said that earlier that night he had been sent by Lieutenant Colonel Camilo Hernández to reinforce troops to the north of the UCA and that he went to the traffic circle in San Benito, one block from the home of U.S. Ambassador William Walker.

Testimony of Other Members of the Security Command

During the first two weeks of July 1990, Judge Zamora cited other officers who comprised the Joint Command of the Military Complex Security Command and took other steps to establish what went on at the Academy that night. It is striking that none of the men responsible for intelligence and operations at the Academy even admit knowing that the Atlacatl commandos searched the UCA on November 13, and only one, Major Miguel Castillo González, recalled that the Atlacatl commandos were assigned to the Security Command during this period. Their ignorance of what went on at the Academy is not credible. DNI Lieutenant Cuenca Ocampo said, for example, that he learned casually that the search was to be conducted while visiting the institution to obtain the daily password.

Capt. Julio Armando García Oliva, deputy chief of S-3 (Operations) in the Security Command told the judge on July 4, 1990 that he remembered seeing some Atlacatl men at the Academy when the offensive began, but denied any had been placed under the special command. Only Colonel Benavides could issue orders, García Oliva said. He mentioned hearing combat from around the UCA at a time when his troops were fighting in the Antiguo Cuscatlán park, but insisted he did not know which units were in the university area.

Maj. Herbert Oswaldo Vides Lucha, in charge of intelligence, S-2, also testifying on July 4, stated he knew of no Atlacatl presence at the Academy, nor whether the commandos had searched the UCA. Each section, he said, maintained a Diary of Operations or Intelligence, which was kept in the Center of Tactical Operations of the Military Complex Security Command. Incredibly, the intelligence officer maintained that he learned of the Jesuit murders through the newspapers.

Maj. Miguel Castillo González, head of S-3 (Operations) was the sole officer to admit that the Atlacatl commandos were assigned to the Academy, though he claimed not to recall their November 13 search or having recorded such a mission in the Diary of Operations that he maintained. He would have been aware of all missions that went through the official command structure, he testified on July 6, 1990.

On August 13, Lieutenant Francisco Mónico Gallardo Mata, head of S-4 (Logistics) testified that he did not issue weapons to Atlacatl members, nor provide them with any food, supplies or transport during this period. Furthermore, no weapons at all were issued on the night of November 15-16, 1989, nor did the Academy even have any AK-47s in its arsenal.[325] He was not aware that any units even left the Academy on the murder night.

Radio Transmissions

Questions about radio transmissions have repeatedly surfaced during the investigation. Some witnesses stated that they heard the murders mentioned over the radio shortly after the crime, while many others have referred to the Army's communications network. According to Maj. René Guillermo Contreras Barrera of C-2 (Intelligence), the COCFA normally had a "communications specialist" on duty whose job was to "maintain radio contact [*enlace*] with the military units in the central area."[326] An interview with this radio technician might

325 In June 1991, the Academy submitted its logistics registry to the court. It included a notation for January 11, 1990 indicating that the Academy loaned an M-60 to the Atlacatl on November 13, 1989. This M-60 and the AK-47s were turned over to the Honor Commission on January 11, 1990, according to the logistics registry. This notation provides proof that while the AK-47s might not have been officially in the Academy's arsenal, they were indeed on hand there. One source who requested anonymity told the Lawyers Committee that an AK-47 used in the crime belonged to Lt. Col. Camilo Hernández. According to this account, this rifle, a gift from General Ponce to Lieutenant Colonel Hernández, was displayed on the wall of Hernández's office and had to be cleaned before it would fire. In his extrajudicial confession, defendant Antonio Ramiro Avalos Vargas related that the AK-47 was assigned to Oscar Amaya Grimaldi because he knew how to manage it and that the weapon had to be cleaned before the commandos left the Military Academy for the UCA on the night of November 15-16, 1989. Amaya Grimaldi himself confessed extrajudicially to using an AK-47 to kill three of the priests -- later identified as Fathers Ellacuría, Martín-Baró and Segundo Montes.

326 Testimony of Maj. René Guillermo Contreras Barrera, Fourth Criminal Court, Nov. 1, 1990.

have shed light on what was known at Joint Command headquarters as the mission at the UCA unfolded, but this never occurred.

On March 7, 1990, National Police agent Pedro Anselmo Arévalo Coreas, repeating his statement to the SIU, testified in court that around 6:00 a.m. on November 16 he heard a voice on a military radio frequency say, "they've killed Ellacuría, now . . ." followed by vulgarities.[327]

Testifying on March 30, Treasury Police agent David Antonio Girón Valencia said he was stationed at the Democracy Tower that night and learned what had happened "around six in the morning on the radio."

The Moakley task force urged the judge to look into the question of the radio call Lieutenant Espinoza said he received at 10:15 p.m. on November 15, instructing him to bring his troops back to the Academy. This call was made shortly before Colonel Benavides allegedly ordered Espinoza to murder the priests. It is not clear who placed the call to Espinoza. This is about the time that the meeting at the Joint Command was breaking up. This means that Colonel Benavides was either still at the Joint Command at this hour, on his way back to the Academy or just beginning the briefing he gave his own men.

On June 11, 1990, Judge Zamora asked Lieutenant Colonel Rivas to provide information concerning radio communication by the Academy from November 13-16; the kind of radios used; frequencies; names of operators, etc. Having received no reply, Zamora repeated the request on July 9. Colonel Benavides testified in July 1990 that the Joint Command had access to transmissions between the Academy and its units. The answer that the military finally provided to the court contained no useful information.

Capt. Julio Armando García Oliva told the SIU on December 6, 1989 that he was not able to establish radio communication with his troops in the UCA area at 1:30 a.m. on November 16 and was forced to send someone personally to check on the situation. Confirmation that radio communication around the UCA was interrupted during the murder period also came from a civilian neighbor to the UCA. A man living near the campus who has a powerful radio said he tuned into nine different military frequencies during the offensive. But on the murder

327 *See supra* Chapter III: "The Myth of Good Police Work." Arévalo Coreas changed his story when he repeated it in court, saying that what he heard was guerrilla interference, an obvious attempt to implicate the FMLN.

night he turned on the radio when he heard fierce shooting nearby and wanted to know what was going on. None of the frequencies were broadcasting at the time, he told the Jesuits.

Capt. Luis Parada Fuentes told the court on May 28, 1991 that DNI Captain Herrera Carranza collected five MX radios assigned to the DNI on November 14 or 15 in order to loan them to the newly formed Security Command. It was over this type of radio on a restricted military frequency that Herrera Carranza heard the news of Father Ellacuría's killing, "while resisting arrest," Parada testified.

Congressman Moakley's August 1990 Statement

On August 15, 1990, Congressman Moakley again released a statement that proved to be a turning point in both the judicial investigation and public perceptions of Army cooperation. Following a visit to El Salvador by task force staff, Congressman Moakley stated that,

> I believe that the High Command of the Salvadoran Armed Forces is engaged in a conspiracy to obstruct justice in the Jesuits' case. Salvadoran military officers have withheld evidence, destroyed evidence and repeatedly perjured themselves in testimony before the judge. I do not believe this could be done without at least the tacit consent of the High Command.[328]

Like the group's April report, Congressman Moakley's statement provoked a strong reaction in El Salvador. *Diario de Hoy* headlined its response, "Moakley Forgets Thousands of Deaths During Offensive." Another *Diario de Hoy* article said the military found Moakley's statement lacking in "any veracity, groundless, and speculative." An Army press release said the "comments of the congressman are political in nature, and besides lacking any legal basis, diminish the prestige of El Salvador's governmental institutions and the Armed Forces, as well as the administration of justice."[329]

The congressional group's August 1990 statement made public what had been whispered for months. That the Salvadoran Armed Forces had engaged in a coverup was no longer in dispute, even among many U.S. officials. Despite its defensive response, the High Command made a gesture of

---

328 Statement by Congressman Joe Moakley on the Jesuits' Case and the Salvadoran Negotiations, released Aug. 15, 1990.

329 *Diario de Hoy*, Aug. 18, 1990; *Prensa Gráfica*, Aug. 18, 1990.

cooperation toward judicial authorities just five days later. On August 20, the entire High Command plus President Cristiani met for three hours with Judge Zamora and Supreme Court President Dr. Mauricio Gutiérrez Castro, at the Supreme Court building. According to *Diario de Hoy*, the officers sought to offer the court "broader cooperation using more agile procedures." President Cristiani said "it is important for the government and the Army that justice is imparted in absolute transparency."[330]

The meeting was initiated by President Cristiani who offered his total personal cooperation, offering to appear in court to testify if necessary. The unwillingness of top officers to submit to cross examination in court had been identified as a major obstacle in the investigation. By appearing in court – as he did on September 7, 1990 – Cristiani, as commander-in-chief of the Armed Forces, hoped to set an example to the officer corps. Several of the officers present stated that the military had never sought to impede the court's work, and offered to streamline procedures for communication. Judge Zamora also reportedly expressed his interest in obtaining a list of officers present at the Joint Command meeting on the evening of November 15, 1989.

Judge Zamora was apparently pleased with the spirit of cooperation expressed by the officers, and optimistic about what his investigation might be able to establish. As a result of this meeting, he began investigating the November 15, 1989 meeting at the Joint Command and recalling Atlacatl soldiers, hoping that this time they would have been instructed to tell the truth.

330 *Diario de Hoy*, Aug. 21, 1990. *See also El Mundo*, Aug. 21, 1990.

CHAPTER VII: TO COURT

(August 21, 1990 to December 6, 1990)

On August 20, 1990 the Jesuit case entered a new phase and again made history when President Cristiani and the entire High Command appeared at the Supreme Court to meet with Judge Zamora and Dr. Gutiérrez Castro. Ostensibly a show of support and commitment to cooperate, the meeting came only five days after Congressman Moakley's harsh critique of the High Command's role in the case. On the heels of the session came the first arrests for perjury. High ranking officers were called to testify about the November 15 meeting at Joint Command headquarters and, after President Cristiani set the example, five colonels waived their right to avoid a court appearance and submitted themselves to cross examination.[331]

These uncomfortable sessions, some of which lasted for hours, were unprecedented events in El Salvador. None, however, yielded significant new evidence. The show of Army cooperation also proved short-lived; no officer waived his privilege to submit written testimony after October 2, 1990. Most notably, current Defense Minister Ponce consistently failed to follow the example set by his commander-in-chief, instead submitting to the court four written statements.[332]

Like other events outside the judicial process that greatly affected what went on in court, the August 20 meeting clearly emboldened court officials, who in subsequent weeks took steps – albeit cautiously – to look at the issue of whether Colonel Benavides was acting on higher orders.

---

331 Col. Nelson Iván López y López and Col. Héctor Heriberto Hernández appeared in court on September 14, 1990; Vice-Minister of Defense Col. Juan Orlando Zepeda, on September 18, 1990; Col. Oscar Alberto León Linares, on September 26, 1990; and Col. Benjamín Eladio Canjura, on October 2, 1990.

332 Others who opted to give their testimony in writing were then-Minister of Defense Gen. Rafael Humberto Larios, Col. Juan Carlos Carrillo Schlenker, director of the National Guard, and Col. Dionisio Ismael Machuca, director of the National Police. Colonel (and later General) Ponce offered on several occasions to appear in person, for example in a letter to Senator Christopher Dodd in August 1991. In fact, General Ponce was never asked by Judge Zamora to appear in person to give testimony; the four requests from the court sought only written responses.

Despite newspaper accounts of a meeting at the Joint Command which had been attended by Benavides hours before he allegedly ordered the killings on November 15[333] and rumors of the possible criminal involvement of the Vice Minister of Defense, Col. Juan Orlando Zepeda, no attempts were made to question Zepeda and the 23 other officers who attended the meeting until September 1990, eight months after the existence of the gathering became public.[334]

Not surprisingly, none of those interviewed revealed information that could illuminate the question of higher orders. All who testified denied that there was any discussion of the UCA or the Jesuits during the meeting. Their testimony, did, however, clarify the official command structure in place at the time of the killings. Several officers indicated that Colonel Benavides answered operationally to Colonel Ponce, though theoretically orders which originated with Ponce could be transmitted by others. These high ranking officers uniformly indicated that Benavides and his Security Command reported to Colonel Ponce. It was Ponce who decided that the Atlacatl commandos would undertake the search of the UCA and be assigned to the military complex security zone during the period November 13-16, 1989.[335]

The hope that military witnesses would begin telling the truth and cooperate with the court proved illusory, however. Confronted with obvious deception, Judge Zamora ordered the detention of Sgt. Oscar Armando Solórzano Esquivel for perjury on August 24, 1990. Testifying before the court for the second time, Solórzano contradicted key aspects of earlier testimony, refusing even to identify himself in a photo. Judge Zamora ordered his immediate detention on charges of "false testimony" or perjury. Accompanied by fellow members of the Atlacatl Battalion, Solórzano fled the courtroom, escaping in a vehicle whose motor was running. The incident was recorded by Salvadoran news cameras and figured prominently on nightly news and in the press the following day. Embarrassed by the publicity, the military apprehended Solórzano and brought him before the judge on August 28. Perjury charges were filed that same day against another soldier, and later against two more.

---

333 *See San Francisco Examiner*, Feb. 5, 1990; *Boston Sunday Globe*, Feb. 4, 1990; *Christian Science Monitor*, Feb. 7,1990; *Baltimore Sun* , Feb. 4, 1990; *Miami Herald*, Feb. 5, 1990. For an account of the meeting, *see supra* Chapter II: "Chronology of the Crime."

334 Col. Carlos Armando Avilés told the court on June 27, 1990 that he attended the meeting but denied that the Jesuits had been discussed.

335 *See e.g.* Testimony of Col. Joaquín Arnoldo Cerna Flores, Fourth Criminal Court, Sept. 21, 1990.

Who Led the Atlacatl Commandos from November 13-16?

While by definition a military chain of command should be easy to establish, the court encountered serious difficulty in determining who was actually giving orders to the Atlacatl troops during this period. It was not until late August 1990 when Colonel Ponce submitted his second sworn statement that the court learned that it was he who had ordered the Atlacatl units into the capital on November 13 to join the newly established Security Command based at the Military Academy. Yet the unit's first mission in the capital, the UCA search, had been ordered by Ponce through C-3 (Operations) chief Colonel Cerna Flores, bypassing the Security Command structure. No testimony to date has indicated that Colonel Benavides was informed of the search order or the mission's results.[336] Colonel Benavides has denied giving any orders to the Atlacatl during the time they were under his command.

Testifying on September 26, 1990, former Atlacatl commander Lieutenant Colonel León Linares asserted that "once the commando unit had passed under the orders of the Security Command, the Joint Command could not continue to give them orders." León Linares claimed not to have contact with his troops while they were at the Academy and said he was eager to have them rejoin the rest of the battalion in Zacamil. According to León Linares, during the November 15 meeting he had asked Colonel Ponce to return the commandos to his control, since he needed additional troops to handle the large and extremely conflictive zone for which he was responsible. He recalled that Ponce said the commandos would be returned in the future. For his part, Colonel Ponce said that during the November 15 meeting he promised to return the men on the morning of November 16, in order to avoid a night-time transfer. In fact, the commandos were returned to León Linares' control at 6:00 a.m. on November 16, just hours after they killed the Jesuits.

Colonel Cerna Flores of C-3 gave a different account. He said that León Linares began asking him – by telephone, radio and in person – to transfer the commando unit back to him in Zacamil on November 14. While unsure of his memory, Cerna Flores believed he had passed Ponce's instructions to send the commandos to Zacamil to Colonel Benavides on November 14 or 15, thus suggesting that Benavides had ignored the order.

---

336 If the extrajudicial statements of Lieutenants Espinoza and Guevara Cerritos are accurate, however, someone who did know about the search and its results informed Benavides by November 15, as he reportedly chose Lieutenant Espinoza and his unit to kill the Jesuits because his men already knew the site.

Maj. Samuel Ramírez, a U.S. adviser from Ft. Campbell, Kentucky, whose statement was provided to the court in May 1991, told the U.S. Federal Bureau of Investigation that he knew Colonel León Linares was not in touch with the commandos in the days surrounding the murders because the colonel's subordinate had difficulty making contact with the commandos in San Salvador; the U.S. trainers were attempting to reclaim their night vision equipment that the Atlacatl men had taken with them to San Salvador.

By Benavides' admission, the commandos were officially under his command, yet the search was ordered by the Joint Command. Thus, it remains unclear who was really directing the Atlacatl commandos.

To Whom Did Benavides Report?

While it is widely assumed that Colonel Benavides did not act on his own in ordering the UCA murders, the investigation accomplished little in determining who might really have given orders to Colonel Benavides. Colonel Ponce explained that the Security Command was under the control of the Joint Command. Colonel Zepeda affirmed in court on September 19, 1990 that Benavides "received orders through C-3 (Operations) of the Joint Command, whose chief was Col. Joaquín Cerna Flores, who was under" Colonel Ponce. Colonel Cerna Flores also seemed to shift blame to Colonel Ponce for not investigating the murders, saying that Colonel Ponce was "the person in charge of questioning Colonel Benavides as head of the Security Command regarding the failure of the security provisions around the UCA, given that armed persons had penetrated [the area] and then killed the Jesuits. . . ."

Col. Benjamín Eladio Canjura introduced a new element into the scenario when he testified on October 2, 1990, asserting that Benavides' Security Command answered to the Center of Tactical Operations (COT), not directly to the Joint Command, as others had said. According to his testimony, during the offensive the rotating responsibility for the center also included the Minister and Vice-Minister of Defense. Thus, the "responsibility for operational decisions would also fall to whomever was in charge of the COT, depending on the rotation."[337] This testimony appears to contradict Zepeda's

337 COT and COCFA seem to be used interchangeably by various witnesses in the court record. COT stands for *Centro de Operaciones Tácticas*, the command center at a garrison or other military unit. COCFA stands for *Centro de Operaciones Conjuntas de la Fuerza Armada* and is the official name of the Joint Command's command central.

assertion that as vice-minister of defense he had nothing to do with operational decisions. According to the State Department, Colonel Benavides would have reported to Colonel Zepeda or to Colonel Cerna Flores on the night of November 15-16, 1989.[338]

Col. Carlos Armando Avilés Buitrago told the court that the sound of the explosions and shooting was so intense during the murder operation that those in Joint Command headquarters feared the complex had come under guerrilla attack.[339] Avilés said he did not remember if Ponce was in the COCFA at the time, but that the potential danger was so great that the COCFA duty officer would have notified Chief-of-Staff Ponce, who was in the building at the time. All members of the Joint Command were in the headquarters, the Estado Mayor, during the UCA operation.

U.S. Intelligence Advisor Lt. Col. Lanning Porter, who was not in the Estado Mayor on the night of November 15-16, 1989, nonetheless said that the standard reaction to such strong detonations "was simply to discover where they were and what was going on. [. . . .] I can only assume that those reports would have gone to" the COCFA.[340] Through court testimony it was established that normally responsibility for the COCFA rotated among the heads of C-1 to C-6 at the Joint Command. During the offensive, members of the High Command itself participated in the rotation. Also on duty at any given time were an officer from C-2 (Intelligence) and C-3 (Operations), an Air Force officer and a radio specialist. It was not until June 1991 that General Ponce told the court in writing that Col. Iván López y López, head of C-1 (Personnel), was in charge of the COCFA that night. In June 1991, General Ponce also provided the names of the C-2 and C-3 officers on duty at the time, unfortunately too late to be of any use. Timely interviews with the men on duty at the COCFA on the murder night, especially the radio operator, might have proved fruitful.

President Cristiani Appears in Court

At the end of the work day on Friday September 7, President Cristiani made legal history in El Salvador by appearing

---

338 Letter dated Feb. 9, 1990 to Congressman Joseph Moakley from Janet G. Mullins, Assistant Secretary for Legislative Affairs, Department of State.

339 Testimony of Col. Carlos Avilés, Fourth Criminal Court, Oct. 31, 1990.

340 Deposition of Lt. Col. Lanning Porter, dated Aug. 5, 1991, *In Re Letters Rogatory From the Fourth Criminal Court Judge of San Salvador, El Salvador*, at 9-10 (D.D.C. 1991).

personally before Judge Zamora. His scheduled appearance had been kept secret, and neither attorneys for the defense or prosecution were notified, nor were they present.

His short statement nonetheless contained some revelations.[341] President Cristiani said that at about 10:30 or 11:00 p.m. on the night of November 15, Defense Minister Larios called him at the home of his personal secretary, Arturo Tona, where he was staying. Cristiani and Tona agreed to come to Joint Command headquarters, where Cristiani met with General Larios, Vice-Ministers Zepeda and Montano and Colonel Ponce. The president met with the High Command until about 12:30 a.m., when he went to COCFA for a briefing, leaving the complex about 2:00 a.m. Cristiani was thus at Joint Command headquarters while the Jesuit murder operation was unfolding less than a mile away.

In the COCFA were two or three U.S. advisors, with whom Cristiani said he did not converse. These advisors have never been identified. The president said he was called to the complex because the officers sought his approval for their decision to use tanks and artillery "for the first time." Cristiani said he granted their request, since they sought to use the weapons outside the city limits in areas that had largely been evacuated by civilians. At no point during the evening were the Jesuits mentioned, he said. It is noteworthy that Cristiani waited 10 months to admit that he was at Joint Command headquarters on the murder night, and has yet to give substantive testimony that could help solve the crime. For example, having been briefed in the COCFA, the president no doubt knew that Col. Iván López y López was on duty that night.

Major Eric Buckland Testifies in San Salvador

Still greater security and secrecy surrounded the testimony of Maj. Eric Buckland, who flew into El Salvador on the morning of September 28, 1990. Fearing for his safety, U.S. officials flew Buckland back to a U.S. Army base in Panama before nightfall, after testifying for six hours at the home of the Deputy Chief of the U.S. Mission.

Judge Zamora had requested the appearance of the U.S. advisor on July 12, 1990 sending the petition through diplomatic channels. After an exchange of diplomatic notes

---

341 The president's entire statement was reprinted in *Prensa Gráfica*, Sept. 10, 1990. *See also Diario de Hoy, El Mundo,* and *Diario Latino*, Sept. 10, 1990.

and deliberations among several U.S. government agencies over the terms of Buckland's appearance, the State Department agreed on a limited waiver of diplomatic immunity, with strict conditions. It is noteworthy that the Bush Administration set the terms of Buckland's appearance, communicating their decision to the Salvadoran Foreign Ministry; Judge Zamora was not consulted.

Off limits to Judge Zamora and the prosecution and defense lawyers were any questions concerning events following Buckland's January 6, 1990 departure from El Salvador. The implications of that prohibition were not apparent until late October 1990, when Congressman Moakley revealed the existence of the additional statements from Major Buckland which had been recorded by the FBI after he returned to the United States. Consistent with the State Department's decision to conceal the bulk of Major Buckland's account, the ban on questions concerning the period after January 6 was clearly designed to ensure the coverup of the major's "prior knowledge" testimony.

Upon discovering that Buckland would not answer questions about his interview with Congressman Moakley earlier in the year in Washington, defense counsel refused to continue cross-examination, characterizing the testimony as "partial." The court record notes the dissatisfaction of the defense attorneys, who pointed out that the agreement between the Foreign Ministry and the State Department had "no validity" because under Salvadoran procedures only the judge can determine whether a question is out of order.

Accompanied by two Pentagon attorneys, Buckland recounted that he and Colonel Avilés had rapidly developed a strong and trusting friendship when he was temporarily assigned to C-5 (Psychological Operations) in June 1989. The two men exchanged gifts when Buckland left El Salvador in July, and Avilés phoned Buckland twice at his home in the United States.

According to Buckland, Avilés requested the major's permanent assignment to C-5, a fact which has been corroborated by Buckland's superiors, and he returned to El Salvador on October 16, 1989. He said that his work with C-5 consisted of "instruction related to civic actions, civil defense, psychological operations, and coordination with the Agency for International Development (AID)." Regarding the Jesuit case, Buckland said that he spoke daily about it with Avilés, since it was C-5's job to "protect and defend the image of the government." It was during one of these conversations that Avilés, based on information received from Colonel López y

López, indicated to Buckland that Benavides directed the murder operation.

Several days after the first conversation with Avilés, Buckland said he raised the issue again with the Salvadoran colonel and asked if Colonel Ponce knew about Benavides' role. Buckland remembered that Avilés raised his hands and asked rhetorically, "What if the superiors ordered the assassination of the Jesuits?" After this exchange, Buckland told Judge Zamora he "realized he had a problem because he was no longer sure what was going on." On December 28, Buckland said he lunched with Avilés and others just back from a training course at Ft. Benning, Georgia. "Colonel Avilés mentioned that he had seen Colonel Benavides but not spoken with him. But he noted that Benavides looked like he wasn't sleeping or eating well . . . and looked worried."[342]

The SIU's Lieutenant Colonel Rivas Mejía Testifies

SIU chief Lt. Col. Manuel Antonio Rivas Mejía appeared in court on October 19, 1990. Over nine hours of questioning, the judge attempted to establish the veracity of Major Buckland's account, which had implicated Lieutenant Colonel Rivas in the coverup. Seeking to determine what, or who, guided the SIU's decision-making, the judge also probed the unit's work.

Lieutenant Colonel Rivas' patent denial of the Buckland account made big headlines in the Salvadoran press. Pointing out that Rivas was the third Salvadoran officer to deny the story, *El Mundo* quoted Rivas saying, "I would like to have supernatural power to know how it occurred to North American Major Eric Buckland to say that Colonel Benavides confessed to me his role in the crime of the Jesuit fathers."[343]

Lieutenant Colonel Rivas' court performance went a long way in undercutting any notion of the SIU's "good police work." His testimony made it clear that the SIU failed to follow obvious leads, was careless with physical evidence in its custody, did nothing to examine the chain of command above Colonel Benavides, made no attempt to determine responsibility for glaring attempts at coverup, and ceased working actively on the case once arrests were made in January 1990, despite uncompleted ballistics tests, among other shortcomings.

---

342 Testimony of Maj. Eric Warren Buckland, Fourth Criminal Court, Sept. 28, 1990.

343 *El Mundo*, Oct. 20, 1990; *see also Prensa Grafica*, Oct. 20, 1990; *Diario de Hoy*, Oct. 21, 1990.

Explaining why the unit had made no attempt to identify the Academy sentinels that night, Rivas said that they had planned to do so in January, but once the suspects were charged, further investigation would have interfered with the judicial process and "said interference supposes that once the material authors and the intellectual author alluded to are established, that marks the end of the investigative unit's investigations. . . ." Lieutenant Colonel Rivas admitted that the SIU had not attempted to:

- find out the source of the bogus intelligence report of an attack on the UCA a few hours before the murders; [344]
- investigate the Joint Command's role, "since this institution is in charge of the whole country. . . .";
- investigate the various reasons given for the November 13 search of the UCA;
- investigate the open-mike which broadcast threats over a military-controlled radio station against the Jesuits in the days preceding their murder;
- question Lt. Col. Camilo Hernández, deputy Academy director, or Colonel León Linares, Atlacatl chief, because the Atlacatl commando unit "was not his responsibility" at the time;
- examine the DNI;
- locate the ninth defendant who fled, Sierra Ascencio, "because [the SIU was] more interested in the defendants who were present"; and
- question Colonel Benavides initially, "because there was no indication that people from the Military Complex were the authors of the crime."

Lieutenant Colonel Rivas also stated several falsehoods during the court testimony on October 19, contradicted by the testimony of others and in some cases his own actions:

- While acknowledging that he knew Richard Chidester, the legal officer in charge of the case at the U.S. embassy and

---

344 SIU's Lieutenant Preza Rivas explained more specifically that the unit had not looked into this element of the coverup "because this report had no relevance to the investigation." Testimony of Lt. José Luis Preza Rivas, Fourth Criminal Court, Oct. 18, 1990.

embassy liaison to the U.S.-funded SIU until June 1991, Rivas said he had "never met with him concerning the [Jesuit] investigation." During his tenure as SIU liaison, Mr. Chidester participated in the unit's weekly meetings and took a very hands-on approach to both the operation of the unit and the Jesuit case in particular. In his letters rogatory deposition Mr. Chidester said "It was my responsibility to monitor progress, so we discussed every aspect of the case."[345] Mr. Chidester added that he "was in daily communication with Colonel Rivas and others at the SIU."

- He stated he had no contact with Colonel Benavides in the weeks after the killings, yet Mr. Chidester said in his letters rogatory deposition that he had accompanied Rivas to the Academy in early December 1989 to talk to Benavides.

- He does not know if murder witness Lucía Cerna had been interviewed by the FBI, though he himself questioned her "and some FBI members were present."

- He stated that he learned from newspaper reports that the Academy logbooks had been burned. In fact, Rivas had told the judge in late March 1990 that the logbooks had been "misplaced." On May 23, he again wrote to Judge Zamora, officially informing him that the registries had been incinerated, citing the Academy director. The May 23 letter is on SIU letterhead, signed by Rivas and stamped with the SIU's seal.

- That the SIU did not take unrecorded investigatory steps.

Lt. José Luis Preza Rivas, who actually directed the SIU investigation, appeared on October 18, and provided testimony similar to his boss, Lieutenant Colonel Rivas. He said the unit had not attempted to identify the duty officer at the Joint Command that night "since they had no relation to the assassination." Lieutenant Preza Rivas only deepened the confusion surrounding the chain of custody of the weapons tested, confirming the unit's lack of attention to detail.

Indicative of the problems faced by the public prosecutors on the case – Henry Campos and Sidney Blanco – Attorney General Roberto Mendoza Jerez attempted to prohibit them from attending the testimony of Lieutenant Colonel Rivas, and barred them from posing questions during the appearance of Lieutenant Preza Rivas. Defying their boss' directions, the two

---

345 Deposition of Richard Chidester, Aug. 6, 1991, *In Re Letters Rogatory From the Fourth Criminal Court Judge of San Salvador, El Salvador*, at 8 (D.D.C. 1991).

attorneys attended the Rivas session anyway, buttressed by the judge's support. Long simmering disagreements over management of the case had escalated after Campos and Blanco gave a long interview to *Diario Latino* in which they criticized the SIU investigation and its failure to examine the chain of command above Colonel Benavides. Following publication of the article on October 4, 1990, the Attorney General banned them from further contact with the press and took steps to limit their active participation in the case by transferring duties to other prosecutors in his office.

Terrorism Charges Filed

On November 16, 1990, the anniversary of the killings, Judge Zamora set another legal precedent in El Salvador, by filing additional charges against the defendants for the commission of acts of terrorism – for the attack on the CRT and nearby vehicles – and charged some of them with related charges of preparation for acts of terrorism and planning and conspiring to commit acts of terrorism.[346] Never before have members of the Salvadoran Armed Forces carrying out official missions been accused of engaging in terrorist acts.

Defense counsel strenuously objected on November 29, 1990, arguing that members of the Armed Forces cannot commit acts of terrorism, much less conspiracy to commit terrorism, simply by virtue of being members of the Armed Forces, a legally established institution with a constitutionally mandated mission.[347] Defense counsel asserted that, under Article 402 of the Criminal Code, acts preparatory to terrorism could be committed solely by "clandestine" organizations, and the Salvadoran Army clearly did not qualify. Soldiers could only, they said, violate Chapter III of the Code of Military

---

346 Charges for acts of terrorism were filed against Benavides, Mendoza Vallecillos, Espinoza Guerra, Guevara Cerritos, Avalos Vargas, Zarpate Castillo, Pérez Vásquez, and Amaya Grimaldi; charges for acts preparatory to terrorism were brought against Mendoza Vallecillos, Espinoza Guerra, Guevara Cerritos, Avalos Vargas, Pérez Vásquez, and Amaya Grimaldi; charges for proposition and conspiracy to commit acts of terrorism were filed against Mendoza Vallecillos, Espinoza Guerra, Guevara Cerritos, and Benavides.

347 The argument was contained in a November 29, 1990 motion to the court asking that the additional charges be revoked. The defense had made the same request on November 16, 1990 in a motion to dismiss, unsuccessfully arguing, as they had in the past, that the extrajudicial declarations were not admissible as they had not been recorded within the requisite 72 hours after detention.

Justice covering crimes against the rights of persons, destruction, pillage and sabotage.

In rejecting this argument, Judge Zamora indicated that "it is no less certain that within this constitutional mission are not included the perpetration of assassinations, nor any other conduct that would constitute crimes that are typified and sanctioned in our substantive law. . . ."[348]

While he did not cite international humanitarian law, the judge's argument on terrorism charges is firmly grounded in this tradition. Generally accepted as applicable to the internal armed conflict in El Salvador are Common Article 3 of the four Geneva Conventions of 1949, as well as Additional Protocol II of 1977.[349] Protocol II, which covers civil wars, explicitly mentions terrorism as a violation in Article 4 and does not limit its application to insurgent forces.[350]

On December 6, 1990, just over a year after the murders, Judge Zamora raised the case to the plenary, or trial phase. He ordered that all nine defendants be tried for crimes of homicide, acts of terrorism, planning and conspiracy to commit acts of terrorism, acts preparatory for terrorism and the destruction of evidence; robbery charges were dismissed. Lt. Col. Camilo Hernández and Lt. Yusshy Mendoza Vallecillos were also ordered to stand trial for destruction of evidence. While the charges of murder, acts of terrorism and acts preparatory to terrorism were to be tried before a jury, Judge Zamora himself would rule on the charges of planning and conspiracy to commit acts of terrorism and destruction of evidence.

---

348 Fourth Criminal Court, "Decree Elevating Case to Plenary," Dec. 6, 1990.

349 The four Geneva Conventions, August 12, 1949, were ratified by El Salvador in resolution No. 173, of December 10, 1952, and published in *Diario Oficial*, No. 37, of February 24, 1953. Additional Protocol II of the Geneva Conventions relating to the protection of victims of non-international armed conflicts was ratified by legislative decree No. 12, of July 4, 1978 and published in *Diario Oficial* No. 158, of August 28, 1978.

The application of these instruments to the Salvadoran armed conflict was reaffirmed and codified by the parties to the conflict in the human rights accord signed by the Cristiani government and the FMLN on July 26, 1990, in San José, Costa Rica, under United Nations auspices.

350 Article 144 of El Salvador's Constitution establishes that international treaties take precedence over domestic law, although in this case there is no contradiction, since both murder (Article 154) and terrorism (Article 400) are defined in the country's Criminal Code.

Also in his December 6 decision, Judge Zamora withdrew all requests already issued for witnesses, saying that they would not provide new evidence.

Evidence Against the Defendants

Judge Zamora's rulings of November 16 and December 6, 1990, summarized the evidence against each defendant. The main evidence against seven of the defendants – Lieutenants Mendoza Vallecillos, Espinoza Guerra and Guevara Cerritos; Sub-sergeants Zarpate Castillo and Avalos Vargas; Corporal Pérez Vásquez; and Private Amaya Grimaldi – consisted of their extrajudicial confessions rendered to SIU detectives in National Police headquarters on January 13 and 14, 1990. Given the military's total lack of cooperation, no additional evidence against these defendants was developed during the judicial investigation.

Not surprisingly, defense counsel sought repeatedly to challenge the admissibility of these confessions, which formed the bulk of the case against these men. The defense argued that the defendants were actually detained on January 5 and 8, 1990, and therefore their confessions were taken after the 72-hour period of administrative detention allowed by law. Judge Zamora held that their period of administrative detention only began to run once they were turned over to the SIU on January 13. Prior to that, they had been confined as part of the Army's own internal investigation handled by the special Honor Commission. The court's conclusion was supported by the testimony of military authorities. (In response to defense appeals and habeas corpus petitions, the intermediate appellate court and the Salvadoran Supreme Court subsequently confirmed Zamora's decision regarding the validity of these confessions.)

These confessions constituted powerful evidence against the defendants. The four enlisted men actually admitted to their role in the killings. Corporal Pérez Vásquez admitted to having killed Father López y López, who had been wounded by another soldier; Sub-sergeant Zarpate Castillo admitted to having shot the two women, whom he left for dead, although the testimony of Avalos Vargas indicates that they were actually finished off by the absent defendant, Sierra Ascencio; Sub-sergeant Avalos Vargas confessed to having killed two of the priests on the lawn behind the residence, and Private Amaya Grimaldi admitted to killing the other three priests.

The three lieutenants were less candid about their roles, denying any responsibility, although all three place themselves inside the UCA at the time of the attack. Guevara Cerritos admits to passing Benavides' order along to the troops. Neither he nor any of the others place him at the actual murder scene. Lieutenant Espinoza Guerra, head of the commando unit, recounts receiving the order from Benavides to have his troops use the same tactics they used to carry out the search and then going with them to the UCA. While Espinoza places Military Academy Lieutenant Mendoza Vallecillos firmly in charge of the operation, Mendoza shifts the responsibility to Espinoza in his declaration. Undeniably, however, the three officers were inside the UCA and directing the troops, as no one suggests either that the troops were acting on their own or that someone other than the lieutenants was giving orders. All evidence, including the confessions of the lieutenants, points to a large-scale, pre-planned, official operation.

More complex is the evidence against Colonel Benavides, who never confessed to any role in the killings and was charged with *autoría mediata*, as the person who must have given the order, and authorized the deployment of troops and the use of Military Academy weapons.[351] While the judicial investigation failed to establish any direct evidence against Benavides, it did establish various facts which through a rational system of deductions lead inexorably to his responsibility. In his decision that there was sufficient evidence to take Benavides to trial, Zamora cited the following elements:

a) the record reflects that Benavides was named head of the Security Command of the Military Complex on November 13, 1989, and that the UCA was located within his area of responsibility;

b) the Armed Forces formal command structure authorizes a commander to give operational orders "without the necessity oF consulting them beforehand with his immediate superiors"; the judge also noted that the record established that the Security Command was under the operational control of the Joint Command of the Armed Forces;

c) the record established that the Atlacatl Commandos, headed by Lieutenant Espinoza Guerra and Second Lieutenant Guevara Cerritos, had been placed under the operational control of the Security Command on November 13, 1989; also that Lieutenant Mendoza Vallecillos was assigned to the Military

---

351 Article 44 of the Salvadoran Criminal Code includes *autoría mediata* as a type of criminal responsibility. Article 46 defines *autores mediatos*, in part, as: those who by means of physical force compel another to commit a crime; those who oblige another to commit a crime; those who cooperate in such a necessary manner that without it, the crime could not be carried out.

Academy, which means that the immediate commander of the commando unit and of Mendoza Vallecillos, in terms of operations, was Colonel Benavides;

d) that the Army regulations establish the hierarchical ability to give orders (Article 8), and Article 9, paragraph 2, second section, states "the superior officer bears the responsibility for all the orders that he gives";

e) testimony from top-ranking military authorities, Colonels Zepeda and Ponce, establishing that "because he was the commander of the zone where the crime was committed, he is responsible for it" (Zepeda); "any member of the [military] who gives an order contrary to the legal order is personally responsible for the results and subject to the appropriate sanctions"; "the Commander of any military organization is directly responsible for the events which occur in his area" (Ponce); and

f) ballistics examination performed by the SIU matched an M-60 machine gun assigned to the Academy and an AK-47 rifle with shells found at the crime scene; testimony in the record indicated that the only person who could authorize the use of these weapons was Colonel Benavides as Director of the Military Academy.

Relying on this evidence and the rules cited, Judge Zamora concluded that there was ample evidence to take Benavides to trial on the basis of *autoría mediata.*

CHAPTER VIII: THE FINAL ACT
(December 7, 1990 to September 1991)

With the decision to raise the case to the plenary or trial stage, defense attorneys found themselves one step closer to the day in court they sought to avoid. On December 19, 1990, they appealed Judge Zamora's ruling, thereby sending the case to San Salvador's First Appeals Court. This was the first of several stalling mechanisms used by defense during the next period, and for a time the case lay largely dormant, as magistrates began the lengthy process of reviewing voluminous case files. The appeals court could ratify the judge's decision to try all nine defendants, opt to try only some of them, modify the charges filed or throw out the case entirely. According to the law, the appellate court must rule within 30 days, though like most time requirements in El Salvador's justice system, the deadline is regularly disregarded.

While a decision is on appeal, no new action may be taken by the trial judge and no new evidence entered into the record. Despite the lack of activity in court, the case stayed in the public eye. On January 8, 1991, Henry Campos and Sidney Blanco, the principal public prosecutors working on the case for most of the last year, resigned in protest, saying they had been prohibited by the Attorney General from aggressively pursuing the investigation.

While officials in both San Salvador and Washington reacted with surprise, the tensions between the prosecutors and their superiors in the Attorney General's office (*Fiscalía*) had long been apparent, building since autumn 1990. In fact, on December 3, 1990, the two attorneys had submitted their written resignations to Attorney General Dr. Roberto Mendoza Jerez, who suggested they take a few days off to rethink their position. This was the second time they had discussed resigning with Dr. Mendoza.

In the weeks preceding their resignations, the attorneys' proposed pleadings had been rejected by their superiors, and their names had ceased to appear in pleadings filed in court. In a January 9 press conference, Sidney Blanco said the Attorney General had reprimanded them for requesting the detention of military witnesses on perjury charges, and forbid them from pursuing additional perjury charges. Henry Campos said that

> [w]ith our resignation we are showing that the space that we had to act has been closed. While we had

> accepted certain conditions and limitations, we did so in order that we would have the opportunity to make a small contribution, but our work makes no sense, and helped nothing if we were just [serving] as ornaments, if they were not going to let us work.[352]

Sidney Blanco said he thought,

> the way the Attorney General's office ought to have behaved would have been to say, "look, gentlemen, the military is obstructing the process totally, and we won't get any further if the military doesn't budge." But the Attorney General's office is perfectly content with the military's claim that the judicial process is going well. The Attorney General's office could play an important role in denouncing to the world that the military does not wish to cooperate.[353]

Reactions to the Resignations

Reeling under the blow to the credibility of the legal process, Salvadoran and U.S. officials attempted to downplay the resignation. Attorney General Mendoza said that "[a]s far as I know, there have been no differences. . . . Their motives . . . have to do with the fact that they want to pursue their profession freely."[354] Others suggested that Campos and Blanco were merely "junior" members of a larger team of more seasoned professionals. But while other members of the human rights division of the Attorney General's office had entered appearances in the case, Campos and Blanco had played the most active role and all of the major documents submitted to the court by the office had been signed by these two men. A State Department spokesman told the press on January 10 that "[w]e have known for some time that two junior prosecutors in the Jesuits' case had planned to resign in order to enter private practice."[355]

On January 11, the Central American Province of the Society of Jesus issued a communiqué which observed that

---

352 *Prensa Gráfica*, Jan. 10, 1991.

353 Press Conference with SPCA, the Foreign Press Association, Jan. 9, 1991, *as reported in Proceso*, #460, Jan. 30, 1991.

354 *Al Día*, Channel 12, Jan. 8, 1991.

355 Richard Boucher, State Department Regular Briefing, 12:45 P.M. EST, Jan. 10, 1991.

> by its indifferent attitude toward the clear ramifications of the case, the Attorney General's office is falling into complicity with those who have hidden evidence and lied throughout the judicial process.
>
> Until now the Society of Jesus has had relative confidence in the Attorney General's office, despite the irregularities committed by that office in the early days of the case (during the tenure of Attorney General Colorado), and the passivity and lack of personal interest in the case exhibited by the current Attorney General. Our confidence was based on the work of the prosecutors who have just resigned.
>
> We would like to publicly state that the Society of Jesus is considering the possibility of contracting private prosecutors to represent the families of the assassinated Jesuits. To that end, we have begun conversations with the former prosecutors, Sidney Blanco and Henry Campos, to explore the possibility of contracting their services.

On January 14, Dr. Mendoza said that the *Fiscalía* would "redouble its efforts to investigate thoroughly the truth behind the [Jesuit murders] and discover the identity of all those who may have been involved in it, whether they were intellectual authors, direct authors, or accomplices, whatever their condition or status in society."[356] He added that his office would continue to investigate the case "alone or in cooperation with private prosecutors." Yet the following day, Dr. Mendoza suggested that "if the ex-prosecutors in the Jesuit case sign a contract as private prosecutors, the responsibility to investigate the case will fall on them."[357]

The change in Mendoza's attitude was the first sign of an effort to discredit Blanco and Campos. The two had been forewarned that their reputations had been likely to come under attack. The news article quoting Mendoza ended by citing information gathered in "courthouse corridors" that the attorneys' "honoraria and other benefits [as private prosecutors] would be more than 2,000% the salary of a public prosecutor." In fact, when the Society of Jesus did hire Campos and Blanco as legal advisors in late January, they were paid the same salary they were receiving in the *Fiscalía*.

A series of articles followed in Salvadoran newspapers accusing the two of "a lack of professional ethics," being

---

356 *Diario de Hoy*, Jan. 15, 1991.

357 *Diario de Hoy*, Jan. 16, 1991.

"mercenaries of justice" and of having ambitions to run for public office.[358] Dr. Juan José García Aguilar, an attorney and member of the ARENA party, told the press that Blanco and Campos resigned "for purely economic reasons and with the objective of gaining notoriety. . . ." Doctors Gutiérrez Castro and García Aguilar are said to be close professionally and García Aguilar has represented the Supreme Court in several matters. Supreme Court President Mauricio Gutiérrez Castro expressed the view that if the Jesuits were to hire the attorneys as private prosecutors it would be "a very wise decision of the Jesuit fathers." Dr. Gutiérrez Castro also praised the work done by Campos and Blanco while at the *Fiscalía.*[359]

High Command Letter

On February 22, 1991, Defense Minister Ponce and the other four members of the High Command sent a letter to Justice Minister René Hernández Valiente in his capacity as chairman of the Commission on Investigations. The Commission is a largely inactive civilian body which was created to oversee the work of the SIU. In their letter, General Ponce and the other senior officers wrote that they were "conscious of the transcendence and social commotion" caused by the Jesuit murders. "Given that the judicial process has not yet concluded," they said, "as members of the High Command of the Armed Forces, we consider it of urgent necessity that some complementary investigatory steps be taken that could help clear up the truth in this delicate case." Further, the five officers asserted that they are "totally sure that there is no institutional responsibility [within the Armed Forces] for planning and carrying out" the murders.

They asked the SIU to look into "some events prior to the crime," mentioning a meeting held on the evening of November 15, 1989, at the Military Academy at which Colonel Guillermo Benavides presided. Attending that meeting were 10 officers, some of whom formed the general staff of the special command then in place at the Academy. The officers also suggested that Colonel Carlos Mauricio Guzmán Aguilar, chief of the DNI intelligence agency in November 1989, and Lieutenant Héctor Ulises Cuenca Ocampo, a DNI agent who participated in the search of the Jesuit residence two days before the assassination, be questioned again concerning the search and the DNI meeting held on the morning of November 16.

---

358 *See El Mundo*, Jan. 18 & 19, 1991; *Prensa Gráfica*, Jan. 20, 1991; *Diario de Hoy*, Jan. 21, 1991.

359 *El Mundo*, Jan. 15, 1991.

It is noteworthy that all but three of the officers cited in the letter had already testified in the case. Further, the investigative steps which the High Command urged should have been requested 15 months earlier. And, the naming of mostly junior officers traced the chain of command downward, and did not encourage investigation of those above the most senior officer in the military hierarchy charged so far, Colonel Benavides.

News of the letter appeared in *The Washington Post* on March 13, 1991, coinciding with an appearance by Bernard Aronson, the Assistant Secretary of State for Inter-American Affairs, at a hearing in the House of Representatives and with the March 15 deadline for the release of U.S. military assistance to El Salvador. In Washington, much was made of the letter. Both *The New York Times* and *The Washington Post* ran articles. According to *The Times*, Mr. Aronson, "characterized the letter as an important step forward." He called the letter a "break-through" and a "serious development."

But in El Salvador, the High Command's letter was greeted more cautiously. Coverage was a bit delayed and based on U.S. news stories. Further, it quickly became clear that the U.S. news articles were based on an erroneous translation of the Spanish text of the letter which had been distributed by the State Department. *The Post*, for example, reported that General Ponce had written that "it was `urgently necessary that we [meaning the Armed Forces] initiate a complementary investigation' and `expand the investigation' to include a dozen named officers at the military school and the intelligence directorate."

Yet the Spanish text, which circulated later, clearly asked the SIU to investigate the men listed and the two meetings. The State Department never corrected the erroneous translation or adjusted its upbeat spin on the matter. While U.S. officials, including Assistant Secretary Aronson, hailed the letter as a "breakthrough," it seemed to have far more importance in Washington – where it was first released – than in San Salvador. Indicative of how the matter was handled, the High Command failed even to send Judge Zamora a copy of its letter to the Minister of Justice. There was speculation that the letter was written at Washington's suggestion, and timed to congressional discussions concerning military aid allocations.

As a result of the High Command's letter, the SIU did briefly resume work on the case. Its findings, 50 pages in all, were submitted to Zamora on May 20, but they provided no new elements.

On April 8, the appellate court upheld Judge Zamora's decision to elevate the case to the plenary stage. The court upheld Zamora's ruling in every aspect and rejected the defense's perennial contention that the defendants' extrajudicial confessions lack validity. The appeals court also rejected the defense argument that members of the military cannot be charged with acts of terrorism. In issuing its opinion, the appellate court harshly criticized the defense, warning it to "abstain from making affirmations that are not found in the record and which have no legal basis."

Defense Files Habeas Corpus Petitions

On April 16, before the case was returned to the trial court, Rosario Elizabeth Torres de Benavides filed a habeas corpus petition in the Constitutional Chamber of the Supreme Court on behalf of her husband, Colonel Guillermo Benavides. Mrs. Benavides attributed her husband's imprisonment to "international pressure." She said: "This is a disgrace against the Armed Forces as an institution, given that its members are fighting in a situation of conflict and fulfilling their constitutional obligations."[360] Dr. Salvador Urrutia López, president of the Federation of Lawyers' Associations, was named on April 18 as the "judge executor" to study and issue an advisory opinion on the legality of Benavides' detention.

On April 26, the parents of Lieutenant José Ricardo Espinoza Guerra filed a similar petition for their son. Apparently wishing to head off further habeas petitions by the defense which would delay the process, the Supreme Court on its own initiative decided to examine the legality of the detention of all the defendants. On May 8, the country's highest court ruled that the case against all nine defendants should continue.

Private Prosecutors Enter An Appearance

On May 6, amidst great public expectation, the two former public prosecutors entered their appearance in court as private prosecutors in behalf of the victims' families.[361] Blanco and Campos had been serving as legal advisors to the Society of Jesus since late January 1991. In explaining their decision, the attorneys said they

---

360 *El Mundo*, April 16, 1991. *See also Diario Latino*, April 16, 1991; *Diario de Hoy*, April 17, 1991.

361 *See* "Por qué y para qué la acusación particular en el caso de los jesuitas?" *ECA, #510,* April 1991, at 327-334.

> are making a new appearance in this case, grounded in the same general concept of prosecution and with the same zeal as when we carried out these functions as public prosecutors in the Attorney General's office. But this time we hope to conduct our work with all the freedom that should be afforded each party to a case, without any adverse pressure on fundamental ethical principles and with the keen desire to breathe life into the country's legal system.[362]

In launching the private prosecution, the attorneys filed a 36-page brief which described the victims, their lives and work in the context of Salvadoran society, arguing that the UCA murders did not occur in isolation. The document sought to build the case that the killings resulted from a collective criminal plan that implied institutional responsibility on the part of the Armed Forces and, quite possibly, culpability on the part of the High Command.

Further, the document examined the case in the context of the responsibilities of the state to protect the lives of its citizens and indicated that the families of the victims would seek civil damages in the future. The prosecutors also asserted that in killing the Jesuits and the two women, the military not only violated the Salvadoran Criminal Code, but also international treaties ratified by El Salvador.

In analyzing the crime, the prosecutors offered two hypotheses: that the assassination was a massacre authorized by members of the High Command, or could be seen as a "collective criminal enterprise, the result of a criminal partnership at the core of the Armed Forces for the purpose of committing numerous crimes. . . ."

> Although the methodology is different in each of these two hypotheses, a single conclusion is inevitable: it is essential that full criminal responsibility be investigated at all levels of the Armed Forces hierarchy. This means considering a far broader range of responsibilities than those entertained to date.[363]

Predictably, the prosecutors' suggestions that those who masterminded the murder plot must be identified drew a vociferous response. On May 7, the day after the private

---

362 Private Prosecutors' Brief filed May 6, 1991, Fourth Criminal Court, at 2. The brief was reprinted in *ECA*, #511, May 1991, at 486-504.

363 Nota Informativa para la Prensa, at 3 (May 6, 1991). This document summarizes the private prosecutors' brief of the same date.

prosecutors entered their appearance in court, General Ponce threatened to initiate libel proceedings against the lawyers if they could not prove their allegations. According to the Salvadoran daily newspaper *Diario Latino,* General Ponce said that "the accusations made yesterday against the High Command of the Armed Forces are very serious and if these [attorneys] do not have proof of the complicity of the [High Command]" the military will "proceed legally."

Col. Inocente Orlando Montano, Vice-Minister of Public Security and a member of the High Command, criticized the private prosecutors in strong terms: "I believe the position of these two lawyers is rather unfair and irresponsible. As someone said on the television, they are eager for notoriety, perhaps looking for economic benefit, perhaps serving an ideological line, they have made statements that are reckless."[364]

Diario de Hoy, another Salvadoran newspaper which over the years has been harshly critical of members of the Society of Jesus as well as opposition political figures and others, described the document as "slander directed against an entire institution," referring to the Armed Forces.[365] In keeping with its history of threats, *Diario de Hoy* quoted unnamed sources who said that the "assassinated priests were in their time the intellectual authors of the atrocities that the guerrillas have committed since they unleashed the so-called final offensive and have caused the deaths of tens of thousands of innocent civilians."

In his homily on May 12, 1991 the Auxiliary Bishop of San Salvador, Gregorio Rosa Chávez, said he "lamented" General Ponce's comments and said they could cause "sick minds" to take action against the attorneys.

Eight-Day Evidentiary Period

The eight-day evidentiary period opened on May 23 and ended on June 3.[366] For the new private prosecutors, the period offered an opportunity to lay out their views on the case's progress and to request evidence which could further

364 *Al Día*, Channel 12, May 15, 1991, as printed in INSISTEM.

365 *Diario de Hoy*, May 7, 1991.

366 Following the judicial investigation, Salvadoran procedure allows for a final eight-day period during which both sides may submit additional evidence or witnesses may be called. Judge Zamora's decision to count only working days was criticized by both the defense and the *Fiscalía*.

the investigation, clear up contradictions and strengthen the judicial case.

Before opening the evidence period, Judge Zamora added the Scotland Yard report to the file, as well as the transcript of Major Buckland's videotape and a 200-odd page transcript of an interview with the major conducted in November 1990. Both documents had been received by Zamora while the case had been on appeal.

Neither defense attorneys nor the public prosecutors requested the appearance of any witnesses during the eight days; the judge called some witnesses on his own motion. The private prosecution made most of the requests, many of which were denied by Judge Zamora.

While viewing the period as a last chance to fill in some of the gaping holes in the judicial process before the trial, Father Tojeira was aware that dramatic revelations were unlikely.

> It's a short period of time. I don't expect spectacular results from this phase of the case, but I do believe that it's possible to round out the evidence. That is, to help make the existing proof against the defendants more solid, and also to contribute to establishing more clearly that there are intellectual authors.[367]

In the days preceding the evidentiary period, San Salvador was rife with rumors about ground-breaking evidence and surprise witnesses to be unveiled by the new private prosecutors. The military reportedly feared that damaging testimony would emerge.

The bulk of Judge Zamora's requests consisted of an attempt to ratify the SIU's extrajudicial investigation of the High Command's February 22, 1991 letter proposing the questioning of several officers. The judge requested sworn declarations from all the signatories to that February 22 letter. He also summoned two SIU agents who had conducted the recent investigation, Catarino Lovato Ayala and José Ismael Parada Cáceres.

Of those interviewed, only Capt. Luis Parada Fuentes, formerly of the DNI, had offered anything new, revealing that news of Father Ellacuría's death had been broadcast early on the morning of November 16 over a military radio frequency. Parada further indicated a closer relationship between the DNI and Benavides' Security Command, noting that the DNI had

---

367 *Buenos Dias*, Channel 12, May 29, 1991.

provided the Security Command with some five MX radios, possibly hooking up the Security Command with the intelligence agency's internal network. He said that the DNI and the Security Command "coordinated" their efforts, and mentioned that four DNI agents were stationed along the Southern Highway just beyond the UCA on November 15-16, 1989.[368]

Requests by the Private Prosecution

On May 22, Campos and Blanco presented a 50-page document which analyzed the investigation to date, the work of the Honor Commission, the judicial investigation and the role of the SIU. In the view of the attorneys:

> In synthesis, it has been adequately demonstrated in this case that there has been a conspiracy to systematically block the investigation, which to a great extent has been successful. In particular, members of the SIU, the Honor Commission and the High Command of the Armed Forces itself have given to history the lie as a method of defense, and the bitter experience that in our country it is not easy for the judicial branch to confront a powerful military apparatus which with great solidarity protects members of the army who are involved in crimes.

The private prosecutors submitted to the court 30 requests for information from the Ministry of Defense, 11 of which were rejected by the judge. Many of the requests sought records which the SIU should have secured early in the investigation. Among these were the identity of the unit attacked from inside the UCA, the alleged reason for the November 13 search; transcriptions of radio broadcasts threatening the Jesuits; circumstances of the desertion of the absent defendant, Jorge Alberto Sierra Ascencio; proof that the AK-47 murder weapon really belonged to the Military Academy; and the DNI's logbooks on operations and intelligence.

In several instances, Judge Zamora's reasons for rejecting investigatory steps seemed dubious. A Military Academy logbook covering the period March through November 1989 which the current Academy director said had not been destroyed was not solicited because according to the judge it had been burned. In fact, the record is ambiguous on this point. Judge Zamora refused to seek information concerning the deaths of

368 Testimony of Capt. Luis Parada Fuentes, Fourth Criminal Court, May 28, 1991.

two officers involved in the case who were killed under mysterious circumstances, because their deaths had "no relation to the events under investigation."[369] A similar request concerning the death of Atlacatl Corporal Santos César Cotta Hernández, allegedly involved in the murder of Father López y López, was also rejected.

Campos and Blanco also requested documents from President Cristiani and the National Police chief; the U.S. embassy was asked to provide the Buckland videotape. The embassy responded via the Foreign Ministry on June 20, 1991, offering to arrange a "private showing" of the video "to the Fourth Criminal Judge and judicial representatives who are a party to the case and who are authorized by the court that they have demonstrated their legal need to evaluate the evidence in this case." The embassy declined to turn the video over to the court, "out of respect for the privacy of Major Buckland."

According to Article 215ff of El Salvador's Criminal Procedure Code, witnesses who have contradicted one another can be brought face to face. The private prosecutors requested four such "confrontations," only one of which was granted by Zamora. In the end, even this did not occur, as one of the officers involved, Lieutenant Colonel Contreras Barrera, was undergoing training at the School of the Americas at Ft. Benning, Georgia.[370] Judge Zamora based his decision to deny requests for other confrontations on the argument that officers of this rank were exempt from testifying in person.

The testimony of six ranking Salvadoran officers was also sought by Campos and Blanco; the judge rejected all of these requests, based again on their exemption, except for General Larios, whom he said had already testified and was unlikely to

---

369 The private prosecutors had asked the Minster of Defense to provide information about circumstances surrounding the deaths of Captains José Alfonso Chávez García and Carlos Fernando Herrera Carranza of the DNI. Chávez García is the officer known as "*el Chileno*" who was implicated in the killings in one of the "Young Officers" letters. *See* note 319 *supra.*

370 Confrontations were sought between Generals Ponce and Zepeda; Colonels Guzmán Aguilar and León Linares; Colonels Machuca and Rivas (about the role of the Honor Commission and the SIU); and between Colonel Equizábal and Major Contreras Barrera (about who was responsible for the false report attributing the crime to "delinquent terrorists").

say anything useful.[371] On his own initiative the judge cited Guzmán Aguilar, and granted the request to cite Colonel Rivas, who failed to show up, claiming privilege; he subsequently submitted a written declaration. Declarations in writing were also received from Colonels León Linares and Machuca. Judge Zamora also asked for written statements from members of the High Command concerning their February 22, 1991 letter.

Despite the court's request that Major Eric Buckland return to testify, the paperwork involved in requesting his return through diplomatic channels was not expedited sufficiently to allow the court to schedule his testimony during the eight-day period. Anticipating the summons, the Pentagon had sent Buckland to Panama.

The private prosecutors also requested a series of new witnesses; the only request granted was for an expert military witness from Argentina. Judge Zamora turned down requests to interview the director of Radio Cuscatlán, which broadcast death threats against the Jesuits just before their murder; the director of *Diario de Hoy,* which published similar threats on numerous occasions; Colonel Elena Fuentes, the hard-line head of the First Brigade, whose members bragged about the Jesuit killings on a megaphone on November 16, 1989; and Colonel Inocente Montano, the Vice-Minister for Defense and Public Security.

Expert Witness from Argentina

Argentine Col. José Luis García, who taught for 14 years at his country's National Defense College and served as a witness in the trials against the leaders of the Argentine juntas, testified on May 27. His six-hour questioning covered how an army is organized and functions, especially during combat against irregular forces. Appearing that evening on the Channel 12 television news broadcast, Colonel García said

> . . . in an Army responsibilities are very clear. It is not possible that an intermediate command here could be the only one responsible for committing aberrant acts without there having been an immediate reaction by higher commands. It can happen that at an intermediate level, such as that of the Military Academy Director

---

371 Those officers who Judge Zamora declined to cite were Generals Ponce and Zepeda and Colonels León Linares and Machuca. All of these officers were later asked to submit written statements, though not all of the questions which the private prosecutors posed were included on the questionnaires.

> and his subordinates in operations, someone acts outside the rules and commits an aberrant act; this is possible. What is not possible is that the command at issue in this case, the security command that operated in the Military Academy, was not immediately investigated . . . and those who committed such a barbarity placed at the disposition of the justice system.

In his court testimony, García also said that the November 13, 1989 search of the Jesuit residence did not have the characteristics of a search for arms and terrorist hiding places, but of reconnaissance of terrain (*reconocimiento del terreno*).[372]

> A search to verify the presence of . . . the enemy, weapons, munitions deposits, or other signs which would confirm an enemy presence requires an operation that is designed with utmost precision. First you must conduct general reconnaissance to determine the enemy presence and eliminate the enemy in combat. Once sure that the terrain is free of the enemy, a search should be conducted of all potential hiding places for people as well as materiel. In order to do this it is indispensable that all locked buildings are opened.[373]

Defense attorneys and Salvadoran officers reacted defensively, calling his testimony "foreign intervention." Colonel Montano protested that

> . . . the intervention of foreign persons alien to the case coincides not with a legal role but a political one. The comments made by Colonel José Luis García, and this is the first time I have heard of this person, seem rather out of place, out of time and outside the circumstances. He is talking as if he were paid to do so, as if he were a person who was trying to damage the institutionality of the Salvadoran State, hurting the

---

372 Agreeing that the search "does not appear to have been meticulous," Scotland Yard cited the soldiers' descriptions of the "superficial" nature of the search and said the number of soldiers participating was too few to have dealt with the guerrillas reportedly inside the UCA. The search had "various characteristics that could contribute to this more sinister interpretation," observed the British detectives, suggesting support for the theory that the killers reconnoitered the site on November 13 for the November 15-16 murders. Scotland Yard, *supra* note 227, para. 1268-1269, at 357.

373 Testimony of Col. José Luis García, Fourth Criminal Court, May 27, 1991.

very Government of El Salvador, the administration of justice. . . .[374]

Colonel Benavides and Lieutenant Espinoza both were recalled on May 29, at the request of the private prosecution. Both vehemently declared their innocence. Benavides said he had a clear conscience, and that "I am the person most interested in having a full investigation."[375] Lieutenant Espinoza again denied that he had made any extrajudicial declaration, though his SIU statement appears in the court record. "All of us who are implicated in the Jesuit case are innocent," he told the press.[376]

Rather than presenting witnesses, the defense chose to impugn the victims and, by implication, to justify the crime. The defense requested that two right-wing diatribes against the Jesuits be included in the court record,[377] and also asked for the service records of the four officers charged. They also asked for a list of those killed by the FMLN since November 1989 as well as safehouses found in the neighborhood in which UCA is located.

Results of the Eight-Day Period

As noted, Judge Zamora denied many of the evidence requests made by the private prosecutors. Despite the High Command's public commitment to support the investigation, no member of the High Command appeared in court during the eight-day period, nor did any other military officer who could invoke privilege. For his part, Judge Zamora made no efforts to encourage officers to appear. Former SIU chief Colonel Manuel Antonio Rivas Mejía, then deputy director of the National Police, declined a summons to appear in court, though he had testified earlier. Nor did the military make any attempt to recall Lieutenant Colonel Contreras Barrera from the United States where he was in training. The officers' cursory written responses suggest they were impatient to put the case behind them.

---

374 Salvadoran television, May 28, 1991, *as cited in* INSISTEM.

375 *Prensa Grafica*, May 30, 1991.

376 *Diario Latino*, May 30, 1991.

377 F. Delgado, *La Iglesia Popular Nació en El Salvador: Memorias de 1972 a 1982*, at 42 (no date or publisher appears on the booklet, which circulated in late 1988) *and* A. Jerez Magaña, *La Infiltración Marxista en la Iglesia*, at 23 (Editorial Dignidad, Instituto de Relaciones Internacionales, San Salvador: 1989). For more on these books, *see supra* Chapter I: "Death to Intelligence."

In response to specific requests from the private prosecutors, General Ponce said he was unable to identify the unit posted at the main UCA gate on the evening of November 13, 1989 that identified Father Ellacuría, or to identify the unit that was fired on that day from inside the campus, the purported justification for the search. Although Ponce had earlier claimed in written testimony that the Atlacatl commandos had requested permission from the Joint Command before entering the UCA on November 13, the general now said he could not identify the officer who had sought authorization to conduct the search.

General Ponce also revealed that Col. Nelson Iván López y López, head of C-1 (Personnel) was at the helm of COCFA on the murder night, identifying as well those on duty for C-2 and C-3. He did not, however, clarify which members of the High Command were also present that night.[378] Some of the documents provided by the military in response to requests by the private prosecutors added important elements, such as the chain of custody of the M-60 machine gun and the AK-47s, and intelligence reports, or lack of reports, for the UCA area.

Letters Rogatory

One investigatory step granted by Judge Zamora was the questioning of nine U.S. citizens, six of them military advisors posted in El Salvador at the time of the murders, two embassy officials and the sister of Major Buckland. Buckland himself was added to the list when arrangements could not be made for his personal appearance during the eight-day evidentiary period. The testimony was recorded under a procedure known as letters rogatory, which allows for the gathering of evidence by a judge in a foreign country.

Those asked to answer a questionnaire submitted by Judge Zamora were:

- Col. Milton Menjívar, chief U.S. Military Advisor
- Maj. Stephen Donehoo, Assistant Army Attaché
- Capt. Carlos A. Puentes, advisor, psychological operations, Major Buckland's housemate and subordinate at C-5
- Lt. Col. Lanning Porter, Milgroup Intelligence Officer, advisor to C-2 (Intelligence) at Joint Command
- Maj. Douglas Richard Lewis, National Intelligence Training Officer

---

378 On October 23, 1990, Ponce had told the court that after meeting with President Cristiani late in the evening of November 15, "all members of the High Command remained in the COCFA until about 2:00 a.m. the following day."

- Lt. Col. William C. Hunter, Jr., Senior advisor to the joint staff, and Major Buckland's immediate superior
- Janice Elmore, political/military officer, U.S. embassy
- Richard J. Chidester, legal officer, U.S. embassy
- Carol Elizabeth Buckland, CNN reporter and sister of Major Buckland

All except Carol Buckland enjoyed diplomatic immunity, which they voluntarily waived.

On behalf of the Central American Province of the Society of Jesus, the Lawyers Committee asked to be present when the testimonies were recorded. The Jesuits believed that serious questioning of these diplomats concerning what they saw and heard in the days surrounding the killings might prove fruitful, given their responsibilities and contacts in El Salvador at the time. "If these people talked" Father Tojeira told the Associated Press, "they could help us more in the search for the intellectual authors than in confirming the guilt of the accused triggermen."[379]

Adopting a narrow interpretation of the law, the U.S. Justice Department rejected the Jesuits' request, explaining that the presence of the Jesuits or their representatives would have a "chilling effect" on the witnesses. The spokesman said the deponents had agreed to participate voluntarily and that this spirit of cooperation was predicated on the absence of the Lawyers Committee and the Jesuits.

A subsequent letter to the Lawyers Committee from the Justice Department's Criminal Division stated that "[c]onsistent with normal legal procedures, the proceedings will take place without the presence or participation of representatives of your organization." The letter continued: "To the extent you have additional questions, you are, of course, free to present them to the court in El Salvador and request that additional letters rogatory be issued." This was, of course, impossible, given that the evidentiary period had ended.

The Justice Department's decision, delivered on July 29, followed weeks of stonewalling on the part of the departments of Justice, State and Defense. "You guys have really paralyzed the lawyers up in Washington," an embassy official told the Lawyers Committee in July 1991. In a letter dated August 7, 1991, the General Counsel's office of the Department of Defense wrote to the Lawyers Committee saying the department had been "cooperating to the fullest extent possible with the investigation being conducted by Judge Zamora." Further, the

379 *El Mundo*, July 31, 1991.

General Counsel said he understood "that the Department of Justice has determined that attendance and participation by the Lawyers Committee on Human Rights [sic] at the questioning of the witnesses would not be appropriate. Accordingly, the Department of Defense will defer to the Department of Justice in this regard."

Speaking at a press conference in San Salvador, Father Tojeira said the decision by the U.S. government to deny the Jesuits a chance to cross examine the witnesses was another example of how the Bush Administration's repeated pledges to cooperate in the investigation never materialized. Tojeira said the "State Department of the United States is seriously slowing down the investigation of the case, preventing people who should be questioned about it from responding to questions that our representatives could make." [380]

A State Department spokesman told the Mexican news agency, Notimex, that the interviewers "would be provided details on the case and they will be prepared to pose follow-up questions, in order to ensure that all the questions be answered as fully as possible. This procedure is the quickest way to fulfill the judge's request." [381]

A review of the depositions indicates, however, that the interviewers did not pose follow-up questions and that important investigatory opportunities were missed. Present were attorneys for the departments of Defense, Justice and State. The Justice Department attorney read aloud the question to the witness, who had been given the questions in advance.

Numerous opportunities for follow up questions were overlooked, either by design or ignorance. Lieutenant Colonel Lanning Porter, an intelligence officer, revealed, for example, that his Salvadoran counterpart was at one time Colonel Benavides, yet Porter was not asked to expound on their relationship or his knowledge of the colonel. Legal officer Richard Chidester was asked, "Did Colonel Benavides provide you or anyone else with oral or written information" after the crime? Mr. Chidester answered simply, "He provided oral – he gave us an oral briefing as to what happened that night." [382] No one expressed interest in knowing what Colonel Benavides had

---

380 *Washington Post*, July 31, 1991. *See also Miami Herald*, July 31, 1991; *El Mundo*, July 31, 1991.

381 *Diario de Hoy*, Aug. 1, 1991.

382 Deposition of Richard Chidester, Aug. 6, 1991, *In Re Letters Rogatory From the Fourth Criminal Court Judge of San Salvador, El Salvador* (D.D.C. 1991).

told Salvadoran and U.S. officials in that early December 1989 encounter. At numerous points in the questioning the tape recorder was turned off, leaving gaps in the record when either the interviewer, the deponent or one of the attorneys attached to the State or Defense Departments wished to discuss something privately.

The U.S. government's attorneys were seemingly uninterested in the quality of the information recorded, and allowed several witnesses to provide useless answers.[383] Asked the names of embassy officials who formed a special working group on the murders, Mr. Chidester replied, "[e]mbassy agencies were represented on the group." Janice Elmore, who was present at the historic encounter in Colonel Ponce's office when Major Buckland and Colonel Avilés confronted one another, was asked to "describe in detail" what took place. Her response in full was as follows: "I'm going to describe some of the meeting. I don't remember all the details. I was not present for the entire meeting. While I was present, Col. Menjívar and Col. Ponce discussed it. Col. Ponce called Col. Aviles, who denied the allegations."[384]

While little was revealed in the depositions, they did bolster Major Buckland's account that he received information about Benavides' role in December 1989. The statements also confirmed that Colonel Rivas, accompanied by U.S. embassy personnel, visited Colonel Benavides in the Military Academy in early December 1989, something Rivas had denied under oath in October 1990 court testimony.

In the end, it was, as one Milgroup member put it, "a non-event." A review of the statements that were recorded in Washington in August 1991 confirms that by excluding questioners who knew the case and would insist on pursuing leads, the Bush Administration ensured that the letters rogatory became a meaningless exercise during which little useful testimony was recorded. With the submission of the statements taken pursuant to the Letters Rogatory to the Salvadoran court, the evidence period closed.

---

383 The closed, in-house nature of the proceedings made it difficult to determine in whose interests each attorney was acting. Technically, the Justice Department was acting on behalf of the Salvadoran court and should have ensured the most complete answers possible.

384 Deposition of Janice Elmore, Aug. 6, 1991, *In re Letters Rogatory From the Fourth Criminal Court Judge of San Salvador, El Salvador* (D.D.C. 1991).

CHAPTER IX: THE DENOUEMENT

(September 1991 to December 1992)

Once the evidence period had ended, final preparations began for the trial, or *vista pública.* [385] Stories immediately began to appear in the Salvadoran press that the long awaited day in court was imminent.[386] On September 6, the private prosecutors filed a civil action on behalf of relatives of the victims, the UCA and the Salvadoran Technical Education Society (SALVATED)[387] against the defendants and the State. The suit sought two million *colones* ($250,000) in damages for the 15-year-old son of the murdered housekeeper, Elba Ramos; compensation for the physical damages to the CRT, estimated at 363,345 *colones* ($45,420); and a symbolic one *colón* for the relatives of the five Jesuits born in Spain. Explaining the decision to file a civil suit, IDHUCA observed that

> The demand for indemnification is grounded in the obligation of the State to ensure the victim adequate compensation for human rights violations. It is evident that one can never repair the damage done by an assassination; nonetheless, the act of acknowledging responsibility and providing a just indemnification to the families of the victim should have a dissuasive effect on the State.[388]

The filing of a civil suit for damages stemming from a human rights crime was unprecedented in El Salvador. Father Tojeira stated the motivation simply: "What interests us is that the State assume its responsibility."

Reacting to the filing of the suit, defense attorneys argued that the State could only be held responsible for damages

---

385 For a more detailed account of the trial, *see* Appendix C, the report of the Lawyers Committee's trial observer, Prof. Robert Goldman of the Washington College of Law at The American University, Washington, D.C.

386 A banner headline across *Diario Latino* on Aug. 29, 1991, read "JURY TRIAL IN JESUIT CASE IMMINENT." Dr. Mauricio Gutíerrez Castro, the Supreme Court President, told *La Prensa Gráfica* on September 18 that the trial would be held before Christmas.

387 SALVATED is the legal entity which owns the Pastoral Center, which is the property of the Central American Province of the Society of Jesus, and not of the UCA.

388 "Caso jesuitas: la acción civil," *Proceso,* #486, Sept. 4, 1991, at 10.

caused by "public functionaries and employees," which in their view did not include members of the Armed Forces. "What they have requested is unconstitutional," said defense attorney José Adalfredo Salgado.[389] Yet the *Fiscalía*, representing the State, did not argue that the State could not be held responsible for damages caused by military men. Perhaps in anticipation of such a suit, Colonel Benavides had sold his home on January 2, 1990, the day that Major Buckland revealed his role.

On September 6, *Diario Latino*, citing a courthouse "leak," fixed the date for the criminal trial at September 20, further heightening the anticipation that had gripped San Salvador. In fact, plans were underway to stage the trial a week later. On September 24, the parties were called to the Fourth Criminal Court, where in the presence of the Papal Nuncio, Dr. Manuel Monteiro de Castro, the jury list was drawn by the chief defense attorney, Dr. Carlos Méndez Flores.[390] To ensure that an adequate number of jurors would appear when cited, Judge Zamora asked the parties not to publicize the trial date, which he then fixed at September 26. Dr. Méndez said he would not respect the judge's wishes, and said he planned to complain publicly that court authorities were more interested in notifying foreign observers than in keeping the Salvadoran people informed. Complaining that the trial had been moved up a day, Dr. Méndez said everything was being done "in a rush" and that "more is known abroad than in our own country about the decisions being taken concerning this case."[391] Specifically, Méndez was referring to the arrival several days earlier of a large Spanish observer delegation, which included the Under Secretary of Foreign Affairs; two official government observers (one a criminal law professor and the other a former ambassador to El Salvador); and five members of the Congress of

---

389 *El Mundo*, Sept. 11, 1991; *Diario Latino*, Sept. 17, 1991. Article 245 of the Constitution states: "Public functionaries and employees shall answer personally, and the State subsidiarily, for material or moral damages that they cause as a consequence of violating the rights consecrated in this Constitution." Yet Article 146 of the Criminal Code -- which exempts the State from civil responsibility in cases involving its employees -- has not been made consistent with the 1983 Constitution, which supersedes the Code. Article 271 of the 1983 Constitution provides that all secondary legislation shall be brought into harmony with the new Constitution by December 20, 1984, that is, one year after it took effect. For the most part, that did not happen and there are a number of such discrepancies.

390 While unusual, the court viewed the presence of the Papal Nuncio as providing credibility and security to the process.

391 *El Mundo*, Sept. 24, 1991.

Deputies, including the chairman of the Commission on Foreign Relations.

Hoping to improve chances that the jury would actually appear, the judge set the trial date for September 26, just two days after the jury list was drawn.[392] On September 25, the prospective jurors were notified in person by court officials accompanied by the Nuncio's secretary. It was only possible to notify eight of the 12 potential jurors. Seven of these appeared at the Supreme Court the following day. One pleaded illness and was excused. A jury of three men and two women was chosen by lot and seated; an additional woman served as alternate. Following Salvadoran practice, the parties did not seek to recuse any of the jurors.

Some aspects of how the trial was conducted were particular to the Jesuit case. The trial was held adjacent to the office of Supreme Court President Gutiérrez Castro, who also controlled access to the courtroom. The proceedings were broadcast live on television, yet discussions among judge, jury and the parties often took place out of earshot of both observers and television microphones.

Other aspects of the trial were determined by Salvadoran criminal procedure, or simply by custom. Often feeling intimidated, Salvadoran juries rarely exercise their right to question either the defendants or witnesses. Judge Zamora rejected the private prosecutors' request to include in the index to the case, the *minuta*, the testimony of Colonel Nelson Iván López y López, who had been belatedly identified as the officer in charge of the Joint Command's command central, the COCFA, on the night of the murders. Because López y López' testimony was not included in the *minuta*, the jury could not recall him as a witness.

The observer sent by the International Commission of Jurists found Salvadoran criminal procedure too wedded to formalisms and lacking flexibility. For the judge, the observer argued for a more active role during the trial:

> In the opinion of the observer, if it is desired that the administration of justice function adequately, criminal procedure must be modified to make it more flexible, less dependent on formalisms, and above all to modify the norms regulating the jury's functioning and forensic practice. The judge should also be granted a role in

---

392 According to Article 336 of the Criminal Procedure Code, not more than 15 days may elapse between choosing the jury list and the actual trial.

> orienting the jury. Without influencing the jury, he should bring to their attention certain substantive and procedural issues which affect criminal responsibility, the circumstances which modify criminal responsibility and the validity of evidence according to law. Given how the process functions now, it can easily end in an arbitrary result in any kind of case, not only in those which are particularly sensitive.[393]

The fact that the trial took place at all was a clear blow to the Armed Forces. Several ranking officers appeared among the defendants' families and a demonstration of the wives of top officers noisily interrupted the proceedings while a defense attorney delivered not so veiled threats to the jury. The entire trial was broadcast on Salvadoran television. For the first time, uniformed members of the Salvadoran Armed Forces – among them four officers – faced the public as accused murderers.

The oral arguments were highly emotional. The defense attorneys barely mentioned the crime itself. Throughout six hours of "*debate*," lawyers offering a joint defense of all nine military defendants focused on a few themes. One was an appeal to the jury to reject foreign intervention. It was stated several times in different ways that the trial was only being held because foreigners – *los cheles*, as Salvadorans refer to light-skinned people – had demanded a trial. In encouraging the jury to acquit the defendants, one attorney said, "We are going to work as Salvadorans and not capitulate to foreign pressure." Emphasis was placed on the fact that five of the murdered priests were Spanish born and that the courtroom was full of foreigners.[394]

---

393 *El Salvador, Una brecha a la impunidad, aunque no un triunfo de la justicia, El Juicio por el asesinato de los Jesuitas*, International Commission of Jurists, at 65 (Nov. 1991) [hereinafter ICJ].

394 The ICJ commented on the defense's argument, acknowledging that "it is true that there was great international concern that those who killed the Jesuit priests be investigated and prosecuted. And it was this international interest -- manifested in many ways, including by UN bodies such as the Subcommission on the Prevention of Discrimination and Protection of Minorities, by many NGOs, by many legislatures, including those of the United States and Spain -- that made the investigation and the trial possible. But in the opinion of this observer, it is now clear in the international fora, which concern themselves with making human rights effective, that demanding justice as a means to prevent future violations is not meddling nor engaging in `undue interference in internal matters of the State.' It is making international law work. On the other hand, various international treaties -- for example the American Convention on Human Rights and the International Covenant on Civil and Political Rights -- obligate

Another predominant defense theme was the inherent injustice in the trial itself. The defense lawyers stressed that Salvadorans ought to be grateful for the job the military had done throughout the decade-long "terrorist aggression." There were repeated references to the violence prevalent in Salvadoran society. Given this climate, they argued that the military had carried out their tasks in an almost heroic manner.

Following the closing arguments, the jury deliberated for nearly five hours. On September 28, Judge Zamora read aloud the 80 criminal charges that the jury had been asked to decide, followed by the jury's decision. Colonel Benavides was convicted on all eight murder counts. His deputy at the Academy, Lt. Yusshy René Mendoza Vallecillos, was convicted of the murder of 16-year-old Celina Mariceth Ramos, but acquitted on all the other murder charges. The remaining defendants, including the confessed triggermen, were absolved of all charges. All defendants were acquitted of terrorism charges.

Most of the independent observers who attended the trial later concluded that these verdicts defied both logic and the weight of the evidence. No witnesses had suggested that Colonel Benavides ever went to the murder site; Lieutenant Mendoza, by all accounts, did not fire his weapon. There is no more reason to link Mendoza to the killing of Celina Ramos than to any other murder. Celina died embracing her mother, Julia Ramos, the Jesuits' cook, with whom she shared a sofa bed that night. It is highly likely that whoever killed Celina also killed her mother. Argentine attorney Eduardo Luis Duhalde, who observed the trial for the American Association of Jurists, called Mendoza's conviction "totally incomprehensible factually and legally."[395] Amnesty International, which also sent a trial observer, was "concerned at apparent inconsistencies in the jury's verdict" and called the conviction of Lieutenant Mendoza "a seemingly inconsistent decision."[396]

---

the Republic of El Salvador to investigate, to prosecute human rights violations and to indemnify the victims or the families of those who have died. The Salvadoran State cannot avoid these obligations while it is a party to these treaties (Article 144 of the Constitution)." *Id.*, at 63-64.

395 *El Proceso por el Asesinato de los Sacerdotes Jesuitas en El Salvador*, Informe del Observador Eduardo Luis Duhalde, Asociación Americana de Juristas, at 78.

396 Amnesty International, *El Salvador: Army Officers Sentenced to 30 Years for Killing Jesuit Priests*, AMR 37/WU 01/92, at 5 (Feb. 7, 1992) [hereinafter Amnesty report].

The jury's unpredictable and illogical decisions led some to speculate that there must have been jury tampering. José María Tamarit, a criminal law professor who observed the trial at the request of the Spanish government, said the most "credible hypothesis" concerning the verdict was that someone "influenced [the jury] in one form or another . . . to predetermine its decision. It is not easy to imagine that a [Salvadoran jury] would spontaneously come up with such a solution . . . . The verdict fulfills all the conditions of a political decision."[397] Amnesty International concluded that "the verdict, which absolved those who pulled the trigger, and limited the investigation of chain-of-command responsibility, appeared to have been influenced by political considerations."[398]

Calling the trial "a grave disappointment," Congressman Moakley said he could not

> rule out the possibility that the military interfered with the outcome of the trial. The verdict is too inconsistent to be rationally explained and fuels suspicions that the jury may have been manipulated. My suspicions are based on conversations that I had with senior Salvadoran officials prior to the trial, during which they predicted the jury would convict the senior officer involved, Col. Guillermo Benavides, while letting the other defendants go.[399]

Congressman Moakley said he was also "disappointed by the silence" of the State Department and President Alfredo Cristiani.

> A terrible injustice has been done. The people who actually carried out the murders, who made these six respected and courageous men of God lie down in the dirt and shot them in the back of the head, the men who ordered that two women be riddled with bullets while they lay, moaning and wounded, in each others arms, have escaped justice. Where is the outrage? Where is the leadership? It is an old but true saying that for evil to triumph, all that is required is that good men do nothing.

---

397 *Informe sobre el proceso judicial por los asesinatos de Seis Jesuitas y dos Colaboradoras en El Salvador*, prepared by José María Tamarit for Ministry of Foreign Affairs of Spain, at 19-20 (1991).

398 Amnesty report, *supra* note 396,

399 *Washington Post*, Oct. 14, 1991.

An October 1 communiqué said the Central American Province of the Society of Jesus

> respects the jury's verdict and understands it as a condemnation of those who gave the order to kill the UCA Jesuits and leave no witnesses. In convicting Colonel Guillermo Alfredo Benavides and his assistant, Lieutenant Yusshy Mendoza, the jury wanted to underline that responsibility for this assassination must be found within the highest echelons of the Armed Forces. Consequently, the task remaining is the investigation of those who masterminded the massacre at the UCA.

San Salvador's Auxiliary Bishop, Gregorio Rosa Chávez, said the verdict set an ominous precedent. "It is very dangerous to acquit the triggermen because it could serve as a signal to others who may proceed in the same fashion in the future."[400]

By contrast, the U.S. State Department's spokeswoman, Margaret Tutweiler, called the conviction of Benavides "an historic achievement for the Salvadoran justice system and for the cause of human rights." Ms. Tutweiler said the conviction "sent an important signal that human rights violations by the security forces will no longer remain in impunity." Asked if Benavides' conviction indicated a coverup of the role of higher ranking officers, Ms. Tutweiler said that "if more evidence exists" the Salvadoran authorities should investigate. She added "that the United States had no knowledge of such evidence."[401]

An editorial in the October 1 issue of the Spanish newspaper *El Independiente* took a very different view. It was entitled, "The trial in El Salvador: A Farce." Under the headline, "Shame," another Spanish newspaper, *El País*, observed that the "formal aspects of the trial, characterized by the most ridiculous histrionics, have been a good example of the extent to which the exhibition of collective hypocrisy can be taken."[402]

Other observers noted the utility of the verdict from the military's point of view. "In short, the jury's decision approximated more the way military men reason than a civilian jury," commented the trial observer from the International Commission of Jurists.[403]

---

400 *El Mundo*, Sept. 30, 1991.

401 Reuters, *as printed in Prensa Gráfica*, Oct. 1, 1991.

402 *El País* (Madrid), Oct. 1, 1991.

403 ICJ, *supra* note 393, at 63.

Observers emphasized that the two convicted officers had been holding desk jobs at the Military Academy, without combat troops under them. Convicting them was less apt to stir up discontent among younger officers. The *tandona*, the large class from the Military Academy that has dominated the Salvadoran military in recent years, may have decided that it had to allow someone to be held accountable for this particular crime. The conviction of Colonel Benavides, a member of the *tandona*, was the price that had to be paid to keep U.S. aid flowing to El Salvador.

It is noteworthy that the conviction did not touch the powerful Atlacatl Battalion, the U.S.-created and trained elite unit that carried out the murders. The 1992 peace accord called for a vast reduction in the size of the army, with the elite battalions to be gradually disbanded. Yet the accord left open the question of whether current members of the Atlacatl and other battalions were to be reassigned or discharged. Convictions of skilled commandos would no doubt have been a blow to the morale of Atlacatl fighters.[404] "By exonerating the triggermen, the verdict leaves intact troop morale while weakening the rule of law," observed two attorneys from the Bar Association of San Francisco, who travelled to San Salvador.[405] While the International Commission of Jurists viewed the Jesuit case as a "breakthrough in the wall of impunity," it observed that "when the final result of a case is neither just nor conforms to the law, one must conclude that the trial was not just. In the [Jesuit] case, the result was essentially arbitrary."[406]

Ultimately, only time will tell just what lessons were learned from the trial, or if any precedent was set. The case undoubtedly served to highlight the justice system's structural problems, and provoked widespread questioning of El Salvador's current jury system. The observers from the Bar Association of San Francisco wrote that

> the consequences for future prosecutions are only moderately hopeful. The outcome here confirmed that it is possible to obtain convictions of military officers.

---

404 The Atlacatl Battalion was disbanded two months behind schedule, on December 8, 1992.

405 "Report of the San Francisco Observer Delegation to the Jesuit Murder Trial in El Salvador," submitted to the Bar Association of San Francisco, at 12 (Oct. 9, 1991) [hereinafter BASF report].

406 ICJ, *supra* note 393 at 64.

> However, the failure of such a "showcase" investigation and trial to produce convictions of the triggermen, and above all the clear limits placed on the investigation upward into the military hierarchy, signal to judges and prosecutors the limits of the permissible. The military has learned that the destruction of evidence, perjury, and stonewalling can be effective in reducing the likelihood of convictions.[407]

Developments Since the Trial

Following the jury trial, Judge Zamora still had to rule on certain lesser charges, which included planning and conspiracy to commit terrorist acts and charges related to the coverup of the crime. While the sentences for those convicted of murder should have been issued within 30 days, the period was extended to allow the judge to consider these lesser charges and for the evidence phase of the civil action requesting monetary damages. On October 31, 1991, the defense filed the first of two recusal petitions, citing Judge Zamora's admission during the trial that he once taught law at the UCA. The attempt to raise the issue at such a late date provoked angry impatience from the appeals court. It warned the defense team "to abstain from continuing to present petitions whose sole objective is to delay the process and complicate the matter."[408] Both recusal petitions were declared inadmissible.

The defendants who were acquitted were released from custody on October 3 and returned to active duty. Lieutenants Espinoza Guerra and Guevara Cerritos were released on their own recognizance (*bajo palabra*) on October 11, despite pending charges on the lesser offenses. They also returned to active duty. Only the two officers convicted on murder charges were expelled from the Armed Forces. They are now housed in specially prepared cells at Santa Ana prison. Defense attorney Adalfredo Salgado said high security cells had been prepared for the two officers because their lives might be in danger. The political prisoners' organization, COPPES, issued a press release reporting that soldiers of the Second Brigade were constructing an "exclusive apartment" for the officers.[409]

---

407 BASF report, *supra* note 405, at 12-13.

408 First Criminal Appeals Court, San Salvador, Nov. 20, 1991.

409 *See Diario Latino*, Oct. 9, 1991; *El Diario de Hoy*, Oct. 10, 1991.

Jesuits Request Investigation

On December 18, 1991, Jesuit Provincial José María Tojeira and UCA Rector Miguel Francisco Estrada presented a petition to the Salvadoran Legislative Assembly asking that a commission be appointed to investigate the "intellectual authorship" of the crime. Article 131, paragraph 32 of El Salvador's Constitution allows for the appointment of "special commissions to investigate issues of national interest. . . ." Father Tojeira had indicated the Jesuits' intention to file the petition during an address at the UCA on November 13.[410] Responding to Father Tojeira's announcement, the president of the Assembly, ARENA member Roberto Angulo, opposed the suggestion. He said that to comply with the Jesuits' proposal would "politicize" the case. He stressed that the matter belonged strictly to the courts.

The Jesuits' petition argued that resolution of the case was a "matter of national interest." It asserted that "inadequate" steps had been taken to investigate who gave the order to kill the priests. Accompanying the petition was a document offering some "logical evidence indicating intellectual authorship" of the crime. The judicial investigation, argued the Jesuits, produced a wealth of circumstantial evidence indicating that Colonel Benavides could not have acted on his own.

The ARENA majority in the assembly, including the rightist Authentic Christian Movement (MAC) and the Party of National Conciliation (PCN), voted against the Jesuit petition and therefore it did not pass. The opposition Convergence coalition and the Christian Democrats voted to appoint the commission. Referring to the recently negotiated peace settlement, ARENA members and their allies urged that bygones be bygones. ARENA deputy Raúl Peña Flores said it was "time to stop sowing hate. . . ."[411] Undeterred, Father Tojeira responded: "To ask that the truth of the Jesuit fathers' assassination be cleared up does not foment hate. Killing is what foments hate."[412] On January 10, the Assembly rejected the petition, refusing even to refer it to committee for further study. MAC member Guillermo Antonio Guevara Lacayo

---

410 *See* Tojeira, "El caso de los jesuitas dos años después," *ECA*, #517-518, Nov.-Dec. 1991, at 1034-1044.

411 *Diario de Hoy*, Dec. 18, 1991.

412 *El Mundo*, Dec. 19, 1991.

"said it was not the right moment to keep rubbing salt in the wound. . . . The crime is painful and well known by everyone, but now is the time to let the dead rest in peace."[413] Echoing the military's message, Renato Pérez of ARENA said "international Communism is relying on this crime in order to attack justice and the Armed Forces of El Salvador." Another ARENA deputy, Mauricio Zablah, invoked the Pope in rejecting the Jesuits request:

> In doing this they want to use the Jesuit case politically. John Paul II can forgive the person who wanted to assassinate him, but they don't. This is the line the Jesuit priests should take. These holy Jesuits are already buried, and by forgiving and forgetting they can be left in peace. This is a theme exploited by the forces of the left. We are members of the Legislative Assembly. The Jesuit case is already annoying, it has been exploited, we are not investigators. It's time to let these men rest in peace and not continue exploiting them.

Another ARENA member, Gloria Salguero Gross, objected to the proposal because it would set a "precedent" and "hundreds and hundreds of the families of the assassinated throughout the 10 years of war could come to the Assembly" asking for investigations.

On January 5, 1992, the Fourth Criminal Court announced it had accepted the withdrawal of the civil action filed by the victims' representatives. The Salvadoran government had offered an out of court settlement in December, providing an undisclosed compensation to Elba Ramos' son and covering expenses incurred in repairing the Pastoral Center.

Amnesty Follows Peace Accord

Early on New Year's Day 1992, representatives of the Salvadoran government and the FMLN signed a peace accord in New York City. The agreement had been nurtured to fruition by representatives of United Nations Secretary-General Javier Pérez de Cuéllar. The Secretary-General was anxious to finalize the text before he left office at the end of 1991. The accord called for a January 16 signing in Mexico City, and February 1 installation of COPAZ, the National Commission for the Consolidation of Peace,

413 These statements were recorded by a Lawyers Committee representative present in the gallery during the Assembly debate.

a multiparty body to oversee implementation of the peace accord and to propose language and concrete proposals on various issues. The ARENA government had argued that an amnesty was necessary in order for the FMLN members of COPAZ to even enter the country and participate in the commission's work, a position that was backed by the U.S. Department of State. Gathered in Mexico City in mid-January for the signing of the peace agreement, COPAZ met to work out the language.

The Legislative Assembly unanimously approved the amnesty decree in an extraordinary session late on Thursday, January 23. The law adopted permitted the granting of amnesty to all those persons who participated directly; as *autores mediatos*;[414] or accomplices in the commission of political crimes, common crimes related to political crimes, and common crimes committed by no less than 20 persons, prior to January 1, 1992, and excluding in all cases, the crime of kidnapping.

The decree also provided that amnesty was not to be granted to those who have been convicted by a jury for any of the crimes included in the amnesty. Nonetheless, rumors persisted in the weeks leading up to the amnesty that the military sought to include Colonel Benavides and Lieutenant Mendoza within the terms of the amnesty. According to Assembly member Mario Aguiñada of the opposition National Democratic Union (UDN), Gen. Juan Orlando Zepeda, the Vice-Minister of Defense, went to the Mexico ceremony specifically to lobby for their pardon. "He was there to win Benavides' freedom," said Aguinada.[415]

Throughout the fall and winter, various members of the U.S. Congress had written to President Cristiani and Secretary of State Baker, expressing their opposition to pardons for those convicted of the Jesuit murders. On November 4, 1991, eight prominent Republican Senators told Mr. Cristiani that a pardon for Colonel Benavides and Lieutenant Mendoza would be "unwise." Lest the message was not clear, the Senators concluded, "We respectfully urge you to carefully consider the negative impact a pardon of the Jesuit case murderers would have in the United States Senate."[416]

---

414 *Autoría mediata* includes some forms of what is known as accomplice and accessory criminal responsibility. The Spanish term does not seem to have an exact English equivalent. The crime is defined in Articles 44 and 46 of the Salvadoran Criminal Code. *See* note 351 *supra*.

415 *Los Angeles Times*, Jan. 24, 1992.

416 Letter to His Excellency Alfredo Cristiani from Senators Bob Dole, John H. Chafee, James M. Jeffords, John McCain, Bob Packwood, Alan K. Simpson, Mark O. Hatfield, Bill Cohen, Nov. 4, 1991.

Sentencing Decision Issued

Judge Zamora announced his sentence on January 24, one day after the amnesty decree and four months after the verdict. Colonel Benavides and Lieutenant Mendoza both received the maximum 30-year sentence for murder. Benavides was also convicted for the crime of intent and conspiracy to commit acts of terrorism. Lieutenant Mendoza was also given a three-year term for destruction of evidence and for the same terrorism charge, to be served concurrently. Lieutenants Espinoza and Guevarra Cerritos were sentenced to serve three years for intent and conspiracy to commit acts of terrorism. This is the first time a member of the Salvadoran Armed Forces has been charged or convicted, on terrorism charges; formerly only FMLN members had been so charged. Col. Carlos Camilo Hernández was sentenced to a three-year term for destruction of evidence – for ordering the burning of the Academy logbooks. Should these convictions be upheld on appeal, these men should automatically be discharged from the military.

The defense attorneys were formally notified of the sentence on Monday January 27. Citing "irregularities in the investigation," they appealed the sentence on January 30, sending the case to the *camara,* or appeals court, where it is still pending.

Jesuits Request Pardon

On November 16, 1992, the third anniversary of the murders, the Central American Province of the Society of Jesus issued a communiqué indicating the Jesuits' intention to request a pardon for Colonel Benavides and Lieutenant Mendoza. The communiqué stated:

> The reasons that motivate us are the following. Having from the very first given Christian forgiveness, we conditioned a legal pardon in the Jesuit case on a process of truth and justice. We believe that with respect to these two persons, truth and justice have been sufficiently established and what remains is a legal pardon, which we will request in the next few days.

The Jesuits also reiterated that they would not oppose a pardon in the case of the intellectual authors of the crime, but that those who ordered the murders must also go through a process of truth and justice. On December 16, 1992, Father Tojeira wrote to Roberto Angulo, President of El Salvador's Legislative Assembly, requesting a pardon for the two convicted officers. The Jesuit Provincial also wrote to President Alfredo Cristiani, asking him to support the request.

On December 9, 1992, Father Tojeira challenged General Ponce to debate him publicly on the question of the existence of additional, as yet unnamed, intellectual authors of the UCA murders. In his most direct attack on the Jesuit Provincial in the three years since the killings, General Ponce called Tojeira "cynical" and the entire case a "political game."[417] "I'm not going to lend myself to any propagandistic show," said General Ponce. "Lamentably, Father Tojeira is a foreigner and maybe he does not know well or has forgotten that in our country there are laws and legal procedures which is the forum in which the guilt of a person should be proven."

417 *Diario Latino*, Dec. 9 & 10, 1992; *Diario de Hoy*, Dec. 10, 1992.

CHAPTER X: WASHINGTON"S MIXED MESSAGES

The assassination of the Jesuits provides an occasion to purify two things in El Salvador: 1) the radical sectors of ARENA, the death squads and 2) the radical sectors of the military, those who killed the Jesuits. Cristiani has this big opportunity, but he can't do it alone.... He needs external support to achieve this "purification." The U.S. government has the capacity to support this process, but I don't think the government of the United States has the political will to achieve this "purification." As an example of this, just look at their signals on the Jesuit case.... If the U.S. government could have gotten away with blaming the Jesuit murders on the FMLN, they would have done so.

Monsignor Arturo Rivera Damas
Archbishop of San Salvador
February 1990

Throughout the Jesuit case, U.S. officials have sent a series of mixed messages, with some branches of the government working against the efforts of others. The work of Congressman Moakley and his task force, which sought consistently to establish the full truth, was at times undermined by Administration officials. Statements by representatives of the U.S. embassy in San Salvador also sent mixed messages which undermined the investigation. Some five days after the crime, U.S. Ambassador William Walker met with Father Tojeira at the Jesuit Curia. Father Tojeira told the ambassador that he believed the Salvadoran Armed Forces had killed the priests, to which Walker reportedly replied that the action must have involved "a special unit over which we have no control." Yet the ambassador and other U.S. officials continued to suggest publicly that the killers could just as easily have been the FMLN. In Washington on January 2, 1990, Mr. Walker told Congressman Moakley that the Jesuits could have been killed by FMLN guerrillas wearing Salvadoran Army uniforms. According to Moakley, Walker said, "anybody can get uniforms."[418] What the ambassador did not know but soon learned, was that his staff in San Salvador had confronted Colonel Ponce with Major Eric Buckland's revelation implicating Colonel Benavides in ordering and supervising the commission of the crime.

418 *New York Times*, Jan. 16, 1990.

Before Buckland came forward, the embassy's legal officer Richard Chidester, who functioned as the point person within the embassy on the Jesuit case, argued that guerrilla combatants could have slipped through Army lines by traveling along a ravine, occupied the UCA campus for several hours and then killed the Jesuits. He maintained this theory despite the fact that the killers used an inordinate amount of firepower, shot bullets from an M-60 stationary machine gun, set fire to the building, shot off flares, etc., all in an area under military control and without being detected by Salvadoran soldiers or by those on duty at DNI intelligence or Joint Command headquarters, both less than half a mile away. Once Colonel Benavides was implicated in the crime, Mr. Chidester substituted Benavides for the guerrillas, using the same *barranca* (ravine) theory to explain how Benavides' men could have reached the UCA without being detected by the some 300 other troops stationed around the campus. Under this revised scenario Chidester acknowledged that Colonel Benavides was involved, but argued strenuously that he was acting on his own and not following higher orders.

U.S. officials never aggressively pursued the question of whether top officers, especially General Ponce, were involved in the crime, vociferously rejecting the notion publicly, despite information to the contrary which made its way to the embassy. The Administration's attitude is summed up in the comment one top ranking U.S. official made to the Lawyers Committee: "You asked for a colonel and we gave you a colonel. What more do you want?" The embassy left then Colonel Ponce dangling as defense minister-apparent for months, refusing to support his candidacy until his name was cleared in the Jesuit case. Finally in September 1990, Ponce acceded to the post anyway, when he was ultimately viewed as the lesser of several evils. Some on the far-right had promoted the candidacy of Air Force chief Gen. Juan Rafael Bustillo, who Congressman Moakley believes masterminded the Jesuit murders. Others favored Col. Carlos Alfredo Rivas, said to be a confidante of Maj. Roberto D'Aubuisson, the late ARENA leader known as the "father of the death squads."

Unwillingness to Follow U.S. Leads

U.S. officials repeatedly stated their desire to establish the full truth. Yet of the scores of U.S. personnel in El Salvador, only one came forward to share information about the case. And given how Major Buckland's allegations were handled, it is understandable that others were hesitant to cooperate. At no point did the United States attempt to seriously survey its own personnel for what they might have seen and heard going on around them in the days surrounding the assassination. U.S. trainers were scattered throughout the Salvadoran Armed Forces. The CIA has a significant presence in El Salvador, and its agents are attached to many Salvadoran units, including DNI intelligence and San Salvador's First Brigade. The CIA was historically close to El Salvador's Air Force and its longtime chief, Gen. Juan Rafael Bustillo. U.S. military advisors had an office just outside the COCFA, the military's command central in Joint Command headquarters, where at least one American was on duty at any given time and usually two at night. President Cristiani mentioned the presence of two U.S. advisors during the briefing he was given as the UCA operation was unfolding.[419] Both U.S. civilian and military personnel taught at the Military Academy. One U.S. official, Amado Gayol, was among the first outsiders at the murder site that morning. Yet, no Americans offered any testimony, and at times U.S. officials actively took steps to block efforts to obtain information from U.S. citizens.

One example of Washington's unwillingness to follow investigatory leads involving U.S. citizens concerns the 13 members of the U.S. Special Forces unit from Ft. Bragg, North Carolina, who trained the Atlacatl commando unit charged with the crime. Six members of the commando unit they were training were tried in September 1991. All were acquitted. The Green Berets were conducting a routine teacher-training exercise when the offensive broke out, and continued the program until November 13, when their students were sent to San Salvador. The Lawyers Committee repeatedly urged the Pentagon and the State Department to make these trainers available for questioning, believing that they could possibly shed light on the question of when the murder plot was launched.[420] "Lots of people were trained by the United States," a top ranking U.S. official told the Lawyers Committee in April 1990. "What's the point of pointing out that [the Jesuits' killers] were trained by `some Americans'? I wouldn't be surprised if Americans were training them. What's the relevance to the Jesuit case?"[421] In its report to Judge Zamora, Scotland Yard recommended that Salvadoran authorities

> investigate the U.S. instructors of the 7th Group of Special Forces to determine any useful information they might have about the emotional state [*animo*], conduct, morale and discipline of members of the Atlacatl Battalion that might be relevant to their supposed subsequent behavior.[422]

---

419 Testimony of President Alfredo Félix Cristiani Burkard, Fourth Criminal Court, Sept. 7, 1990.

420 *See* Lawyers Committee for Human Rights, Memo to the U.S. Jesuit Conference, *et al.*, 1990, at 17 (July 27, 1990).

421 Lawyers Committee interview, Department of State, April 18, 1990.

422 Scotland Yard, *supra* note 227, at 2769.

Despite this recommendation, the United States government never made these instructors available for questioning.

One indication that some U.S. personnel might have gleaned useful information from Salvadoran colleagues was the testimony of Maj. Samuel Ramírez, a U.S. advisor attached to the training center for immediate reaction battalions adjacent to Atlacatl headquarters. Having received a tip that he might have something to offer, the FBI interviewed Ramírez at Ft. Campbell, Kentucky on December 20, 1990. Ramírez stated that he worked closely with Lieutenant Espinoza, who served as a point of contact for U.S. trainers.[423] Ramírez also revealed that without authorization the Atlacatl commandos had taken with them to San Salvador night vision equipment belonging to the U.S. trainers.

While the Ramírez statement was recorded in December 1990, U.S. officials did not reveal its existence until it was learned that others knew of it. Having been told that Congressman Moakley was aware that the interview had occurred, Defense Department officials approached the task force staff, and finally shared the statement. The Congressman urged that it also be provided to Judge Zamora. During the eight-day evidence period in May-June 1991, the Department of Defense finally provided the court with a copy of Ramírez' statement, marked "SECRET Edited Transcript." The Pentagon has never provided a copy of the statement of a second U.S. officer interviewed by the FBI at the same time, reportedly because he slurred a prominent Salvadoran officer.

The Moakley Task Force

On December 6, 1989, Thomas Foley, Speaker of the U.S. House of Representatives, appointed a task force of 17 House Democrats to monitor the Jesuit murder investigation.[424] As chairman he chose Boston Congressman Joe Moakley, who had been introduced to the situation in El Salvador by refugees living in his district. Congressman Moakley and his staff took the mandate seriously – perhaps more so than House leadership intended – and set a new standard for congressional activities in the field of human rights. Throughout the case, task force staff visited El Salvador regularly

423 For more on Major Ramírez' contact with Espinoza, *see* Appendix D.

424 The group was officially named the Speaker's Special Task Force on El Salvador. Its members were: David Bonior, George Crockett, Dan Glickman, Lee Hamilton, Steny Hoyer, Barbara Kennelly, H. Martin Lancaster, Frank McCloskey, Dave McCurdy, Jim McDermott, Matthew McHugh, George Miller, Joe Moakley, John Murtha, David Obey, Larry Smith, John Spratt and Gerry Studds. The group is often called the "Moakley task force." Several Republican members of the House accompanied the task force during its February 1990 fact-finding mission to El Salvador.

and issued frequent reports and statements which served to move the case forward at critical junctures. In welcoming Congressman Moakley to the campus in July 1991, UCA Rector Miguel Francisco Estrada, S.J., highlighted the importance of the group's work.

> Over the last decade of civil war, the United States government has used its influence and pressure selectively, at times with good effect. But we had historical reasons to fear that, once the outrage had died down, Washington would lose interest in our Jesuit case and move on to other issues. The Moakley task force made such forgetfulness impossible. Its reports and the Chairman's public statements soon became front-page news in El Salvador as well as the United States. In April of 1990, the publication of the *Interim Report* changed perceptions in the United States of how the case was proceeding and who was to blame for blocking the legal investigation.[425]

The Salvadoran Armed Forces itself provided proof of the effectiveness of the task force's work following Congressman Moakley's July 1, 1991 speech to an overflow crowd in the UCA's auditorium. On that occasion, he re-emphasized themes that had come to characterize the task force's view of the case:

- He rejected the notion that the murders were the "acts of individuals." Moakley concluded that the Armed Forces as an institution bore responsibility for the crime. "General," the congressman said, addressing himself directly to Defense Minister Ponce, "believe me, you have an institutional problem."

> . . . you have an institutional problem when it is the institution that instills fear in potential witnesses; when it is the institution that teaches its officers to be silent, to be forgetful, to be evasive, to lie; when it is the institution that demands loyalty to the armed forces above loyalty to the truth or to honor or to country.

- Moakley charged that an institutional coverup had been orchestrated, including efforts to implicate the FMLN at the crime scene; a phony firefight; and evidence withheld and destroyed. Congressman Moakley concluded that "even the special military Honor Board appointed by President Cristiani to review the case lied about it."

- The Congressman stressed that the whole truth must be established. "Without the truth, the Armed Forces will never be

---

425 "Welcoming remarks by Father Miguel Francisco Estrada, S.J., Rector of the University of Central America (UCA), San Salvador, El Salvador, July 1, 1991," *as cited in Proceso*, #480, July 3, 1991.

cleansed of its responsibility for this crime, and for shielding those involved in it. Without the truth, this government cannot lay claim to truly democratic institutions. Without the truth, the argument that those in opposition to the government should lay down their arms is undermined. Without the truth, the path towards peace in El Salvador will grow steeper still."

The Armed Forces, supported by ranking ARENA politicians, reacted quickly and vehemently to Congressman Moakley's message. The next day, a headline in *Diario Latino* read, "Moakley Has No Proof, Says Ponce." The Armed Forces took out a paid advertisement in several newspapers on July 9, "categorically rejecting the accusations made by Congressman Moakley."

> Evidently, the critics find it easier to make accusations based on anonymous witnesses or secret informers than to take steps to produce authentic evidence that helps clear up the facts; it is ironic that at the same time that they solicit the testimony of unknown soldiers who they say have some information, they do not provide the names of their secret informers, they spread rumors and unfounded accusations against the armed institution.[426]

The military said it considered "these actions as the start of a propaganda campaign destined to negatively influence the allocation of military aid to El Salvador . . . ."

President Cristiani told the foreign press that he shared the military's views. "This was not an institutional crime," he said, "but carried out by members of the Armed Forces who acted on their own." Mr. Cristiani told the Spanish newspaper *El Sol* that "if more people were involved in this, we don't know about it."[427] The remarks of San Salvador mayor Dr. Armando Calderón Sol, who is also the ARENA party president and a presidential hopeful, received wide coverage. The July 14 headline in the newspaper *Latino* concerning his remarks read: "ARENA Offended by Moakley's Speech." The paper quoted Calderón saying that "El Salvador deserves respect." The mayor asked that Moakley "legislate in his own country, and not in ours." *El Diario de Hoy* reported on July 11 that Dr. Calderón Sol "publicly demanded of Moakley that he `not involve himself in El Salvador's internal affairs nor accuse the Armed Forces without having any proof'."

> As a Salvadoran and as a nationalist I have sufficient moral authority and courage to tell any North American senator that he shouldn't come here trampling on

426 *See e.g. Diario Latino* July 9, 1991.

427 *El Sol* (Madrid), July 8, 1991. *See also* Notimex, July 4, 1991, *as printed in El Mundo*.

> Salvadorans. They've been elected by North American voters and we Salvadorans elect our deputies and representatives. I think you have to remind these senators of this now and then because they forget it, given that they are arrogant simply because they have technological and economic superiority.

Congressman Moakley Names Names

While the military's reaction to the congressman's speech in July 1991 was strong, it paled in comparison with the military's assault on Moakley following a statement he issued on November 18, 1991. In this statement, made shortly after the second anniversary of the murders, Mr. Moakley released information he had received from confidential sources indicating that top Salvadoran officers had decided to kill the Jesuits at a meeting on the afternoon of November 15, 1989, just hours before the UCA operation. He reported that among those who attended the meeting at the Military Academy were Gen. René Emilio Ponce, then chief of staff and now Defense Minister; Gen. Orlando Zepeda, Vice Minister of Defense; Col. Francisco Elena Fuentes, then head of the First Infantry Brigade in San Salvador; Gen. Juan Rafael Bustillo, the longtime Air Force chief who abruptly and unexpectedly resigned his command just six weeks after the crime; and Col. Guillermo Alfredo Benavides, the director of the Military Academy who was ultimately convicted for the murders. According to Congressman Moakley, "[r]eportedly, the initiative for the murders came from General Bustillo, while the reactions from the others ranged from support to reluctant acceptance to silence."[428] In support of this conclusion, Congressman Moakley offered *inter alia* the following evidence:

- "an allegedly eyewitness account of the meeting by an individual known to have been present at the military school that afternoon";
- "confirmation by another individual that the officers listed above were at the military school on the afternoon of November 15";
- "the secret destruction, by military officers, of the logs indicating the identity of those who came and went from the military school that afternoon";

428 Statement of Rep. Joe Moakley, Chairman of the Speaker's Task Force on El Salvador, Nov. 18, 1991, at 4.

- an allegation that General Ponce was told in January 1990 that the logs were destroyed, a fact which he concealed from the investigating judge;

- a report that Colonel Benavides told Academy officers on the night of November 15 that he had "received the green light" to conduct an operation against the Jesuits;

- another report that on the same night, General Bustillo told fellow Air Force officers that a decision had been made to kill Father Ellacuría;

- evidence that a U.S. military advisor was told by a Salvadoran officer on the afternoon of November 15 that "something was going to go down at the UCA" that night;

- additional evidence that one of those later tried for the murders confessed his role to his commanding officer in mid-December 1989. According to this evidence, General Ponce was notified of the role of this Salvadoran military officer, but he did not pass this information on to investigators.[429]

Congressman Moakley concluded "that it is possible – not certain, but very possible – that senior officers other than Colonel Benavides ordered the murders. [. . . .] I personally find this version of events more credible than the alternative, which is that Colonel Benavides acted on his own, notwithstanding the chain of command, and took upon himself the awesome responsibility for these crimes."

El Salvador's senior military officials reacted harshly to Congressman Moakley's allegations. They declared their innocence, demanded proof and decried the "politicization" of the case. According to the Salvadoran daily newspaper *Diario de Hoy*, General Bustillo said that though Moakley is a self-described conservative, he is in reality on the side of the leftists.[430] "Moakley is a politician without scruples or professional ethics who respects neither individuals nor institutions," said Bustillo.

Col. Francisco Elena Fuentes, whose First Brigade troops have been implicated in some of the Army's worst human rights violations, said Moakley has a notoriously close relationship to the FMLN, "to the point that there is a suspicious coincidence between the declarations of the terrorist leader Joaquín Villalobos

---

429 *Id.* at 5.

430 "Moakley is a Liar, Affirms General Bustillo," *Diario de Hoy*, Nov. 22, 1991

and the honorable Mr. Moakley."[431] In a press communiqué Elena Fuentes charged that during visits to El Salvador the congressman spent most of his time with "sectors allied with the guerrilla strategy of destruction of the FMLN." The colonel said he would hold Congressman Moakley "responsible for any verbal or physical attack on my family or on me." On the afternoon of the assassination, First Brigade sound trucks drove around San Salvador announcing, "Ellacuría and Martín-Baró have fallen. We are going to continue killing communists!" General Bustillo and Colonel Elena Fuentes, who was reassigned in mid-January 1992, said they were considering a slander suit against Congressman Moakley.

Generals Ponce and Zepeda held a press conference on November 19 to refute the charges, which they attributed to "internal political problems among the congressmen."[432] They also released an Army communiqué saying, "It is totally illogical that persons who supposedly were inside the Military Academy on the afternoon of November 15 who are said to have verified that the meeting took place but who did not participate in the meeting could have knowledge of what the meeting was about and what was decided during that meeting."[433] The wording is curious, especially in light of an exchange between General Ponce and a journalist at the press conference:

> Q: You also deny that [the meeting] took place at the Military Academy?
>
> A: I deny it categorically because I was not at the Military Academy. I was here at my command post at Joint Command headquarters.

The government of President Alfredo Cristiani issued a communiqué in Salvadoran newspapers on November 19. Without naming Congressman Moakley, the government criticized "persons or groups" who have the "evident goal of manipulating politically and attacking personalities of the Armed Forces and the institution itself. This has been done with absolute irresponsibility, with no foundation and based on purely partisan speculation."[434] In Washington, State Department spokesman Richard Boucher said that Congressman Moakley's charges provided "accusations but no direct evidence."[435]

---

431 *Diario de Hoy,* Nov. 21, 1991. Joaquín Villalobos of the ERP, a faction of the FMLN, was a top guerrilla military strategist throughout the war.

432 *Diario de Hoy,* Nov. 20, 1991.

433 Armed Forces communiqué, Nov. 19, 1991, *as cited in Diario de Hoy,* Nov. 20, 1991.

434 *See e.g. La Prensa Gráfica, El Mundo, Diario de Hoy,* Nov. 19, 1991.

435 UPI, Nov. 18, 1991, *as cited in Diario de Hoy,* Nov. 19, 1991.

Lucía Barrera de Cerna

A series of incidents occurred within a week of the Jesuit murders which set the stage for how the U.S. government would later handle the case. Several of these incidents involved an eyewitness to the army's presence at the UCA, Lucía Barrera de Cerna. Mrs. Cerna was a housekeeper for the Jesuits and the UCA who sought refuge in an unoccupied UCA residence on the night of November 15-16, 1989. She had fled her family's home in the war-ridden neighborhood of Soyapango with her husband and young daughter.[436] Awakened by the sound of gunfire inside the campus, Mrs. Cerna crept to a window overlooking the entrance to the murder site where she saw five men in military uniform. At 6:00 a.m. when curfew was lifted, Mrs. Cerna covered the short distance to where the bodies were lying, leaving the scene immediately in order to inform Jesuit Provincial José María Tojeira of the murders.

Mrs. Cerna's testimony was subsequently recorded in the presence of court officials at the Spanish embassy on November 22, 1989 and the following morning at the French embassy in San Salvador. The Jesuits arranged for the protection and departure of the Cerna family in cooperation with French and Spanish diplomats. The French State Secretary of Humanitarian Affairs, who happened to be in El Salvador at the time, agreed to accompany the family to Miami, which the Cernas had chosen over sanctuary in Spain or France.

At approximately 1:30 a.m. on the day the Cernas were scheduled to leave, Father Tojeira received a telephone call from U.S. embassy legal officer Richard Chidester. The Jesuits had not notified U.S. embassy officials of the Cernas' travel plans. Mr. Chidester offered to accompany the family to Miami. Father Tojeira told Mr. Chidester that this would not be necessary since they would be accompanied by European diplomats and met by the French and Spanish consuls in Miami, who would then turn the Cernas over to Jesuits in Florida. After Mr. Chidester insisted on accompanying the Cernas in order to facilitate their entry into the United States, Father Tojeira finally agreed.

The completion of Mrs. Cerna's judicial testimony on November 23 took longer than expected and by the time the entourage reached Comalapa Airport, the TACA flight had already departed, though the Salvadoran airline had promised to hold the plane for the Cernas. Several hours passed before a French military

436 For a more complete account of what happened to Mrs. Cerna and her family, *see* Lawyers Committee for Human Rights, "The Jesuit Murders: A Report on the Testimony of a Witness" (Dec. 15, 1989).

jet was diverted from Belize to pick up the party. Father Fermín Saínz, the Jesuit who directs Loyola Center, had accompanied the family to the airport and waited with them. During the hours of waiting, U.S. Ambassador William Walker, Mr. Chidester and Ed Sánchez, an FBI agent, arrived at the airport. The U.S. diplomats got into an argument with the French diplomats, who saw no reason for the Americans to be on the flight. In the end, Mr. Chidester and his FBI colleague were included in the group accompanying the Cernas to Miami. Though U.S. officials played no role in preparing the Cernas' departure, Ambassador Walker later defended what had happened by telling a U.S. reporter that the "second objective [of sending Lucía Cerna abroad] was to find out as much as she possibly knew – what she saw, what she heard the night that the Jesuits were killed."

While Mr. Sánchez was introduced to Father Saínz as an FBI agent, U.S. embassy officials had made no mention of plans to involve the FBI to Father Tojeira. Mr. Walker did mention the possibility of changing Ms. Cerna's identity for her own protection in the United States. In Miami, the Cernas were taken through immigration by U.S. officials and ultimately taken to a hotel where they were held by the FBI for a week of incommunicado questioning.[437] According to what the Cernas subsequently told the Lawyers Committee, the questioners suggested Mr. Cerna had ties to the FMLN, that he was "effeminate," and insinuated that his wife might have had sexual relations with the Jesuits. Intimidated and wishing to end the ordeal, Mrs. Cerna recanted after four days in FBI custody, saying she had seen no soldiers on the campus on the murder night, and indeed, had not even gotten out of bed.[438] "They pressured me and they pressured me," Mrs. Cerna told the Lawyers Committee on December 3, 1989, the day she was finally released to the Jesuits. "They pressured me until I couldn't stand it any more."

Mrs. Cerna repeatedly failed lie detector tests on the basis of her revised story. Lt. Col. Manuel Antonio Rivas Mejía, the SIU chief, also participated in the questioning, leaving San Salvador in the crucial early days of the Jesuit investigation.[439] Neither Mr. Chidester nor FBI agents told the Cernas that Lieutenant

---

437 As soon as they learned of the Cernas' arrival in Miami, U.S. Jesuit officials informed the State Department that they were prepared to take responsibility for the family as soon as they were released to their care. When asked when the release could occur, State Department officials indicated that the FBI needed a period of time to perform a risk assessment to determine the level of protection the Cernas would require. *Id.* at 16-17.

438 For an account of the Cernas' questioning by the FBI, *see id.* at 19-31.

439 On the SIU's performance in the first period, *see supra* Chapter III: "The Myth of Good Police Work."

Colonel Rivas was a Salvadoran officer. Admitting he had not identified Rivas, Mr. Chidester told a visiting U.S. church group in February 1990 that to have done so would have frightened the Cernas unnecessarily.[440]

U.S. officials then began to leak news of Mrs. Cerna's recantation to the press, saying that she admitted having lied. Further, these officials spread the story that Mrs. Cerna had been coached by María Julia Hernández, director of the human rights office of the Archdiocese of San Salvador, *Tutela Legal*. President Cristiani told reporters at a December 9, 1989 news conference that Mrs. Cerna was lying. In Washington, Mr. Chidester proposed to U.S. Jesuit officials that they hold a joint news conference to announce that Mrs. Cerna now admitted she had seen nothing on the murder night.

Angered at the attack on Ms. Hernández and the attempt to discredit Mrs. Cerna and her very limited testimony, Archbishop Arturo Rivera y Damas denounced the behavior of U.S. officials in uncharacteristically harsh terms. The Archbishop said Mrs. Cerna had been subjected to "aggressive and violent" interrogations, and continued: "Instead of being protected, as officials in the U.S. embassy in El Salvador had promised, she was subjected . . . to a veritable brainwashing and to the blackmail that she would be deported if she was not telling the truth."[441]

U.S. Ambassador William Walker responded by saying the "version that was provided to the Archbishop is incorrect" and that he was misinformed.[442] During this period, the U.S. embassy staff also summarily dismissed the substantial circumstantial evidence implicating the Salvadoran Armed Forces in the murders. They argued that the crime could just as easily have been committed by the FMLN.

In an attempt to further discredit the Cerna testimony, the embassy spread a variety of rumors about the couple. In the weeks and months following the incident various U.S. officials told the Lawyers Committee and others that

---

440 In August 1991 Mr. Chidester revised his story and said he "asked Lucia first if she would be willing to talk with investigating authorities from the government of El Salvador. She said that she would be willing to talk to those authorities. And at that point I called Col. Rivas and asked him if he would like to come up and talk to Lucia." Deposition of Richard Chidester, Aug. 6, 1991, *In re Letters Rogatory From the Fourth Criminal Court Judge of San Salvador, El Salvador*, at 8-9 (D.D.C. 1991).

441 *Los Angeles Times*, Dec. 11, 1989.

442 *Id*; U.S. embassy communiqué, Dec. 10, 1989.

- the Cernas made up the story because they wanted to emigrate to the United States;
- Jorge Cerna had been in a fight in which he killed a man, as evidenced by the scar on his face;
- Mrs. Cerna had four children by another man, whom she had abandoned in El Salvador, proof that she was an unfit mother; and
- the Jesuits and María Julia Hernández had persuaded Lucía Cerna to make up the story; Mrs. Cerna acquiesced out of devotion to the church and the Jesuits.

Mrs. Cernas' testimony was of course later corroborated by other information gathered by the court.[443] While her testimony itself was not central to the case, it helped shape public perceptions about the manner in which the U.S. government was responding to the case. For other Salvadorans with information to share, the message was clear. "Because of how the *Señora* was treated in the United States, we were afraid for our families," a night watchman at the UCA said.[444]

Major Eric Warren Buckland

A second early episode in the case which shaped perceptions about Washington's role in the investigation pertained to the testimony of U.S. Maj. Eric Buckland, the senior U.S. military advisor attached to C-5 (Psychological Operations) at the Joint Command.[445] His revelation unleashed a sequence of events culminating in President Cristiani's January 7, 1990 announcement that members of the Armed Forces were responsible for the murders. Like that of Mrs. Cerna, the handling of Eric Buckland became an issue in its own right, diverting attention from the core of his story. It was 10 months after the murders that Buckland first appeared before Salvadoran judicial authorities and 11 months before the second portion of his testimony was leaked out of

---

443 Scotland Yard said Mr.and Mrs. Cerna's testimony "has been confirmed." In the view of the British investigators, the couple "told the truth about what little they saw and heard of the crime." Scotland Yard, *supra* note 227, para. 1276, at 361.

444 Lawyers Committee interview, Feb. 1990.

445 The Moakley task force report commented on Major Buckland's relationship to his Salvadoran commander, Col. Carlos Avilés Buitrago, and the work of C-5: "Colonel Avilés and the American Major worked together closely. Their joint task, among other things, was to improve the image of the Salvadoran armed forces and demoralize the guerrilla opposition. In both respects, the murder of the Jesuits, and the accompanying suspicion of military involvement, was a serious problem." Interim Report, *supra* note 129, at 27.

Washington. To date, the complete account of what he knew and when he knew it has never been established. Major Buckland's story was revealed in bits and pieces over the course of nearly two years, making it impossible for investigators to piece it together and follow its leads. It is impossible to know with hindsight what turn the investigation might have taken had the court been aware of the full scope of his account in January 1990. Because of the manner in which it was revealed, observers only belatedly appreciated the significance of Major Buckland's role.

Major Buckland's story can be summarized as follows. About December 20, 1989, Col. Carlos Armando Avilés Buitrago, the C-5 chief, told Major Buckland that the Atlacatl commando unit, working out of the Military Academy, committed the killings at the UCA on the orders of Col. Guillermo Alfredo Benavides Moreno. Avilés said he had received this information from Col. Iván López y López, who in turn had been briefed by SIU chief Lt. Col. Manuel Antonio Rivas Mejía. The chain of information was thus as follows:

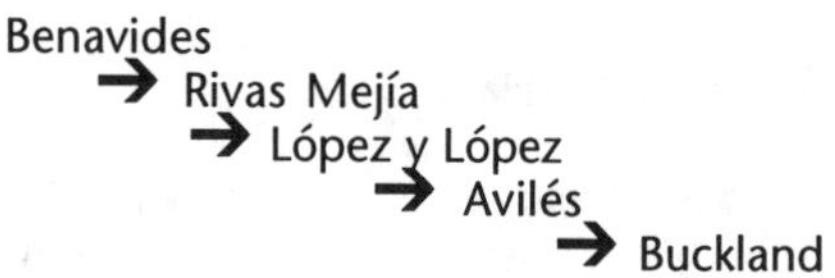

In a one-page statement written in San Salvador on January 3, 1990, Buckland said that,

> Colonel López y López had told [Avilés] that Lieutenant Colonel Rivas had told him Colonel Benavides had admitted his responsibility in the slayings of the Jesuits. Again – when the investigation of the killings had started Colonel Benavides had approached Lieutenant Colonel Rivas and said something to the effect of, "I did it. What can you do to help me?" According to Colonel Avilés, Lieutenant Colonel Rivas was scared and did not know what to do. As a result, the investigation slowed and eventually, Colonel López y López went to talk to Lieutenant Colonel Rivas. During the conversation Lieutenant Colonel Rivas told Colonel López y López about Colonel Benavides' comments.[446]

Avilés had emphasized that Buckland was only to make use of this information on a "Break in Case of Emergency" basis. According to Buckland, Avilés said, "In the event the Jesuit investigation did not unfold properly or if he (Avilés) should be

446 Statement of Maj. Eric W. Buckland, San Salvador, Jan. 3, 1990 (on file at Lawyers Committee for Human Rights).

killed, then it was his desire that this information be made available to the appropriate authorities."[447] When asked if Colonel Ponce knew, Avilés said he "believed that he did, but wasn't sure. [Avilés] did not feel that it was his place to tell him," Buckland said in his written account of the conversation. Colonel Avilés said that "nothing could be done until the investigation was completed." In retrospect, Buckland told his superiors that he assumed that the Salvadoran investigation would proceed apace and that arrests were imminent.[448] Buckland shared the information about Colonel Benavides with his sister, first in a telephone call and subsequently in more detail in a letter dated December 25, 1989.[449] Buckland said he also told his U.S. roommate, Capt. Carlos Puentes, on December 28.

It was some 12 days later when Major Buckland first mentioned the conversation to his immediate superior, Lt. Col. William C. Hunter, senior U.S. advisor to the Joint Command. Major Buckland told Colonel Hunter that he had learned of Benavides' role in the crime from his Salvadoran colleague, Colonel Avilés. Buckland could not remember the date on which the conversation allegedly took place, but he and his superiors ultimately placed the conversation on December 20, 1989. Buckland recalled in the videotaped version of his statement: "So on the 2nd of January, Colonel Hunter, for some reason, God, had the occasion to walk up into my office." The conversation took place in Buckland's office in the annex at Joint Command headquarters in the early afternoon of January 2, 1990.

Lieutenant Colonel Hunter immediately went to the U.S. embassy and briefed Col. Milton Menjívar, the MilGroup

---

447 Sworn statement of Maj. Eric Warren Buckland to the FBI, Jan. 11, 1990, Washington, D.C., at 4 (on file at Lawyers Committee for Human Rights).

448 Buckland recalled: "I asked Colonel Avilés, `Why don't they arrest Benavides right now?' He told me that under El Salvadoran law the investigation must be fully completed before arrests are made. I felt confident with his answers because of the trust I had in him and felt that justice would be served." *Id.*, at 6-7.

449 Carol Buckland's testimony was recorded in Washington in August 1991. Ms. Buckland confirmed her brother's account and said "[m]y brother went on in the letter to ask me to sit on this information. He said if it did not come out, say, in two months or if something happened to him, I might consider, in his words, letting the cat out of the bag." Ms. Buckland says she turned the original copy of Eric Buckland's hand-written letter over to the FBI when they interviewed her early on. Deposition of Carol Elizabeth Buckland, Aug. 14, 1991, *in re Letters Rogatory From the Fourth Criminal Court Judge of San Salvador, El Salvador*, at 7 (D.D.C. 1991). While the U.S. embassy has stated that the letter was delivered to Judge Zamora, it has never been entered into the court record.

commander. Colonel Menjívar subsequently sought further information from two other embassy employees who were well connected to the military, political officer Janice Elmore and Steve Donehoo, of the Defense Attaché's office. Both Elmore and Donehoo said they knew nothing. Menjívar, accompanied by Elmore, then proceeded to Joint Command headquarters to lay out the story for Colonel Ponce. Asked what he knew about the matter, Colonel Ponce said, "I haven't the slightest idea." Ponce was surprised that the Americans had this information, and as the conversation progressed, he became increasingly agitated at the suggestion that he had been briefed previously about Benavides' role. In August 1991, Colonel Menjívar recalled that "[f]irst of all, Ponce seemed surprised, then he was sort of disappointed and then outraged. He didn't believe – he wanted to know where the information came from."[450]

Colonel Avilés was called to Colonel Ponce's office; he arrived about an hour later and denied his role in the affair. Avilés repeated his denial after Buckland joined the meeting, accompanied by Hunter.[451] When Colonel Ponce was unable to locate Colonel Iván López y López, the second link in the chain, Avilés said he knew where to find him, and volunteered to phone López y López, who showed up about half an hour later. "By then the story had been fixed," one source close to the case told the Lawyers Committee. "López y López showed up and denied everything."

Early the next day, January 3, 1990, Colonel Menjívar met with members of the High Command of the Salvadoran Armed Forces. Menjívar repeated the story to Defense Minister Gen. Rafael Humberto Larios López; Cols. Inocente Orlando Montano and Juan Orlando Zepeda, Vice Ministers of Defense; Deputy Chief of Staff Col. Gilberto Rubio Rubio; and Colonel Ponce. "Their faces were as white as sheets," a source with knowledge of what transpired at the

450 Deposition of Col. Milton Menjívar, Aug. 7, 1991, *in re Letters Rogatory From the Fourth Criminal Court Judge of San Salvador, El Salvador*, at 25 (D.D.C. 1991).

451 According to accounts in the U.S. press, Avilés was punished for having violated the strict code of silence imposed on members of the Salvadoran Armed Forces. According to the *Miami Herald*, he was "placed in temporary confinement" and a pre-announced posting as defense attaché to the Salvadoran embassy in Washington was canceled. *See Miami Herald*, Jan. 16, 1990; *Los Angeles Times*, Jan. 12, 1990; *New York Times*, Jan. 14, 1990.

In an interview with *60 Minutes*, Col. Sigifredo Ochoa Pérez, a prominent former officer and ARENA leader, was extremely critical of the U.S. embassy for having revealed the source of its intelligence implicating Benavides. "The American officer put the informant in a very difficult situation, so dangerous he could have been killed." *60 Minutes, supra* note 23.

meeting told the Lawyers Committee. "They were nervous about how much more [the Americans] knew. All five were scared." Montano was the first to respond. "There may be some truth to what you are saying," he reportedly told the U.S. officer.

That morning, Major Buckland prepared a one-page written statement outlining what he knew and how. Concerned that embassy staff had turned against Buckland, the U.S. military sent a military attorney from the U.S. Southern Command in Panama to El Salvador to provide Major Buckland with legal counsel. Buckland refrained from signing his statement until the arrival of the attorney, who helped Buckland clarify the statement's wording. It was subsequently transmitted to General Larios under Colonel Menjívar's signature.

Major Buckland was sent to Washington on January 6. On January 10 and 11, the FBI recorded an affidavit in which Buckland indicated for the first time that he had had prior knowledge that a group of Salvadoran officers planned to kill some Jesuits, including Father Ellacuría. On January 12, the FBI recorded a videotape in which Major Buckland presented the most complete account of his "prior knowledge" of the crime.

Major Buckland told the FBI that at some point in late October or early November 1989, Col. Carlos Armando Avilés asked Buckland to accompany Avilés to the Military Academy. During their visit Colonel Avilés met with Colonel Benavides for about 15 minutes. Avilés told Buckland that Colonel Ponce had sent him there to "solve a problem with Colonel Benavides." After meeting with Colonel Benavides, Colonel Avilés told Major Buckland that Benavides "wanted to do something about the priests and things coming out of the UCA. Benavides told Avilés that Ella Coria [sic] was a problem." Buckland's affidavit says "Avilés told me they wanted to handle it in the old way by killing some of the priests."

Explaining why he had done nothing to prevent the killings, Major Buckland said,

> I felt unconcerned that it would happen because other people were talking along those lines and I didn't feel that the El Salvadoran Armed Forces would do something about it. Also because Chief of Staff Ponce assigned a senior Colonel (Avilés) to address the problem I felt

> that if there was any validity to this talk it would not happen.[452]

One week later, Major Buckland officially recanted the prior knowledge story to the FBI at Fort Bragg, North Carolina. He first indicated his intention to recant in a January 14 telephone call to the FBI. An FBI agent's note to the file indicates that Buckland "said he was `uncomfortable' with his statement . . ." and that he felt "pressured by the interviewer" and was in "a poor mental state." In a sworn statement recorded by the FBI on January 18, Buckland said, "I do not recall and am not aware of any specific information regarding any proposed threat to or attack on the University of Central America, including any of the Jesuit priests prior to the incident on November 16, 1989. I wish to specifically retract information or comments or statements made to FBI agents last week to that effect."

In this January 18 affidavit, Buckland did, however, tell about visiting the Academy before the murders with Colonel Avilés, who had been sent by Colonel Ponce to talk to Colonel Benavides. But Buckland added, "I do not recall any specific discussion about Colonel Benavides planning to do anything or any discussion by anyone, including Colonel Avilés on any proposed or possible attack or threat to the University of Central America or any persons associated with that university." The January 18 statement contains elements of Buckland's earlier "prior knowledge" story. Yet there is a striking difference in style between Buckland's January 10-11 affidavit and his January 18 retraction. While the earlier statement is rambling and emotional, the retraction is carefully worded and more restrained in its tone. It reads more like a formal affidav it, suggesting that Major Buckland may have been assisted by an attorney.

Major Buckland's January 11 affidavit and the videotape were turned over to Richard Chidester, legal officer at the embassy, by the FBI on January 13, 1990. Mr. Chidester as well as his superiors at the embassy were briefed by the FBI on the contents of the statements. Ranking State Department officials in Washington were also briefed.[453] They decided not to disclose this informa-

452 Sworn statement by Eric Warren Buckland, Jan. 11, 1990, hand written addendum, Washington, D.C., at 10 (on file at Lawyers Committee for Human Rights). A previous Lawyers Committee report, *The Jesuit Case a Year Later: An Interim Report* (Nov. 15, 1990) incorrectly reported that part of Buckland's testimony was hand-written by the major. The handwritten portion was in fact written by one of the FBI agents.

453 Ambassador Walker told the Lawyers Committee on November 21, 1990 that he himself was not briefed by the FBI. "In any case, it would be too formal to say anyone was briefed." Lawyers Committee interview, San Salvador.

tion publicly, or to share it with the court. More than just concealing the evidence, State Department and Pentagon officials actually denied its existence when *The New York Times* printed rumors suggesting that a U.S. officer had prior knowledge of the murder plot. A Pentagon spokesman told *The Times* on January 13, "I have seen absolutely nothing to indicate that" Major Buckland had prior knowledge.

While the gist of Major Buckland's story as well as his role in late December 1989 and early January 1990 had appeared in both the Salvadoran and U.S. press,[454] the account was first laid out in full in the *Interim Report* published by the Moakley task force on April 30, 1990. The congressional task force respected the wishes of the Pentagon by not publishing Major Buckland's name, referring simply to "an American major."

The inappropriateness of the embassy's handling of Buckland is evidenced by the fact that it was not until May 29, 1990 – one month after the story appeared in the Moakley report – that Judge Zamora felt he had the backing even to request a copy of Buckland's statement.[455] Neither the embassy nor military authorities had seen fit to submit a copy of the document to the court. The document was not added to the court record until June 6, 1990. On July 18, the Foreign Ministry requested that Buckland appear before the judge. He finally appeared over two months later, on September 28, 1990. The State Department, in consultation with the Pentagon, dictated the terms of Buckland's appearance, under a limited waiver of diplomatic immunity. Judge Zamora was not consulted about the terms. The decision followed months of wrangling between U.S. and Salvadoran officials, and disagreement among branches of the U.S. government about the appropriateness of even a partial waiver of diplomatic immunity.

The State Department's efforts to conceal Buckland's admissions about "prior knowledge" actually began to unravel in the days preceding his court appearance in San Salvador. A new embassy official found the second set of documents in embassy files which indicated that Buckland had prior knowledge of a plot to kill the Jesuits. This employee raised the issue with his superior. With only days until Buckland was scheduled to appear in San Salvador, it was decided in consultation with Department of Defense officials not to reveal the existence of the prior knowl-

---

454 *See Miami Herald*, Jan. 16, 1990; *New York Times* , Jan. 14, 1990. It is noteworthy that in reporting the arrests, Salvadoran newspapers did not mention and failed to credit Major Buckland's revelations, focusing instead on the work of the SIU and the Honor Commission.

455 U.S. officials refused Congressman Moakley's request for a copy of Buckland's January 3 one-page statement, which he ultimately received from a Salvadoran officer.

edge story, confirming the decision made in January 1990 when the testimony was first recorded by the FBI.

Major Buckland was flown to the U.S. Southern Command in Panama, and from there into El Salvador only for one day, September 28, 1990. Under tight security, he testified for eight and a half hours at the home of the Deputy Chief of the U.S. Mission. Buckland was accompanied by two Pentagon attorneys, Cols. John C. Cruden and David E. Graham. Defense attorneys lodged a protest when Buckland refused to answer questions concerning meetings with the Moakley task force in Washington, since questions regarding what happened after January 6, 1990 were prohibited, according to the terms set by the State Department. In San Salvador, Major Buckland confirmed his January 3 account and buttressed his credibility by offering additional details.[456]

The significance of the ban on questions dealing with the period after January 6, 1990 was not apparent for another three weeks, when the Moakley staff learned of the existence of Buckland's additional statements about his prior knowledge of the crime.

Moakley Publicizes Buckland's Additional Affidavits

On October 18, 1990, Congressman Moakley issued a statement concerning the additional Buckland statements recorded by the FBI on January 10, 11, 12, and 18. Mr. Moakley said that "[i]f the information is accurate, Salvadoran military authorities should have considered Colonel Benavides the prime suspect immediately after the murders took place." While it was still not known who had access to Buckland during the critical week in January 1990 and therefore might have been in a position to influence him, in a short piece entitled, "Cracking the Major," *Newsweek* quoted a Bush administration source who said, "He was grilled and grilled until he cracked."[457]

---

456 Testimony of Maj. Eric Buckland, Fourth Criminal Court, Sept. 28, 1990.

457 *Newsweek*, Nov. 19, 1990, at 6. "The administration `didn't want that story to come out,' sources said, because it `wasn't productive to the conduct of the war," *Newsweek* continued. One U.S. official close to the case called the *Newsweek* account "completely specious," and said that *Newsweek* had been "advised to retract it and refused." Lawyers Committee interview, Mar. 15, 1991.

Mr. Moakley called the failure of U.S. officials to share this potentially important testimony with Salvadoran judicial authorities "an unbelievable and inexcusable error in judgement ...."[458] In an article published on October 19, 1990, the day after the Moakley task force released its statement, *The Washington Post* quoted a State Department official who said it was "not correct" that Judge Zamora had only been provided with the evidence as a result of Mr. Moakley's protests. "When the Embassy came upon [Buckland's January 11 and 18 affidavits] again," he said, "they felt it was something worth pursuing" and gave it to the judge.[459] Yet according to a court press release, Judge Zamora did not receive the affidavits until October 22 at 1:30 p.m. when "a series of photocopies was presented to this court . . . through private channels by two employees of the U.S. Embassy . . . not by means of appropriate channels."[460]

The timing of the delivery of the documents to Judge Zamora is noteworthy. While the embassy official discovered the documents on the eve of Buckland's arrival in San Salvador, it was not until one month after his testimony – and five days after Moakley's statement – that the affidavits were delivered. If U.S. officials were genuinely interested in fully exploring all investigatory leads, they should have immediately made the additional testimony available to Salvadoran judicial authorities, who precisely at that moment were preparing for Buckland's deposition in El Salvador.

In explaining the decision, one ranking U.S. diplomat suggested that

> Judge Zamora was not in a good position to evaluate the affidavits. In fact, Zamora was reluctant to accept the affidavits because it complicates his job. He said he didn't want to see the videotape because he can't use it. It's not admissible. Also, we had to practically force him to take the affidavits.[461]

On October 24, René Emilio Ponce, by now a general and the Minister of Defense, wrote to Congressman Moakley "to explain that in reality [Buckland's] information is false" because of a few errors in fact and logic. General Ponce ended by repeating that "we

458 Statement of Rep. Joe Moakley, Chairman, Speaker's Special Task Force on El Salvador, at 3 (Oct. 18, 1990).

459 *Washington Post*, Oct. 19, 1990.

460 Comunicado Oficial, Juzgado Cuarto de lo Penal, Oct. 22, 1990. The communiqué refers to embassy legal officer Richard Chidester and his assistant.

461 Lawyers Committee interview, U.S. embassy, Nov. 21, 1990.

all want to see justice done in the Jesuit case. Any information that helps clarify this matter is welcome. As you know, we have been and will continue assisting Judge Zamora in his investigations." Colonel Avilés was less diplomatic, echoing language heard in the U.S. embassy. "It is totally false," the colonel told the Associated Press. "The only explanation for these statements is that Buckland is completely unstable emotionally. He is crazy."[462]

In its own way, the U.S. embassy in San Salvador also reacted to the firestorm. The Associated Press reported on October 25 that "embassy spokeswoman Pamela Corey-Archer said the State Department has ordered all embassy officials to refuse comment on the affidavit." Once the ban was lifted, embassy officials blamed the failure to provide the documents on the FBI, who they said forbade them from sharing the evidence. "Once they develop the information, it's their information," a top embassy official told the Lawyers Committee. "The embassy is prohibited from passing the evidence."[463] In answer to a question posed during the Letters Rogatory process, Richard Chidester said,

> It would not have been my responsibility to provide that to the Salvadoran court. They were FBI documents. I had only partial sets of those documents. And unless the FBI had authorized us or ordered us to share those documents, I could not share those documents.[464]

Embassy officials also renewed their criticism of Major Buckland, who one diplomat told the Lawyers Committee was "unstable" and "confused." Another said, "Eric lost it at some stage of the game."[465]

Presented with the more damaging version of events in Buckland's prior knowledge story, embassy staff now said they thought Buckland's first version was true. Yet they failed to acknowledge that if Buckland was telling the truth about the Benavides to Rivas to López y López to Avilés chain of information, Lieutenant Colonel Rivas, the SIU chief who headed the police investigation, was actively involved in the coverup of the crime.

---

462 Associated Press, Oct. 25, 1990; *see also* INTERJUST, Oct. 31, 1990.

463 Lawyers Committee interview, U.S. embassy, Nov. 21, 1990.

464 Deposition of Richard Chidester, Aug. 6, 1991, *In re Letters Rogatory From the Fourth Criminal Court Judge of San Salvador, El Salvador*, at 12 (D.D.C. 1991).

465 Lawyers Committee interviews, U.S. embassy, Mar. 15, 1991 and Sept. 6, 1991.

On November 1, 1990, the Supreme Court asked the Foreign Ministry to request the Buckland videotape through diplomatic channels. The court also requested "all documents and elements related to the criminal case against Col. Guillermo Benavides and others."[466] In response, the U.S. embassy in a Diplomatic Note dated June 12, 1991 offered a "private showing" at the embassy for "the Fourth Criminal Judge and judicial representatives who are interested parties and who are authorized by the judge, having demonstrated their legal necessity to review the evidence in this case." With respect to the additional documentation requested, the embassy said it would "maintain its practice of voluntarily providing information related to the case. Nonetheless, this Mission is not willing to respond to requests for documents which are imprecise and general." The Diplomatic Note cited Article 24 of the Vienna Convention concerning the inviolability of embassy archives.[467]

In November 1990, Major Buckland was again interviewed at length by Maj. John L. Plotkin of the Pentagon's Judge Advocate General's office. Also present were Col. Glen La Force, of Ft. Bragg's U.S. Trial Defense Service, representing Buckland, and FBI agent Rick Staver. The major was granted immunity from criminal prosecution in advance to "remove any hesitation about providing [. . .] accurate information . . . ." Buckland's response was to repeat that he had no prior knowledge of the Jesuit murders. Buckland blamed the FBI agents for pressuring him into fabricating his "prior knowledge" account.[468]

In early 1991, Salvadoran court officials began to consider recalling Buckland to San Salvador for further testimony. Their first opportunity to do so was in late May, when the court opened an eight-day period for the introduction of new evidence. Sensitive to charges that Washington was not cooperating, the State Department flew Buckland to Panama so that he could reach San Salvador on short notice. The United States Information Service (USIS) went so far as to put out a press release saying that Buckland had been "placed at the disposition of the judge" and is waiting at "a nearby location." But the Salvadoran Foreign Ministry reportedly failed to expedite the paperwork, and the major was ultimately questioned along with nine other U.S. citizens under the Letters Rogatory process in Washington, D.C., on August 7, 1991 (see below).

---

466 INTERJUST, Nov.1, 1990.

467 Diplomatic Note, #421, June 20, 1991 (Lawyers Committee translation).

468 Transcript of sworn statement of Maj. Eric Buckland dated Nov. 1990 (no specific date is provided; on file at Lawyers Committee for Human Rights).

The Official Reaction to Buckland's Testimony

The April 1990 *Interim Report* of the Moakley task force found that the "timing of events is such that it is not clear whether the case ever would have broken if the American Major did not come forward."[469] *The Miami Herald* quoted a diplomatic source who agreed that Colonel Benavides probably would not have been charged if Major Buckland had not linked him to the crime. "What is evident is that if Avilés had not come through, the involvement of the top colonel maybe would not have been mentioned at all."[470] Both Salvadoran and U.S. officials tried to downplay Buckland's role and the importance of his testimony early on. In January 1990, a Pentagon spokesman dismissed Major Buckland's information as a "rumor."[471]

There are several parallels between the embassy's handling of the Cerna and the Buckland testimonies. As with Mrs. Cerna, U.S. diplomats took steps which had the effect of cordoning off and discrediting information implicating the Salvadoran Armed Forces. In Buckland's case, they did so even when the source was an embassy colleague. The actions of the embassy staff served to undermine any follow-up investigative efforts. Legal officer Richard Chidester immediately phoned Lieutenant Colonel Rivas and told him the story, despite the fact that Rivas himself was implicated in the coverup. Though the gist of Buckland's account was quickly borne out and arrests were made, embassy officials dismissed the story, saying that lie detector tests taken by both Buckland and Avilés had been "inconclusive."[472]

In preparing its April 1990 report, the Moakley task force interviewed Buckland and concluded that he was "telling the truth." The *Interim Report* observed that "It is simply not credible to imagine that he concocted a story that just coincidentally

---

469 Interim Report, *supra* note 129, at 32.

470 *Miami Herald*, Jan. 16, 1990.

471 *Miami Herald*, Jan. 16, 1990.

472 Major Buckland was polygraphed both in San Salvador and Washington by the FBI. An FBI report on tests conducted on January 11, 1990 concluded that it is the "opinion of the examiner that the results of this examination were inconclusive." Buckland "indicated deception" when he responded negatively on two occasions to the question: "Have you deliberately provided us with false information regarding the Jesuit killings?" Likewise, deception was indicated when he answered "No" to the question: "Did you make up the information you provided about the Jesuit killings?" Yet the FBI found that Buckland also exhibited deception when he negatively responded to the question: "Did you have prior knowledge that the Jesuits would be killed?" Polygraph report of Maj. Eric Warren Buckland, dated Jan. 24, 1990 (on file at Lawyers Committee for Human Rights).

happened to be true. . . . This premise is supported by the fact that, in coming forward ten days to two weeks after the event, he was subjecting himself to potentially serious criticism."[473] Buckland did not previously know Benavides, and in fact was initially unable to provide his sister with the Salvadoran colonel's complete name.

Major Buckland himself came under attack, and, like Mrs. Cerna, was treated as a hostile witness. One embassy official charged that Buckland "went native and became more Salvadoran than any Salvadoran."[474] Several U.S. officials referred to Buckland as "unstable" and an "emotional basket case." This theme was picked up by Salvadorans who found it convenient to dismiss Buckland's account. Buckland was hurriedly sent out of the country on January 6. The reluctance of U.S. officials to make Buckland available for questioning was explained as both a desire to protect Buckland's privacy and safety, and because they said he was emotionally wrought. Yet privately, U.S. officials were unrelenting in their criticism of Buckland, and admitted "he should never have served in El Salvador."

Perhaps most remarkable is that U.S. officials failed to examine the role of the Special Investigative Unit (SIU), whose integrity was called into question by Buckland's testimony. If Colonel Benavides in fact confessed to Lieutenant Colonel Rivas, who failed to act on the information, Rivas himself was criminally liable for his role in the coverup. Furthermore, Rivas could have testified against Benavides, augmenting the limited evidence that was admissible against him. Asked whether allegations about Rivas' wrongdoing were being investigated, the State Department responded:

> The U.S. MilGroup major learned from Colonel Avilés that Colonel Benavides had approached Rivas; Avilés heard the story from Colonel López y López. At best, we had uncorroborated third-hand information. The U.S. officer and Colonel Avilés both failed polygraphs trying to establish this point.[475]

The embassy consistently protected Lieutenant Colonel Rivas and defended the SIU's work on the case. "They were trying to do everything they could to justify their program," one source close to

---

473 Interim Report, *supra* note 129, at 32.

474 Lawyers Committee interview, U.S. embassy, San Salvador, Feb. 1990.

475 Cited in Storrs, "El Salvador--Legal System, Judicial Reform, and Major Human Rights Cases Involving the Military: A Compilation from State Department Reports and Other Sources," at 19 (Congressional Research Service, Mar. 23, 1990).

the case told the Lawyers Committee, referring to embassy efforts to protect the SIU. "They took the easy way out by focusing on Buckland. Why not focus on the others in the chain?"

Impact of the State Department's Handling of Buckland's Testimony

In withholding this evidence, U.S. officials denied Salvadoran judicial authorities an opportunity to test Major Buckland's allegations in a timely fashion and to pursue leads his testimony may have helped to suggest. If accurate, Major Buckland's testimony provides important evidence that ranking officers – including Defense Minister Gen. René Emilio Ponce – launched a coverup, knowing that Colonel Benavides had just days earlier indicated his intentions to kill the Jesuits to Colonel Avilés. Major Buckland's testimony also means that General Ponce, knowing of Colonel Benavides' intentions, placed Benavides in charge of a special security zone which included the Jesuit university; placed the elite Atlacatl troops later charged in the crime under his command; and ordered a search of the Jesuit residence two days before the assassination. Further, since Major Buckland was not a defendant in the case, his testimony against Colonel Benavides would have been admissible under Salvadoran law.

In the end, the various affidavits, hand written addenda, the videotape and the polygraph results suggest more questions than answers. It is not clear if the major is telling the story piecemeal, or if the second version is an embellishment. No element of the testimony directly contradicts another, though it seems unlikely that Buckland would have forgotten, as he says, having been told in advance of the plan to kill Father Ellacuría, and not had his memory jogged until December 20, when he learned from a Salvadoran informant of Benavides' role in the Jesuit murders.

While the court was ultimately provided with a transcript of the videotape on January 22, 1991 – over a year after it was recorded – the failure of the State Department to ever turn over the tape itself impeded the investigatory process. The videotape version is the most complete account of Buckland's supposed prior knowledge about the plot. In the video, the major adds details such as the presence of Atlacatl commander Colonel León Linares at the Military Academy when he visited with Avilés; the information he received on the afternoon of November 15 that "the military was going to go in and clean out the UCA. [. . . .] to get the dirty people in there";[476] and the visit by Avilés precisely

476 Buckland videotape transcript, Jan. 12, 1990, Washington, D.C., at 10-11

as the murder operation was unfolding.[477] Several embassy and State Department officials told the Lawyers Committee that they believed that if they turned over the videotape it "would turn up the next day on CNN."

The decision to withhold the evidence was, as Congressman Moakley expressed it, at best an "error in judgement." The Bush administration, whose officials repeatedly stated their commitment to pursue the investigation wherever it might lead, had denied Salvadoran authorities the opportunity to examine the evidence, and in doing so undermined due process in a case where its application would potentially harm U.S. policy.

Speaking of the decision by U.S. officials to conceal Buckland's full testimony, a State Department official told congressional staff members in March 1991 that there is "no question in anyone's mind that it was a screw-up. [. . . .] it was a foul-up that should not have happened." Despite this admission of wrongdoing, there is no indication that anyone was ever held accountable for what amounts to withholding evidence.

Letters Rogatory

The existence of the Buckland and Ramírez testimonies suggested that other U.S. advisors and diplomats might have other relevant information that could be productively pieced together with other facts already on the public record. Yet Washington's response in the Buckland incident made it clear that if not officially approached by the court, U.S. officials would not offer any information. Consequently, at the request of the private prosecutors, Judge Zamora requested the testimony of nine U.S. citizens: six U.S. military advisors serving in El Salvador in November 1989; two U.S. diplomats; and Carol Buckland, the sister of Maj. Eric Buckland. Carol Buckland was the only one of the nine who did not have diplomatic immunity.[478]

Citing "normal legal procedures," the U.S. Justice Department refused a request by the Jesuits and the Lawyers Committee, as the Jesuits' legal counsel, to be present during the letters rogatory interviews. The Justice Department's reliance on what it termed "normal legal procedure" is debatable. U.S. law stipulates that if the requesting judge does not specify a specific procedure to be

477 Buckland says that Avilés visited him and Captain Puentes in the early morning hours of November 16, 1989, and told them they should "stay down. There's fighting going on, just stay down." Buckland says he thought Avilés wanted to establish an alibi proving that he was not involved in the murder operation. *Id.* at 14.

478 On the letters rogatory, *see* Chapter VIII: "The Final Act."

followed in the administration of the letters rogatory, the Federal Rules of Civil Procedure for the taking of evidence and depositions apply, regardless of whether or not the action is criminal or civil. In practice, there is significant leeway in how letters rogatory are handled with a trend toward flexibility. For example, the legislative history related to the applicable U.S. law states: "In exercising its discretionary power, the court may take into account the nature and attitudes of the government of the country from which the request emanates and the character of the proceedings in that country. . . ."[479] Salvadoran criminal procedures allow for follow up questions by the parties, including the victims of crimes or their representatives, in this instance the Jesuits. The victims may be represented by a private prosecutor (*acusador particular*), who participates actively in the discovery process and the trial itself. Witness statements are recorded in public. The parties must be notified in advance. Far from attempting to approximate conditions in a Salvadoran court, these U.S. citizens were questioned in a carefully controlled fashion behind closed doors and lawyers for the Jesuits were expressly forbidden from participating.

While the Bush administration's denial of the Jesuits' request to participate did not violate the letter of the law, the refusal did contradict its stated commitment to explore all investigatory opportunities and to cooperate with judicial authorities. By making the investigatory process as open as possible, the administration could have taken steps toward undoing its image of non-cooperation. Instead, it chose to block the participation of the victims' representatives. The reaction of U.S. officials to the filing of letters rogatory ranged from annoyance to anger. One called the "whole thing silly." Another labelled the questions, which were prepared by the private prosecution, "inane."[480]

One U.S. official involved in the exercise told the Lawyers Committee in March 1992 that "none" of the officials administering the Letters Rogatory at the Departments of State, Justice and Defense "were interested in learning any more. They were clearly afraid of something and wanted to distance themselves from the whole process," he said.

---

479 H.R. Rep. No. 1952, 88th Cong., 1st Sess. (1063); S. Rep. No. 1580, 88th Cong., 1st Sess. (1963) (identical to House Report), reprinted in [1964] U.S. Code Cong. & Admin. News 3782. In *In Re Letter of Request From Crown Pros. Serv.*, 570 F. 2d 686 (D.C. Cir. 1989), the court held that in enforcing letter rogatory from the United Kingdom the district court had wide discretion and that evidence taken from a U. S. citizen for the purpose of assisting a British criminal investigation was to be supplied in a form appropriate for use in British court.

480 Lawyers Committee interviews, U.S. embassy, San Salvador, July 1991 and Sept. 6, 1991; and in Washington, D.C., May 1991.

CHAPTER XI: EL SALVADOR'S LEGAL SYSTEM

The following describes Salvadoran legal procedure and the institutions involved in the administration of justice, emphasizing criminal procedure in murder cases as relevant to the Jesuit case. A number of changes called for by the 1992 peace accords are also highlighted.

Justice of the Peace

When a murder occurs a Justice of the Peace examines the body and undertakes the initial investigation. A judge may undertake an investigation upon learning of a crime or after receiving a report or complaint. If a Justice of the Peace initiates an investigation, he or she has 12 days to transfer the case to the appropriate Judge of First Instance. In the Jesuit case, Justice of the Peace Rosario Góchez Castro de Paz transferred the case to Judge Ricardo Zamora, a First Instance Judge, one day after the crime, on November 17, 1989.

Police Investigation

Cases are investigated by the "auxiliary organs" of the courts designated in Article 11 of the Criminal Procedure Code. During the period in which the Jesuit case unfolded, these were the three Security (or police) Forces: the National Police, National Guard and Treasury Police. The auxiliary organs cooperate in the administration of justice by investigating crimes and identifying suspects who are then turned over to the court along with all collected evidence.[481] They also carry out investigations requested by the court. Until recently, all three Security Forces were under the jurisdiction of the Armed Forces responsible to the Defense Ministry and specifically to the Vice Minister of Defense and Public Security, then Col. Inocente Orlando Montano. Officers in the Security Forces followed the same career path as officers in other military divisions. There was thus a clear conflict of interest when those suspected of having committed a crime were themselves members of the Armed Forces. In the Jesuit case, for example, prominent members of the Armed Forces were publicly blaming the FMLN for the murders while lower ranking officers were responsible for carrying out the investigation in an impartial fashion.

---

481 Criminal Procedure Code, Art. 137.

All three Security Forces also had full combat units, further blurring the distinction between them and other branches of the Armed Forces. According to the 1992 peace accord signed by the Salvadoran government and the FMLN, the National Guard and the Treasury Police were to be dissolved by March 1, 1992 and a new civilian police force gradually built. Yet the bodies continued to exist as Security Forces until the Assembly passed the corresponding legislation on June 28. Some members remain in militarized units under a different name and some members were transferred to the National Police. Meanwhile, plans for the new National Civilian Police, which will replace the current National Police, remain seriously behind schedule.

Given the nature of the crime, the Jesuit murder case was immediately assigned to the Commission on Investigation founded in 1985 to investigate human rights cases in which the military was implicated.[482] The Commission is nominally led by a civilian committee comprised of the Minister of Justice, the Vice-Minister of Interior and a delegate of the president. The Commission is not functioning at this time and the civilian leadership is virtually invisible. In response to an inquiry by Senator Patrick Leahy, the State Department explained why the oversight commission was not functioning: "After taking office in 1989, President Cristiani consolidated the control of the [SIU] in the hands of the Minister of Justice, feeling that he could provide the necessary oversight."[483]

The Commission is nominally the parent organization of a Special Investigative Unit (SIU) and a Forensic Unit (FU) which are under an Executive Unit currently headed by Lt. Col. José Reynaldo Ayala Rodríguez. In practice, the SIU has functioned

---

482 The Commission is known in Spanish as the *Comisión de Investigación de Hechos Delictivos*. For an overall evaluation of the Commission's work, *see* Lawyers Committee for Human Rights, *Underwriting Injustice: AID and El Salvador's Judicial Reform Program*, at 43-55 (1989). Since its founding, the U.S. government has provided a substantial portion of its budget. The UN Independent Expert on El Salvador, citing the fact that the Commission has been operating within the Justice Ministry under the control of "serving officers of the armed forces and staffed to a large extent by military personnel" went on to say: ". . . [T]he Commission has been perceived in some quarters as one of the causes, by reason of its lack of results at least, of the impunity with which violations of human rights have been committed." Situation of Human Rights in El Salvador, UN Doc. A/47/596, at 38 (Nov. 13, 1992).

483 Letter to Senator Patrick Leahy, Chairman, Subcommittee on Foreign Operations, Committee on Appropriations, United States Senate, from Janet G. Mullins, Assistant Secretary, Legislative Affairs, U.S. Department of State, July 23, 1991.

independently of any civilian leadership. During the Jesuit investigation the unit was led by Lt. Col. Manuel Antonio Rivas Mejía.[484] The SIU consists of between 25 and 30 detectives, all of whom are active duty members of the Security Forces who, until recently, were subject to military discipline and dependent on the military for career advancement.

The Criminal Procedure Code does not name the Special Investigative Unit (SIU) as an auxiliary organ for the administration of justice. However, it has effectively acquired that status because its investigators are Security Force members; most are from the National Police.[485] If the Special Investigative Unit decides to act on a case, no other auxiliary organ may become involved; if another security force has undertaken an investigation, its investigative files must be turned over to the SIU.[486] Thus, in the Jesuit case, National Police detectives who conducted preliminary investigations ended their efforts and turned their records over to the SIU.

Article 138 of the Criminal Procedure Code establishes the "Obligations and Powers" of the auxiliary organs. Among these are preservation of the crime scene; detention of suspects; collecting evidence at the crime scene and arranging for photographs, laboratory examinations, etc.; and questioning victims, neighbors and witnesses. The auxiliary organs must record all investigative steps, witness declarations, and other steps undertaken. Original records must be sent to the appropriate judicial authority, while a

---

484 Lieutenant Colonel Rivas was previously the second in command under Col. Iván López y López. Col. Carlos Armando Avilés was the first head of the SIU. All three former SIU chiefs played a role in the Jesuit case and are implicated in the coverup by Major Eric Buckland.

485 The SIU's legal status has been an issue of considerable debate. A San Vicente appellate court held that the SIU was not an auxiliary organ of the court in a ruling on the 1988 San Francisco massacre of 10 peasants. The authorizing legislation for the Commission classed it as "transitory and its objectives and results will be evaluated two years after its creation . . . by the Revisory Commission on Salvadoran Legislation," which should then make a recommendation on institutionalizing the project. Defense attorneys in the Jesuit case raised this issue informally, but at trial restricted their attacks to the quality of the SIU's work, not its legal status. Supreme Court President Mauricio Gutiérrez Castro had maintained that the Legislative Assembly should clarify the SIU's status. That never happened, and courts continued to rule on a case-by-case basis. Presumably, the issue will finally be resolved as secondary legislation is brought into compliance with constitutional changes stemming from the peace process.

486 *Ley de Creación de la Comisión de Investigación de Hechos Delictivos*, Art. 10.

copy is to remain with the investigating auxiliary organ.[487] In the Jesuit case, the SIU failed in its obligation to turn over the entire record of its investigation to the court and to document all investigative work.

The SIU is unlikely to continue in its present form. Since Fiscal Year 1991, the U.S. Congress has withheld U.S. funding – $1.5 million has been allocated yearly – pending a plan to civilianize the unit. During 1991, Salvadoran officials debated the merits of various possible parent organizations for the SIU. The Supreme Court favored converting the unit into a Costa Rican-style Judicial Police, while others argued that it should be placed within the Attorney General's office.

In the end, the decision grew out of the peace talks, and was included in a constitutional reform package on judicial issues that was ratified by the Legislative Assembly in late 1991. A new civilian criminal investigatory unit is to be formed within the Attorney General's office. Implementing legislation has not yet been approved. The future of the SIU, its staff and resources has not yet been determined. According to the peace accord, the chief of the new unit is to be named by the head of the National Civilian Police in consultation with the Attorney General and the president of the Supreme Court.

The Role of the Armed Forces

Because they are not auxiliary organs of the court, the Armed Forces have no legal role in criminal investigations. In exceptionally sensitive and high-profile cases, the Minister of Defense has convened a military Honor Commission. This formula was used both in the 1988 San Francisco massacre case and in the Jesuit case. Just what the Honor Commissions actually did in either case has never been revealed. Apparently, their role was to identify the defendants for the Special Investigative Unit and limit institutional responsibility.

The military justice system is used to try military personnel for specifically military offenses such as desertion and insubordination. Prior to the recent constitutional reforms, civilians accused of certain "political" crimes were consigned to military courts when constitutional guarantees were suspended under a state of

487 Criminal Procedure Code, Art. 142.

exception.[488] Thus, persons accused of participating in the FMLN offensive, collaborating with the FMLN, engaging in "acts of terrorism" such as burning buses or dynamiting electric posts, during the period when guarantees were suspended, were consigned to military courts. The murders at the UCA, however, were considered common crimes to be handled by civilian courts.

Judicial Investigation

The judge has extensive investigative responsibilities in criminal cases in El Salvador, as in other civil code systems. In reality, however, until defendants have been identified by the Security Forces, the court's role is usually rather limited. Before defendants are consigned to the court, other investigative bodies act independently to develop evidence. The Security Forces must either release a detainee within 72 hours or turn him over to the court. Once a formal accusation has been made and the defendant consigned to the court, all evidence must be submitted to the court by the investigating body. Consigning defendants to the court does not, however, end the police responsibility to continue their investigation.[489] Notwithstanding, after delivering the defendants to court in January 1990, the SIU took few investigatory steps on its own.

The judge must initially order suspects' detention for the inquiry period (*término de inquirir*) of 72 hours, during which he must determine whether there is sufficient evidence to justify their provisional detention.

Judicial Declaration

The judge is obligated to record the suspect's declaration no later than 24 hours after the person is turned over to the court.[490] The defendant cannot be required to swear to the truth of his statement nor may the judge use coercion or deception. Suspects can decline to testify when first brought to court, but must ultimately make a statement. In the Jesuit case, six of the

---

488 Constitution, Arts. 29 and 30. A state of exception -- commonly called "state of siege" -- was in effect from March 1980 until January 1987 and from November 12, 1989 until April 10, 1990, although due process rights were restored in March 1990. The provision of Article 30 which established military court jurisdiction for political crimes during the suspension of constitutional guarantees was abolished in the constitutional reforms stemming from the peace process.

489 Criminal Procedure Code, Art. 143.

490 Criminal Procedure Code, Art. 189.

defendants declined to testify when brought to court alleging that they felt ill; the following day they gave statements.

Only the judge can direct questions to the defendant; if the parties wish to formulate additional questions they must be presented through the judge who will pose them if he finds them appropriate.[491] If there is more than one defendant, their declarations are to be taken separately without allowing them to listen or communicate among themselves.[492] There is no limit on the number of times a defendant may declare.[493]

Provisional Detention

Provisional detention of a suspect requires that the judge find sufficient evidence that a crime has been committed and sufficient indication of the defendant's participation.[494] In the Jesuit case, Judge Zamora found sufficient evidence to decree the defendants' provisional detention based primarily on the extrajudicial confessions of seven defendants as well as the judicial testimony of another soldier. A fugitive from justice such as private Jorge Alberto Sierra Ascencio in the Jesuit case can be tried *in absentia* when codefendants are in custody. Once the court has decreed provisional detention, the case enters the investigative (*instrucción*) phase.

Detention of Military Defendants

In most instances, the judge determines where defendants will be held, usually a nearby prison. Yet Salvadoran law allows the Armed Forces to designate where military personnel are held for both the inquiry and provisional detention periods as long as they remain on active duty. In the Jesuit case, the Ministry of Defense did not always inform the judge of the defendants' whereabouts, in violation of the code. In February 1990, the foreign press reported that Colonel Benavides had been seen at a military beach resort. In June 1991, Lieutenant Espinoza Guerra was spotted socializing and circulating among the guests at a party at Treasury Police headquarters, where he was detained.

---

491 Criminal Procedure Code, Art. 191. The parties in the case are the defense attorney (*defensor*) and the public prosecutor (*fiscal*) from the Attorney General's office. El Salvador's Civil Law system also allows for a private prosecutor (*acusador particular*) representing the "offended party," that is, the victim and his or her family.

492 Criminal Procedure Code, Art. 194.

493 Criminal Procedure Code, Art. 195.

494 Criminal Procedure Code, Art. 247.

Military defendants charged with certain crimes – kidnapping, extortion and various drug-related offenses – must be cashiered when provisional detention is decreed.[495] In cases involving other crimes, including murder, dismissal from the military remains optional until the case is brought to trial.

In cases in which the military as an institution is not necessarily implicated, military defendants are often promptly dismissed. Failing to cashier the defendants and thus controlling the place and conditions of their detention has important consequences. For example, in the Jesuit case the possibility that any of the defendants might opt to cooperate with the investigation was greatly diminished by their continued status as active duty members of the military.

By not expelling the Jesuit case defendants from the Armed Forces, the Salvadoran Army violated its own rules as set out in its Normal Operating Procedure (PON) published by the Joint Command in April 1990. According to the PON, enlisted men detained in connection with a crime will be dismissed from service when they are transferred to the investigating Security Force. The PON provides that even officers and commanders are normally to be dismissed. The Minister of Defense is to be notified of the charges against the officer and within 72 hours must issue the order he deems "appropriate" (*lo que estime pertinente*). If the Ministry fails to act within 72 hours, the defendant is turned over to the court and the Ministry notified so the defendant can be cashiered. Only if the crime was committed through negligence or other factors foreclose criminal responsibility may the defendant continue on active duty.[496] Yet the PON, drafted by C-5 (Psychological Operations) is not legally binding.

The Investigation (*Instrucción*) Phase

After the decree of provisional detention, the case remains in the "instruction" or investigative phase until the court determines that sufficient evidence has been collected, largely in the form of testimony, to dismiss the case or take it to trial. The goal of this phase is to carry out the steps necessary to prove the existence of the crime and establish the identity of those responsible as well as the circumstances which could exclude, attenuate or aggravate

---

495 Criminal Procedure Code, Arts. 246 & 247.

496 Estado Mayor Conjunto de la Fuerza Armada, Unidad de Derechos Humanos C-5, *Procedimiento Operativo Normal para las Detenciones Efectuadas por Elementos de la Fuerza Armada*, April 1990.

their criminal responsibility.[497] Additional charges and defendants may be added during this period.

Because admissible evidence must be developed in this phase and must be obtained under court order, the judge must repeat much of the police investigation while pursuing additional leads. The instruction period is supposed to be concluded within 90 days, but can be extended to 120 days.[498] In actuality, this time limit is honored in the breach, especially in complex cases. The instruction phase in the Jesuit case lasted nearly one year, from January to December 1990, more than 320 days.

Witnesses

All witnesses called are obliged to testify about what they are asked, unless the witness fits into one of the exceptions established by law.[499] The judge must summon as witnesses all persons named by the investigating police as having knowledge of the crime or the circumstances surrounding it; the persons whom the defendant or his attorney designate as useful for the defense; and any person who can provide useful information.[500] The judge is to use his discretion to limit the number of witnesses to those necessary to establish the truth. Most witnesses in the Jesuit case were selected by the court although the prosecutors and, to a lesser extent, the defense attorneys, also requested that the court cite certain individuals. No witness may listen to another witness' testimony. Cramped courthouses only permit court staff to take one statement at a time, further slowing progress on the case. Although the judge prepares the questionnaire, he is often not even present when the answers are recorded.

Witnesses who fail to appear when cited can be sanctioned and a witness who refuses to testify without legal basis can be provisionally detained by order of the court, after which a separate criminal case is initiated.[501]

Certain persons are excused from appearing before the court; these include the President and Vice President, government ministers, members of the legislature, magistrates of the Supreme Court and the appellate courts, the Attorney General, the Archbishop and other Bishops, heads of diplomatic missions,

---

497 Criminal Procedure Code, Art. 115.

498 Criminal Procedure Code, Art. 123.

499 Criminal Procedure Code, Art. 198.

500 Criminal Procedure Code, Art. 199.

501 Criminal Procedure Code, Art. 207.

Generals and full Colonels with command positions in the Armed Forces. All of these may instead provide sworn statements in writing.[502] This cumbersome procedure requires the judge to send a questionnaire to the witness, who then sends back a reply, often after a delay of days or even weeks. If the answers provided raise additional questions or other issues have surfaced in the interim, the judge must again direct a petition to the witness. This procedure also denies the parties any opportunity for cross examination.

In court, witnesses are asked to give testimony under oath or to promise to tell the truth on their word of honor.[503] When a witness appears to have lied (*falso testimonio*), the judge may order his provisional detention and try him separately. While many witnesses appear to have committed this crime in the Jesuit case, only four were charged with perjury. When two witnesses have given conflicting testimony they may be recalled for a "confrontation" (*careo*) in which they will be asked to address the essential points on which they differ. The judge may also allow the two witnesses to question each other.[504] Although numerous military witnesses contradicted one another during Jesuit case testimony, no "confrontations" were held, despite requests by the private prosecutors.

Habeas Corpus Petition (*Recurso de Exhibición Personal*)

Defendants can challenge the legality of their detention at any time by interposing habeas corpus petitions. These petitions are normally directed to the Supreme Court, which follows a cumbersome procedure established in the Law of Constitutional Procedures. A lawyer or law student is named to serve as a "judge executor," who collects information about the case and gives an opinion on the detention's legality. The judge executor's non-binding report is then submitted to the Supreme Court which issues its own decision. During this period, which in practice may last for months, the case is transferred from the trial court judge to the Supreme Court, thereby interrupting the proceedings. Even if only one of several defendants presents a habeas corpus petition, the case against the others cannot proceed until it is resolved. There is no limit on the number of petitions that can be presented.

---

502 Criminal Procedure Code, Art. 205.

503 Criminal Procedure Code, Art. 210.

504 Criminal Procedure Code, Art. 216.

Evidence

In common crimes, as the Jesuit murders were defined, extrajudicial confessions are adequate proof to decree provisional detention and to take the case to the jury[505] if the following requisites are met:

1) There are two reliable witnesses to the confession, even if they heard the confession at different times and in different places; and
2) If the confession is consistent with other elements of proof in the same case.

Extrajudicial confessions rendered in police custody must also:

1) have been rendered within 72 hours of detention; and
2) be signed by two adult witnesses who heard the confession and saw that the defendant was not subject to physical force or intimidation.

Extrajudicial confessions are often unreliable and their use remains controversial. A recent report by the Director of the Human Rights Division of the United Nations Observer Mission in El Salvador (ONUSAL) noted,

> the widespread conviction among the legal community and society in general that extrajudicial confessions are often obtained by means of violence or coercion. The Revisory Commission on Salvadoran Legislation (CORELESAL), established in 1984 by the Government of El Salvador to suggest ways of reforming the criminal laws, said that extrajudicial confessions ". . . are most frequently obtained in auxiliary organs [Security Forces] through violence or intimidation . . ." The Mission has ascertained that such practices exist. . . .[506]

The Technical Support for Judicial Reform (ATJ), a newly formed team of experts working within the Ministry of Justice, has drafted legislation which would eliminate the use of extrajudicial confessions. The Justice Ministry has circulated the draft bill for comment, but has yet to submit it to the Legislative Assembly.

---

505 Criminal Procedure Code, Art. 496.

506 The Situation in Central America: Threats to International Peace and Security and Peace Initiatives, UN Doc. A/46/935, S/24066, at 7 (June 5, 1992) [hereinafter ONUSAL report].

Co-defendant testimony is specifically excluded except in cases of kidnapping, extortion and certain drug-related crimes.[507] These exceptions were introduced in 1986 to facilitate the conviction of former military officers and their right wing associates accused of participating in a kidnapping for profit ring. Because these exceptions do not extend to murder cases, the extrajudicial testimony of the defendant lieutenants in the Jesuit case that they received orders from Colonel Benavides was not admissible against Benavides although it can be considered as circumstantial evidence (*indicios*). This distinction is nearly meaningless in practice given that the jury heard the extrajudicial confessions of the colonel's codefendants.

Evidence is to be evaluated under the rules of sound judgment "*sana critica*," using a rational system of deductions in accordance with the other evidence in the case.[508] Scientific evidence such as ballistics testing and handwriting analyses is also admissible.

Plea Bargains or Reduced Sentences

Plea bargaining is not used in Salvadoran courts. Nonetheless, the Criminal Code does provide for a reduction in criminal responsibility in certain cases, including where a judicial confession has been made before the case is elevated to the trial stage.[509] A 1986 amendment to the Criminal Code further empowers the court to reduce a sentence to as little as half of the minimum provided by law:

> when there are several defendants, any or several of them, in the extrajudicial and judicial phase or only the latter, have confessed and collaborated in an effective fashion with the administration of justice in the prudent opinion of the Judge.[510]

In the Jesuit case, the joint defense strategy pursued by the army and defense counsel made it particularly unlikely that any of them would provide information against others in the military.

Plenary (Trial) Stage

Upon completion of the investigation phase, the judge may dismiss the charges against a defendant, or, if the evidence is

507 Criminal Procedure Code, Arts. 499 & 499-A.

508 Criminal Procedure Code, Art. 488.

509 Criminal Code, Art. 41.8(a).

510 Criminal Code, Art. 70(4o).

sufficient, elevate the case to the plenary phase, the adversarial stage of the proceedings. From this point on, the parties' presence is mandatory and the proceedings must be carried out in public. The decision to take a case against a defendant to the plenary phase, or the decision not to do so, is appealable. Once the time period for filing an appeal has passed, or the superior tribunal has confirmed the judge's order, the judge opens an eight-day period for the presentation of additional evidence.[511] During the eight-day period, new witnesses may be called, previous witnesses recalled and witnesses who have contradicted each other may be asked to confront one another.

After the conclusion of the evidence period, the judge formulates the index (*minuta*) of the case, starting with evidence that establishes the existence of a crime, followed by that referring to the defendants' participation and, finally, evidence relevant to mitigating or aggravating circumstances, indicating the page in which each item appears.[512] Unlike many civil law systems, in El Salvador the judge who conducts the investigation (*juez de instrucción*) also presides at trial and imposes a sentence (*juez de sentencia*). Commenting on this aspect of Salvadoran procedure, the observer who attended the Jesuit trial from the International Commission of Jurists said:

> In the opinion of the observer, this is not a good solution because it does not create the best conditions for the Defense or the Public Prosecutors to arrange, for example, for carrying out certain evidentiary steps that were denied to them during the investigation (or Summary) stage. In effect, there is little possibility that certain legal steps will be taken, since the attorneys have to request permission to carry out these steps from the same judge who denied them previously, because he did not consider them pertinent.[513]

A recent United Nations report also identified this as a "structural defect" in Salvadoran criminal procedure:

> One example of those defects, organic in nature, is that the examining magistrate who investigates the facts of the case is at the same time the presiding judge who directs the proceedings and passes sentence. There will be no basic solution unless the independence and impartiality of the judiciary is upheld, and there is an increase in the number of judges, as well as an improvement in their

511 Criminal Procedure Code, Arts. 299 & 300.

512 Criminal Procedure Code, Art. 329.

513 ICJ, *supra* note 393, at 30.

training and of the human and material resources that support their work.[514]

Most crimes punishable with more than three years in prison are subject to jury trial, although the tendency has been to exclude various crimes, such as kidnapping, extortion and drug-related offenses. The murder and terrorism charges in the Jesuit case went before the jury while the charges for crimes with lesser penalties – planning and conspiracy to commit acts of terrorism and coverup – were decided by the judge.

Jury Selection (*Insaculación y Sorteo*)

A jury is made up of five persons. Jurors must be at least 21 years old, know how to read and write, be of "good conduct" and engaged in a known occupation, profession or artistic endeavor. Jury lists, based on town records, are notoriously inadequate because of the mobility – and displacement – of the population. A new system for jury selection was established by the 1991 reforms to the Criminal Procedure Code, but the revised system was not used in the Jesuit case. Once the judges have definitive jury lists, each judge is to put together lists of 12 jurors that include both men and women as well as a variety of occupations and places of residence.

The list of jurors drawn for a particular case is chosen by lot in the presence of the parties. The names of the jurors are to be sealed until the time of the trial. Supposedly, only the judge and his assistant who cites the jurors know the names. Despite these precautions, Salvadoran jurors have been subject to threats and bribes. No more than 15 days may elapse between choosing the jury list and the actual trial.[515] Jurors who fail to appear may be fined. Jurors are questioned to make sure that they meet legal requirements. Prosecution and defense counsel have no real opportunity to disqualify or recuse jurors as challenges must be for cause, presented in writing and supported by evidence. False (or unconfirmable) allegations can result in sanctions against the attorney.[516] The judge ultimately determines whether there is sufficient evidence to disqualify the juror.[517]

---

514 ONUSAL report, *supra* note 506. Both the Ministry of Justice and the Supreme Court have expressed support for the separation of investigating and sentencing functions between two different judges, and have stated that a proposal is under preparation.

515 Criminal Procedure Code, Art. 336.

516 Criminal Procedure Code, Arts. 342 & 343.

517 Criminal Procedure Code, Art. 343.

The Jury Trial (*Vista Pública*)

Often, several attempts must be made to seat a jury because jurors do not appear when cited or are disqualified. Once sworn in, the jury is read the passages contained in the index prepared by the judge. Members of the jury may ask the defendant or a witness or expert already examined to clarify or amplify their testimony; in practice, this rarely happens. The defense and prosecution may not recall witnesses, but can ask the judge to pose further questions to witnesses called by the jury. If the defendant testifies differently before the jury than in his previous declaration, the judge will order the previous declaration read and will note the contradictions. Either party may request a new witness by petitioning the judge five days before the trial with a list of questions to be asked the new witness.

Once the evidence has been presented, the judge will ask the private prosecutor, if any, then the public prosecutor and finally the defense to make their oral arguments. Each side may have up to three hours for its first intervention and up to two hours for the second round. The parties are not limited to admissible evidence, although their arguments are not to go beyond matters in the case record. The judge must ensure that neither side pursues issues or arguments which are "irrelevant to the establishment of the truth." At the same time, he is bound to ensure that he does not suppress the legitimate exercise of the prosecution and the freedom of the defense."[518] At the jury trial in the Jesuit case, Judge Zamora imposed almost no restrictions on counsels' arguments, which often strayed far afield.

The jury must answer the following question for each defendant and each charge: Does the jury have the intimate conviction that defendant X is guilty? No clear distinction is made between issues of fact and issues of law. There is no requirement that jurors be instructed on the law. The jury is not bound by rulings of law made by the courts, by the law itself, logic or even the weight of the evidence. The jury's verdict may be challenged through a petition of annulment if, for example, one or more votes were obtained through bribery, intimidation or violence or other irregularities in the jury process.

Appeals

The judge must sentence the defendants within 30 days of the finding of guilt. Sentences issued by the First Instance court go as a rule to the appellate court (Second Instance) even if the parties

---

518 Criminal Procedure Code, Art. 340.

accept the sentence or fail to appeal. Only sentences of under three years are not automatically reviewed by an appellate court. Cases dismissed must also be reviewed by the appellate court. The appellate court's ruling can be further appealed (*en casación*) to the Criminal Chamber of the Supreme Court.

Role of the Attorney General's Office and the Defense Attorneys

The Public Ministry, which includes the Attorney General's office, *Fiscalía General de la República*, is mandated to prosecute all criminal and civil actions in the public domain. The *Fiscalía* is not an auxiliary organ nor does it have resources to conduct investigations.[519] Instead, the *fiscales* or prosecutors must ask the competent judge to undertake the necessary investigative steps and must turn over whatever information they possess about the crime and those presumed to be responsible.[520] The *Fiscalía* may be present when witnesses make declarations in court and can present questions which the judge may pose to the witness. The absence of the prosecutor, however, does not prevent the court from taking a witness statement or conducting other kinds of investigations.[521] Defense counsel can also suggest investigatory steps to the judge and likewise has the right to be present when witness statements are recorded and during other investigatory steps.[522] The victim only has a right to intervene in the process through a private prosecutor or a civil action.[523]

The Attorney General was previously chosen by a simple majority of the Legislative Assembly, making him in essence a political appointee. Recent constitutional reforms stipulate that the Attorney General will be elected by a two-thirds majority of the Assembly.

519 The peace accords have granted the Attorney General's office new responsibility for criminal investigations.

520 Criminal Procedure Code, Art. 40.

521 Criminal Procedure Code, Art. 118.

522 Criminal Procedure Code, Art. 119.

523 Criminal Procedure Code, Art. 120.

The Supreme Court

The 14-member Supreme Court is responsible for naming all lower court judges and for ensuring that justice is administered promptly and fully (*pronta y cumplida*). The Constitutional Chamber of the court hears habeas corpus petitions while the Criminal Chamber is the court of last resort in criminal appeals.

As a result of recent constitutional reforms, members of the Supreme Court of Justice will be appointed for staggered nine-year terms by a two-thirds vote of the Legislative Assembly. The current court was appointed in June 1989 by an ARENA-dominated Assembly and has come under heavy criticism for its partisan actions and direct intervention in individual cases.[524] Nonetheless, court president Dr. Mauricio Gutiérrez Castro supported Judge Zamora throughout the Jesuit case, providing important political backing and facilitating the investigation that Judge Zamora undertook, however limited. Dr. Gutiérrez Castro's views on the case frequently appeared in Salvadoran newspapers and he was integrally involved in planning the jury trial. The Supreme Court issued frequent press releases about developments in the case. The jury trial was held in the Supreme Court building and Dr. Gutiérrez Castro issued credentials to foreign observers.

---

524 The UN Independent Expert on El Salvador stated: "The Independent Expert received various complaints alleging that the President of the Supreme Court of Justice had pressured a number of judges to take or abstain from taking a particular course of action. When confronted with this in an interview with the Independent Expert, the President of the Court said that, fundamentally, that allegation lacked all basis. None the less, he acknowledged that in some cases, there had been historic circumstances which had compelled him to follow developments in order to protect the judge from political pressure, since the majority of judges were ill-prepared to deal with a particular political environment. He explained that, even in those situations, he merely made suggestions and never attempted to impose anything. In the Independent Expert's view, the very fact that such situations can arise `in exceptional cases' bears out his opinion that the potential scope for hierarchical influence over the judge undermines the total independence which his office warrants." Situation of Human Rights in El Salvador, UN Doc. A/47/596, at 42-43 (Nov. 13, 1992).

POSTSCRIPT, JULY 1993

On the night of 15 November 1989, then Colonel René Emilio Ponce, in the presence of and in collusion with General Juan Rafael Bustillo, then Colonel Juan Orlando Zepeda, Colonel Inocente Orlando Montano and Colonel Francisco Elena Fuentes, gave Colonel Guillermo Alfredo Benavides the order to kill Father Ignacio Ellacuría and to leave no witnesses.

Truth Commission[1]
March 15, 1993

With my hand on the bible, you can be sure and you can testify to the fact that General Ponce at no moment gave the order to assassinate the Jesuits.

General René Emilio Ponce
Minister of Defense
March 25, 1993[2]

The news that Defense Minister Ponce, two additional members of the Armed Forces' High Command and two other prominent officers ordered the Jesuit murders led all press accounts coming out of New York City as the long-awaited report of the Truth Commission on El Salvador was released on March 15, 1993.[3] No doubt in anticipation of the blow, on

---

1 "From Madness to Hope: The 12-year war in El Salvador," Report of the Commission on the Truth for El Salvador, UN Doc. S/25500, April 1, 1993, at 46. Hereinafter, "Madness to Hope."

2 Frente a Frente, Channel 12, Mar. 25, 1993, as recorded by INSISTEM, at 9.

3 The Truth Commission was established by the government of El Salvador, the FMLN and the United Nations in the April 1991 Mexico round of peace talks. The Commission had a broad mandate to examine past abuses and document responsibility. Specifically, it was charged with "investigating serious acts of violence which have occurred since 1980." In determining its portfolio, the Commission was to consider cases' impact on society, their "characteristics and repercussions," as well as the "social commotion they generated." The Commission was directed to make recommendations based on its findings, including measures to prevent the repetition of these kinds of crimes as well as initiatives promoting national reconciliation. The Commissioners were former Colombian President Belisario Betancur, former Venezuelan Foreign Minister Reinaldo Figueredo and U.S. law professor Thomas Buergenthal.

March 12 General Ponce had unexpectedly offered his resignation to President Cristiani, who never accepted it.[4] While Congressman Joe Moakley had held virtually the same group of officers responsible some 15 months earlier, the imprimatur of the United Nations made it official. Of the ten officers named in the report, all but Bustillo, who had resigned in 1991, were still on active duty. Most were also likely named by the Ad Hoc Commission established to purge the Armed Forces of egregious human rights violators.[5] Issued in late September 1992, the findings of the Ad Hoc Commission were to have been implemented by President Cristiani by November 23, 1992.

The Truth Commission account provides the first confirmation of what transpired at the large gathering of officers at Joint Command headquarters on the evening of November 15, 1989.[6] In court, officers who attended had denied there was any mention of the Jesuits or even any suggestion of moving against guerrilla "ringleaders." Yet according to the Truth Commission, "Colonel Ponce authorized the elimination of ringleaders, trade unionists and known leaders of FMLN.... The Minister of Defense, General Rafael Humberto Larios López, asked whether anyone objected. No hand was raised. It was agreed that President Cristiani would be consulted about the measures."[7]

Rumors had circulated since the murders about a second meeting held that evening. In fact, in early 1990, Colonel Sigifredo Ochoa Pérez, a prominent former army officer and ARENA leader, had told *60 Minutes* that some officers had stayed behind after the larger gathering. His account proved

---

4 According to *The Washington Post* on June 2, 1993, "Ponce made it clear to Cristiani that the resignation should not be accepted, and Cristiani publicly said Ponce should stay until the end of his term in 1994."

5 Under military pressure, President Cristiani attempted to allow 15 officers named by the Ad Hoc Commission to remain on duty. Seven of these were assigned abroad as military attachés. In January 1993, the Secretary General told him this was unacceptable. Though the identity of those on the list has never been confirmed, it is widely believed that among the 15 were the leading members of the *tandona*.

6 *See* Chapter II: Chronology of the Crime, at 54-61.

7 *Madness to Hope*, at 50.

accurate.[8] The Truth Commission said Colonels Ponce, Francisco Elena Fuentes (then commander of the First Infantry Brigade), Juan Orlando Zepeda and Inocente Orlando Montano, both vice-ministers of defense, and General Juan Rafael Bustillo, the Air Force Commander, sat discussing decisions taken earlier. They called over Colonel Benavides, and Colonel Ponce "ordered him to eliminate Father Ellacuría and leave no witnesses." Ponce told Benavides to use the Atlacatl commando unit then temporarily under his command.

Returning to the Military Academy, Colonel Benavides reported to his men on the decisions taken at Joint Command headquarters. According to the report, Benavides said extraordinary measures had been adopted to combat the FMLN offensive and that it was "necessary to eliminate all known subversive elements." He said he had been ordered to "eliminate Father Ellacuría and leave no witnesses." Benavides asked any man who did not agree with the order to raise his hand; none did so. Major Carlos Camilo Hernández, the acting Academy deputy director who was sentenced to a three-year jail term for his role in the coverup, organized the operation. His own Soviet-made AK-47 rifle was used since having been captured from the guerrillas, it could not be traced. The use of the FMLN's most common weapon was one of several steps taken to implicate the guerrillas.

Major Hernández assigned Lieutenant Edgar Santiago Martínez Marroquín, whose name had not previously surfaced in connection with the case, to coordinate troop movements in the area around the UCA. Confirmation of Martínez Marroquín's role suggests strongly that the murder mission was a full-scale military operation using the armed forces' standard operating procedures. After curfew, in the midst of a guerrilla offensive, soldiers on duty would obviously have been under orders to shoot at anything that moved. Had they not been briefed that the Atlacatl would be passing through their lines, men stationed around the UCA would have engaged the Atlacatl commandos in combat. With these additional revelations, the Truth Commission report depicted a crime of much wider scope, involving more Army units and implicating the Armed Forces on an institutional level.

---

8 *See* Chapter II: "Chronology of the Crime," at 60-61.

The Coverup

Finding: Colonel Manuel Antonio Rivas Mejía, Head of the Commission for the Investigation of Criminal Acts (CIHD), learnt the facts and concealed the truth; he also recommended to Colonel Benavides measures for the destruction of incriminating evidence.[9]

Major Hernández and Lieutenant José Vicente Hernández Ayala -- an Academy officer who had not previously been linked to the crime -- went to Joint Command headquarters on the morning of November 16 and gave Chief of Staff Ponce a full report on the operation. They took with them a suitcase containing the $5,000 in prize money which Father Ellacuría had received in Spain. (The court had never been able to determine who had stolen the money and robbery charges were dropped in December 1990.) The officers told Ponce that the suitcase also contained photographs and documents. Colonel Ponce -- recognizing that the existence of the suitcase implicated the Army in the murders -- ordered its destruction. It was later destroyed at the Military Academy.

According to the Truth Commission, the role of the Special Investigative Unit (SIU) in the coverup was far more extensive and active than had been known. While the SIU's handling of the case had generally been viewed as merely passive and incompetent, the Truth Commission attributed to it a much more aggressive role in the coverup. After the murders, Colonel Benavides confessed his role in the killings to SIU chief Lieutenant Colonel Manuel Antonio Rivas Mejía, and secured his help. Lieutenant Colonel Rivas told Benavides he should destroy the barrels of the weapons used in the crime, since the SIU would run ballistics tests on them. Atlacatl Commander Lieutenant Colonel Oscar Alberto León Linares helped destroy the barrels. Rivas later tipped off Benavides that a request would be made for the Academy's logbooks, suggesting that Benavides eliminate anything incriminating in the registries. The logbook in which exits and entries to the Academy were recorded likely contained a notation indicating when the troops departed for the UCA on the night of November 15-16, 1989. Benavides ultimately ordered his subordinates to burn the books for 1988 and 1989.

---

9 *Madness to Hope*, at 46-47. The Commission for the Investigation of Criminal Acts is the official name of the Special Investigative Unit, or SIU.

This account coincides with the testimony of U.S. Major Eric Buckland, who had been told by a Salvadoran officer that Benavides had confessed to Rivas and sought his help. Rivas, a U.S. favorite, was reportedly on the list of officers whose transfer was ordered by the Ad Hoc Commission. Until the Truth Commission report appeared, he was also the leading candidate for deputy director of the new National Civilian Police.

Assisting Rivas at the SIU in the coverup, according to the Truth Commission, was Colonel Nelson Iván López y López. Colonel López y López, personnel chief at the Joint Command, was placed at the SIU by Colonel Ponce. López y López, it was belatedly learned, was in charge of the COCFA during the murder hours. The report says López y López "learned what had happened and concealed the truth."[10] In January 1990, Major Buckland had also mentioned the role of Colonel López y López. Had the leads provided by Major Buckland been seriously explored in early 1990, confirmation of the military coverup might well have come a lot sooner.[11]

Further, the SIU worked hand in hand with the Military Honor Commission. Previously it was believed that the SIU had put its investigation on hold while the military conducted an in-house probe. By contrast, the Truth Commission describes the two units working in concert under military control. Lic. Rodolfo Antonio Parker Soto, a civilian attorney who works for the Armed Forces and served as counsel to the Honor Commission, censored the extra-judicial confessions made by the defendants. Lic. Parker Soto was present when the SIU recorded the confessions and ensured that all references to higher orders and higher ranking officers were excluded, especially mention of Lt. Col. Camilo Hernández. Hernández and Ponce are said to have remained close since the younger man served under Ponce at the Third Brigade. Indeed, the AK-47 used to kill Fathers Ellacuría, Martín-Baró and Montes had been a personal gift from Ponce to Hernández.

By early January 1990, when the arrests were made, the High Command understood that some scapegoats needed to be offered up. The challenge was to craft a credible version of events which could serve as a basis for limited prosecutions, while insulating the High Command from the crime.

General Gilberto Rubio Rubio, who served as Chief of Staff until July 1, 1993, joined Generals Ponce, Zepeda and Montano throughout the two-year judicial process in pressuring junior

---

10 *Madness to Hope,* at 54.

11 *See* Chapter X: "Washington's Mixed Messages," at 221-231.

officers "not to mention higher orders in their testimonies before the court," according to the report. Throughout the judicial investigation, witnesses were regularly coached by ranking officers and their attorneys in preparation for sessions before the judge.

Naming Names

The publication of *From Madness to Hope* was a major political event in El Salvador. In the days leading up to March 15, speculation about who would be named in connection with the Jesuit killings and other celebrated cases reached a level of mass hysteria. Much of this speculation concerned ARENA party members who were said to be death squad sponsors; ultimately no civilians were named in this context. President Cristiani sent emissaries to New York in early 1993 to urge postponement of the report until after the March 1994 elections, and withholding the names of those held responsible for violations.

This controversy over "naming names" became a constant drumbeat in the weeks preceding the report's release. The pressure was so great that it drew a two-paragraph commentary in the report itself. The Commissioners said that at the outset of their work Salvadoran authorities had argued that "institutions do not commit crimes, and for this reason, those responsible should be named specifically."[12] Later, the Commissioners again came under pressure -- this time *not* to name names -- in order to protect people who had played a positive role in facilitating the peace process. This was widely viewed as a reference to General Ponce, who is said to have been crucial to making the peace settlement palatable to his fellow officers. President Cristiani said that revealing the names would bring "grave consequences." He went on, "There are opportune moments to divulge certain things and there are inopportune moments."[13] The Mexican daily *Excélsior* quoted Mr. Cristiani saying unequivocally: "There will be violence if [the names are published] now."[14] General Zepeda told Salvadoran journalists that "it is a question of evaluating how important and how opportune it would be for the population to know the full names of those responsible."[15]

12 *Madness to Hope,* at 4.

13 Notimex, as printed in *Diario de Hoy,* Mar. 2, 1993.

14 IPS, Mar. 11, 1993, as printed in *Diario Latino*, Mar. 11, 993.

15 *Latino,* Mar. 2, 1993.

Under the banner headline "Government Does Not Guarantee the Security of Truth Commission Witnesses," the Salvadoran newspaper *Diario Latino* reported that President Cristiani had written to Secretary General Boutros-Ghali and the Commissioners saying it would be impossible for the Salvadoran government to guarantee the security of those who had provided testimony to the Truth Commission.[16] The rightist press set out to rob the report of its legitimacy, describing it as unconstitutional and an affront to national sovereignty. The character of two of the commissioners also came under assault. *Diario de Hoy,* which generally represents the views of the most right-wing officers and civilians, quoted a law professor at an unnamed private university who asserted that the Commission violated El Salvador's "magna carta" because "no entity except the courts have the power to judge."[17] An ARENA member of the Central American Parliament said "We're not afraid of the truth, but of the Commission. The result will be purely propagandistic even though they may try to give it a moral cast."[18]

The Commissioners showed no signs of caving in to the pressure. The Salvadoran Armed Forces had received another blow in mid-February when the Clinton Administration froze $11 million in military aid until the Ad Hoc recommendations were fully implemented. No doubt aware that his name would lead the account of the Jesuit murders, General Ponce appeared to buckle. Ponce, whom *The Washington Post* described as "quiet and generally regarded as unflappable," gave an angry press conference, offering Cristiani his resignation, which he said stemmed from "foreign pressure."[19]

---

16 IPS dispatch from New York, as printed in *Diario Latino*, Mar. 3, 1993. UN sources confirm that such a letter was sent.

17 *Diario de Hoy*, Mar. 12, 1993.

18 *Id.*

19 *Washington Post*, Mar. 14, 1993.

According to *The Los Angeles Times*, the general said he offered to step aside "as a soldier who wants to better serve our country. I do it because I have to live here in El Salvador. I do it for the present and future generations of El Salvador."[20]

Asked if Washington had exerted pressure, the ranking U.S. diplomat in El Salvador, Peter Romero, admitted there had been "pressure in the sense that we could not continue military assistance without a final and total resolution of the recommendations which form part of the implementation of the peace."[21] *The Washington Post* said the resignation "was due largely to U.S. pressure that has left the Salvadoran military feeling bitter and betrayed by the nation that once was its staunchest supporter and protector...."[22] Salvadoran officers did not hide their resentment. "We fought this war, yes, for ourselves, but also for the United States. We feel betrayed when the United States turns around and...attacks us like the enemy," a senior officer told *The Post*. For his part, General Ponce acknowledged that he felt besieged: "No one is unaware of the national and international pressures that exist, and the possible threats and pressures that could come in the future. The $11 million in U.S. military aid has already been suspended. That is an act of pressure, and there could be more."[23]

The Jesuits React

A communiqué issued on March 16 by the Central American Province of the Society of Jesus said:

> The report makes clear that both parties to the conflict committed abuses throughout the war. It is then, an obligation of the belligerent parties -- the Government and the FMLN -- to ask the Salvadoran people for forgiveness and to provide guarantees that these kinds of tragedies do not occur again.

---

20 *Los Angeles Times*, Mar. 13, 1993.

21 *Diario de Hoy*, Mar. 15, 1993. Romero added that pressure had also been exerted by the UN and the four "*países amigos*," the four friends of the Secretary General which have supported El Salvador's peace process: Mexico, Spain, Colombia and Venezuela. *Diario Latino*, Mar. 15, 1993.

22 *Washington Post*, Mar. 14, 1993.

23 *Id.*

> Throughout the last few years the Society of Jesus has emphasized the necessity of a process of reconciliation that contains the triple dimension of truth, justice and forgiveness. Given the report, we feel it is important to broaden the truth that it describes, and embark on the path to justice and forgiveness for all those who are named in the report. At no point should the necessary law of national reconciliation -- that we are requesting today -- prohibit amplification of the truth, supersede minimum requisites of justice, or reinforce the structure of impunity that has existed in the country.
>
> We invite those implicated in the case of our assassinated brother Jesuits to the reconciliation found in the truth. The more quickly they recognize the truth in what happened, the more quickly can be set in motion the mechanisms of justice and legal forgiveness so needed by them as well as by our society. For our part, we have never harbored hate toward these people, and we have extended Christian forgiveness to them from the beginning. In order to help them with legal forgiveness they must recognize their participation in the crime, or be convicted at trial.

Though they had consistently insisted that the "intellectual authors" of the crime must be identified, once the names were public, the Jesuits sought to focus attention on the institutional nature of human rights abuse in El Salvador. Appearing on Salvadoran television on the morning of March 16, Father José María Tojeira, the Jesuit Provincial for Central America, said that while those named in connection with the Jesuit case should be held legally accountable, "what really matters is to reflect more thoroughly on the attitudes. Now is the time to be tough on the attitudes and structures that foster these kinds of crimes, rather than on the individuals involved. With individuals you have to be understanding. But I think that given this report you have to come down extremely hard on the structures and attitudes."[24]

---

24 Buenos Dias, Channel 12, Mar. 15, 1993, as recorded by INSISTEM.

Father Rodolfo Cardenal, an UCA vice rector who lived with the men who were murdered in November 1989, added,

> The most important aspect of the report is not the names, but that the report shows that the Army, the justice system and the State as a whole has failed in its constitutional mission and that it must be restructured and fundamentally reformulated.... But what we do emphasize is that we harbor no hate, no resentment against any of them, nor against anyone who has been named in the report.[25]

Writing in *The Christian Science Monitor*, Father Tojeira echoed this theme: "That members of El Salvador's military high command ordered the Jesuit murders confirms the institutional nature of the crime. [....] Indeed, the report as a whole makes a compelling case that the abuse of human rights in El Salvador was systematic and institutionalized."[26]

Those Named React

Several of those named by the Truth Commission in connection with the Jesuit case attempted a showy public defense. Asked the next day for his opinion of the report and the accusations made against him, former Air Force Commander Juan Rafael Bustillo called the report "garbage" that had "caused this great problem here in our country...."[27] General Bustillo suggested that President Cristiani had been remiss in not calling him to discuss the Jesuit case so that his alleged participation could be clarified. Further, he called on Generals Ponce, Zepeda and Elena Fuentes "to manifest publicly, from a position of honor and professional ethics, if in any time or place I met with them to plan" the murders. According to the General, the Jesuit murders deprived the Armed Forces of the "sacrifice" they had made in achieving a "military victory" during the guerrilla offensive.

Several outspoken rightists criticized President Cristiani for ever agreeing to the formation of the Truth Commission. Calling Mr. Cristiani "irresponsible," General Bustillo said the "president and his advisors should be more careful when signing

---

25 El Noticiero, Mar. 15, 1993, as recorded by INSISTEM.

26 *Christian Science Monitor*, April 13, 1993.

27 Megavision, Mar. 16, 1993, as recorded by INSISTEM.

agreements that involve the destiny of the nation."[28] Cristiani's own vice-president, Francisco Merino, said it was an "error" to have appointed the Commission because similar efforts elsewhere had promoted reconciliation, but "here we didn't get what we expected."

Generals Zepeda and Ponce, appearing together on a morning TV talk show, sought to discredit the Truth Commission findings in a confused torrent of countercharges and distortions. General Ponce laid out three theses which he found contradictory and speculative -- "none are supported by any verifiable evidence or concrete testimonies."[29] To present the "Jesuit thesis," Ponce read from an UCA article and a brief filed by the private prosecutors stating simply that Benavides was acting on higher orders. In one revealing statement, Ponce attributed his second thesis -- the similar version put forward by Congressman Moakley -- to the proverbial Jesuit conspiracy: "The thesis of the Moakley Commission is nurtured and based on the passage that I read from the Jesuits because the influence of the Jesuit Congregation in the world is extensive and about this we have to be very clear." Additionally, Ponce accused Moakley and his staff of "coercion," claiming they had pressured some of the defendants to make statements supporting Moakley's account in exchange for help, which the general termed "direct intervention in the internal affairs of our country." Ponce said he had invited the congressman to El Salvador to conduct a thorough investigation. The Defense Minister said Moakley -- whose charges had "definitively hurt our dignity as individuals and that of our families" -- had not answered his invitation.

The third thesis, according to General Ponce, was that put forward by Major Buckland, who said Colonel Avilés had been sent by Ponce to try to persuade Benavides from killing the Jesuits. The Defense Minister said that the Truth Commission report contained elements of all three theses, which were mutually exclusive, ergo the report was a "lie." Ponce read aloud a long portion of *From Madness to Hope*, pointing out that the officers met in "such a small room -- how were we going to meet in groups to plan an assassination of such magnitude?" And seeking to further disprove the Commission's version of events, the Defense Minister said he would not be apt to conspire with General Bustillo because through the years

---

28 *Washington Post*, Mar. 19,1993.

29 Frente a Frente, Channel 12, Mar. 25, 1993, as recorded by INSISTEM.

they had had many "differences."[30] Asked about the report's inclusion of his accusations that "terrorist strategy was planned" inside the UCA, General Zepeda said he was just repeating what was common knowledge. The general said that "it was almost proven and there was a general consensus, that the universities, both the National University and the UCA, were planning centers for terrorism....I was not accusing individuals or institutions, as the Jesuits have tried to say, nor was I accusing the Jesuits, I said the National University, the UCA. (sic)"[31]

On March 23, General Ponce read a lengthy statement on television blasting the report as "unfair, incomplete, illegal, unethical, biased and insolent." Ponce, who was flanked by the rest of the High Command plus brigade and military detachment chiefs, was introduced by Mr. Cristiani's spokesman. The military threatened to take "legal measures" against those who "promote the destruction" of the institution. While the statement did not mention the Jesuit case specifically, the rejection of the Commission and its legitimacy was total:

> The "Truth Commission" has exceeded the powers that it was given by the Peace Accords, invading constitutional terrain and the jurisdiction of governmental bodies themselves and the proper administration of justice. Furthermore, the Commission does not recognize in its report the nature and origins of the communist attack against El Salvador. Nor does the Commission recognize the legitimate right of defense of any legally constituted government in the face of any kind of aggression.
>
> At no time were those accused given an opportunity to argue their cases or publicly defend themselves against the charges made. The report marginalizes any proper process of the rule of law.
>
> ...we affirm that the report defrauds the hope and faith of all Salvadorans. We hoped for a serious and impartial document that would help heal the wounds inflicted during the 12 years of war and that would

---

30 On this point, Ponce's argumentation rings true; the enmity between the hard-line Air Force chief and the *tandona* is well known.

31 Frente a Frente, Channel 12, Mar. 25, 1993, as recorded by INSISTEM, at 10.

> uphold the process of moral and material reconstruction of the country.[32]

When opposition politicians questioned the constitutionality of the military's attack on the report, President Cristiani said he had authorized the presentation because he believed that the Armed Forces had the right to defend itself. Rubén Zamora of the Democratic Convergence said, "We have a crisis and the question is: Who is running the country, a defense minister who resigned or the president who has not yet accepted his resignation?"[33]

The Joint Command's legal advisor, Rodolfo Antonio Parker Soto, the only civilian named by the Truth Commission in connection with the case, wrote a letter to the United Nations Secretary General, which appeared as a paid advertisement in Salvadoran newspapers. The advertisement began: "I, Rodolfo Antonio Parker Soto, before the national conscience declare: Above any personal interest, we are and WE WILL CONTINUE UNFLINCHINGLY, at the service of our El Salvador."[34] Parker Soto denied altering any statements or excluding the names of higher ranking officers, since he said he had heard no such testimony. "The nonexistent cannot be altered." Parker Soto did not take issue with the report's account of how the crime was ordered, but stated that "neither the undersigned nor the members of the Honor Commission ever had any knowledge that Benavides had received higher orders."

ARENA Reacts

Government officials and their allies uniformly attacked the report, raising doubts about their will to comply with the extensive recommendations made by the Commission. Dr. Oscar Santamaría, the minister of the presidency who headed the government side at the negotiating table, charged that the report will lead to "confrontation, not reconciliation....It is a

---

32 Posición de la Fuerza Armada de El Salvador ante el Informe de la Comisión de la Verdad, Mar. 23, 1993, as published in *Diario de Hoy*, Mar. 24, 1993. The assertion that those mentioned by the Truth Commission were not given an opportunity to "defend themselves against the charges made" is not true. All those mentioned in the report or involved in the cases covered were invited to an interview with Commission staff.

33 *Washington Post*, Mar. 26, 1993.

34 *Diario de Hoy*, Mar. 22, 1993. Emphasis in the original.

step backwards, not serious, not complete...not balanced."[35] General Mauricio Vargas, who served as deputy chief of staff until July 1 and was the only officer on the negotiating team, called the report "biased, incomplete, unfair, totally unacceptable....This lousy document must be rejected totally....They talk about autonomy and reconciliation and then attack the sovereignty of the state!"[36] President Cristiani took to the airwaves on March 18 to present the government's official position. He reminded the nation that the Truth Commission was an "integral part" of the peace accords. Yet he said the report failed to meet the Salvadoran people's "yearning" with respect to national reconciliation "which is to forgive and forget this painful past."[37] Vice President Francisco Merino and San Salvador Mayor Armando Calderón Sol came to the defense of ARENA founder Roberto D'Aubuisson, to whom the Commission not surprisingly assigned responsibility for the 1980 murder of Archbishop Oscar Romero and whom it accused of sponsoring widespread death squad activity. Mr. Merino called the charges against D'Aubuisson an "insult."

In arguably its most controversial recommendation, the report called for the resignation of the entire Supreme Court. The failings of El Salvador's justice system were the document's leitmotif. "The judiciary was weakened as it fell victim to intimidation and the foundations were laid for its corruption," the Commissioners observed. "Since it had never enjoyed genuine institutional independence from the legislative and executive branches, its ineffectiveness steadily increased until it became, through its inaction or its appalling submissiveness, a factor which contributed to the tragedy suffered by the country."[38] Characteristically feisty, Supreme Court President Mauricio Gutiérrez Castro, of ARENA's right flank, responded that "only God" could remove him from his post. Of the creation of the Truth Commission, Mr. Gutiérrez said: "it was not an error, it was a stupidity."[39]

---

35 Channel 12, Mar. 19, 1993, as cited in El Rescate: Report from El Salvador, Vol. 4, No. 11.

36 Interview, JSU radio, Mar. 20, 1993, as quoted in El Rescate: Report from El Salvador, Vol. 4, No.11.

37 INSISTEM, Mar. 18, 1993. See also, *Los Angeles Times*, Mar. 19, 1993.

38 *Madness to Hope*, at 172-173.

39 TCS News, April 15, 1993, as recorded by INSISTEM.

Reactions in the United States

The findings of the Truth Commission also made big news in the United States, where El Salvador once again dominated headlines for weeks. Congressman Moakley noted that the report reinforced his own findings, and called it a "road map for El Salvador's future":

> In the case of the murders at the University of Central America in 1989 (the Jesuits' case), the Commission's findings are similar to those of the Speaker's Task Force on El Salvador, which I chaired, and which released its own report more than a year ago. The Commission's findings underline my own conclusion that members of the Salvadoran High Command were involved in ordering and in covering up these cold-blooded murders. *Accordingly, it is my personal view that no further U.S. military aid should be delivered or obligated to El Salvador as long as senior military officers named in both the Truth Commission and Ad Hoc Commission reports remain in uniform.*
>
> Finally, the Commission's report reminds us that truth, no matter how difficult, remains a far better basis than denial or concealment for uniting a people and building a nation. Every page screams out the truth that political tolerance and respect for law are essential to the fabric of any society and to the happiness and well-being of its people. In this vital sense, the Truth Commission's report, while necessarily focusing on El Salvador's past, has provided a road map for El Salvador's future.[40]

With some politicians and observers expressing surprise at the litany of abuses attributed to government forces -- 95% of the complaints received by the Commission -- coverage focused on what the Reagan and Bush Administrations knew and when they knew it. One refreshingly candid article attempted to put that question to rest. Benjamin Schwarz, the author of a critical Rand Corporation study of U.S. policy toward El Salvador produced for the Defense Department, said "Of course we knew."

---

40 Statement by Congressman Joe Moakley (D-MA) on the Salvadoran Truth Commission Report, Mar. 15, 1993. Emphasis in the original.

> The recently released United Nations report on the atrocities of El Salvador's civil war confirms what we have long shrunk from confronting: In El Salvador, Americans were dancing with the devil. If our policy toward that country is faced honestly, then there is ample blame to be distributed among us all: Democrats and Republicans, "liberals" and "conservatives."
>
> The report provokes a number of questions about American policy in El Salvador, and the supposedly "difficult" one can be put immediately to rest: Of course we knew.
>
> The American project in El Salvador gave the U.S. government and military access to every facet of Salvadoran public life. American officials have therefore always known *more* than the human rights groups, journalists and non-partisan experts who for 14 years have chronicled the brutality and corruption of the Salvadoran military.[41]

What the Bush Administration should have known about the Jesuit case was that the High Command -- including Defense Minister Ponce -- had ordered the murders and that a massive institutional coverup was launched by the Armed Forces. After the report was issued Congressman Moakley said that the Bush Administration "was either involved in the coverup or they had very incompetent and insensitive people."[42] While the U.S. Embassy temporarily blocked René Emilio Ponce's promotion to defense minister until his name was cleared, they ultimately gave him the green light when he was considered the most attractive of several potential ministers. As the peace process progressed, U.S. officials openly praised Ponce for the positive role they felt he was playing in coaxing the military to accept a negotiated settlement to the war. By late 1990, Embassy officials admitted privately that the High Command was engaged in a coverup of the Jesuit murders, but argued that continuing to push for more accountability would only derail the greater good -- achieving a negotiated end to the bloodshed. Moakley told *The New York Times* that United States officials repeatedly withheld evidence from him and that when he tried to trace the chain of command upward after the

---

41 *Washington Post*, April 8, 1993.

42 *New York Times*, Mar. 21, 1993.

trial in September 1991 "the Administration wanted us to keep quiet and go away."[43]

For its part, the State Department's response was bland and understated. Richard Boucher, the spokesman who had also served under President Bush, declined to comment specifically on the report, observing merely that the "examination of human rights abuses on both sides during the conflict is a critical step towards building national reconciliation."[44] According to press accounts, Mr. Boucher said the department had "cooperated fully and helped fund" the Truth Commission's work.[45] Asked if the Republican Administrations had failed to protect the human rights of Salvadorans, the spokesman said, "That's something that the analysts and the historians can try to judge. I'm not going to try to make that judgment at this point."[46]

Several press accounts retold the story of how Ambassador Walker had suggested to Congressman Moakley, as late as January 2, 1990, that the FMLN might have killed the Jesuits. Mr. Walker says he had argued that all possibilities should be explored. *The Washington Post* noted prominently that Mr. Walker had referred to the Jesuit murders in November 1989 as a "management problem":

> Management control problems exist in a situation like this. And it's not a management control that would lend itself to Harvard Business School analysis. I mean, this is war. It's fighting, it's death....I really think President Cristiani is under a barrage from all sides and all sorts of events. I think some things are happening that he would prefer not to happen.[47]

Perhaps surprisingly, the U.S. responsibility for events in El Salvador over the last decade only drew one comment from the Truth Commission, which pointed out that Washington had "tolerated" the activities of Salvadorans living in Miami who "directly financed and indirectly helped run certain death

---

43 *Id.*

44 *New York Newsday*, Mar.16, 1993.

45 *Id.*

46 *New York Times*, Mar. 16, 1993.

47 *Washington Post*, Mar. 21, 1993.

squads."[48] Asked by a Spanish reporter how U.S. advisors could not have known about the Jesuit murders, Commission President Belisario Betancur answered: "You are asking me a difficult question. I would like to believe (*Me hago la ilusión*) that it passed by unnoticed, that it was known by individuals but not institutionally."[49]

The Jesuit Provincial was more direct in holding Washington accountable. Father Tojeira told Spanish radio that he believes "there is a lot more responsibility that does not appear in the report on the part of some sectors of the U.S. Embassy. I believe that [U.S. diplomats in El Salvador] did know what happened from the very first moment and they positively covered it up and this aspect is not in the report yet is just as real as the part which accuses the Salvadoran army."[50]

Secretary of State Warren Christopher pointed out that although the report "contains no explicit criticism of the U.S. government or its representatives....when questions arise that challenge our commitments [to human rights], we have an obligation to seek answers." The Administration's response was to appoint a panel to "examine the implications" of the Truth Commission report for the "conduct of U.S. foreign policy and the operations of the Department of State." The panel, consisting of two retired ambassadors and an academic advisor, was mandated to examine: 1) responsiveness to Congressional and public inquiries; 2) human rights reporting 3) and the "degree to which we encouraged State Department officers to conduct a full and independent inquiry of abuses by both sides." Not mandated to re-examine U.S. policy toward El Salvador, the panel would instead conduct a narrow examination of the performance of State Department and Embassy officials. No such study was launched of the behavior of personnel attached to the Pentagon, FBI, CIA or any of the other intelligence agencies which have worked in El Salvador since the 1960s. Responding to a congressional request, President Clinton promised to release documentation concerning the 32 cases in *From Madness to Hope*. The President said that the declassification, to be completed by September 30, 1993, would include the files of not only the

---

48 *Madness to Hope*, at 137.

49 *Diario 16* (Madrid), Mar. 16, 1993.

50 *El País* (Madrid), Mar. 17, 1993; see also Notimex, Mar. 17, 1993, as printed in *El Mundo*, Mar. 17, 1993.

State Department, but also the Pentagon and the Central Intelligence Agency.[51]

March 20 Amnesty Decree

In El Salvador, ARENA officials wasted no time in heading off any attempt to file legal proceedings. On the eve of the report's release, President Cristiani appeared on a nationwide television broadcast calling for "maturity and patriotism," while indicating his intention to implement an immediate general amnesty. Heeding the president's call, ARENA assembly deputies, supported by two other conservative parties, pushed through an immediate, unconditional and far-reaching amnesty late on the evening of Saturday, March 20, 1993. Opposition political parties and nongovernmental organizations objected to the fashion in which it was adopted -- rapidly and without consensus -- yet most were on record in support of an amnesty at some point after the report's publication. The Democratic Convergence had argued that an amnesty should be conditioned on compliance with Truth Commission recommendations. According to Convergence leader Rubén Zamora, "A full-speed-ahead amnesty gives the impression of wanting to silence the Truth Commission."[52] The amnesty's critics cited several areas in which the amnesty was unconstitutional. For example, Article 244 of the Constitution denies amnesty to government functionaries -- including high-ranking officers -- during the term of the president in office at the time the crime was committed. This provision makes Colonel Benavides ineligible for a pardon until President Cristiani leaves office in June 1994.

Oddly, the amnesty also included a chapter in the penal code dealing with crimes committed by lawyers and judges, none of which fall within the definition of political crimes eligible for amnesty. Perhaps fearful that the Truth Commission's emphasis on judicial complicity in impunity might result in prosecutions of civilian officials,[53] the law's authors expanded the scope of "political offenses" to include

---

51 Letter to the Honorable John Joseph Moakley from President William Clinton, June 7, 1993; *see* also *New York Times*, June 13, 1993.

52 Channel 21, Mar. 15, 1993, as quoted in El Rescate: Report from El Salvador, Vol. 4, No.11.

53 For example, the Truth Commission found that two officials, Supreme Court President Gutiérrez Castro and Joint Command legal advisor Parker Soto had interfered with investigations. *Madness to Hope*, at 121, 54.

crimes such as coverup and willfully improper judicial rulings (*prevaricato*). By characterizing such offenses as political per se, they foreclosed prosecution of any and all legal system abuses, regardless of whether they bore any relation to politically motivated acts such as those investigated by the Truth Commission.

The amnesty also flouted international law, which requires the Salvadoran government to afford victims and their families adequate judicial redress. In some respects the law was even more egregious than other amnesties in the region that had previously been declared unlawful by the Inter-American Commission on Human Rights, which has jurisdiction over El Salvador. In its pre-emptive haste, the Legislative Assembly largely robbed Salvadorans of both the chance to reflect on the Truth Commission's findings and how best to promote reconciliation. In addition, the amnesty, under color of law, corrupted the legal system by reprieving those who had subverted it. That this extended even to acts unrelated to El Salvador's political conflict mocked the drafters' claim to be seeking "consolidation of the peace."

San Salvador's Archbishop Arturo Rivera Damas quickly expressed the Church's rejection of the amnesty and concern about the "desperate maneuver of the government to forget and maintain impunity in [the Archbishop Romero] and other cases."[54] Writing in *El País*, José María Tojeira termed the amnesty "an affront to justice."[55]

> Few people in El Salvador doubt the necessity of seeking mechanisms for legal forgiveness after a civil war that lasted more than a decade, but the capricious, non-consensual, indiscriminate and apparently illegal character of the current amnesty law suggests a mockery of justice that achieves everything but reconciliation in society.
>
> This amnesty law is...an affront to the poor of El Salvador. It reaffirms the idea that the life of the poor has no value or interest in the country. It is more

---

54 Radio YSAX, Mar. 21, 1993, as quoted in El Rescate: Report from El Salvador, Vol. 4, No.11.

55 *El País* (Madrid), April 12, 1993.

> important to save a military officer the shame of being confronted with his crimes -- though he would ultimately be forgiven -- than to make amends for, in some way, the memory of innocent victims. The more than 100 children assassinated in cold blood at El Mozote do not merit even an official request for forgiveness from the institution which perpetrated this massacre. By contrast, they want to oblige the poor to forget the past so that some very few -- in power -- do not have to assume any responsibility for their atrocious crimes. [....] to justify this law, the government has resorted to lying publicly and systematically manipulating information.

In their public communiqué and in numerous interviews in March and April, the Jesuits laid out a novel two-step approach to forgiveness. "For our part, we have never harbored hate toward these people, and we have extended Christian forgiveness to them from the beginning. In order to help them with legal forgiveness, they must recognize their participation in the crime, or be convicted at trial."[56] Father Tojeira said on a morning talk show that "Christian forgiveness and social, legal forgiveness must not be confused. These are two very different things. I have forgiven the common criminals, but society has not given them legal forgiveness" and they are in jail.[57] "To achieve a pardon I believe that the concrete mechanisms should be as follows: that the person admit his crimes and ask Salvadoran society for forgiveness." For those who do not admit their participation in the crimes in which they are accused, Tojeira proposed that they should stand trial. "For those who are found guilty, we will be the first to ask for a pardon, as we have for those who have already been convicted. So these are the two routes: confess and ask society for forgiveness or stand trial. I think that's the rational formula for putting forward a 'Law of Reconciliation' in the country, a law that has to come. There must be legal forgiveness in this country."[58]

UN Secretary General Boutros-Ghali expressed "concern at the haste with which this step had been taken" and his opinion that "it would have been preferable if the amnesty had been promulgated after creating a broad degree of national consensus

---

56 Public Communiqué, Society of Jesus, San Salvador, Mar. 15, 1993.

57 Frente a Frente, Channel 12, Mar. 15, 1993, as recorded by INSISTEM, at 7.

58 *Id.*, at 8.

in its favor."[59] Before the amnesty was adopted, Senator Christopher Dodd, who chairs the Senate Foreign Relations Committee, said a blanket amnesty "would be a major step backwards; it would send the message that there is no price anyone pays."[60] *The New York Times* condemned the amnesty in the strongest terms, calling it an affront to the "United Nations-sponsored peace process, international human rights law and the memory of El Salvador's victims." The editorial observed: "Commit atrocities on a large enough scale and you can get away with it, on the argument that full accountability would destabilize the political order. That's the callous conclusion invited by El Salvador's sweeping amnesty law...."[61]

Saying they were "stupefied" by the amnesty, the families of the five Spanish-born Jesuits wrote to President Cristiani to express their "righteous indignation at what is...a new transgression of the most elementary principles of justice [....] behind this amnesty is hypocrisy, bad faith, an eagerness to hide the truth and impede justice. It protects the impunity that has existed until today and it encourages public criminals in their arrogance and in placing themselves above the law. The only thing the authors of this amnesty cannot hide is that by adopting the law, they admit that those whom they are trying to protect really are guilty of crimes against humanity."[62]

Three Salvadoran human rights groups filed constitutional challenges to the amnesty, but the Constitutional Chamber of the Supreme Court refused to consider their petitions, arguing that to rule on the constitutionality of the amnesty would violate the division of powers. The Supreme Court is not competent to consider "purely political questions," it ruled.[63] The grandiloquent ruling issued by the Chamber ironically supports the charges that the Court is politicized. Reading more like a sociology text than a legal brief, the ruling discusses the roots of the word sovereignty in the French and

---

59 "Report of the Secretary-General on the United Nations Observer Mission in El Salvador," UN Doc. S/25812, May 21, 1993, at 2.

60 *Washington Post*, Mar. 17, 1993.

61 *New York Times*, Mar. 25, 1993.

62 Letter to President Alfredo Cristiani, dated Mar. 26, 1993, signed for the families by Juan. A. Ellacuría.

63 Sala de lo Constitucional de la Corte Suprema de Justicia, May 20, 1993, No. 10-93, at 11.

American revolutions; the definition of what is political; and discusses the Greek origin of the word amnesty. The document offers a survey of literature on the subject, buttressing its rejection of the challenge by citing a duke who served as advisor to France's King Charles X who wrote that "a pardon is more judicial than political. Amnesty is more political than judicial." Somebody spent a lot of time trying elegantly to duck the issues at hand.

Given the strong rejection of *From Madness to Hope* by ARENA officials, prospects for full implementation of the Commission's extensive recommendations seem slim. Supreme Court President Gutiérrez Castro has repeatedly expressed his view that the peace settlement is a political agreement and as such, has nothing to do with the justice system.[64] President Cristiani and his vice president have stated more than once that since the judicial branch is independent of the executive branch, their government was powerless to ask the Supreme Court to resign.[65] According to the UN Secretary General, Cristiani wrote to him saying he was "willing to comply strictly with those of the Commission's recommendations which fell within his competence, were consistent with the Constitution, were in harmony with the Peace Accords and contributed to national reconciliation."[66] This wording leaves Cristiani a lot of room for maneuver. Mr. Boutros-Ghali indirectly expressed concern about the depth of the Government's will to comply, and noted, "At the same time, spokesmen of the Government accused the members of the Commission of having exceeded their mandate and in particular of having purported to assume judicial functions."[67]

There were other signs that publication of the Truth Commission report might not provide the hoped-for turning point in El Salvador's polarized society. A paid advertisement in the afternoon newspaper, *El Mundo*, blamed the Truth Commission and peace process itself on a "Jesuit document" published more than a decade ago which laid out a "nefarious

---

64 *See* for example, the Supreme Court's rebuttal to the Truth Commission, published in *Diario Latino*, Mar. 29, 1993.

65 *See* for example comments by Vice President Francisco Merino, Al Día, Mar. 18, 1993, as recorded by INSISTEM.

66 "Report of the Secretary General," *supra* note 59, at 13.

67 *Id.*

plan" for a negotiated solution to the conflict.[68] One week later, a full-page ad from the Civic Movement for a Free El Salvador, entitled "The Jesuit Document and the Annihilation of the Army," declared that the Ad Hoc and Truth Commissions were part of a longstanding plot to "do in the Army."[69]

Where are they now?

On March 31, San Salvador's First Criminal Appeals Court -- where the case had been sitting since the defense attorneys challenged the sentences -- decreed that the amnesty applied to those convicted in the Jesuit case. That same afternoon, the Fourth Criminal Judge signed release papers for Colonel Guillermo Alfredo Benavides and Lieutenant Yusshy René Mendoza Vallecillos. Both men left the Santa Ana prison on April 1. The cases against the other men convicted on lesser charges were also dropped. The release of Benavides and Mendoza fulfills the only recommendation made by the Truth Commission concerning the Jesuit case: that the two men should not remain in jail while others responsible for planning the killings and carrying them out remained at liberty.[70]

Colonel Nelson Iván López y López, who most recently commanded the Third Brigade, and Fourth Brigade Commander Colonel Oscar Alberto León Linares, who headed the Atlacatl Battalion at the time of the Jesuit murders, were both placed on "unassigned" status in the April 30, 1993 General Order of the Armed Forces. It was widely believed that these moves were linked to the Ad Hoc-mandated "purge." General Montano had earlier been sent to Mexico as Military Attaché; Colonel Francisco Elena Fuentes was sent to Guatemala as envoy to the Central American Defense Council. It was later revealed that he too had been placed on "unassigned" status as his retirement papers were processed.

On July 1, Generals Ponce, Zepeda, Rubio and Vargas retired with full military honors, having completed 30 years of service in the Armed Forces.[71] Calling it a day of "great

68 *El Mundo*, Mar. 8, 1993.

69 *Prensa Grafica*, Mar. 15, 1993.

70 *Madness to Hope*, at 54.

71 According to General Ponce, Generals Rubio and Vargas were not on the Ad Hoc list. Channel 6 News, June 30, 1993, as cited in Report from El Salvador, Vol. 4, No.24. Vice Minister of Defense Juan Orlando Zepeda

transcendence," President Cristiani said they had performed with "merit, efficiency, and loyalty to the highest duties that the nation can demand.... We want to express our recognition and our gratitude....[72] General Ponce told reporters he was considering running for public office.

On July 6, General Juan Rafael Bustillo announced his candidacy for the presidency of El Salvador on the ticket of the the Party of National Conciliation (PCN), the traditional party of the Armed Forces. "As a soldier I fulfilled my duty, in strict accordance with the law and the Constitution and respectful of the rights of others," said Bustillo. "But now the theater is different and I am ready to continue fighting for the good of the country."[73] Six weeks after the Jesuit murders, General Bustillo had unexpectedly resigned as commander of the Air Force, which he had led for an unprecedented ten years. Bustillo was assigned as Military Attaché in Israel, and resigned from the military in 1991, amid rumors that he would make a presidential bid.

Secretary General Boutros-Ghali informed the Security Council on July 7 that the Salvadoran government was now in "broad compliance with the Ad Hoc Commission's recommendations, although with a delay of several months...." His letter said the 15 officers had been "placed on leave with pay pending completion of the procedures for their retirement, which would take place not later than 31 December 1993."[74]

---

officially retired on March 31, though he participated in the ceremony in full dress uniform.

72 Discurso del Señor Presidente de la Republica y Comandante General de la Fuerza Armada, Lic. Alfredo Felix Cristiani en Ocasión al Traspaso de Mando de la Fuerza Armada, July 1, 1993, as printed in *Diario de Hoy*, July 2, 1993.

73 *Diario de Hoy*, July 7, 1993.

74 Letter Dated 7 July 1993 from the Secretary-General Addressed to the President of the Security Council, UN Doc. S/26052, July 8, 1993.

Commenting on the retirement of the High Command and the long-awaited departure of the *tandona*, Father Rodolfo Cardenal said: "We cannot say that they have been forgiven without them having recognized their role in the events. This would be to forget and we cannot do that. Also, the person who is going to be forgiven has to demonstrate it, and these officers who are resigning have not demonstrated that they want to be forgiven. [....] They have prevailed over civil society, retiring when they wanted to and in the manner they chose. And it's no secret they are leaving with their pockets full."[75]

75 *Diario Latino*, July 3, 1993.

ATLACATL COMMANDOS

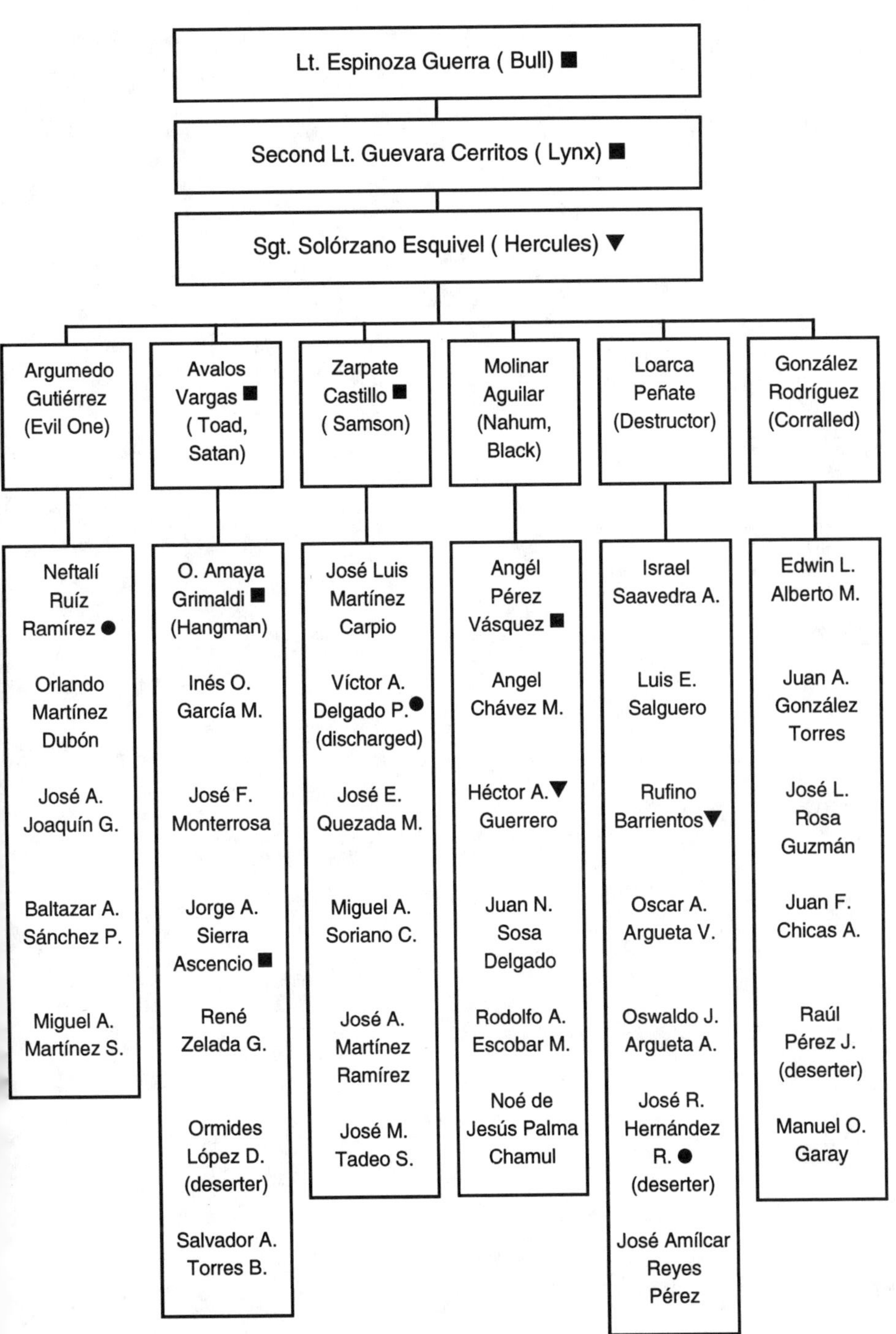

■ Charged with murder
▼ Charged with perjury
● Ballistics match-up

Appendix A

CHRONOLOGY OF THE UCA ASSASSINATION CASE

October 1989

16 U.S. military advisor Major Buckland returns to El Salvador on permanent assignment at C-5 (Psychological Operations).

31 Colonel Avilés leaves for vacation in New Orleans, returning to El Salvador on Nov. 14.

November 1989

10 U.S. Special Forces from Ft. Bragg, North Carolina initiate a training course for elite Atlacatl troops at battalion headquarters at Sitio del Niño, La Libertad.

11 3:30 p.m. to 5:35 p.m., Vice President Merino visits Atlacatl headquarters.
8:00 p.m. FMLN offensive commences in San Salvador and other cities around the nation.
By 11:00 p.m., all radio stations are pressured into joining a nationwide hook-up, which broadcasts death threats against the Jesuits and members of the political opposition.

12 President Cristiani declares a State of Exception and 6:00 p.m. to 6:00 a.m. curfew. National Guard Director Colonel Carrillo Schlenker is named *Jefe de Plaza* during the State of Exception, with ultimate authority over the metropolitan area.
Threats against the Jesuits continue to be broadcast over the national radio network.
11:30 a.m. Weapons left by fleeing guerrillas found by Treasury Police at Loyola Center near the UCA.

13 U.S. training of Atlacatl commandos is suspended. Atlacatl troops are transferred to San Salvador, where they are billeted at the Military Academy near the UCA.
UCA rector, Father Ellacuría, arrives in San Salvador in the afternoon.
A Special Security Zone is created to defend Joint Command headquarters and neighboring military installations. Placed in charge of the Army's most important zone is Colonel Benavides, commander of the Military Academy.
5:45 p.m. Father Ellacuría arrives at the UCA.
6:30 p.m. Within two hours of their arrival in San Salvador, Atlacatl units under the command of Lieutenant Espinoza search the Jesuit residence on the UCA campus. Lieutenant Cuenca Ocampo, who is attached to the military intelligence body, DNI, participates in the operation.

14 Atlacatl troops arrest a woman a few blocks from the UCA.

15 3:00 p.m. Over 100 Atlacatl troops occupy Loyola Center near the UCA.

Early evening. Lieutenant Espinoza meets with Ambassador Walker and top U.S. military advisor Colonel Menjívar at the ambassador's home.
Evening. Atlacatl patrols stationed on north, southeast, southwest and west sides of the UCA.
Ranking military officers hold several meetings throughout the day. Twenty-four top officers meet in closed door session from 6:30 p.m. to 10:30 p.m.
8:00 or 9:00 p.m. A National Guardsman is killed by "friendly fire" near Cine Colonial, four blocks from the UCA.
10:30 p.m. President Cristiani is summoned to Joint Command headquarters, where he meets with Chief-of-Staff Ponce, Defense Minister Larios, and Vice Ministers Zepeda and Montano. Colonel Benavides meets with Military Academy officers to report on the meeting at the Joint Command headquarters.
10:30 p.m. Lieutenant Espinoza of the Atlacatl is ordered by radio to gather his men.
11:30 p.m. Colonel Benavides gives Lieutenants Espinoza and Mendoza the order to kill the Jesuits.

16 12:30 a.m. President Cristiani is given a briefing on San Salvador's military situation in the COCFA, where he says two or three U.S. military advisers are present.
1:00 a.m. The operation against the UCA commences. Colonel Cerna Flores ends his period as COCFA duty officer.
2:30 a.m. Atlacatl commandos execute two women and six Jesuit priests inside the walled UCA campus. The Oscar Romero Pastoral Center (CRT) is also ransacked, burned and barraged with an M-60 machine gun. Mrs. Cerna and her family hear gun fire; she observes military officers on the UCA campus.
2:30 a.m. President Cristiani leaves Join Command headquarters.
6:30 a.m. UCA gardener Obdulio Ramos, husband of the murdered cook, Elba Ramos, informs the Jesuits of the assassinations.
Ellacuría's death is announced at the daily meeting of the National Intelligence Directorate (DNI). The officers present reportedly break into applause.
News of the multiple murder spreads, and scores of people arrive at the scene, including San Salvador Archbishop Rivera y Damas and judicial authorities.
9:10 a.m. The SIU arrives at the crime scene.
During the day, First Brigade megaphones announce, "Ellacuría and Martín-Baró have fallen. We are going to continue killing communists."
Archbishop Rivera y Damas and Jesuit Provincial Father Tojeira announce that circumstantial evidence points toward the Armed Forces.

17 Police stationed in the vicinity during the murder hours inform the SIU that they saw Atlacatl pass by.

18 President Cristiani asks forensic experts from Spain, USA, Great Britain and Canada to collaborate with the SIU investigation.
Attorney General Colorado writes to Pope John Paul II, suggesting that bishops who "have persisted in keeping alive this questionable ideology of the "church of the poor" be sent out of the country.

19 Defense Minister Larios condemns the murders, placing blame on the FMLN.

20 The SIU begins interviewing witnesses.

21 Father Estrada tells the SIU that Atlacatl members searched the Jesuit residence on November 13.

22-23 Before flying to Miami, Mrs. Cerna, a Jesuit housekeeper, testifies before Judge Zamora to the presence of armed men in military uniform on the campus while the murders took place.

23 President Cristiani calls Cerna's testimony "inconclusive."

24 The Attorney General dismisses the importance of Cerna's testimony.

28 Father Estrada is named UCA Rector.
Mrs. Cerna and her family begin a week of incommunicado interrogation by the FBI and Lieutenant Colonel Rivas of the SIU. On the third day, Cerna recants her testimony under pressure.

30 *Tutela Legal*, human rights office of the Catholic Archdiocese of San Salvador, publishes a report, concluding that the Salvadoran Armed Forces are responsible for the murders, and demonstrating the use of U.S.-supplied bullets in the crime.

December 1989

1 Colonel López y López, a former SIU chief, is temporarily reassigned to the SIU.

3 Mrs. Cerna and her family are turned over to U.S. Jesuits. U.S. Embassy legal officer Richard Chidester and Lieutenant Colonel Rivas return to San Salvador and within days meet with Colonel Benavides at the Military Academy.

4 The Cristiani government launches an international diplomatic offensive to "neutralize disinformation" concerning the murders. Delegations visit Europe, South America and Washington.

6 The Speaker's Special Task Force on El Salvador is appointed, headed by Congressman Moakley.

8 Colonel Ponce, chief of the Joint Command, provides written testimony to the Judge.
Fathers Ibisate and Estrada tell the court that the Atlacatl searched the Jesuit residence on November 13.

9 President Cristiani offers a $250,000 reward to anyone offering information leading to killers' identification.

10 Archbishop Rivera y Damas accuses U.S. authorities of mistreating witness Lucía Cerna while in FBI custody in Miami.

13 Lieutenant Espinoza is questioned by the SIU. In subsequent days, other Atlacatl commandos also give statements.
DNI Lieutenant Cuenca Ocampo prepares a report on the November 13 search of the UCA residence for his superiors.

18 Colonel Ponce sends the SIU a report of events in the UCA area on the night of November 15-16 which includes an entry indicating that "delinquent terrorists," the Army's appellation for the FMLN, assassinated the Jesuits at 12:30 a.m.

20 Major Buckland is told by Colonel Avilés of Colonel Benavides' role in the murders.

22 Fathers Tojeira and Estrada are given what the U.S. embassy calls a "full and detailed briefing" by Colonel López y López and Lieutenant Colonel Rivas of the SIU. Neither the Atlacatl Battalion nor Colonel Benavides is mentioned.

25 Major Buckland writes a letter to his sister, Carol Buckland, telling her of what he has been told of Colonel Benavides' role in the murders.

29 Ballistics tests begin on weapons assigned to those soldiers who encircled the UCA on November 15-16.

Late Dec. Over several days, the SIU stages reconstructions of the November 13 search of the Jesuit residence, using soldiers who conducted the operation. Numerous contradictions emerge.

January 1990

1 Colonel Guzmán Aguilar, head of the National Intelligence Directorate (DNI), is named military attaché in Costa Rica.

2 Colonel Menjívar informs Colonel Ponce that Major Buckland has implicated Colonel Benavides in the killings. Ponce summons Buckland and Avilés to Joint Command headquarters.

3 SIU says ballistics tests give first positive results, proving that shell casings found at the UCA were shot from weapons assigned to Atlacatl soldiers.
Major Buckland prepares a written statement containing his account of what he learned from Colonel Avilés.

4 In response to an SIU inquiry, Colonel Benavides denies that his troops used flares known as Bengal lights.

5 General Larios appoints a military Honor Commission to examine the evidence.
Future murder defendants Avalos Vargas, Zarpate Castillo and Pérez Vásquez are detained at National Police headquarters; Guevara Cerritos and Amaya Grimaldi at Treasury Police; and Espinoza Guerra at the National Guard.

6 Major Buckland leaves El Salvador.

7 President Cristiani announces that men of the Salvadoran Armed Forces are implicated in UCA killings and that a military Honor Commission will "deduce responsibility" and "clarify the truth in all its magnitude."

8 Future defendant Lieutenant Mendoza Vallecillos is detained at National Police headquarters and Colonel Benavides at the National Guard.

10-11 Major Buckland makes a sworn statement to the FBI in Washington revealing that there may have been prior knowledge that the murders would occur.

11 Ballistics tests indicate that an AK-47 rifle and an M-60 machine gun obtained from the Military Academy were used during the murder operation. The AK-47 was used to kill three priests.

12 The Honor Commission delivers its report to President Cristiani.
The Commission names nine suspects and excludes the possibility that other military men are involved.
In Washington, the FBI records a videotape of Major Buckland telling his story about prior knowledge of the murder plot.

13 U.S. embassy legal officer Richard Chidester receives Major Buckland's additional statements and the videotape. U.S. officials do not share this evidence with Salvadoran judicial authorities.
President Cristiani publicly names the nine defendants.

16 Eight defendants brought before San Salvador's Fourth Criminal Court Judge, Dr. Ricardo A. Zamora. A ninth suspect reportedly fled in late December.

17 The defendants begin to give statements to the court.The SIU provides the judge with six volumes on its investigation and considers its work on the case terminated.

18 In a new affidavit, Major Buckland recants his story about prior knowledge of the plot to the FBI.
Judge Zamora orders the detention of the nine defendants.

20 Jesuit Provincial Tojeira says the investigation has not sufficiently examined the question of who ordered the killings.

22 President Cristiani admits that the investigation is incomplete.
In late January or early February, Cristiani is privately shown the Buckland videotape at the home of U.S. Ambassador Walker.

February 1990

7 *The Washington Post* and other U.S. newspapers cite intelligence and military sources concerning meetings of ranking officers held before and after the assassination.

11 The Moakley task force arrives in El Salvador.

22 Judge Zamora decides to ask President Cristiani to provide the names of the officers who participated in the Honor Commission.

March 1990

5 Judge Zamora officially requests Honor Commission names from President Cristiani.

16 Judge Zamora requests the logbooks of entries and exits to the Military Academy during the month of November 1989 as well as the names of guards on duty on the night of November 15-16, 1989.

22 Defense attorneys petition to transfer the case to Santa Tecla.

23 Father Tojeira writes to the judge asking that members of the Honor Commission be cited to testify.

28 Court receives a letter from President Cristiani dated March 21 providing the names of Honor Commission members.

29 SIU provides the judge with names of cadets on Military Academy guard duty on November 15-16. The SIU informs the court that the logbook of entries and exits to the Military Academy has been "misplaced."

30 Judge Zamora has already questioned more than a hundred witnesses.

April 1990

10 Judge Zamora rejects the defense's petition to transfer the case to Santa Tecla.
Four Military Academy cadets are cited to testify.

22 Retired Colonel Ochoa of the ruling ARENA party tells *60 Minutes* that Colonel Benavides orchestrated the killings on orders from his superiors.

27 House Foreign Affairs Committee votes to cut U.S. military aid to El Salvador by 50%.

30 Moakley task force publishes its *Interim Report*.
Defense attorneys again request that the case be transferred to Santa Tecla.
The judge begins to cite members of the Honor Commission to testify.

May 1990

1 Commanders from around the country publish a communiqué rejecting Colonel Ochoa's allegations.
An anonymous communiqué from "Young Officers" implicates high ranking officers in the crime and endorses the statements of Colonel Ochoa.

3 Colonel Casanova Sandoval, the new director of the Military Academy, informs the court that the four cadets cited to testify are outside the country.

7 Vice Minister of Defense Colonel Zepeda rejects suggestions that he was involved in the crime and asserts that Colonel Benavides reported that night to Colonel Ponce, head of the Joint Command.

9 Vice-Minister of Defense and Public Security Colonel Montano says he believes Colonel Benavides is innocent.
Fiscalía says case should be transferred to Santa Tecla.
Judge Zamora reaffirms his decision not to transfer the case to Santa Tecla.

11 Testifying before the court, two of the four cadets identified by Academy Director Colonel Casanova Sandoval say they were not on duty the night of the killings.

14 The court asks the SIU and the Military Academy to explain why incorrect names were provided and requests that those cadets who were on duty be delivered to the court. The Director of the Military Academy is asked to explain how the logbooks were "lost."

18 Colonel Ochoa provides written testimony.

23 Judge Zamora asks President Cristiani to provide the court with the report he received from the Honor Commission on January 12.
Lieutenant Colonel Rivas of the SIU reports that the Military Academy's logbooks have been burned on the orders of interim Deputy Academy Director Lieutenant Colonel Hernández.

25 Lieutenant Colonel Rivas of the SIU says an "involuntary error" caused him to provide the judge the wrong names of cadets who were on duty the night of the murders.
President Cristiani sends the Honor Commission report to Judge Zamora, who does not receive it until May 28.

28 Judge receives the list of cadets who in fact were on duty that night.

29 Judge Zamora requests Major Buckland's January 3 statement.

30 Judge concludes questioning of Honor Commission members.

31 Judge Zamora cites Lieutenant Mendoza and the Military Academy's archivist to question them about the burning of the logbooks.
General Larios provides the court with Major Buckland's January 3 statement.

June 1990

1 DNI's Lieutenant Cuenca Ocampo testifies that he participated in the November 13 UCA search on the orders of DNI Captain Herrera Carranza, who has since been transferred to Morazán.

4 Military Academy archivist testifies. Judge Zamora cites Colonel Avilés to appear in court.

6 Lieutenant Mendoza testifies, blaming Lieutenant Colonel Hernández for ordering burning of the logbooks.
Legislative Assembly names Dr. Roberto Mendoza as the new Attorney General, bypassing Dr. Colorado for reappointment.

8 Cadets on duty at the Military Academy on the murder night begin to testify.
The SIU sends the court statements from 15 DNI officers who attended the early morning intelligence meeting on November 16, 1989; they provide no useful information.

11 Judge cites Lieutenant Colonel Hernández. He also asks the SIU's Lieutenant Colonel Rivas to clarify various points concerning the cadets and radio transmissions. Further, Zamora asks the Minister of Defense if there are standing orders to burn logbooks.

13 New Attorney General Mendoza announces that prosecutors from his office will play a more active role in the case.

14 Minister of Defense Larios informs the court that there are no standing orders to burn logbooks.

15 Lieutenant Colonel Hernández testifies before the court.

21 Colonel Casanova Sandoval, new director of the Military Academy, turns over a Book of Operations. Suspecting that it might be falsified, the judge sends it to the FBI in Washington for analysis.

26 Provisional detention is ordered for Lieutenant Colonel Hernández on charges of destruction of evidence.

27 Colonel Avilés denies in court that he told Major Buckland that Colonel Benavides ordered the killings.

29 U.S. Ambassador Walker tells the Salvadoran press that "In my country, destruction of evidence is also a crime."

July 1990

2 Colonel Benavides refuses to testify, citing illness.

11 Colonel Benavides testifies for eight hours.

12 President Cristiani admits publicly for the first time that he authorized the search of the UCA on November 13, 1989, and alleges erroneously that weapons were found in the Jesuit residence.

13 Former DNI Captain Herrera Carranza testifies, saying it is common for intelligence agents to participate in searches.

14 Father Tojeira says President Cristiani has been misled by the military about the search of the Jesuit residence and criticizes the authorities' attempt to disassociate the search from the assassination.

17 Lieutenant Colonel Hernández' defense attorney resigns, citing "threats."

18 Major Buckland is cited through Foreign Ministry channels to appear in court on July 30.

20 Defense attorneys again request that the case be transferred to Santa Tecla, this time relying on a provision which allows for appeal.

26 FMLN says President Cristiani bears "political responsibility" for the crime because he authorized the November 13 search, "providing a decisive step in the chain of decisions and orders" leading to the murders.

27 Lieutenant Colonel Hernández is brought before the judge.

August 1990

11 Father Tojeira states that several U.S. intelligence agencies have documents concerning the case and considers it "ridiculous" that they have been withheld "for reasons of national security."

15 In Washington, Congressman Moakley charges that he believes the High Command of the Salvadoran Armed Forces is blocking the investigation.

17 The court rules the petition filed by the defense to transfer the case to Santa Tecla "out of order."
It is reported that Lieutenant Colonel Hernández, out on bail, is wounded in Chalatenango.

20 President Cristiani; Defense Minister Larios; Vice-Ministers Zepeda and Montano; and Colonel Ponce, chief of the Joint Command, meet with Supreme Court President and Judge Zamora, reiterating their support for judicial investigation.

23 During a television interview, Father Tojeira suggests that other ranking officers should be questioned, and names Colonel León Linares, formerly of the Atlacatl Battalion; Colonel Cerna Flores, ex-chief of Operations; and Colonel Guzmán Aguilar, formerly of the DNI.

24 Atlacatl Sergeant Solórzano Esquivel testifies before the Judge, who orders his detention on perjury charges; Solórzano flees.

27 General Larios provides a list of officers who attended evening meeting on November 15 at Joint Command headquarters.

28 Sergeant Solórzano Esquivel is brought back to court to face perjury charges.

29 Colonel Ponce provides written testimony for the second time.

30 General Larios provides a written statement to the court.

September 1990

1 Colonel Ponce is named Minister of Defense.

5 In his acceptance speech, Colonel Ponce states his commitment to clear up the case. No members of the Salvadoran Armed Forces attend the ceremony.
Judge Zamora orders detention of two more military witnesses on perjury charges.

7 President Cristiani appears personally to testify before the judge.

10 Lieutenant Colonel Velasco Alfaro testifies, stating that he was named in early December to replace Colonel Benavides as commander of the special Security Zone, contradicting earlier testimony by other officers.

12 Intelligence officer Lieutenant Colonel Equizábal Figueroa testifies that two U.S. advisors – Colonel Porter and Major Lewis – were working with C-2 (Intelligence) in November 1989. The two are not fully identified until May 1991, when the judge orders witness statements under the Letters Rogatory process.

14 Treasury Police Director, Col. Héctor Heriberto Hernández, testifies.

18 Vice-Minister of Defense, Colonel Zepeda, testifies.

21 Colonel Cerna Flores, chief of C-3 (Operations) at Joint Command in November 1989, testifies.

26 Colonel León Linares, former Atlacatl commander, testifies.

28 Major Buckland testifies in San Salvador at the home of a U.S. diplomat, and flies out of the country before nightfall. Colonel Carrillo Schlenker of the National Guard sends the judge an unsolicited written statement.

30 President Cristiani says at a press conference at United Nations headquarters that the Jesuit investigation is proceeding well. He announces that a group of prominent U.S. attorneys have been invited to El Salvador to monitor the case.

October 1990

1 SIU detectives Lovato Ayala and Parada Cáceres testify, revealing several irregularities in the SIU investigation. Attorney General rejects the suggestion of a judicial "confrontation" to resolve differences in the testimonies of Buckland and Salvadoran officers.

2 Public prosecutors say the SIU and Army officers have shown a "lack of will" to facilitate and advance the investigation.

5 Former DNI chief Colonel Guzmán Aguilar testifies.

15 Archbishop Rivera y Damas says he is convinced more intellectual authors remain to be identified.

18 SIU Lieutenant Preza Rivas testifies. Congressman Moakley reveals existence of additional statements made in January 1990 by Major Buckland which U.S. officials have concealed from Salvadoran judicial authorities. Moakley receives State Department assurances that they have been delivered to Judge Zamora, who announces that he has not received the material.

19 SIU Lieutenant Colonel Rivas Mejía testifies and is unable to answer numerous basic questions concerning the work of the SIU. U.S. Senate votes to cut military aid to El Salvador by 50%.

22 The Fourth Criminal Court issues an official communiqué reporting that Major Buckland's January 10 and 18 affidavits were delivered through private channels by two U.S. embassy officials. Embassy officials continue to withhold Buckland's videotape.
Colonel Carrillo Schlenker submits second written statement.

23 Minister of Defense, Colonel Ponce, provides written testimony for the third time amplifying earlier statements.

24 Defense Minister Ponce writes to Congressman Moakley, asserting that Major Buckland's testimony is false.

30 Father Tojeira provides the court with 17 heavily censored documents from the U.S. Defense Intelligence Agency, and suggests that the judge request the documents in their entirety from U.S. authorities.

31 Colonel Avilés testifies in court, saying officers in Joint Command headquarters were extremely concerned by the fierce attack nearby in the early morning hours of November 16, and that they feared the headquarters was under siege. He told reporters that Major Buckland is "unstable, unbalanced and deceitful." Defense attorney Carlos Méndez Flores says "Buckland's falsehoods are clear."
Through diplomatic channels, Judge Zamora requests U.S. authorities to deliver all Buckland documents and his videotaped declaration.

November 1990

1 Supreme Court asks the Foreign Ministry to request through diplomatic channels the Buckland videotape and other documents.

7 SIU ballistics expert González García tells the court that the SIU has not finished ballistics testing and therefore cannot submit a final report. Zamora orders the SIU to submit the results and conclusions of the ballistics tests done to date, and describe those still pending.

8 Zamora asks National Police for intelligence reports about the alleged presence of guerrillas in the UCA in November 1989.

9 Major Contreras, C-2 counterintelligence chief at the Joint Command, declares that he heard heavy detonations around the UCA early on November 16, but did not investigate.

12 SIU Lieutenant Preza Rivas replies to Judge Zamora's November 7 request for ballistic test results, reporting that 32 other shells remain to be analyzed.
The UCA initiates a week of academic, cultural and religious activities commemorating the first anniversary of the assassinations.

13 Speaking at Georgetown University, Congressman Moakley says "it is inconceivable to me that officers would intentionally lie and destroy evidence unless they felt that these actions would be approved or – in fact – had been ordered, by their superiors."

16 First anniversary of the assassinations at the UCA.
Judge Zamora files additional charges against the defendants for terrorism, the first time Salvadoran soldiers have been so charged.
The European Economic Community expresses concern over the case's lack of real progress.

20 Former DNI intelligence officer Captain Herrera Carranza killed in Morazán while serving under former Atlacatl commander Colonel León Linares.

29 Attorney General's office asks the judge to raise the case to the trial stage.
Defense moves to have terrorism charges dropped.

December 1990

6 Judge Zamora ends the investigative phase, elevating the case to plenary. All nine defendants are ordered to stand trial, but robbery charges are dismissed.

7 Judge Zamora, frustrated at the uncompleted ballistics tests, criticizes the SIU for having "little seriousness in its work."

8-13 Moakley task force staff visits El Salvador.

9 Archbishop Rivera y Damas criticizes decision to raise case to plenary, saying the investigation should continue because there are more intellectual authors.

11 Central American Province of the Society of Jesus issues a communiqué, stating that while the Jesuits consider the investigation incomplete, there is sufficient evidence to try the case.

13 U.S. Ambassador Walker says "my government and I are doing everything possible to achieve justice in this case," explaining that some portions of documents given to the Jesuits under the Freedom of Information Act were blacked out, as U.S. law permits.

19 Defense attorneys challenge the decision to take the case to trial.

20 Major Ramírez, a U.S. military adviser in El Salvador in November 1989, gives a sworn statement on the case to the FBI at Ft. Campbell, Kentucky. U.S. officials do not share his testimony with Salvadoran judicial authorities.

January 1991

1 Defense Minister Ponce, Vice-Minister Zepeda and Colonel Rubio Rubio, head of the Joint Command, are promoted to general. Lieutenant Colonel Rivas Mejía of the SIU is promoted to full colonel and named second-in-command of the National Police. Lieutenant Colonel Aguilar Alfaro later takes over the SIU.
Judge Zamora admits the defense's challenge to take the case to trial.

8 Public prosecutors Campos and Blanco resign in protest from the *Fiscalía*. Attorney General Mendoza says "[t]heir resignation won't affect the case."

9 At a San Salvador press conference Blanco says they resigned because of the Attorney General office's "lack of seriousness and responsible intent."

11 Central American Province of the Society of Jesus says the "resignation under pressure . . . causes us to lose our relative confidence in the Attorney General's office." Jesuits say they are considering hiring Blanco and Campos as private prosecutors.

15 Judge Zamora admits the defense's challenge, referring the case to a San Salvador appeals court.
President Bush says withheld U.S. military aid will be released, but waits 60 days, pending progress in the case, among other conditions.

18 An ARENA attorney attacks Blanco and Campos, calling them "mercenaries of justice." Others join the chorus of attacks.

22 U.S. embassy says a transcript of Buckland's videotape and a Spanish translation have been provided to the Foreign Ministry; Zamora receives the documents sometime in March 1991.

February 1991

22 The High Command sends a letter to Justice Minister Hernández Valiente rejecting any institutional responsibility for the crime, but suggests further interviews with 12 officers. The letter was first released in Washington prior to congressional consideration of the release of aid to El Salvador; the High Command does not send a copy to Judge Zamora.

March 1991

6 UN Human Rights Commission says some within the Armed Forces have "obstructed the complete clarification of the crime and application of the law for those responsible."

15 The U.S. State Department releases $21.5 million, 50% of the U.S. military aid for El Salvador in FY 1991.

19 Attorney General's office repeats its position to the appeals court, recommending that all nine defendants stand trial.

22 Supreme Court delivers Scotland Yard's report to the court.

April 1991

1 UCA Rector Father Estrada says U.S. is participating directly in a coverup of the crime and accuses the military of obstructing the judicial investigation.
Father Tojeira says the State Department does not want to collaborate in identifying those who ordered the killings.

8 Appellate court upholds Zamora's decision to try the case.

16 Mrs. Benavides files a habeas corpus petition on behalf of her husband, Colonel Benavides.

17 Supreme Court names Dr. Urrutia López, head of the Salvadoran lawyers' association, to review the habeas petition.

26 Parents of Lieutenant Espinoza Guerra file a habeas petition in behalf of their son.

29 Dr. Urrutia upholds Zamora's decision to send the case to plenary.
Supreme Court says it will examine the legality of detention of all nine defendants.

30 Relatives of the defendants criticize Urrutia's decision, attributing the detentions to "international pressure."

May 1991

6 Blanco and Campos enter an appearance in court as private prosecutors acting in behalf of the victims' families.

7 General Ponce threatens to initiate libel proceedings against Blanco and Campos, who suggested Benavides was acting on higher orders and that the investigation should continue.

8 Supreme Court upholds Urrutia's opinion and rules that the case against all nine murder defendants and that against Lieutenant Colonel Hernández should continue.

12 San Salvador Auxiliary Bishop Rosa Chávez "laments" General Ponce's statements and says they could cause "sick minds" to take action against the private prosecutors.

14 Relatives of three soldiers detained for perjury file habeas petitions in their behalf.

22 Private prosecutors file a 50-page brief requesting a series of investigatory steps.

23 The eight-day period for the introduction of new evidence opens in Fourth Criminal Court.

24 Judge Zamora asks Supreme Court to initiate diplomatic proceedings so that Major Buckland may again appear to testify in San Salvador.

25 Supreme Court asks the Foreign Ministry to process the judge's request for Major Buckland to appear in court to testify.

27 Argentine Colonel (ret.) García appears as an expert witness for the prosecution.

28 Former DNI Captain Parada Fuentes testifies in court that it was announced over a closed circuit military frequency early on the morning of November 16, 1989 that Father Ellacuría was "killed resisting arrest."

30 Judge Zamora asks Supreme Court to petition U.S. government to turn over Buckland videotape.

June 1991

3 The eight-day evidentiary period ends, but Judge Zamora allows a 90-day extension for the testimonies of 10 U.S. citizens to be recorded in the United States.
At request of the defense, Zamora adds to the court record the book, *Marxist Infiltration in the Church*, a right-wing diatribe attacking the Jesuits.
U.S. embassy announces that Major Buckland is "in a country near El Salvador" (later identified as Panama) so he can arrive quickly if asked to testify.

4 Father Tojeira appears at an UCA forum on the case with private prosecutors Henry Campos and Sidney Blanco.

5 Judge Zamora informs the Supreme Court that Buckland's testimony will be recorded through the Letters Rogatory process.

17 Judge Zamora adds the transcript of U.S. military advisor Major Ramírez to the court record, after Moakley learns of its existence.

20 U.S. embassy offers Zamora a "private showing" of the Buckland videotape at the embassy but declines to turn over the tape, out of "respect for Major Buckland's privacy." Embassy deems the judge's additional request for documents related to Buckland "imprecise or general," and states it therefore cannot comply.

27 General Ponce says Colonel López y López was COCFA head on the murder night.
Bush administration announces the release of $21 million in withheld military aid.

29 Former Attorney General Colorado writes to the Archbishop, indicating that his November 1989 letter to the Pope suggesting that the Archbishop should be withdrawn from El Salvador "could have contributed to dissuading any extremists," thereby saving Rivera y Damas' life.

30 Congressman Moakley interviews Lieutenants Espinoza Guerra and Guevara Cerritos in detention at Treasury Police headquarters.

July 1991

1 Congressman Moakley addresses a standing-room only crowd at the UCA, suggesting the Armed Forces had institutional responsibility for the crime.

2 General Ponce attacks Moakley, saying "Moakley has no proof."

4 ARENA's Dr. Calderón Sol accuses Moakley of interfering in the country's internal affairs.
President Cristiani answers the judge's written questions.
Cristiani tells Notimex the assassination was "not an institutional crime, but was carried out by members of the Armed Forces who acted on their own."

9 The Armed Forces place a paid advertisement in the press strongly condemning Moakley's views.
Defense attorney Dr. Méndez Flores says Congressman Moakley is "violating the country's sovereignty."

14 ARENA's Calderón Sol says Moakley should "legislate in his own country, and not ours."

30 Father Tojeira says the State Department is obstructing the investigation by barring attorneys for the Jesuits from being present during the questioning of 10 U.S. citizens in the United States.

August 1991

5-14 Declarations are taken in Washington from 10 U.S. citizens. Jesuits' attorneys are banned from the sessions.

September 1991

3 Congressman Moakley writes to President Cristiani asking him to "make a clear statement at the earliest possible time" opposing amnesty for the defendants.

6 The private prosecutors file a civil action demanding indemnification for the son of victim Julia Ramos, damages to the UCA, and a symbolic one *colón* (12 cents) for each of the Jesuits.

10 Defense attorney Dr. Méndez Flores criticizes Moakley's opposition to amnesty, saying, "Who's Moakley, to be running around meddling in questions which are only the business of Salvadorans?"

26 The public trial begins at noon in the Supreme Court building.

28 10:30 a.m. During oral arguments by the defense, some 200 demonstrators outside the Supreme Court building chant slogans in favor of the defendants, interrupting the process inside.
4:45 p.m. Oral arguments end and jury begins deliberation.
10:30 p.m. Judge Zamora begins reading the verdict. Colonel Benavides and Lieutenant Mendoza are convicted of murder; the other defendants are acquitted on all charges.

October 1991

3 Those acquitted are released from custody and remain on active duty.

10 Judge Zamora blocks pretrial release on bail for three Atlacatl soldiers charged with perjury.

11 Lieutenants Espinoza Guerra and Guevara Cerritos are released on bond, pending the court's decision on a lesser charge.

14 Non-jury charges are heard by Judge Zamora.

16 Evidentiary period opens for civil action.

31 House and Senate Democrats write to Secretary of State Baker asking for a report on conduct of the Jesuit case.

November 1991

1 Recusal petition filed by the defense is admitted to the appellate court. Defense argues that Judge Zamora should excuse himself from the case because he once taught at the UCA.
Defense attorneys file habeas petitions in behalf of three soldiers held on perjury charges.

4 Eight prominent Republican Senators write to President Cristiani, opposing a pardon for Benavides and Mendoza.

7 Appellate court rejects recusal petition.

8 Judge appointed to consider habeas petitions.

13 Father Tojeira addresses the UCA community on the case, announcing that the Central American Province of the Society of Jesus will ask the Legislative Assembly to form a commission to identify who ordered the murders.

14 Second petition seeking the recusal of Judge Zamora is filed by the defense.

16 Second anniversary of the assassination is commemorated with a mass on the UCA grounds.

18 Congressman Moakley releases a statement outlining his hypothesis of how the murder was planned.
Chief instigator, he says, is former Air Force chief General Bustillo.
Defense Minister Ponce was also present at the meeting at which the murders were planned; Poncepromptly denies the charges.
Bustillo says Moakley is a "liar."

19 Second recusal petition admitted to appeals court.

20 Appeals court again rejects recusal petition.

December 1991

10 Court agrees to end civil action at the request of the victims' relatives.

18 Fathers Tojeira and Estrada petition the Legislative Assembly to appoint a commission to investigate who ordered the murders.

January 1992

1 The Cristiani government and the FMLN sign peace accords in New York City under the auspices of the UN.

5 The court announces the end of the civil action, which concluded with an out of court settlement, providing compensation to Elba Ramos' son and to the UCA.

10 Legislative Assembly rejects the Jesuits' petition. An ARENA deputy says it is "time to stop sowing hate."

16 The peace accords are finalized in Mexico City at a ceremony attended by UN Secretary-General Boutros-Ghali and foreign diplomats and other guests.
ARENA party president Calderón Sol says he supports a pardon for Benavides and Mendoza.

23 Amnesty decree approved by the Legislative Assembly. Those already convicted by a jury are not eligible.
Judge Zamora sentences Benavides and Mendoza to 30-year prison terms. Lieutenants Espinoza and Guevara Cerritos are sentenced to three years for proposition and conspiracy to commit acts of terrorism.

30 Defense attorneys appeal the sentences.

February 1992

1 A ceasefire begins and FMLN leaders return to San Salvador.

22 Retired General Bustillo, saying he was "falsely accused" by Congressman Moakley, "demands justice" because his "reputation has been impugned. . . ." Writing in *The Washington Post*, Bustillo challenges "Moakley to join me in El Salvador to publicly debate these charges."

May 1992

15 "Ad-hoc Commission," established under the terms of the peace accords, begins a review of the Armed Forces in order to purge those unfit for service.

July 1992

14 Three foreign notables forming a "Truth Commission" begin examining a decade of acts of violence by the FMLN and Armed Forces.

31 José Eduardo Pineda Valenzuela, chief public prosecutor on the case, is shot and wounded by two gunmen who forceably enter his home. The men steal nothing from the home, but take one of the family's two cars.

August 1992

12 Jesuit Provincial Tojeira issues a communiqué indicating that the order is considering requesting a pardon for Colonel Benavides and Lieutenant Mendoza.

17 The same gunmen who shot public prosecutor Pineda Valenzuela on July 31 return to his home and threaten his wife, warning her against cooperating with the criminal investigation into the July 31 incident. Like the earlier attack, the men take nothing from the home, but steal the second of the family's two cars.

September 1992

23 Ad-hoc Commission delivers its findings to the UN Secretary-General and to President Cristiani. The names of those to be dismissed from the military are not made public, and the mid-November deadline for the dismissals passes without action.

November 1992

16 The third anniversary of the murders is commemorated with a mass at the UCA. Father Tojeira reiterates his call for identification of the officers who ordered the crime, and indicates his intention to officially ask for a pardon for the two officers convicted.

December 1992

9 Father Tojeira challenges General Ponce to a public debate on the question of the "intellectual authorship" of the UCA murders.

10 General Ponce calls Father Tojeira "cynical" and says he will not participate in a "propaganda show."

16 Father Tojeira writes to Roberto Angulo, President of El Salvador's Legislative Assembly, officially requesting a pardon. He also writes to President Cristiani, asking him to support the request.

January 1993

7 UN Secretary-General Boutros-Ghali informs the UN Security Council that the Cristiani government has refused to remove 15 officers from their commands, as called for by the Ad-Hoc Commission. Boutros-Ghali says he has asked Cristiani to "take early action to regularize the position of the 15 officers in respect of whom the Ad-Hoc Commission's recommendations have not yet been fully implemented."

11 U.S. Senators Christopher Dodd and Patrick Leahy call on the Bush administration to withhold U.S. military aid to El Salvador until the Cristiani government complies fully with the peace accords.

Appendix B

ATTACKS ON EL SALVADOR'S JESUITS*

1971

Immigration authorities threaten to cancel the residency permits of Father Ignacio Ellacuría and six other foreign priests, accusing them of "subversive and antidemocratic activities."

1973

Spring and Summer. Jesuits teaching at the Jesuit high school, Externado San José, are accused of teaching Marxism and turning child against parent. Considering criminal proceedings for teaching "communist, anarchic or antidemocratic doctrines," the Attorney General's office holds hearings. Father Juan Ramón Moreno, Externado rector, is called in to testify.

1975

July 30. Security Forces fire on a demonstration of university students, including some from the Central American University José Simeón Cañas (UCA), killing 12 people and wounding 20. Forty more students are detained. The students were protesting repression and the government's expenditure of $3.5 million on the Miss Universe contest. On August 7, the UCA Superior Council condemns "exaggeratedly violent repression" of the demonstration.

Television spots announce that a priest, a nun and a politician would be killed. Though no names are mentioned, Jesuits learn that the targeted priest is Jon Sobrino, S.J., who had recently moved to El Salvador.

1976

January 6. The offices of the UCA journal, *Estudios Centroamericanos (ECA)*, bombed.

January 15. Declaration by the Agricultural Front for the Eastern Region (FARO), a right wing landowners' association, appears in newspapers attacking the Jesuits because of their support for agrarian reform. The ads, which mention by name Jesuits working in Aguilares and the UCA, warn, "either obey our laws and respect our government or leave the country."

March. UCA administration building bombed.

---

* During the period described, there were also numerous attacks on Catholics other than Jesuits. Two of the most prominent cases were the March 1980 murder of Archbishop Romero and the December 1980 murders of four U.S. churchwomen.

August 23. *ECA* offices just off the UCA campus bombed about midnight. The house is nearly destroyed.

September. Two small propaganda bombs explode in the UCA. The flyers contain attacks on the Jesuits.

December 2-3. UCA administration building bombed at night. Father Francisco Javier Ibisate and others are still in the building when the blast occurs. A death squad calling itself the White Warriors Union assumes responsibility.

December. The death of an Aguilares landowner is blamed on the Church and Jesuits in particular. Both are attacked in a newspaper campaign, which mentions Father Rutilio Grande,
S.J., and another priest by name.

1977

January 4. Two ex-Jesuit seminarians working in Aguilares expelled.

February. Former Jesuit, Juan José Ramírez, interrogated, beaten, tortured with electric shock for 10 days and expelled. He is later located in a Guatemalan prison.

February 21. Father Benigno Fernández, S.J., a Spanish citizen working in Aguilares, is refused re-entry to the country.

February 22. Father Luis de Sebastián, S.J., a naturalized Salvadoran, UCA Vice-Rector and economics professor, refused re-entry to the country, told his life was in danger.

February 22. Father Ignacio Ellacuría, S.J., naturalized Salvadoran, refused re-entry to the country.

March 12. Rutilio Grande, S.J., assassinated on his way to say mass in El Paisnal. Also murdered were two parishioners, Manuel Solórzano, 72, and Nelson Rutilio Lemus, 15. Well known and respected throughout the country, Father Grande's killing shocked Salvadorans, who did not suspect that the rhetoric directed against the church would translate into this kind of violence. Some 100,000 people attended his funeral on March 20.

April 22. Foreign Minister Mauricio Borgonovo kidnapped by the Popular Liberation Forces (FPL). A communiqué in *La Prensa Grafica* places responsibility for the kidnapping on "Jesuit priests and other communist priests of the Popular Revolutionary Bloc (BPR), front for the FPL. If [Borgonovo] is assassinated, it will be an eye for an eye."

May 6. Father Jorge Franklin Sarsanedas del Sid, S.J. a Panamanian citizen, is kidnapped on May 1 but the Jesuit Provincial is not notified until five days later that he is in the custody of the National Guard. He is held with his hands and feet tied, blindfolded and only fed twice. The first night he is kicked and beaten. Expelled from the country, the 30-year-old priest is charged with "participation in subversive activities." Archbishop Romero refuses to sign the National Guard document releasing Sarsanedas to him because of numerous inaccuracies.

May 11. Father Alfonso Navarro, the parish priest in the Miramonte section of San Salvador, is assassinated the day after Foreign Minister Borgonovo's body appeared. A 15-year-old youth is murdered with Navarro.

May. Flyers and radio announcements urge "*Haga Patria, Mate un cura*" (Be a Patriot, Kill a Priest).

May 19. In "Operation Rutilio," the military lays siege to the town of Aguilares. Sealing off a 500-square mile area, they search every house. While the government acknowledges seven deaths, witnesses place the number at around 50. Among those killed is the sacristan, who was shot while ringing the church bell warning of the troops' arrival. Father Grande and three other Jesuits had worked in the area since 1972. The church is occupied by troops for the next month.

May 19. Fathers Salvador Carranza, S.J., José Luis Ortega, S.J., and Marcelino Pérez, S.J., all working with Father Rutilio Grande around Aguilares and Guazapa are detained at 5:00 a.m., handcuffed, mistreated and deported to Guatemala at mid-day. They remain jailed in Guatemala until May 25, incommunicado.

June 20. The White Warrior's Union death squad issues an ultimatum for all 47 Jesuits to leave the country within 30 days.

October 25. A State Department Bureau of Intelligence and Research report entitled "The Catholic Church and Human Rights in Latin America" reports the Salvadoran government's charges that the Jesuits were abetting a leftist guerrilla organization, the Popular Liberation Movement (FLP) [sic]. Further, the report notes the threat made by the right-wing death squad White Warriors Union (UGB) against all Jesuits who had not left the country within 30 days.

1978

January 1. The Curia, seat of the Province of Central America of the Society of Jesus, is broken into and equipment stolen.

January. Father Robert Drinan, a U.S. Jesuit and member of the U.S. House of Representatives, visits El Salvador. ANEP, the business association, and the Front of Salvadoran Women, publish attacks on Drinan.

March. Roberto Zarruck, a Jesuit student, is refused entry to El Salvador.

July 8. One of the Jesuit residences in Jardines de Guadalupe, then known as UCA II, searched at 2:00 p.m. by over 50 agents of the Security Forces who said they were looking for weapons. Soldiers take up positions on the roof and block off traffic in the surrounding streets. The troops – who arrive in six police cars and two trucks – bring along cameras and medical equipment, in case of casualties.

1979

February 3. Monsignor Pedro Arnoldo Aparicio y Quintanilla, Bishop of San Vicente, is quoted in *Diario Latino* saying that "some Jesuits are responsible for the situation" of violence in El Salvador. The headline reads, "Monsignor Aparicio Blames the Jesuits."

September. A homily by Monsignor Aparicio triggers paid ads in support of his views and further attacking the Jesuits. Aparicio charges that the left itself killed four priests, among them Father Rutilio Grande, who was supposedly murdered by the left because they were "afraid that Grande would discover that his Jesuit comrades were inciting the insubordination of the peasantry against the State, against the government and against the Church."

December. A newspaper column signed by "Josefo" directly attacks Luis de Sebastian, S.J. and Archbishop Romero.

December 27. Three bombs explode outside the UCA computer center.

1980

January 5. Members of the death squad White Warriors Union (UGB) machine-gun the Jesuit high school, Externado San José.

February 16. Jesuit residence known as UCA II fired upon by machine-guns and G-3s; 100 bullet holes are later found.

February 18. Bomb destroys part of UCA library.

March 22. National Police enter the UCA campus at 1:15 p.m. shooting their weapons. Manuel Orantes Guillén, a math student, is killed and two others arrested.

June 25. Brutal search of Aguilares church.

June 29. At dawn, the Salvadoran Anticommunist Army (EAS) detonates two powerful bombs at the UCA, one in a room used by a student association and another in the printing press, which was largely destroyed.

July 5. Externado San José encircled by some 150 soldiers at 7:00 a.m. The school is searched and the offices of the human rights group, Socorro Juridico, especially examined and documents and money taken. All files on the killing of Archbishop Romero are stolen. Only the doorkeeper, Brother José de la Cruz Alberdi, S.J., is present during the operation. Tanks block off surrounding streets and soldiers posted at the entrance prohibit the entry of the principal, Father José Santamaría. *La Prensa Gráfica* falsely reports that weapons, molotov cocktails and a shooting range were found.

September 24. The Maximiliano Hernández Martínez Anti-Communist Brigade burns the Guazapa parish archive and photos of the Pope and Archbishop Romero. They also burn the convent and threaten the nuns to leave the zone. The Jesuit serving the parish had already been expelled from the country.

September 30. Rafael Santos and Oscar Romano, two primary school teachers at the Externado San José, are assassinated in the doorway of the school.

October 10. Combined Security Forces shoot at the Aguilares church, they enter the church, stealing and shooting up the interior. The parish house is also ransacked and items stolen. The parish clinic is attacked with machine guns and clothing stolen from the parish warehouse.

October 24. Two high potency bombs explode at 2:00 a.m. at UCA II, a residence where 10 Jesuits were sleeping at the time. The first explosive, which was thrown over the wall, left behind a meter-wide hole in the wall of Segundo Montes' bedroom. Father Montes was asleep in bed at the time. Fearing a second explosion, the men got up but did not leave. Minutes later a second bomb exploded at the metal gate, which melted. Later, 10 more small bombs were found which had not gone off.

October 27. UCA II, the same Jesuit residence in Jardines de Guadalupe, is bombed again. Partially destroyed, the house is uninhabitable and the community breaks up and moves elsewhere.

November. *ECA* offices bombed for the fourth time.

Late November. Father Ellacuría flees the country after being tipped off about a military plot to kill him; he remains outside the country until April 1982.

November 28. Armed men in civilian clothing return to occupy the Externado San José and remain for the next two weeks.

December 19. San Antonio Abad residence of Jesuits working at the Externado San José is thoroughly searched by Security Forces.

1981

January 16. Two Jesuit residences, UCA I and II, are searched for an hour and a half at 5:00 a.m. Since UCA II is unoccupied, soldiers break windows and doors and force open cabinets.

January 17. Combined forces occupy the UCA campus.

May 1-2. Father John Willmering, S.J., a U.S. citizen travelling over land from Honduras, is denied entry to the country by the National Guard and turned over to the Honduran police.

October 8. Salvadoran Anticommunist League leaflet: "Out with Marxist Jesuits! Out with the Creators of Violence and Crime in El Salvador. Out with the Founders of the FPL." This new paramilitary group arose following accusations by a Jesuit kidnapped by the Guatemalan Armed Forces (see below).

October 22. The Salvadoran Armed Forces sponsors a press conference at the Military Academy by Father Luis E. Pellecer, a Jesuit kidnapped on June 9 in Guatemala. Pellecer makes a series of accusations against the Jesuits who he says are involved in "subversive activities." A one and a half hour videotape made by the Guatemalan Armed Forces is also aired on Costa Rican television and twice in one week in El Salvador. Held incommunicado for over 100 days by the Guatemalan Armed Forces, Pellecer is believed to have been brainwashed. The Society of Jesus said that Pellecer was being used to "justify religious persecution." After his appearance, the Archdiocese is attacked during curfew hours and the Divine Providence high school dynamited.

1982

June 9. A U.S. embassy cable describes *ECA* as "the most important of the very few non-clandestine pro-FMLN/FDR publications available in El Salvador."

October 7. Bishop Pedro Arnoldo Aparicio y Quintanilla of San Vicente meets with the Armed Forces High Command and later publicly attacks the Jesuits, especially Ignacio Ellacuría, accusing them of subversive activity and promoting violence. *La Prensa Gráfica* says Aparicio has turned over documentation to the government proving the collaboration of 30 priests with clandestine organizations, most of them Jesuits.

1983

August 16. A U.S. embassy cable describes an article in *ECA* as containing a "bias for a negotiated solution to the Salvadoran conflict which will ultimately lead to an authoritarian leftist (but not Marxist-Leninist) regime, and a willingness to forego democratic freedoms such as elections."

September 6. The Secret Anti-Communist Army (ESA) bombs Jesuit residence UCA II and home of UCA professor Italo López Vallecillos. An ESA communiqué accuses Jesuits of "open membership in the terrorist organizations that make up the FMLN" and delivers a "warning to those who are interested in dialogue" with the FMLN.

October 13. Security Forces search Jesuit residence in San Antonio Abad around 10:00 p.m.

November 23. At 7:30 a.m., during a major military operation in the area, UCA I and II are searched by the National Police. Two Jesuits are held for 11 hours, while the soldiers thoroughly examine the house. After 7-8 hours, some 400 books deemed "subversive" are gathered in the dining room to be confiscated. The search is finally called off at 6:00 p.m. after an appeal is made to the President of El Salvador and the U.S. embassy intervenes. Nothing is confiscated. During the search, the back part of the UCA campus is occupied.

1984

January 20. Agents of the Section for Criminal Investigations (SIC) of the National Police raid the Loyola Center during a meeting of COTRAMY, a co-operative, following reports that cannons were being stored there. Loyola director Father Fermín Saínz was present throughout the search, during which 15 people were arrested and 600 *colones* stolen.

December 17. The Traditional Catholic Movement (MTC) publishes an open letter to Archbishop Rivera y Damas blaming the UCA Jesuits for "instigating the assassination of Archbishop Romero" and for promoting a "confrontation among Salvadorans and class hatred and destruction of our country's economic, political and social structures." Father Ignacio Ellacuría is named an "author" of the "poisonous fruit, the most advanced theory of communist Marxism-Leninism. . . ."

1985

September 30. Brother Magdiel Cerón Alvarado, S.J., arrives from Nicaragua to attend his mother's funeral and is detained by the police and accused of carrying information and orders from Nicaragua. He is released after intervention by the Jesuit Provincial.

1986

September. ARENA, supported by some members of the Christian Democratic Party, launches a campaign to strip Father Ellacuría of his Salvadoran citizenship, citing two provisions in the Constitution barring the clergy and foreigners from entering into the country's political life.

September 10. An ARENA Assembly group introduces a bill appointing a Special Commission to investigate Father Ellacuría.

Mid-September. U.S. Jesuit Michael Kennedy is arrested while travelling with staff of the Archdiocese en route to a resettlement site. U.S. consular officers secure his release from the Treasury Police and escort him out of the country.

1987

March 12. Security Forces check the documents of all those Jesuits gathered in El Paisnal to commemorate the tenth anniversary of the death of Rutilio Grande.

June. A media campaign by the Armed Forces and *Diario de Hoy* accuses Father Ellacuría of defending the use of land mines by the guerrillas.

July 20. Salvadoran Institute for Political, Social and Economic Studies (ISEPES), a small right-wing research group, calls for closure of UCA and the National University and outlawing of the UNTS labor federation.

November. Ignacio Ellacuría and eight other theologians are named in a document attacking liberation theology prepared for a meeting of the Conference of American Armies, which includes the armed forces of 15 nations in the Americas, including El Salvador and the United States. "Aligned with Marxist ideology," the document observed, "because of their attitudes and means of operation they have marginalized themselves from serious theological discussion." The theologians are mentioned in a chapter entitled, "Strategy of the International Communist Movement in Latin America through Different Means of Action." Colonel Juan Orlando Zepeda, El Salvador's vice-minister of defense, is part of the working group responsible for the document.

1988

February. Attacks against Rutilio Grande and Jesuits in general again appear in the press. *La Prensa Gráfica* runs a four-part series against Grande.

August. Attacks appear in the press against the National Debate for Peace, sponsored by the Archdiocese. Much of the vitriol was directed toward the Jesuits at the UCA, who provided technical support. An article entitled, "The Basque Curse," accuses the Bishops of getting involved in politics and of being manipulated by the Jesuits and liberation theology.

September 2. A preannounced lecture series by Father Jon Sobrino at the Jesuit-affiliated Rafael Landívar University in Guatemala is protested in the Guatemalan press. Though the lectures were canceled and Sobrino did not go to Guatemala, bombs were set off at the Landívar campus on the day the program was to begin, destroying several cars. Leaflets demanded that the Jesuit theologian leave Guatemala immediately.

October. A media campaign accuses Father Ellacuría of defending the use of car bombs by the FMLN.

1989

March 3. A paid advertisement by the Crusade for Peace and Work denounces what they call "tiny group of satanic brains led by Ellacuría and a pack of communist hounds" who they say are ruining the country.

March 14. A grenade explodes in the UCA electrical plant.

March 18. A paid advertisement by the Civic Patriotic Committee mentions the "deceptive Jesuit Ignacio Ellacuría, Segundo Montes and others, who with their doctrines, are poisoning many young minds. . . ."

April 16. A paid advertisement by the High Command of the Armed Forces of El Salvador charges Father Segundo Montes with defending the FMLN's use of land mines, saying, "In El Salvador there are groups and individuals who insist on defending the terrorism of the FMLN-FDR and its front groups." An ARENA press release calls Montes "inhuman and immoral."

April 20. Col. Juan Orlando Zepeda, then commander of the First Brigade, said the UCA is a "refuge for terrorist leaders, from where they plan the strategy of attack against Salvadorans." Zepeda charges specifically that the FMLN killing of the Attorney General on April 19 was planned at the UCA.

April 28. Three bombs explode at the UCA printing press and the gate off Avenida Einstein and the Southern Highway. No one is injured, but all the windows are broken in the gatekeeper's home.

July 3. Open letter to President Cristiani from the Crusade for Peace and Work demanding capture and summary justice for Fathers Ignacio Ellacuría and Segundo Montes "because they are responsible for all the destruction of the infrastructure and all the vile and cowardly assassinations that have been committed in the name of liberation theology and the Marxist-Leninist doctrine that they want to impose." Also mentioned are leaders of the FMLN, the Democratic Convergence and the labor movement. The letter also calls for the imposition of a death penalty, a state of siege and martial law.

July 22. Four bombs explode at the UCA printing press, the most powerful explosion of the last decade. Three more bombs are deactivated. Footprints of military boots are found. Computers, a photocopier, office equipment, transformers, printing press are all destroyed. The damages exceed $60,000.

November 11-15. Radio Cuscatlán broadcasts threats against the Jesuits of the UCA and Archbishop Rivera y Damas and Monsignor Rosa Chávez. Among these threats were heard: "Ellacuría is a guerrilla, cut off his head" (*que le corten la cabeza*); "Ellacuría should be spit to death!" (*Deberian sacar a Ellacuría para matarlo a escupidas!*) Vice-President Francisco Merino accuses Ellacuría on the nationwide radio hook-up of "poisoning the minds" of Salvadoran youth at the UCA and the Externado San José.

November 13. *La Prensa Gráfica* reports on the broadcast threats, saying, ". . . it is of the utmost urgency that the Jesuits are thrown out of the country because the UCA has been hiding weapons for about the last 10 years. The Spanish Jesuit priest, Ignacio Ellacuría, was named as the principal person responsible."

November 13. The Jesuit residence and the Theological Reflection Center on the UCA campus are searched by men of the Atlacatl Battalion. When Father Ellacuría questions their right to search church property, an officer says the state-of-siege permits anything.

November 16. Six Jesuits – Ignacio Ellacuría, Ignacio Martín-Baró, Segundo Montes, Joaquín López y López, Amando López and Juan Ramón Moreno – and two assistants – Elba Ramos and Celina Ramos – are murdered at the Jesuit residence on the UCA campus around 2:30 a.m. Six members of the Atlacatl Battalion and two officers attached to the Military Academy are arrested in January 1990 and charged with the killings. The Center for Theological Reflection is also assaulted with an M-60 machine gun. Offices are burned and ransacked.

November 16. A military sound truck of the First Infantry Brigade circulating in the neighborhood around the Archbishopric announces: "Ellacuría and Martín-Baró have fallen. We're going to continue killing communists."

November 21. A helicopter gunship dips down into the UCA campus, shooting off a few rounds through the window of Father Ellacuría's office.

1990

March 13. An article entitled "El Salvador: The Bishop-President Speaks," which was published in Spain, is reprinted in Salvadoran newspapers as an op-ed and later as a paid advertisement. An attack on Father Ellacuría, the article also mentions Father Jon Sobrino, S.J., and a Jesuit at the Jesuit Santa Clara University, which has a "sinister" history, according to the piece.

July 19. In a paid ad in *Diario de Hoy*, the Crusade for Work and Peace denounces "pastors who dedicate themselves to serving Satan through Liberation Theology." The same list of persons mentioned in the group's July 3, 1989 letter to President Cristiani is repeated, minus three who were killed in the last year: Ignacio Ellacuría, Segundo Montes and Febe Velásquez, a labor leader who died in the October 1989 bombing of the FENASTRAS office.

August 9. A column in *Diario de Hoy* attacks liberation theology and mentions "prominent members of the Society of Jesus, who helped design this ill-fated theology in Europe and Latin America, which has caused so much damage to the peoples of the Third World and especially Indo-Latin America."

August 27. *La Prensa Gráfica* publishes "Guerrillas are the Jesuits of War," an article suggesting that such Jesuitical qualities as "treachery, surprise, and nocturnal habits" [*nocturnidad*] are "essential elements in the guerrilla struggle."

August 28. An article signed "Don Quijote" in *Diario de Hoy* asserts that the Jesuit Provincial for Central America has "confessed" that Jesuits "have participated and are participating in a war" and that the murdered Jesuits were "involved with the guerrillas." The "majority of these missionaries are foreigners," writes the author, and "nobody likes that . . . foreigners come and stick their noses and hands in our matters." According to "Don Quijote," the Jesuits are to be blamed for the "disrespectful form" in which Salvadoran peasants have chosen to rename their communities after the assassinated priests.

September 6. *Diario de Hoy* publishes an article entitled, "Ellacuría was a Strategist for Marxism, ex-Jesuit Affirms." The article says that Father Ellacuría used the UCA to promote "his strategic militancy in support of Marxism, as well as the theoretical-practical defense of the tactic of the so-called "dialogue negotiation" and the identification of Catholic curia with communism."

1991

April 11. *Diario de Hoy* publishes an article denouncing "exalted priests, many of them mad, who made calls `to the revolution,' incited disobedience of laws and customs, encouraged theft and fomented class hatreds."

September 18. A *Diario de Hoy* column summarizes the historical period when the Jesuits were expelled by the King of Spain, "in order to preserve the tranquility of his people." Motivating the "very Catholic" king, said the column, was that "Jesuits were rebellious, insubordinate and dangerous subjects. . . ." The author proposes that Salvadoran historians bring this history up to date, "given . . . that Jesuit themes are very timely in the media these days."

October 8. "Of the Jesuits, A Brief Account," in *El Mundo*, again tells how the Jesuits were expelled and suppressed and says, "The order is still powerful and . . . dedicates itself to teaching and political intrigue."

October 15. A *Diario de Hoy* columnist attacks Father Tojeira and others for their efforts to identify those who ordered the UCA murders. "We all know that it's very difficult to investigate – if in fact they exist – who are the intellectual authors of these deaths. But that is not what is important. What these people really are interested in is discrediting the Armed Forces, to expose it in the eyes of television viewers abroad as an institution of people with no scruples."

November 11. A *Diario de Hoy* article blames the growth of evangelical sects on liberation theology and says "[l]iberation theology is but debris of the collapse of communism, of the collapse of the utopias."

1992

March 13. Father Steve Kelly, S.J., is deported from El Salvador after having been arrested in the course of a police operation seeking to expel peasants from lands they occupied.

September - October. A series of seven paid advertisements attacking the Jesuits is placed by the Civic Movement for a Free El Salvador in San Salvador daily newspapers *Diario Latino* and *La Prensa Gráfica*. The first installment summarizes a 1981 *ECA* article by former UCA rector Román Mayorga Quiróz, who outlined steps toward a negotiated settlement to the war and social reform. Six subsequent articles signed by Mauricio Morales note the group's surprise at the "almost prophetic analysis" of the "Jesuit document" in predicting many of the reforms that have been realized or are covered by the peace accords. The *ECA* article is called "insurgent, subversive, apologetic and morally bankrupt." The series ends with an appeal to "honest entrepreneurs, businessmen, workers, small merchants, the Salvadoran people . . . for the future of your children and the honor of the Nation, to take matters into your own hands so that our glorious country will not be submitted to this disgraceful future that the Jesuit document lays out, to demand of the government, policitians, leaders, to tirelessly guard the security of the state, to maintain the system in which we live . . . that we shall not be vicitmized by permanent slavery . . . . "

1993

January 13. Government press secretary Ernesto Altschul responds on television to an UCA communiqué urging compliance with the Ad-Hoc Commission's findings. Many of the UCA Jesuits are "foreigners," he says. "They should look for political opportunities in their countries of origin . . . . It is not the business of the Jesuits to evaluate a process of a political nature."

Sources: Salvadoran daily press; R. Cardenal, *Historia de una esperanza: vida de Rutilio Grande* (UCA Editores, 1987); *La Iglesia en El Salvador* (UCA Editores, 1982); *La Vida Religiosa en El Salvador* (CONFRES, 1977); *Envio*, Vol. 9, #102a, January 1990 (Managua); Hearings Before the Subcommittee on International Organizations of the Committee on International Relations, House of Representatives, July 21 and 29, 1977; Arroyo, "El Salvador: Los Riesgos del Evangelio, Iglesia y violencia política," *Estudios Centroamericanos (ECA)*; Lernoux, "Be a Patriot (In El Salvador) and Kill a Priest!" in *Cry of the People*, at 61-80 (Doubleday, Garden City, NY, 1980); T. Montgomery, *Revolution in El Salvador, Origins and Evolution*, at 107-117 (Westview Press, Boulder, CO, 1982); Russell, "The Church," in *El Salvador in Crisis*, at 111-116 (Colorado River Press, 1984); *Proceso* #38, October 11, 1981; *Proceso* #409, November 29, 1989; *Noticias de la Viceprovincia Centroamericana; Noticias de la Provincia Centroamericana S.I.; Noticias S.J.* (1971 to 1990).

Appendix C

REPORT TO THE LAWYERS COMMITTEE FOR HUMAN RIGHTS ON THE JESUIT MURDER TRIAL

BY ROBERT KOGOD GOLDMAN*

Introduction

This report describes the trial of nine members of the Salvadoran armed forces charged with the murders of six prominent Jesuit priests, their cook and her 15-year-old daughter, on November 16, 1989. The trial, which took place in San Salvador from September 26 to 28, 1991, ended with a jury verdict finding Colonel Guillermo Alfredo Benavides Moreno guilty of all eight murders and Lt. Yusshy René Mendoza Vallecillos guilty of the murder of l5-year-old Celina Mariceth Ramos. The other six defendants present, including those soldiers who had confessed to killing the victims, were acquitted on all charges.

This report evaluates the trial, as well as the relevant judicial steps preceding it, in light of Salvadoran law and, particularly, applicable international legal standards.

The Public Trial (*Vista Pública*)

The public trial began at noon on September 26 after the presiding judge, Ricardo Zamora, of the Fourth Criminal Court, had empaneled five jurors and one alternate. The trial was held in a makeshift courtroom located on the fourth floor of the Supreme Court building, which was sealed off from the public by armed Supreme Court security personnel who admitted only persons with official credentials issued by the Supreme Court. Attendance at the trial was limited to members of the diplomatic corps, accredited international observers, members of the Jesuit order, and their associates, friends and relatives of the victims and friends and members of the defendants' families. A substantial contingent of international and domestic press was also present. The entire proceedings were televised on Salvadoran television.

---

* Professor of Law and Louis C. James Scholar; Co-Director, Center For Human Rights and Humanitarian Law, The Washington College of Law, The American University. Member of the Executive Committees of Americas Watch and Middle East Watch, and the Boards of the Washington Office on Latin America and the International Human Rights Law Group.

In order to protect their identities, the jurors were seated behind a ten-foot high wooden partition, shielding them from view of the defendants, the observers and the press. The defendants, all dressed in uniform, were seated in a single row, facing the public with their backs to the judge. Defendants in El Salvador customarily face the public. Yet in this case the fact that the nine defendants were required to face the glare of television lights for more than 33 hours over three days unquestionably created unusual discomfort.

Reading of the *Minuta*

The entire first day and the first three and a half hours of the second day of the trial, totalling 12 hours, was taken up by a reading by court clerks of the *minuta*, *i.e.*, the summary of the 28 volume, 5,600 page record of evidence and supporting materials compiled by Judge Zamora in his capacity as investigating judge. It began with a recitation of evidence establishing the commission of the crime with a description of the murders and the physical scene, followed by a reading of the autopsies and death certificates, ballistic and other forensic reports and a variety of other evidentiary material relevant to each defendant's participation in these crimes.

The Problematical Extrajudicial Confessions

The most detailed information about these murders is contained in the extrajudicial confessions of seven[1] of the defendants which were read, together with the statements of witnesses to each confession, consecutively from l:30 to 7:00 p.m. on September 26. Under Salvadoran law, extrajudicial confessions, when made in police custody, are directly admissible against the declarant/defendant in a murder case if, *inter alia*, the confession is signed by two competent witnesses who attest to having heard the confession and that it was given without intimidation or physical force.

Since these extrajudicial confessions were the most incriminating direct evidence against each defendant, they were of particular interest. While their substance certainly rang true, there was something strange, indeed, troubling, about their format and, particularly, the uncanny similarity between each defendant's confession and the statements of the attesting witnesses.[2]

In order to be admissible, each of these confessions was presumably made freely, spontaneously and in the declarant's own words. The declarant presumably did not engage in an uninterrupted monologue, but was asked at least some questions by the police who recorded his responses. Yet the "confessions" that were read in court were flowing narratives, all in the third person, unpunctuated by any questions and answers and with such exquisite details that they sounded like carefully prepared statements. In fact, what was read in court were not verbatim transcriptions of the seven declarants' own words, but rather, as the

---

1 Colonel Benavides never confessed extrajudicially or otherwise and Private Jorge Alberto Sierra Ascensio allegedly deserted in December 1989 and thus never confessed extrajudicially or entered a plea in court. He was being tried in absentia with court appointed counsel.

2 The coincidence in wording between the statement of the defendant and that of the witness is not uncommon in Salvadoran legal documents.

President of the Salvadoran Supreme Court told this observer, an "accurate summary" of the declarants' statements as taken and written by the police.

Even more remarkable was the virtual coincidence in language between each extrajudicial confession and the two corroborating witnesses' statements that were read to the jury immediately after each confession. So strikingly similar, if not identical, were their content and terminology that initially it seemed that the clerk had been required by some procedural formality to read each confession three times. This similarity perhaps could have been easily explained if what was actually read was each defendant's confession as attested to by each witness before the investigating judge. But this apparently was not the case.

Under applicable procedures, the judge does not summon each witness, read him the pertinent confession and ask him to authenticate it. Rather, the judge questions and takes each witness' statement about the declarant's confession and whether it was freely given. Thus, what was entered into the record, together with each extrajudicial confession, and read from the *minuta* was each witness' *own* statement. How then does one explain the essentially coincident wording of these confessions and witnesses' statements?

The fact that all seven defendants made their extrajudicial confessions to the police without the benefit of legal counsel and within days of having been implicated in these crimes by the Military Honor Commission is cause for additional concern. These confessions, moreover, were not taken or witnessed by members of an independent police force under genuine civilian control, but by persons under the direct control of the chief of the Special Investigative Unit (SIU), Colonel Manuel Antonio Rivas Mejía, an active duty officer in the armed forces, who, according to the testimony of a U.S. military officer, and despite Rivas' denials, had been told by Colonel Benavides of his responsibility for the killings, yet had taken no action.

There are other issues related to these extrajudicial confessions which also raise questions of procedural fairness to one or more of the defendants. One issue concerns what was excluded from the *minuta*. To cite one example, when Judge Zamora took their initial statements in court, all seven defendants maintained their innocence and denied knowing the contents of their confessions, claiming they were coerced into signing them while in police custody. Although these court statements were made part of the official record, none were included in Judge Zamora's *minuta*. Consequently, the jury heard all seven extrajudicial confessions – effectively three times – but was not told by the judge of their subsequent repudiation by defendants. The jury only learned about this issue from defense counsel. Why were the defendants' judicial statements of denial omitted from the *minuta*?

Another set of issues pertain to the admissibility of certain evidence against the defendants. Under Salvadoran criminal procedure, for example, co-defendant testimony is specifically excluded as direct evidence in murder cases. Lieutenants Espinoza and Mendoza said in their extrajudicial confessions that they received orders from Colonel Benavides. Consequently, this testimony should not have been directly admissible against Benavides as the lieutenants were his accomplices. Yet, Judge Zamora did not either during or after the reading of Espinoza or Mendoza's extrajudicial confessions or before the jury began its deliberations publicly admonish the jury to disregard their testimony insofar as it implicated Colonel Benavides.

Although this exclusionary rule may have the effect, rather perversely, of protecting the "intellectual authors" of crimes, it is, nonetheless, the law. It is the judge's duty to apply it. It is not clear why Judge Zamora apparently failed to exclude or otherwise appropriately qualify this testimony. Surely, no member of a lay jury can be expected to know such an esoteric rule of evidence. Without this damning evidence, the case against Colonel Benavides was essentially circumstantial. Judge Zamora's apparent error may have been highly prejudicial to Colonel Benavides, since he was ultimately convicted by the jury on all murder counts.

At the conclusion of the reading of the *minuta* at noon on September 27, Judge Zamora asked the jury if they wished to question any of the defendants or any person whose statement was read from the *minuta*. The jury declined to do so. In response to a suggestion by government prosecutors that they visit the scene of the crime, the jurors indicated that they were familiar with the Central American University (UCA) and preferred not to leave the Supreme Court building. Judge Zamora also denied a request by the private prosecutors to call and question a witness, Colonel Nelson Iván López y López, who was in charge of the Operations Center at the Joint Command headquarters when the murders took place.

Presentation of Legal Arguments (*Debate*)

The trial resumed with the initiation of the "*debate*," the presentation of legal arguments by the parties. The jury heard first the private prosecutors, then prosecutors from the Attorney General's office (*Fiscalía*) and lastly defense counsel. Because of the multiple defendants, Judge Zamora allocated six hours to be shared by the private and public prosecutors and six hours to defense counsel in the first round with a maximum of three hours to each side in the final round of arguments.

In criminal cases Salvadoran procedure apparently allows the parties in their arguments to introduce any *kind* of evidence so long as it does not go beyond matters contained in the official case record. However, as noted, the rule excluding co-defendant testimony was apparently disregarded. Moreover, restrictions on the admissibility of hearsay evidence, as that term is understood in common law, seemed to be nonexistent in these proceedings.

The trial judge has broad, if not absolute, discretion to disallow a particular issue or argument which is "irrelevant to the establishment of the truth." The only parties really in a position to assess the relevance of the statements made by the various counsel for both sides were the counsel themselves and Judge Zamora.

Despite the quasi-adversarial character of this phase of the trial, no witnesses were called. Moreover, counsel were limited to putting on their own case and, only on one occasion did any of them object or otherwise protest, to the judge any argument or characterization of the probative value of evidence made by opposing counsel. Given the judge's exclusive role in this regard, his near total passivity during the 18 hours of oral arguments was somewhat surprising. Judge Zamora interrupted the proceedings only four times, three of which appeared to be on relevancy grounds, all to admonish defense counsel to drop a particular line of argument. Otherwise, counsel, most notably for the defense, were free to make many arguments, frequently replete with hearsay. While not uncommon in El Salvador, the arguments' tone and content would not likely have been tolerated in most civil or common law courts.

The Private Prosecution

The two most logically coherent and skillfully crafted presentations were made by the two private prosecutors, Henry Campos and Sidney Blanco, who represented the victims' families. In his opening argument, Mr. Campos methodically and dispassionately recounted facts establishing Colonel Benavides' responsibility for these crimes. He noted that on November 13, 1989, Benavides was named commander of the security zone of the Military Complex, which included within its boundaries the High Command headquarters, the Defense Ministry, the Military Academy and the UCA. He explained that as the person in charge of this zone – the very nerve-center of the Armed Forces – Colonel Benavides was obliged to protect and defend everything and everyone within its perimeters from rebel attack. Mr. Campos also reminded the jury that six of the other defendants, who were members of the Atlacatl commando unit that was assigned to the Military Academy, were under Benavides' operational control and that the head of that unit, Lieutenant Espinoza Guerra, in his extrajudicial confession, had stated that Colonel Benavides had ordered him to go to the UCA, kill Father Ellacuría and leave no witnesses. Mr. Campos added that under Army regulations, cited by Defense Minister Ponce in his deposition to the court, Benavides had authority to issue orders without prior clearance and was responsible not only for these orders, but for all actions, including abuses, committed by troops under his command.

Mr. Campos argued that, in addition to his "command" responsibility for these crimes, Colonel Benavides was also guilty of committing murder by omission, for failing to protect the victims from foreseeable harm.[3] He told the jury about the campaign of hate and death threats against the Jesuits broadcast over the Armed Forces radio at the beginning of the rebel offensive. In light of these threats, Colonel Benavides had a duty to ensure that soldiers he commanded refrained from hostile acts against the Jesuits. But, instead of protecting them, Colonel Benavides sent a commando unit to assassinate them. He argued that in an attempt to cover up their responsibility for these murders, the commandos, before leaving the UCA, feigned an attack by the rebels against the Pastoral Center and Jesuits' residence, firing hundreds of gunshots and grenade launchers and scribbling on the walls and doors of the residence the initials "FMLN." Mr. Campos noted that despite the noise that was heard coming from within the key security zone that he commanded, Colonel Benavides, incredibly, did nothing to investigate the disturbance in dereliction of his duty. Throughout his presentation, Mr. Campos frequently directed the jury's attention to two large maps, one of the murder scene at the UCA and the other of the Military Complex security zone under Colonel Benavides' command, reconstructed from Colonel Ponce's deposition and information Benavides provided to the SIU, showing the deployment of government forces around the zone and the campus in particular.

Mr. Campos also told the jury that the existence of an armed conflict did not relieve Colonel Benavides of his affirmative duty to protect civilian non-combatants. He pointed out that El Salvador ratified the 1949 Geneva Conventions and Additional Protocol II, whose provisions absolutely prohibit combatants from directly attacking or summarily executing unarmed civilians. He noted that these

---

3 Continental and Latin American law and practice recognize situations in which failing to avert harm is equivalent to positively causing such harm. For an excellent treatment of this subject, see G. Fletcher, Rethinking Criminal Law, at 628-634 (Little Brown, 1978).

provisions are totally consistent with and reinforce comparable prohibitions under Salvadoran law.

Referring to the defendants who had extrajudicially confessed to these murders, Mr. Campos correctly stated that as members of the Armed Forces they were bound to obey only lawful orders. Since Colonel Benavides' order to kill the Jesuits and all witnesses was manifestly illegal, due obedience to his orders was not an acceptable defense in this case.

While acknowledging that this case has attracted international attention, Mr. Campos rejected the charge that the trial was politically motivated for "foreign consumption." He reminded the jury that seven of the defendants were U.S.-trained and had committed the crimes with U.S.- and Soviet-made weapons.

Mr. Campos concluded by observing that the trial did not address the criminal responsibility of those higher up the military command structure who have covered up their involvement in these crimes. "The intellectual authors who are still hiding in the shadows," he said, would have to be unmasked in a later investigation and prosecution. "There is a popular demand for justice in El Salvador and the aspirations of the Salvadoran people are in your hands. You have the opportunity to take a decision on behalf of the Salvadoran people and to break the long history of the military's impunity," he told the jury.

Sidney Blanco, the other private prosecutor, then gave an emotionally charged presentation, primarily designed to strengthen the case Campos had made against Colonel Benavides. Characterizing the evidence against Benavides as "strong and robust," Mr. Blanco drew the jury's attention to the map of the security zone under Benavides' control and the fact that it was ringed by two concentric circles of government troops. Mr. Blanco stated that it was virtually impossible for any combatant, much less the highly trained and well equipped Atlacatl commando unit sent to kill the Jesuits, to have penetrated the UCA without being detected and, given the Army's sophisticated communications network, without Colonel Benavides finding out immediately. He indicated, therefore, that no credence should be given to the suggestion that these crimes were committed by "elements extraneous" to the Armed Forces. He also reminded the jury that as the operational commander of the zone, Colonel Benavides was directly responsible for the security of all persons therein. Mr. Blanco then alluded briefly to the initial testimony of U.S. Major Eric Buckland in which Buckland stated that he had had prior knowledge of a plan within the Salvadoran Army, which included Benavides, to kill the Jesuits.

Mr. Blanco also argued that ballistic reports also implicated Colonel Benavides in these crimes. These reports conclusively established that two of the murder weapons, including the AK-47 used by the defendant Amaya Grimaldi to kill three of the Jesuits, came from the Military Academy. As the Academy's Director, Benavides was the only person who could authorize the removal and use of these weapons.

Mr. Blanco then described the murders as depicted in the other defendants' extrajudicial confessions. Anticipating defense counsel arguments, he told the jury that these confessions, notwithstanding their subsequent repudiation by the defendants, were all witnessed and freely given, and that their validity had been affirmed on appeal by the Appellate Court and the Supreme Court.

The Public Prosecutors

The first member of the prosecution team from the Attorney General's office to address the jury was Eduardo Pineda Valenzuela, who heads the human rights unit. Mr. Pineda said that convicting the defendants on all charges would signal an end to the "dictatorship of violence" and "cycle of impunity" that had placed the Armed Forces above the rule of law.

Referring to the military's "enormous conspiracy of silence," he catalogued how the defendants and others in the military had attempted to cover up these crimes by first blaming the FMLN and later by obstructing the judicial investigation. He recounted a "pattern" of lies and contradictory statements by the Atlacatl commandos, memory lapses by cadets at the Military Academy and the destruction of the Academy's 1989 log books – critical evidence for establishing who entered and left the premises in the period surrounding the murders. He reiterated Mr. Blanco's charge that the Atlacatl commando unit could not have left the Military Academy and entered the UCA without Colonel Benavides' actual knowledge and approval. He told the jury, "we all have one goal here; our dream for El Salvador is a renewal of the administration of justice in this country." He concluded by exhorting the jurors to answer yes to all 80 questions and, thereby, convict the defendants on all counts.

Following Mr. Pineda's presentation the next two government prosecutors made long arguments which were largely repetitive of points already made.

The Defense

During their six hours of oral argument, defense counsel never presented an alternative explanation of the events of November 16, 1989. Instead, their strategy was to turn the proceedings into a political morality play in which their clients – self-confessed assassins and their accomplices – were depicted as heroes who were being martyred to appease the vengeful appetite of the U.S. Congress and other foreigners.

For six hours, they barraged the jury with repeated appeals to Salvadoran nationalism, defamation of individuals and groups, numerous invocations of the Almighty and his predilection for the defendants and some not terribly subtle attempts to intimidate jurors.

The first defense lawyer, Eulogio Rodríquez Barahona, began by appealing to the jurors' patriotism, juxtaposing their humble Salvadoran values against the arrogance of foreign interveners. To illustrate the point, he reminded the jury that most of the Jesuit victims were Spanish born and alluded to the presence of the Spanish Ambassador, the large Spanish observer delegation and other foreign observers. He mentioned the Jesuit Provincial, Father José María Tojeira, a Honduran citizen of Spanish origin, Father Miguel Francisco Estrada, current rector of the UCA, and María Julia Hernández by name, all of whom were present in the courtroom. He accused Ms. Hernández of conspiring to obstruct justice by allegedly tampering with evidence at the murder scene.

He said that because of this foreign interference the Army as an institution was being put on trial. Rodríquez Barahona affirmed the defendants' innocence, stating that their only "sin" was having joined that noble institution. He insisted that their extrajudicial confessions were not valid since they were taken more than 72 hours after the defendants were detained. He then pointed out minor inconsistencies in certain forensic and ballistic reports to impugn the reliability and credibility of the police investigation. He also read selected critical comments from a report by New Scotland Yard, which early on evaluated the SIU's work on the case, to bolster his contentions. He concluded with a defense of the Armed Forces and told the jury that if they had *any* doubt about the defendants' guilt, they could not convict them. This clearly erroneous characterization of the "intimate conviction" standard by which the jury determines guilt was not challenged by Judge Zamora.

The oral argument of the next defender, Raúl Méndez Castro, extolled the institutional history and constitutional role of the Armed Forces, without whom the country could not even administer justice. He told the jury that the country owed a debt to the defendants, all humble Salvadorans, who in the midst of the rebel offensive merely did their duty. Referring obliquely to the concept of due obedience, he said that as soldiers they had to follow superior orders and suggested to the jury that the defendants had risked their lives for the country in the line of duty.

He queried how members of the Armed Forces could be tried for terrorism and acts preparatory thereto when it is their sacred duty to fight terrorists. The notion of clandestine acts, he added, was inconsistent with the role of this national institution. He again raised the issue of foreign interference by saying that the United States does not send money for the people, but arms to fight the war. He concluded by telling the jury that the country's problems would not be solved by convicting the defendants and urged the jury to acquit them.

The third defense lawyer, José Adalfredo Salgado, attempted to discredit the probative value of the defendants' extrajudicial confessions. He compared the confessions of Lieutenants Yusshy René Mendoza and José Ricardo Espinoza and pointed out several, albeit minor, factual discrepancies between them. For example, Mendoza stated that Lieutenants Espinoza and Guevara Cerritos were already with Colonel Benavides when he arrived for the meeting at which Benavides gave the order to kill Father Ellacuría and leave no witnesses; whereas, Espinoza's confession states that Mendoza told him that Benavides wanted to meet with them.

He told the jury that Lieutenant Mendoza not only did not have a lawyer present when he supposedly gave his confession, but that the police barred lawyer(s) from seeing him until Mendoza had confessed. How could it be said, Mr. Salgado asked, that this confession was not coerced? Mr. Salgado also questioned the validity of these confessions as not having been made within the requisite time period. Returning to Lieutenant Mendoza's confession, he noted that Mendoza had said that he did not know the purpose of the mission or where he was going. Mr. Salgado then queried how, given these circumstances, Mendoza could be charged with acts preparatory to terrorism? As for the other charges against Lieutenant Mendoza, Mr. Salgado indicated that no one – including Colonel Rivas, who led the SIU investigation – could explain how Lieutenant Mendoza was linked to the murders. He also wondered on what basis the Military Honor Commission implicated Mendoza and the other defendants in these crimes.

He suggested to the jury that the trial was politically motivated and the result of foreign interference. Indeed, it was the price demanded by "the opposition in the U.S. Congress" for the continuation of military aid. Mr. Salgado viciously attacked the Jesuit order, stating that it "controlled governments and legislatures." He also attacked the presence and motives of the foreign observers, saying that they wanted "to destabilize the government and the Armed Forces." He told the jury that the Jesuits and foreigners would not be content with convictions in this case since they had already talked about a cover-up and the need to investigate and prosecute those higher-up in the military. In this sense, he said, they shared common cause with the FMLN. Judge Zamora interrupted and apparently warned Salgado to stop these attacks.

During Mr. Salgado's presentation, about 200 military supporters, led by a senior officer, staged a noisy demonstration directly in front of the Supreme Court building. They carried placards, chanted, listened to some speeches amplified by megaphones. A sound truck broadcast the national anthem three times and military "Taps" twice. The music and noise were clearly audible by everyone, including the jurors, in the courtroom while Mr. Salgado spoke. The demonstration lasted approximately one hour, beginning at about 10:30 a.m.

From a window I was able to see some of the demonstrators and security guards who, while holding shields, did nothing to stop them. The government permitted this demonstration, which clearly was intended to disrupt the trial and send a message to everyone inside. By contrast, on the previous day, riot police prevented about 70 UCA students and staff from approaching the Supreme Court to demonstrate their support for the prosecution.

Mr. Salgado finished his presentation as the pro-military demonstration ended. With impeccable timing, he told the jurors that for "their own safety and well-being and that of their families" they should ponder the importance of the Armed Forces to the stability of the country. He cautioned them to remember "what the Armed Forces do while we are sleeping, at the cinema or a soccer game. Think about this before you decide." Given the context, his words were clearly meant to intimidate the jurors.

In addition to warning Mr. Salgado to stop his tirade against the Jesuits, Judge Zamora interrupted him on two other occasions. After Salgado had concluded his argument, Judge Zamora warned him that since he had said nothing in defense of the absent defendant, Sierra Ascencio, whom the court had appointed him to represent, Mr. Salgado risked being cited for *patrocinio infiel*, roughly the equivalent of ineffective assistance of counsel. Mr. Salgado then made some brief remarks on Sierra's behalf. The other occasion was when Mr. Salgado incorrectly told the jury that, if convicted, each defendant faced consecutive sentences up to 100 years' imprisonment. Judge Zamora immediately interrupted Mr. Salgado, telling him that he was mistaken (the maximum sentence for each defendant is 30 years) and that it was for the judge, not the jury, to impose the sentence.

The last defense lawyer, Carlos Méndez Flores, focussed on two basic themes, the defendants as scapegoats and the insufficiency and dubious character of the evidence against them. Throughout his presentation, he asserted that the trial was strictly politically motivated and, indeed, would never have occurred had the government, in its desire to continue receiving U.S. aid, not buckled under U.S. pressure. He told the jury, "He who pays the mariachi chooses the song." He suggested that perhaps it was time that Salvadorans picked their own songs instead of having them dictated by the United States and other interlopers. Referring to the presence of foreign observers, he told the jury that they should have spent more time in El Salvador before the trial, implying that the observers did not appreciate the context in which the trial was taking place. He singled out the Spanish Ambassador and his large entourage, which included Spain's Deputy Foreign Minister and members of Parliament, telling the jury that they traveled to and from the court building in an armed caravan.

He reiterated that the case against the defendants was largely based on their extrajudicial confessions which, he asserted, were riddled with inconsistencies and thus unreliable. He reminded the jury of the situation in the capital during the rebel offensive which claimed about 2,000 lives. Alluding to the prosecution's claim that Benavides was solely responsible for events within the military complex security zone, Mr. Méndez implied that the rebels had access to the zone and especially the UCA since the first bombs were planted there on November 11 and a rebel arms cache was discovered in a search of the Loyola Center the next day. He did not mention that the zone as such was not created and Colonel Benavides named its commander until November 13. He suggested that given the military activity and confusion throughout the city during the offensive, it was inappropriate to question the Army's and implicitly Benavides' actions during the offensive.

Mr. Méndez then turned to the testimony of Lucía Barrera de Cerna, who had stated that she saw armed men in uniform at the Jesuits' residence on the night of the murders. He first tried to impugn her credibility by noting the conflicting testimony of night watchmen at the UCA, who first denied, then later confirmed, having seen her on November 16. Mr. Méndez noted, referring to Father Tojeira's introduction to the UCA book *Martyrs of the UCA* (*Mártires de la UCA*), that Ms. Cerna, during intense interrogation by the FBI in the United States, had recanted her original testimony and stated that María Julia Hernández in effect had told her to lie. Holding the book, he exclaimed to the jury that even the FBI mistreats witnesses.

Mr. Méndez also picked away at Father Tojeira's testimony that was part of the court record. He looked directly at Tojeira, who was observing the proceedings, and accused him of "amnesia," telling the jury that Father Tojeira could not remember when he first saw Ms. Cerna or whom he had requested to take her to the Spanish Embassy (where she detailed what she had seen the night of the murders). Mr. Méndez focussed on minor discrepancies in the testimonies of Father Tojeira and Father Estrada, such as which of the two was first notified of the murders. He said despite faulty recollection and conflicting testimony by these and other witnesses, none of them had been cited for perjury. In contrast, his clients were being prosecuted.

Returning to a theme raised by co-counsel, he implied that Father Estrada and María Julia Hernández had obstructed justice by removing evidence, *i.e.*, shell casings, from the scene of the crimes. He attacked Ms. Hernández, who was also present, calling her an "*auto-juez*," or self-judge, for sending this evidence abroad for analysis. He sarcastically told the jury, "some sectors in this country act with impunity."

At one point, he turned toward Judge Zamora and said: "You don't mind if I mention that you teach at the UCA?" Zamora snapped back, saying: "I am not on trial here, but I have taught at the UCA and I'm proud of it." Before concluding his argument, Mr. Méndez reminded the jurors that six members of the military linked to this case had been killed, adding: "How do we know what could happen to any of us when we leave this room?"

He concluded by telling the jury that it was for them to tell Judge Zamora whether they wanted to hear a second or rebuttal round of arguments. After consulting with the jury, Judge Zamora decided to allocate one hour of rebuttal to each side. He then adjourned the court for a short luncheon recess.

Rebuttals

The Prosecution

At 2:30 p.m. Sidney Blanco led off the rebuttal for the prosecution. He told the jury to disregard defense counsels' characterizations of the defendants' extrajudicial confessions as invalid and unreliable. Mr. Blanco said that their validity had twice been sustained on appeal, and, despite their protestations, defense counsel were only interested in being present when Colonel Benavides gave his statement to the police. He reiterated that Benavides was the "closest" intellectual author of these crimes and told the jury that a guilty verdict on all charges would not only end the military's impunity, but would pave the way to identifying those who had covered up their responsibility for these murders.

Henry Campos then told the jury not to be fooled by the defense's repeated references to foreign interference and attacks on the Jesuits and foreigners who were observing the trial. He said the case against the defendants was strong and supported by evidence provided by the military. He charged that defense counsel Eulogio Rodríquez Baharona had deliberately distorted the findings of the New Scotland Yard report by quoting only selected passages and conclusions. Mr. Campos read a conclusion from that report which states that none of the defendants or other members of the Atlacatl commando unit, who gave statements to the police, had provided a "complete and sincere" version of the events.

Mr. Campos reiterated the theme of Benavides' command responsibility for the military complex security zone and his obligation to protect it from attack. Pointing to the map of that zone, he told the jury that on the night of the murders, elements of the Puma Battalion, who were guarding the zone and under Benavides' command, had shot and killed a National Guardsman stationed at the Minister of Economy's residence, located near the UCA. Mr. Campos stated that this incident clearly demonstrated that the Atlacatl commando unit sent to murder the Jesuits could not have penetrated this zone without having been detected by the Puma Battalion, unless Colonel Benavides had approved and coordinated the operation.

Saúl Zelaya then gave the sole closing argument for the Attorney General's office. He told the jury that the prosecution was not accusing the Armed Forces as an institution of wrongdoing or arguing the case in defense of the Jesuits, but was merely seeking the conviction of persons who had violated the law. He reminded the jury that, in addition to the Jesuits, two Salvadoran women, including a minor, had been brutally slain. He praised Judge Zamora for his impartiality and the respect he enjoyed at home and abroad. He denounced the defenses' insulting attacks on Fathers Tojeira and Estrada, exclaiming to the jury, "we are all Catholics." He concluded by urging the jury to find the defendants guilty on all charges.

The Defense

The first two defense lawyers said little substantively, one calling the jurors "good Salvadorans and beautiful people," the other wishing them "a safe trip home." Both exhorted the jury to acquit the defendants on all counts.

The last rebuttal was delivered by lead defense counsel, Carlos Méndez Flores. He said that the prosecution had not proved its case and reiterated that Colonel Benavides' only "sin" was having commanded the zone where the murders occurred, for which he was not legally responsible. He contradicted the prosecution's argument that the evidence against the defendants had been compiled and delivered to the court by the military. He said the Special Investigative Unit was a police unit, independent of the military, but financed by the United States.

The remainder of his time was devoted to attacking the role of the United States in politicizing the trial. He said Major Buckland's statements, made on four different occasions, were inconsistent and contradictory. He alluded to Major Buckland's claim that he was "pressured" by the FBI as evidence that even U.S. military personnel can be interrogated in such a way that they make "untrue allegations" or sign "false statements." He noted that Buckland's judicial statement was not signed as required by Salvadoran law since it was sent to Washington before being transmitted to the court.

Mr. Méndez then referred to Congressman Joe Moakley's report, citing a passage which suggested that it would be difficult to prosecute Colonel Benavides because of the exclusion of co-defendant testimony and the absence of other direct evidence. He told the jury that during Congressman Moakley's July 1991 visit to El Salvador he saw Lieutenants Espinoza Guerra and Guevara Cerritos, then in police custody, and supposedly told them: "I am here because I do not think you are guilty," implying that they were being blackmailed. He said that without U.S. pressure, this trial never would have taken place. Mr. Méndez ended at 4:45 p.m. by calling on the jury to vote "no" on all 80 questions.

This concluded the public phase of the trial, and everyone was escorted out of the courtroom.

The Jury Verdict

Judge Zamora apparently did not instruct the jury before it began its deliberations. Instead he presented them 80 questions to be answered, by majority vote, "yes" or "no." A typical question read as follows: "Do you have an inner conviction that Colonel Benavides was guilty of the murder of Father Ignacio Ellacuría?"

After deliberating nearly six hours, the jury reached its verdict. At 10:30 p.m. the observers and other authorized spectators were permitted to return to the courtroom to hear Judge Zamora read all 80 questions regarding each defendant and the jury's answers. The jury found Colonel Benavides guilty of eight counts of murder, but acquitted him on all terrorism charges. Lieutenant Yusshy Mendoza Vallecillos was found guilty of one count of murder, that of Celina Mariceth Ramos, but also was acquitted of all terrorism charges. The remaining defendants, including the self-confessed executioners, were acquitted on all charges.

The conviction of Colonel Benavides, if not expected, was not altogether surprising. However, the verdict otherwise is deeply disturbing and, in one respect, defies rational analysis. Assuming that the jury freely arrived at its decision, the verdict perhaps can be explained by the peculiar role of the jury of "conscience" in Salvadoran criminal cases.

The allocation of functions between judge and jury in El Salvador is poorly defined and blurred. For example, the jury's role in criminal cases is not that of a finder of facts with a *duty* to apply the law, as *stated* by the judge, to those facts. The judge exercises no effective control over the jury since he is not required to charge them on any matter, including the weight of the evidence or permissible defenses. The jury, moreover, need not be convinced that the State has met a particular burden of proof, such as "beyond a reasonable doubt," in order to convict the defendant of the crime(s) with which he is charged. On the contrary, the law authorizes the members of the jury to virtually ignore the law and the evidence and to render their verdict on the basis of a wholly subjective standard, *i.e.* "inner conviction." This standard is set forth in Article 363 of the Salvadoran Criminal Procedure Code which states:

> The law does not ask jurors how they arrived at a decision; the law does not prescribe for them the rules to be used to deduce if a particular piece of evidence is sufficient; it stipulates that they must ask themselves in silence and spiritual absorption, and seek in the sincere judgment of their consciences, what impression the evidence produced against and in favor of the defendant has had on their judgment. The law does not say: do you take that fact as truth; it asks only one question which circumscribes the limits of their duties: are you personally convinced?

When applied by a jury unconstrained by a judge's instructions, this standard invites irrational verdicts.

Certainly the jury's conviction of Colonel Benavides was not irrational. Although the case against him was circumstantial, it was nonetheless not without merit and well argued by the private prosecutors. The jury might simply have been persuaded that he gave the order to kill Father Ellacuría and the other victims. But by convicting Colonel Benavides, the jury, presumably, would also have had to conclude that the other defendants, who confessed to these crimes, did in fact kill the eight victims, and did so on Colonel Benavides' orders.

One theory that would explain the jury's acquittal of the other defendants for these murders was based on their obedience to superior orders. This is entirely plausible since defense counsel had repeatedly raised this defense and the judge apparently did not take the issue away from, or otherwise instruct the jury on the law. However, if the jury did acquit on this ground, their verdict violates both international and Salvadoran law.

It has been an established principle of international law since the Nuremberg trials that the performance of a manifestly illegal act pursuant to superior orders is not excusable, but can only be considered in mitigation of punishment.[4] This principle is effectively incorporated in Article 40, Sec. 2(c)(c) of the Salvadoran Criminal Code which states that obedience to hierarchy does not excuse one's behavior when the order manifestly entails a punishable act.

Should the Salvadoran military interpret the verdict in this fashion, it would send the worst possible message: soldiers will not be held accountable for their crimes, no matter how heinous, if they allege they merely followed orders. So interpreted, the verdict condones, rather than inhibits, impunity.

If the verdicts against Benavides and those acquitted could be rationally explained, the same cannot be said for the jury's conviction of Lieutenant Mendoza on one murder count. Indeed, the Mendoza

---

4 *See* Control Council Law No. l0, Dec. 20, 1945, Art. 4(a) *reprinted* in 3 International Criminal Law, Enforcement 129, app. 7 (M. Bassiouni ed. 1987); Principle IV, *Report of the International Law Commission to the General Assembly*, 5 U.N. GAOR Supp. (No. 12) at 11-14, U.N.Doc. A/1316 (1950).

verdict is so bizarre and devoid of logic that it has fueled speculation that the jury was tampered with.Congressman Moakley has publicly refused to rule out this possibility, citing his conversations with "senior Salvadoran officials" who, before the trial, had accurately predicted the verdicts.[5]

Various persons, both Salvadoran and foreign, have made similar predictions to the Lawyers Committee. They speculated that the Army's High Command may have "fixed" the verdict because they feared the reaction, including the possibility of open revolt, of junior officers, in the event the Atlacatl commandos were convicted. Supposedly, these junior officers, whose troops were doing the fighting and dying, were furious that their superiors, while having covered up their own responsibility for these murders, had used the Military Honor Commission to "finger" the victims' executioners. According to this theory, the Army's senior officers, most of whom are members of the *Tandona* (1966 graduates of the Military Academy) then decided to sacrifice one of their own, Colonel Benavides and his assistant at the Academy, Lieutenant Mendoza, in order to pacify their restive underlings. These senior officers probably assumed that pardons could be secured for Colonel Benavides and Lieutenant Mendoza, perhaps as part of the general amnesty which followed the UN-brokered peace settlement.

This scenario, if true, could certainly explain the Mendoza and other verdicts. While there is no evidence that the military manipulated the jury, Congressman Moakley is right in not summarily dismissing that possibility. It would take a singular lack of imagination to suppose that an institution which could conceive of and carry out these atrocious crimes could or would not perpetrate a more benign and less visible crime to achieve its ends. Besides, it is common knowledge in El Salvador that juries have been compromised in other cases where the stakes have not been so high.

Concluding Observations

The conduct of this trial does little to inspire confidence in the existing criminal justice system in El Salvador. Both structurally and operationally, it contains features discarded by many other civil and common law systems, such as a trial judge who performs both investigatory and sentencing functions; a jury virtually free to disregard law and reason in rendering verdicts; antiquated evidentiary guidelines with broad exclusionary rules that are selectively applied; and the admissibility of recanted extrajudicial confessions. These features, in combination, seriously erode, if not deny, basic due process guarantees to defendants – which arguably – occurred in this case. If this trial with its unprecedented public scrutiny exemplifies how the system works, then there is cause for concern how defendants in ordinary criminal cases are treated.

Much has been made about the achievement of actually bringing these defendants to trial. But a deferential nod to the technical formality of a trial should *not* obscure the reality that this proceeding was not the result of an unimpeded and impartial administration of

---

5 Moakley, "Justice Disserved in the Jesuit Murders," *Washington Post*, Oct. 14, 1991, at A25.

justice as required by human rights and humanitarian law treaties to which El Salvador is a party.[6]

Virtually all of these instruments contain provisions that expressly mandate trial by independent and impartial tribunals.[7] This requirement is not limited to just the judiciary, but perforce to the entire apparatus responsible for the administration of justice, particularly those bodies that investigate crimes and identify suspects. Unless such investigations are conducted free from political interference and other external pressures, it simply would be impossible to safeguard a suspect's rights or ensure the integrity of the overall trial process.

In this connection, the Inter-American Court of Human Rights, in its landmark decision in the *Velázquez-Rodríguez* case,[8] elaborated on the duty of State Parties to the American Convention to investigate every violation of rights guaranteed therein.

The Court said that such investigations "must be undertaken in a serious manner and not as a mere formality preordained to be ineffective. . . ."[9] In finding that Honduras failed to seriously investigate the disappearance of Manfredo Velázquez Rodríguez, the Court noted, *inter alia*, that the investigation was conducted by the Armed Forces, "the same body accused of direct responsibility for the disappearances" and that "this raises grave questions regarding the seriousness of the investigation."[10] The Court's observations are equally relevant to the facts of the Jesuit case.

When judged against these international standards and the Inter-American Court's authoritative pronouncement on the duty to investigate violations of the American Convention, the proceedings leading up to this trial simply do not measure up. Any fair appraisal of the police and SIU's investigations of these crimes would have to conclude that by any standard they were, with little exception, grossly deficient. These investigations also suffered from the same defect noted by the Inter-American Court in the Honduran case. The police and SIU detectives, who investigated the military's responsibility for these crimes, were themselves members of the Security Forces under the control of high-ranking Army officers. Another governmental organ, the Attorney General's office, so dragged its feet in aggressively pursuing leads that the two principal public prosecutors, Henry Campos and Sidney Blanco, resigned their posts in protest.

Only when faced with mounting international pressure did the High Command take a political decision to permit a trial in this case.

---

6 El Salvador is a party to the American Convention on Human Rights, the International Covenant on Civil and Political Rights and the 1949 Geneva Conventions and its 1977 Second Additional Protocol.

7 See Article 8 of the American Convention; Article l4 of the Covenant; Article 3 common to the Geneva Conventions, and Article 6 of Protocol II.

8 Case Velázquez-Rodríguez, No. 4 (Inter-Am. Ct. H.R. July 29, 1988), judgment finding Honduras responsible for the forced disappearance of Manfredo Velázquez Rodríguez.

9 Id. at 156.

10 Id. at 157.

The Minister of Defense did this by convening a wholly extralegal body – a Military Honor Commission – which promptly implicated the nine defendants and effectively bound them over for trial. The intervention of this ad-hoc body in the midst of an ongoing judicial investigation affronts the notion of due process of law. It also reflects the failure of the criminal justice system to carry out an unimpeded investigation to identify the authors of these crimes.

The High Command's reluctant willingness to deliver these soldiers to the court also was self-serving. It enabled them to further draw a veil of secrecy around the intellectual author(s) of these crimes. Yet, even after delivering the soldiers to the court, the military did its best to prevent building a strong case against them by failing to cooperate with the judge. In the end, the military's own actions are the best evidence of a conspiracy to hide the full truth in this case.

The trial of the nine defendants and convictions of Colonel Benavides and Lieutenant Mendoza, therefore, cannot be seen as a triumph, much less a vindication of El Salvador's criminal justice system. What occurred in the courtroom in San Salvador brought forth little truth and rendered only partial justice. The intellectual author(s) of these crimes still lurk in the shadow of impunity. But the imperatives of justice and, above all, of decency, demand that they be exposed and held accountable for their unspeakable crime.

Appendix D

THE DEFENDANTS

In December 1990, 13 months after the murders took place, Judge Ricardo Zamora decided that there was sufficient evidence to take the case to trial against 10 members of the Salvadoran military. Nine of these men faced a jury trial for the murders and related charges, while Lt. Col. Carlos Camilo Hernández was charged solely in the coverup, a non-jury offense. All of the defendants remained on the military payroll, except Pvt. Jorge Alberto Sierra Ascencio who deserted before charges were brought. The three lieutenants and four enlisted men tried had all confessed to being part of the military operation in the UCA during the early morning hours of November 16, 1989. While the lieutenants denied responsibility for the killings, the enlisted men admitted playing a role in the murders. During pre-trial proceedings, all professed their innocence and denied knowing the contents of the confessions they signed in police custody.

Seven of the defendants were members of the elite Atlacatl Battalion commando unit. A U.S. advisor who worked with the military described the commando unit as "probably [the Atlacatl's] best unit."[1] Major Ramírez explained that the commandos were more motivated and experienced, although they did not have any special training or skills. He also noted that "they have been known to carry AK-47s from time to time" and would disguise themselves as guerrillas to try to infiltrate enemy lines. They were professional soldiers, not new recruits, and were among the chief beneficiaries of U.S. training.

Col. Guillermo Alfredo Benavides Moreno. Colonel Benavides, 44 years old[2], is the highest ranking officer ever to stand trial for a human rights crime in El Salvador. Colonel Benavides is a member of the *Tandona*, the unusually large 1966 graduating class from the Military Academy, which includes the most powerful officers currently in the Armed Forces.[3]

Colonel Benavides began his military career in the Air Force. As a lieutenant colonel in 1984 he was named commander of the Belloso Battalion, and then became commander of Military Detachment 3 in La Unión for a six-month stint in 1986. In 1987 he was named head of Military Detachment 5 in Cojutepeque; the following year he was assigned to head the Intelligence Section (C-2) of the Joint Command, where he remained for a year until he was named Director of the Captain General Gerardo Barrios Military Academy on June 1, 1989.

---

1 Statement of Maj. Samuel Ramírez, Ft. Campbell, Kentucky, Dec. 12, 1990, entered in court record, Fourth Criminal Court [hereinafter Ramírez Statement].

2 The ages given in this appendix are at the time of the crime.

3 *See* Arms Control and Foreign Policy Caucus, *Barriers to Reform: A Profile of El Salvador's Military Leaders, A Report to the Arms Control and Foreign Policy Caucus* (May 21, 1990).

As director of the strategically located Military Academy during the FMLN offensive, on November 13, 1989, he was named head of a special security zone which included the most important military installations in the country and the UCA within its perimeter. Troops from different military units were placed under his operational command, including the Atlacatl commando unit charged with carrying out the murders. Of the nine defendants, he is the only one thought not to have been present when the crime was committed. Instead, he was charged with giving the order to the lieutenants who allegedly directed the operation. He was the only defendant to be convicted on eight counts of murder, although the jury absolved him of the terrorism charges. Judge Zamora sentenced him to the maximum term of 30 years in prison. Finally discharged from the military after his conviction, Benavides was transferred to specially constructed quarters in Santa Ana prison.

Colonel Benavides, who never confessed to any role in the killings, has steadfastly maintained his innocence and professed a total ignorance of any missions (including the November 13 search) carried out by the Atlacatl commandos in the UCA. He was charged as the person responsible for the zone and the troops involved who, according to Army regulations, must have given the order, authorized the deployment of troops and the use of Military Academy weapons.

Colonel Benavides sold his home on January 2, 1990, days before his arrest.

Lt. Col. Carlos Camilo Hernández. Lieutenant Colonel Hernández, 37 years old, was interim deputy director of the Military Academy at the time of the killings. When the Security Command was formed, he was named its coordinator, but was not among those implicated in the crime by the military Honor Commission. He was later charged in the coverup for his alleged role in ordering the destruction of Military Academy records.

In May 1990, the SIU reported that Military Academy registries sought by the court had been burned under the orders of Camilo Hernández; subsequent court testimony by the Academy archivist and defendant Yusshy Mendoza substantiated this charge. Testifying on June 15, 1990, Hernández denied giving any order to have Academy records burned. On June 26 the court charged him with destruction of evidence (*encubrimiento real*). The military was slow in bringing him to court; he did not actually appear until July 18 at which time his lawyer resigned, alleging that he had been threatened. Subsequently, Hernández was represented by the same group of lawyers as the other defendants, despite his obvious conflict of interest with Yusshy Mendoza, who had accused him of ordering the burning of the logbooks.

In 1987-1988, Hernández served under Colonel Ponce at the Third Brigade. At the time he was charged, Hernández was the second-in-command (*Ejecutivo*) of the Belloso Battalion. Freed on bond on July 31, 1991, he returned to the field only to be injured by a guerrilla mine in Chalatenango a few weeks later. Apparently, he was then transferred to a less dangerous position in San Salvador.

Many were surprised when Camilo Hernández was charged in connection with the crime, as he was known as a leader of the younger officers. Some speculate that he was implicated in the case to draw in the younger officers who had been characterizing the crime as entirely the responsibility of the *Tandona*. Others, however, believe that because of Hernández's strategic position at the time of the killings, he must have known more about the actual crime. Judge Zamora convicted him on the non-jury coverup charge in January 1992, however he has yet to be discharged from the army as he awaits the appellate court's ruling on his sentence.

Lt. José Ricardo Espinoza Guerra. Lieutenant Espinoza, 28 years old, studied at the Externado San José while Father Segundo Montes taught there, graduating in 1979. He graduated from the Military Academy in 1984 and, like Colonel Benavides, began his military career in the Air Force. After three years in the Air Force, he was expelled on January 30, 1987, for "serious errors committed within the service." He was immediately reassigned to the Atlacatl Battalion.

A product of U.S. training,[4] Espinoza was sent to the United States on various occasions: for English studies at Oakland Air Force Base in San Antonio, Texas from March 5 to August 9, 1985; as a pilot aviator from August 19, 1985 to September 22, 1985, subsequently extended through December 31, 1985. He was authorized to participate in yet another unspecified official mission in the United States between January 1 and November 25, 1986. In 1988 he again went to the United States for a Special Forces officer training course. Espinoza served as a point of contact for U.S. trainers and, as head of the Atlacatl commando unit, maintained his popularity with U.S. advisors.[5] According to U.S. Maj. Samuel Ramírez, who began working with Espinoza shortly before the November 1989 offensive,

> [h]e was the primary point of contact that we worked with to coordinate the training for this special force. He speaks excellent English and I believe he was trained by our special forces school in Ft. Bragg, North Carolina. If I am not mistaken, he is a pilot . . . . I found out he spoke English and was pretty intelligent. He had been through our pilots course and was helicopter qualified and I know he has been to the special forces course. He is the person I went through to coordinate the training, the requirements, the bedding, the food we were going to need for the special forces team that was going to come down.[6]

Espinoza, codenamed "Bull," was tried for murder, acts of terrorism, planning and conspiracy to commit acts of terrorism and acts preparatory to terrorism. While the primary evidence against Espinoza was his extrajudicial confession taken by the SIU on January 13, 1990, he was also the immediate commanding officer of the troops implicated in the killings.

Espinoza's extrajudicial confession constitutes the most complete account of the events surrounding the crime. He recounts having received the order from Benavides to eliminate Father Ellacuría and to leave no witnesses. According to Espinoza, Benavides assigned Military

---

4 The U.S. Department of Defense acknowledged that Espinoza Guerra attended the Salvadoran Officer Candidate School course at the U.S. Army Infantry School from January-April 1982 and the Special Forces Officer's Course from November 11, 1988 to January 21, 1989 at the Special Warfare Center in Ft. Bragg, North Carolina. His service record, however, indicates considerably more training in the United States.

5 Ramírez Statement, *supra* note 1.

6 *Id.*

Academy Lt. Yusshy Mendoza to head the operation "to make sure there are no problems." Espinoza described how he transported his troops and rounded up three patrols already in the UCA area. Inside the campus, however, Espinoza sought to distance himself from the action, claiming to have retreated from the Jesuit residence with tears in his eyes. (His troops, however, place him closer to the scene.) He further claimed to have lodged a complaint with Benavides who reassured him, "Calm down, don't worry, you have my support, trust me."

Although this testimony was read to the jury, Espinoza was acquitted by the jury on all counts. Judge Zamora subsequently sentenced him to a three-year prison term for the non-jury crime of planning and conspiracy to commit acts of terrorism. He remains in the Armed Forces pending resolution of an appeal.

Lt. Yusshy René Mendoza Vallecillos. Lieutenant Mendoza, 26 years old, graduated from the Military Academy with Espinoza Guerra in 1984 and went on to serve in the Artillery Brigade. On September 1, 1987, he was assigned to the Military Academy as a section leader. Mendoza accompanied Espinoza on the Salvadoran OCS course at the U.S. Army Infantry School in Fort Benning in early 1982. In 1988, he returned to Fort Benning to participate in the commando course.

Mendoza faced charges of murder, acts of terrorism, planning and conspiracy to commit acts of terrorism, acts preparatory to terrorism, and the destruction of evidence (*encubrimiento real*) for his alleged role in burning Academy records. How investigators linked Mendoza to the crime remains a mystery, as SIU records turned over to the court provide no mention of him prior to the completion of the Honor Commission's work, when the names of the nine to be charged in the case were made public. While Mendoza, like Espinoza, denied responsibility, he provided the primary evidence against himself in his extrajudicial confession.

According to Mendoza's account, Benavides ordered him to accompany Espinoza without specifying what the mission involved. He describes witnessing Espinoza's men surrounding the building that included the Jesuit residence, conducting a search and seeing two women sitting on a bed, after which he heard a series of continuous shots. Others involved credit him with a far more active role, assigning the AK-47 rifle to Private Amaya Grimaldi and giving orders.

While Mendoza now denies having made the statements contained in his extrajudicial confession, he subsequently admitted his role in burning Military Academy records, although he claims to have done so at the orders of then Academy Deputy Director Lieutenant Colonel Camilo Hernández and in accordance with routine practice.

The jury inexplicably found Mendoza guilty of just one count of murder, that of 15-year-old Celina Ramos, while Judge Zamora also convicted him of the two non-jury charges. Along with Colonel Benavides, he was discharged and is serving a 30-year sentence in special facilities at Santa Ana prison.

Second Lt. Gonzalo Guevara Cerritos. Lieutenant Guevara Cerritos, 27 years old, joined the Army in 1980 but did not attend the Military Academy, instead working his way up through the ranks. He was promoted to second lieutenant at the end of 1988. He began his military career in the Air Force, subsequently serving in the Belloso Immediate Reaction Battalion from 1982 through 1988, after which he joined the Atlacatl as a section commander. From July through December 1988 he was in the United States, receiving an OCS training course at Fort Benning, Georgia. At the time of the killings, he was the executive (second in command) of the Atlacatl commando unit.

Guevara Cerritos ("Lynx") was tried for murder, terrorist acts, planning and conspiracy to commit acts of terrorism and acts preparatory to terrorism. Along with the other lieutenants, in his extrajudicial confession he denied responsibility while admitting participation in the military operation in the UCA the night of the killings. His confession constituted the major evidence against him. He recounted being present when Benavides gave the order to go to the UCA and told them, "Well *señores*, we are playing for all or nothing. It's them or us. These have been the intellectuals directing the guerrillas for a long time." Although his extrajudicial confession was read to the jury, he was acquitted of all charges by the jury. He remains in the Army pending appellate resolution of Judge Zamora's decision to sentence him to three years in prison for planning and conspiring to commit acts of terrorism.

Sub-Sgt. Ramiro Avalos Vargas. Sub-Sergeant Avalos Vargas, 21 years old, was known as "Toad" or "Satan." He led the second patrol of the Atlacatl commandos. Two other members of his patrol were charged in the killings. He received Small Unit Management Training in the United States from September 30 to December 14, 1988. He was charged with murder, terrorist acts and acts preparatory to terrorism. In his confession to the SIU, he admitted having killed two of the priests (apparently Fathers Amando López and Juan Ramón Moreno). Following instructions from Lieutenant Espinoza, Avalos Vargas claims to have said to Amaya Grimaldi, who was also guarding the five priests, "Let's proceed." After the shooting, as he was leaving the area of the residence, Avalos heard groans coming from a room and told Private Jorge Alberto Sierra Ascencio to go check. When he saw two women lying on the ground, embracing and moaning, Avalos told Sierra Ascencio to finish them off, which he did. In court, Avalos Vargas, like the others, denied that he confessed. Although the jury heard his extrajudicial confession, he was acquitted on all charges.

Sub-Sgt. Tomás Zarpate Castillo. Sub-Sergeant Zarpate Castillo, 28 years old, was the leader of the third patrol of the Atlacatl commandos and was known as "Samson." He was charged with murder and terrorist acts. Like the other enlisted men, he admitted his role in the crime. Specifically, he admitted in his extrajudicial confession to having shot the two women and left them for dead. Nonetheless, he was acquitted of all charges by the jury.

Cpl. Angel Pérez Vásquez. Corporal Pérez Vásquez, 30 years old, was a member of the fourth patrol of the commandos. He was tried for murder, terrorist acts and acts preparatory to terrorism. Like Sub-Sergeant Avalos Vargas, he was sent to the United States for a Small Unit Training Management course in 1987. In his extrajudicial confession he admitted to shooting and killing Father López y López, when the priest was already on the floor (having been previously wounded by another soldier) and had grabbed his foot. The jury absolved him of all charges.

Pvt. Oscar Mariano Amaya Grimaldi. Private Amaya Grimaldi, known as "Pilijay," 26 years old, entered the Atlacatl Battalion in 1982. He had been in the commando unit for 18 months and knew how to use an AK-47 rifle. In his extrajudicial confession, Amaya Grimaldi admitted that he was entrusted with an AK-47 by Lieutenant Mendoza and told that he was the "key man." With this rifle he admitted to killing Fathers Ellacuría, Martín-Baró and Montes. He said he drank a beer in the residence kitchen afterwards and stayed around to join in shooting up the building. Despite hearing his extrajudicial confession, the jury acquitted Amaya Grimaldi on all the charges he faced.

Pvt. Jorge Alberto Sierra Ascencio. Private Sierra Ascencio, 27 years, joined the Atlacatl in July 1985 and the commando unit in 1987. A member of the second patrol commanded by Avalos Vargas, he deserted in December 1989, and therefore did not give an extrajudicial statement or enter a plea in court. He was tried *in absentia*. Charged solely with murder – as the person who finished off the two women at Sub-Sergeant Avalos' direction – he too was acquitted.

Appendix E

LIST OF PERSONS CONNECTED TO THE JESUIT CASE

Victims:

Julia Elba Ramos
Celina Mariceth Ramos
Ignacio Ellacuría Beascoechea, S.J., UCA rector
Amando López Quintana, S.J.
Joaquín López y López, S.J.
Ignacio Martín-Baró, S.J., UCA vice-rector
Segundo Montes Mozo, S.J.
Juan Ramón Moreno Pardo, S.J.

Members of the Society of Jesus:

Father José María Tojeira Pelayo, Provincial, Central American Province
Father Miguel Francisco Estrada Lemus, UCA rector after November 1989
Father Fermín Saínz, UCA psychology professor and Loyola Center director

Catholic Archdiocese of San Salvador:

Archbishop Arturo Rivera Damas
Monsignor Gregorio Rosa Chávez, Auxiliary Bishop
Lic. María Julía Hernández, director of *Tutela Legal*

Defendants:

Military Academy:
Colonel Guillermo Alfredo Benavides Moreno, director
Lieutenant Yusshy René Mendoza Vallecillos
Lieutenant Colonel Carlos Camilo Hernández, acting Academy Deputy Director (charged only in the coverup)
Atlacatl Commando unit:
Lieutenant José Ricardo Espinoza Guerra ("Bull")
Second Lieutenant Gonzalo Guevara Cerritos ("Lynx")
Sub-sergeant Antonio Ramiro Avalos Vargas ("Toad" or "Satan")

Sub-sergeant Tomás Zarpate Castillo ("Samson")
Corporal Angel Pérez Vásquez
Private Oscar Mariano Amaya Grimaldi ("Pilijay" or "Hangman")
Private Jorge Alberto Sierra Ascencio

Salvadoran Officials:

President Alfredo Félix Cristiani Burkard
Vice-President Francisco Merino
Mauricio Eduardo Colorado, Attorney General in November 1989
Dr. Roberto Mendoza Jérez, current Attorney General
Dr. Mauricio Gutiérrez Castro, Supreme Court President
Dr. Ricardo A. Zamora, Judge, Fourth Criminal Court
Colonel (ret.) Sigifredo Ochoa Pérez, ARENA leader
Mauricio Sandoval, head of the government press office, SIN

Members of the Armed Forces:

High Command in November 1989:
General Rafael Humberto Larios López, Defense Minister
Colonel René Emilio Ponce, Chief of Staff (current Defense Minister)
Colonel Juan Orlando Zepeda, Vice-Minister of Defense
Colonel Inocente Orlando Montano, Vice-Minister of Public Security
Colonel Gilberto Rubio Rubio, Deputy Chief of Staff (current Chief of Staff)

Selected Members of Joint Command in November 1989:
Colonel Nelson Iván López y López, Chief of C-1 (Personnel)
Colonel Iván Reynaldo Díaz, Chief of C-2 (Intelligence)
Lieutenant Colonel Juan Vicente Equizábal Figueroa, C-2 (Intelligence)
Mayor René Guillermo Contreras Barrera, counter-intelligence chief, C-2
Colonel Joaquín Arnoldo Cerna Flores, Chief of C-3 (Operations)
Colonel Carlos Armando Salvador Avilés Buitrago, Chief of C-5 (Psychological Operations)

Special Investigative Unit:
Lieutenant Colonel (now Colonel) Manuel Antonio Rivas Mejía, head of SIU in November 1989
Lieutenant José Luis Preza Rivas, Chief SIU investigator
DNI, November 1989:
Colonel Carlos Mauricio Guzmán Aguilar, Chief
Colonel Roberto Pineda Guerra, head of intelligence school in November 1989, later Treasury Police director
Captain Carlos Fernando Herrera Carranza
Captain Luis Alberto Parada Fuentes
Lieutenant Héctor Ulises Cuenca Ocampo ("Charly Coyote")

Honor Commission:
General Rafael Antonio Villamariona, Air Force commander after General Bustillo
Colonel Dionisio Ismael Machuca, National Police director
Lieutenant Colonel Juan Vicente Equizábal Figueroa, C-2 (ntelligence)
Major José Roberto Zamora Hernández
Captain Juan Manuel Grijalva Torres
Dr. Antonio Augusto Gómez, civilian attorney
Lic. Rodolfo Antonio Parker Soto, civilian attorney

Military Academy:
Colonel Ricardo Alfonso Casanova Sandoval, director after Colonel Benavides' arrest

Security Command at the Academy during guerrilla offensive, November-December 1989:
Lieutenant Colonel Carlos Camilo Hernández, acting Academy Deputy Director, coordinator of the Security Command
S-1: Lieutenant Nelson Alberto Barra Zamora
S-2: Major Herbert Oswaldo Vides Lucha
S-3: Major Miguel Castillo González
S-4: Lieutenant Francisco Mónico Gallardo Mata

COCFA During the Murder Hours:
Colonel Nelson Iván López y López, chief*
Lieutenant Raúl Antonio Mejía Chávez, representing C-2*
Major Oscar Joaquín Martínez Orellana, representing C-3*
Colonel Joaquín Cerna Flores, C-3 chief (present until 1:00 or 2:00 a.m.)
High Command (present until 2:00 a.m.)**
President Cristiani (present from 12:30-2:00 a.m.)

Security Force Directors:
Colonel Héctor Heriberto Hernández, Treasury Police
Colonel Dionisio Ismael Machuca, National Police
Colonel Juan Carlos Carrillo Schlenker, National Guard

Others:
Major Mauricio de Jesús Chávez Cáceres, COPREFA chief in November 1989
General Juan Rafael Bustillo, Air Force commander in November 1989
Colonel Francisco Elena Fuentes, Commander, First Infantry Brigade until January 1992
Colonel Oscar Alberto León Linares, Atlacatl commander in November 1989

Chief Public Prosecutor:
Eduardo Pineda Valenzuela

* According to testimony of General Ponce, June 3, 1991.
** According to testimony of General Ponce, October 23, 1990.

Defense Attorneys:

Carlos Alfredo Méndez Flores, lead counsel
José Raúl Méndez Castro
Joaquín Eulogio Rodríquez Barahona
José Adalfredo Salgado

Private Prosecutors:

Edward Sidney Blanco Reyes
Alvaro Henry Campos Solórzano

U.S. Officials:

Bernard W. Aronson, Assistant Secretary of State for Inter-American Affairs
Ambassador William Graham Walker, until end of 1991
Colonel Milton Menjívar, head of U.S. Military Group in November 1989
Janice Elmore, Political/Military Officer, U.S. embassy
Richard Chidester, legal officer, U.S. embassy, throughout most of case
Major Eric Warren Buckland, psychological operations advisor in November 1989

Appendix F

ACRONYMS AND NAMES

AK-47 Automatic assault rifle often used by the FMLN.

ARENA *La Alianza Republicana Nacionalista*, the party currently in power, founded by Maj. Roberto D'Aubuisson, who died in February 1992.

Armed Forces The Armed Forces of El Salvador include all men in uniform and are led by the Minister of Defense. Under the Defense Minister are two vice-ministers, one for defense and the other for public security. The three Security Forces, or police – the National Guard, the National Police and the Treasury Police – were under the jurisdiction of the Vice-Minister of Public Security.

Atlacatl An elite, immediate reaction battalion (BIRI), recipient of considerable U.S. training. Seven of its members were tried for the murders at the UCA. The Atlacatl was disbanded in December 1992, pursuant to the peace accord.

BIRI *Batallón de Infanteria de Reacción Inmediata*, a rapid-reaction infantry battalion; generic name for several elite battalions, among them the Atlacatl, Belloso, Bracamonte, etc.

C-1/6 The Joint Command's operational divisions: C-1: Personnel; C-2: Intelligence; C-3: Operations; C-4: Logistics; C-5: Psychological Operations; C-6: Transmissions.

CEAT Special Anti-Terrorist Commando.

CEBRI *Centro de Entrenamiento de Batallones de Reacción Inmediata*, Training Center for the BIRIs, adjoining Atlacatl headquarters in La Libertad.

CIDAI *Centro de Investigación y Documentación de Apoyo a la Investigación*, a social science research center at the UCA, publisher of *Proceso*.

CIHD *Comisión de Investigación de Hechos Delictivos*, Special Investigative Unit (SIU).

CIN *Centro de Información Nacional*, the governmental National Information Center.

COCFA *Centro de Operaciones Conjuntas de la Fuerza Armada*, the command center at Joint Command headquarters.

COPREFA *Comité de Prensa de la Fuerza Armada*, the Armed Forces press office.

COT *Centro de Operaciones Tácticas*, command center of a garrison or other military unit.

CRT *Centro de Reflexión Teológica*, the Romero Theology Center at the UCA, also known as the Pastoral Center; the building where the priests and women were killed and which was heavily damaged during the murder operation.

DM *Destacamento Militar*, Military Detachment or outpost; each is identified by a number.

DNI *Dirección Nacional de Inteligencia*, a top Salvadoran intelligence agency.

D/T The Army's abbreviation for *delincuentes terroristas*, delinquent terrorists, the usual tag employed by the Armed Forces to name members of the FMLN.

ECA *Estudios Centroamericanos*, the UCA's major academic journal, published 10 times a year.

EMCFA *Estado Mayor Conjunto de la Fuerza Armada*, the Joint Command of the Armed Forces.

FMLN *Frente Farabundo Martí para la Liberación Nacional*, the coalition of five rebel groups founded in 1980, which fought a guerrilla war against the Government of El Salvador until early 1992, when a negotiated ceasefire went into effect.

IDHUCA *Instituto de Derechos Humanos*, the Human Rights Institute of the UCA, founded in 1985 by Father Segundo Montes, S.J.

IUDOP *Instituto Universitario de Opinión Pública*, the UCA's public opinion research institute, founded by Father Ignacio Martín-Baró, S.J.

Milgroup Group of U.S. military advisors attached to the U.S. embassy.

OCS Officer Candidate School.

Proceso A weekly bulletin of social, economic and political analysis prepared by CIDAI and published by the UCA.

RLT *Revista de Teologia Latinoamericana*, a scholarly journal on contemporary Latin American theology published by the Romero Theology Center (CRT) at the UCA.

S-1/4 The operational divisions of a military unit: S-1: Personnel; S-2: Intelligence; S-3: Operations; S-4: Logistics.

SIU Special Investigative Unit, *Comisión de Investigación de Hechos Delictivos*, a U.S.-trained and financed criminal investigatory body whose agents are members of the Security Forces. Its chief is an active duty Army officer.

SJ Society of Jesus/*Compañía de Jesús*, also referred to as "the Society" or "*la Compañía.*"

TL *Tutela Legal del Arzobispado*, the Archdiocesan Human Rights Office, headed by Lic. María Julia Hernández.

Tandona A large *tanda*, the word used to refer to a graduating class from the Military Academy. The *tandona* which graduated in 1966 has for several years occupied most positions of leadership within the Salvadoran Armed Forces.

UCA *Universidad Centroamericana "José Simeón Cañas,"* also known as the UCA.

UES *Universidad de El Salvador,* also known as the National University or "*la UES.*"

Appendix G

OTHER PUBLICATIONS REGARDING THE JESUIT CASE

Lawyers Committee publications:

1. *The Jesuit Murders: A Report on the Testimony of a Witness,* December 15, 1989. *(Summary Available in Spanish: El testimonio de Lucía Cerna: algunas sombras judiciales en el caso de los Jesuitas,* Proceso #413, 10 de enero 1990.)

2. *Status of the Investigation of the Jesuit Murders in El Salvador,* April 12, 1990.

3. *Status of Jesuit Murder Investigation in El Salvador,* July 27, 1990. *(Available in Spanish: Informe sobre la investigación de los asesinatos de los Jesuitas en el Salvador por Lawyers Committee for Human Rights, 27 de julio de 1990, ECA #502* agosto 1990.)

4. *Update on Investigation of the Murder of Six Jesuit Priests in El Salvador,* October 2, 1990.

5. *The Jesuit Case a Year Later: An Interim Report,* November 15, 1990.

6. *Update on Investigation of the Murder of Six Jesuit Priests in El Salvador,* March 25, 1991.

7. *Update,* May 23, 1991 (includes: IDHUCA, "The Jesuit Case: A Break with Impunity?"; Father Tojeira, "Tipping the Scales of Justice"; Letter to Assistant Secretary of State Bernard Aronson; Press summary of May 1991 brief filed by the private prosecutors; Lawyer-to-Lawyer Network case report).

8. *Jesuit Murder Case Update,* August 1991.

9. *The "Jesuit Case": The Jury Trial (La Vista Pública),* September 1991. (Available in Spanish: *El caso de los jesuitas, La vista pública, ECA* #517-518 noviembre-diciembre 1991.)

IDHUCA publications:

1. *El caso de la UCA y los deberes del Estado, Proceso* #452, 14 de noviembre 1990.
2. *El caso de los Jesuitas, una ruptura con la impunidad?, ECA* #505-506 noviembre-diciembre 1990. (Available in English.)
3. *Caso Jesuitas: el problema de investigar a los militares, ECA* #507-508 enero-febrero 1991.
4. *La ética de los ex-fiscales del caso la UCA, Proceso* #460, 30 de enero 1991. (Available in English.)
5. *Por qué y para qué la acusación particular en el caso de los Jesuitas?, ECA* #510 abril 1991.
6. *El caso de los Jesuitas: el periodo de prueba y la búsqueda de la verdad, ECA* #512 junio 1991.
7. *La prueba en el caso de la UCA, Proceso* #480, 5 de junio 1991. (Available in English.)
8. *Las comisiones rogatorias en el caso de los Jesuitas y la respuesta de EE.UU., Proceso* #483, 14 de agosto 1991. (Available in English.)
9. *Caso Jesuitas: La acción civil, Proceso* #486, 4 de septiembre 1991.
10. *Caso Jesuitas: la vista pública y la posibilidad de amnistía, Proceso* #487, 11 de septiembre 1991.
11. *Proceso,* Suplemento especial, #490, 9 de octubre 1991.
12. *El Jurado cuestionado, ECA* #516, octubre 1991.
13. *La Vista Pública en retrospectiva, ECA* #517-518, noviembre-diciembre 1991.
14. *La autoría intelectual en el caso Jesuitas: una investigación pendiente, Proceso* #497, 4 de diciembre 1991. (Available in English.)

Reports by Trial Observers:

1. *Justice in El Salvador: The Jesuit Case, Observations of a visting judge on the trial of nine soldiers accused of murder*, prepared for The International Centre for Human Rights and Democratic Development, Montreal, Quebec, by Brent Knazen, Judge, Ontario Court of Justice (Provincial Division), October 31, 1991.

2. *Affaire du Meurtre des Jésuites à la Universidad Centroamericana de San Salvador le 16 Novembre 1989, Compte Rendu Critique du Proces*, Université du Québec à Montréal Département des Sciences Juridiques, by François Crépeau, Professeur, October 15, 1991.

3. *Report of the San Francisco Observer Delegation to the Jesuit Murder Trial in El Salvador*, Submitted to the Bar Association of San Francisco, by Linda P. Drucker and Naomi Roht-Arriaza, October 9, 1991.

4. *El Salvador, The Jesuit Trial, An Observer's Report*, Americas Watch, December 13, 1991.

5. *Informe del Congreso de los Diputados sobre su viaje a la Republica de El Salvador en Septiembre de 1991 para informar sobre la vista pública del caso de los Jesuitas españoles asesinados en la Universidad Centroamericana (UCA) el 16 de Noviembre de 1989*, Congreso de los Diputados, December 18, 1991.

6. *El Salvador, El juicio por el asesinato de los Jesuitas, Una brecha a la impunidad aunque no un triunfo de la justicia*, Comisión Internacional de Juristas, November 1991.

7. *El Proceso por el Asesinato de los Sacerdotes Jesuitas en El Salvador*, Asociación Americana de Juristas, by Eduardo Luis Duhalde, November 15, 1991.

8. *Report of Observers on the Trial in El Salvador of Military Personnel Accused of Murdering Six Jesuit Priests, A Cook and Her Daughter*, International Human Rights Law Institute, DePaul University College of Law, by Douglass Cassel and Duane Sigelko, January 13, 1992.

9. *Report to the Lawyers Committee for Human Rights on the Jesuit Murder Trial*, by Robert Kogod Goldman (see Appendix C).

Note: Page numbers followed by *n.* indicate material in footnotes. *Italicized* page numbers indicate definitions of acronyms. The following abbreviations are used throughout the index: FMLN *(Farabundo Martí Front for National Liberation);* SIU (Special Investigative Unit); UCA *(Central American University José Simeón Cañas).* In most cases, military officers are listed with their rank at the time of discussion.

INDEX